EXCEL® MODELING IN INVESTMENTS

Fourth Edition

CRAIG W. HOLDEN

Professor of Finance
Kelley School of Business
Indiana University

Boston Columbus Indianapolis New York San Francisco Upper Saddle River
Amsterdam Cape Town Dubai London Madrid Milan Munich Paris Montreal Toronto
Delhi Mexico City Sao Paulo Sydney Hong Kong Seoul Singapore Taipei Tokyo

To Kathryn, Diana, and Jimmy.

VP/Editorial Director: Sally Yagan
Editor in Chief: Donna Battista
Acquisitions Editor: Tessa O'Brien
Editorial Project Manager: Amy Foley
Editorial Assistant: Elissa Senra-Sargent
Senior Managing Editor: Nancy Fenton
Marketing Assistant: Ian Gold

Media Producer: Nicole Sackin
Senior Manufacturing Buyer: Carol Melville
Senior Media Buyer: Ginny Michaud
Cover Design: Jayne Conte
Printer/Binder: Edwards Brothers
Cover Printer: Lehigh Phoenix

Cataloging-in-Publication Data is on file at the Library of Congress

10 9 8 7 6 5 4 3 2 1

Prentice Hall
is an imprint of

ISBN-13: 978-0-13-249787-9
ISBN-10: 0-13-249787-5

CONTENTS

CONTENTS ON CD

📄 **Excel Modeling in Investments Fourth Edition.pdf**

📊 **Ready-To-Build spreadsheets:**

- Ch 01 Bond Pricing - Ready-To-Build.xlsx
- Ch 02 The Yield Curve - Ready-To-Build.xlsx
- Ch 03 Affine Yield Curve Models - Ready-To-Build.xlsx
- Ch 04-05 Portfolio Optimization - Ready-To-Build.xlsm
- Ch 06 Portfolio Diversification Lowers Risk - Ready-To-Build.xlsx
- Ch 07 Stock Valuation - Ready-To-Build.xlsx
- Ch 08 Du Pont System of Ratio Analysis - Ready-To-Build.xlsx
- Ch 09 Asset Pricing - Ready-To-Build.xlsx
- Ch 10 Market Microstructure - Ready-To-Build.xlsx
- Ch 11 Life-Cycle Financial Planning - Ready-To-Build.xlsx
- Ch 12 International Parity - Ready-To-Build.xlsx
- Ch 13 Swaps - Ready-To-Build.xlsx
- Ch 14 Option Payoffs and Profits - Ready-To-Build.xlsx
- Ch 15 Option Trading Strategies - Ready-To-Build.xlsx
- Ch 16 Put-Call Parity - Ready-To-Build.xlsx
- Ch 17 Binomial Option Pricing - Ready-To-Build.xlsx
- Ch 18 Black-Scholes Option Pricing - Ready-To-Build.xlsx
- Ch 19 Futures - Ready-To-Build.xlsx
- Ch 20 Pricing By Simulation - Ready-To-Build.xlsx
- Ch 21 Corporate Bonds - Ready-To-Build.xlsx
- Files in Excel 97-2003 (xls) Format

Preface

For more than 25 years, since the emergence of PCs, Lotus 1-2-3, and Microsoft Excel® in the 1980's, spreadsheet models have been the dominant vehicles for finance professionals in the business world to implement their financial knowledge. Yet even today, most Investments textbooks have little or no coverage of how to build Excel models. This book fills that gap. It teaches students how to build financial models in Excel. It provides step-by-step instructions so that students can build and estimate models themselves (active learning), rather than being handed already completed spreadsheets (passive learning). It progresses from simple examples to practical, real-world applications. It spans nearly all quantitative models in investments, including nearly all niche areas of investments.

My goal is simply to *change finance education from being calculator based to being Excel based*. This change will better prepare students for the 21st century business world. This change will increase student evaluations of teacher performance by enabling more practical, real-world content and by allowing a more hands-on, active learning pedagogy.

Fourth Edition Changes

Derivative

- ⦿ Asian Call
- ○ Asian Put
- ○ Lookback Call
- ○ Lookback Put
- ○ Down-And-Out Call
- ○ Down-And-In Call

Both Direction and Volatility Strategies
Higher Volatility Strategies
 Buying a Straddle
 Buying a Strangle
 Writing a Butterfly Call Spread
 Writing a Butterfly Put Spread
 Buying a Iron Butterfly
 Buy a Condor
 Writing a Calendar Call Spread = Buying R
 Writing a Calendar Put Spread = Buying R
 Buying a Covered Ratio Spread
Lower Volatility Strategies
 Writing a Straddle
 Writing a Strangle
 Buying a Butterfly Call Spread
 Buying a Butterfly Put Spread
 Writing a Iron Butterfly
 Write a Condor
 Buying a Calendar Call Spread = Writing R
 Buying a Calendar Put Spread = Writing R
Both Direction and Volatility Strategies
 Diagonal Spread
 Strip
 Strap
Arbitrage Strategies
 Buying a Box Spread
 Writing a Box Spread
 Buying a Conversion
 Buying a Reversal
 Buying a Forward (Calendar) Spread
 Writing a Forward (Calendar) Spread

The Fourth Edition adds great new investments content:

- Perform either unconstrained or constrained portfolio optimization on any number of risky assets up to maximum of 20 assets
- Immunize bond portfolios against interest rate risk by matching the durations of assets and liabilities, by matching both durations and convexities, or by matching cash flows
- Use simulation to price both path-independent derivatives (e.g., European options, cash-or-nothing options, asset-or-nothing options) and path-dependent derivatives (e.g., Asian options, lookback options, and barrier options) – both with and without jumps
- Analyze trading strategies involving many options, stocks, bonds, and futures either holding to maturity or holding to any date before maturity – it includes a database of 50 trading strategies with bullish strategies, bearish strategies, high volatility strategies, low volatility strategies, combined directional and volatility strategies, and arbitrage strategies
- Price derivatives on alternative types of underlying assets, such as stocks, stock indexes, futures, and foreign currencies
- Determine margin calls and excess margin on futures contracts
- Translate bond pricing into alternative foreign currency values
- Compute the average of a N-step and a N-1-step binomial model to order to gain pricing accuracy
- See how the binomial model converges to the normal distribution
- Use current Trade and Quote (TAQ) data to compute the National Best Bid and Offer (NBBO), the quoted spread, the effective spread, and determine which exchange has the lowest cost of trading

The CD contains **Ready-To-Build spreadsheets**, which are based on the **Excel 2007-2010** (xlsx) file format. However, the CD also contains a folder with Ready-To-Build spreadsheets based on **Excel 97-2003** (xls) format. By default, the explanations in the book are based on **Excel 2010**. However, the book also contains "Excel 2007 Equivalent" boxes that explains how to do the equivalent step in Excel 2007 (when it is different than Excel 2010) and "Excel 97-2003 Equivalent" boxes that explain how to do the equivalent step in Excel 97 through Excel 2003.

The instruction boxes on the Ready-To-Build spreadsheets are *bitmapped images* so that the formulas cannot just be copied to the spreadsheet. Both the instruction boxes and arrows are *objects*, so that all of them can be deleted in one step when the spreadsheet is complete and everything else will be left untouched. Click on **Home | Editing | Find & Select down-arrow | Select Objects**, then select all of the instruction boxes and arrows, and press the delete key. Furthermore, any blank rows can be deleted, leaving a clean spreadsheet for future use.

The book contains a significant number of comparative statics exercises (lower risk aversion, higher short-rate, etc.) and explores a variety of optional choices (alternative models to forecast expected return, alternative spreads and combinations, etc.). In each case, a picture is shown of how things change and there is a discussion of what this means in economic terms. For example, below is Figure 5.14 which explores what happens to the optimal portfolio when risk aversion is lowered?

Files in Excel 97-2003 Format

Excel 2007 Equivalent

To install the Analysis ToolPak in Excel 2007, click on [icon], click on **Excel Options** at the bottom of the drop-down window, click on **Add-Ins**, highlight **Analysis TookPak** in the list of Inactive Applications, click on **Go**, check the **Analysis ToolPak**, and click on **OK**.

Excel 97-2003 Equivalent

To install the Analysis ToolPak in Excel 97-2003, click on **Tools**, **Add-Ins**, check the **Analysis TookPak** checkbox on the Add-Ins dialog box, and click on **OK**.

FIGURE 5.14 Risk Aversion of 16 and 0.4

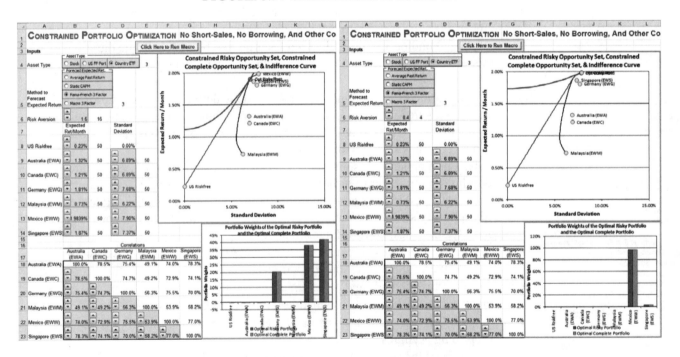

The CD provides **Ready-To-Build Spreadsheets** for every chapter with:

The model setup, such as input values, labels, and graphs

Step-by-step instructions for building and estimating the model on the spreadsheet itself

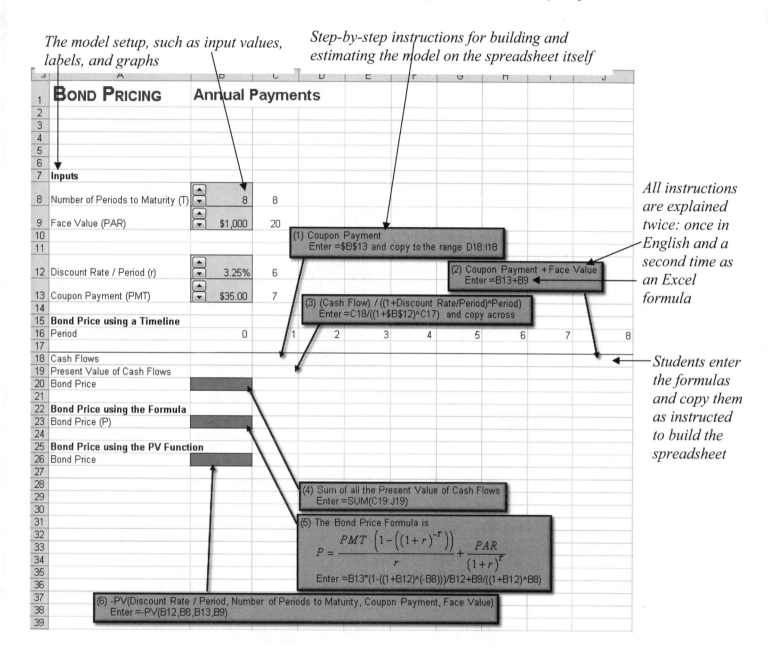

All instructions are explained twice: once in English and a second time as an Excel formula

Students enter the formulas and copy them as instructed to build the spreadsheet

Many spreadsheets use real-world data

ASSET PRICING — Static CAPM Using Fama-MacBeth Method

Inputs

Market Portfolio Benchmark
○ SPDR ETF ○ CRSP VWMR ● DJ World Stock   3

Asset Type
○ Stock ○ US FF Port ● Country ETF   3

	A	B	C	D	E	F	G
7		Stock	Stock	Stock	Stock	Stock	Stock
8		Barrick	IBM	KEP	Nokia	Telefonos	YPF

(1) Monthly Return(Asset i, Month t) - Riskfree Rate(Month t)
Enter =B10-$AC10 and copy to B133:V252

Monthly Excess Returns

	Barrick	IBM	KEP	Nokia	Telefonos	YPF
Dec 2009	-7.75%	3.60%	5.98%	-3.09%	-3.18%	17.39%
Nov 2009	19.37%	5.22%	-1.15%	5.15%	8.07%	2.70%
Oct 2009	-5.20%	0.84%	-8.92%	-13.75%	-4.76%	-0.63%
Sep 2009	9.22%	1.32%	23.40%	4.35%	-5.25%	-2.41%
Aug 2009	-0.58%	0.56%	-7.64%	5.01%	17.57%	9.96%
Jul 2009	4.01%	12.93%	16.25%	-8.51%	-2.48%	16.19%
Jun 2009	-11.90%	-1.75%	0.17%	-4.71%	-1.38%	-10.93%

Spin buttons, option buttons, and graphs facilitate visual, interactive learning

BLACK SCHOLES OPTION PRICING — Continuous Dividend Yield and Alternative Underlying Assets

Inputs

Option Type: ● Call ○ Put   1

Underlying Asset Type: ● Stock ○ Stock Index ○ Futures ○ Foreign Currency   1

Row	Input	Value	
6	Stock Price Now (S(0))	$137.10	137
7	Standard Dev - Annual (σ)	38.67%	3
8	Riskfree Rate- Annual (r)	2.44%	2
9	Exercise Price (X)	$140.00	140
10	Time To Maturity - Yrs (T)	0.4583	4
11	Underlying Asset Yield is Stock Dividend Yield (d)	1.00%	1

Continuous Dividend and Alternative Underlying Assets (chart: Option Price vs Stock Price Now, ranging $0–$50 on y-axis and $100–$180 on x-axis)

Outputs

Row		Value
15	d_1	0.076
16	d_2	-0.186
17	$N(d_1)$	0.530
18	$N(d_2)$	0.426
19	Call Price (C_0)	$13.35
21	$-d_1$	-0.076
22	$-d_2$	0.186
23	$N(-d_1)$	0.470
24	$N(-d_2)$	0.574
25	Put Price (P_0)	$15.32

(1) Copy the basic Black-Scholes formulas from the previous sheet
Copy the range B15:B25 from the previous sheet to the range B15:B25

(2) Add dividend yield (d) to the d_1 formula:
$$\left(\ln\left(S_0 / X\right) + \left(r - d + \sigma^2/2\right) \cdot T\right) / \left(\sigma \cdot \sqrt{T}\right)$$
Enter =(LN(B6/B9)+(B8-B11+B7^2/2)*B10)/(B7*SQRT(B10))

(3) Add dividend yield (d) to the call formula:
$$C_0 = S_0 e^{-dT} N\left(d_1\right) - X e^{-rT} N\left(d_2\right)$$
Enter =B6*EXP(-B11*B10)*B17-B9*EXP(-B8*B10)*B18

(4) Add dividend yield (d) to the put formula:
$$P_0 = -S_0 e^{-dT} N\left(-d_1\right) + X e^{-rT} N\left(-d_2\right)$$
Enter =-B6*EXP(-B11*B10)*B23+B9*EXP(-B8*B10)*B24

What Is Unique About This Book

There are many features which distinguish this book from any other:

- **Plain Vanilla Excel.** Other books on the market emphasize teaching students programming using Visual Basic for Applications (VBA) or using macros. By contrast, this book does nearly everything in plain vanilla Excel.[1] Although programming is liked by a minority of students, it is seriously disliked by the majority. Plain vanilla Excel has the advantage of being a very intuitive, user-friendly environment that is accessible to all. It is fully capable of handling a wide range of applications, including quite sophisticated ones. Further, all that is assumed is that your students already know the basics of Excel, such as entering formulas in a cell and copying formulas from one cell to another. All other features of Excel (such as built-in functions, Data Tables, Solver, etc.) are explained as they are used.

- **Build From Simple Examples To Practical, Real-World Applications.** The general approach is to start with a simple example and build up to a practical, real-world application. In many chapters, the previous Excel model is carried forward to the next, more complex model. For example, the chapter on binomial option pricing carries forward Excel models as follows: (a.) single-period model with replicating portfolio, (b.) eight-period model with replicating portfolio, (c.) eight-period model with risk-neutral probabilities, (d.) eight-period model with risk-neutral probabilities for American or European options with discrete dividends, (e.) full-scale, fifty-period model with risk-neutral probabilities for American or European options with discrete dividends. Whenever possible, this book builds up to full-scale, practical applications using real data. Students are excited to learn practical applications that they can actually use in their future jobs. Employers are excited to hire students with Excel modeling skills, who can be more productive faster.

- **Supplement For All Popular Investments Textbooks.** This book is a supplement to be combined with a primary textbook. This means that you can keep using whatever textbook you like best. You don't have to switch. It also means that you can take an incremental approach to incorporating Excel modeling. You can start modestly and build up from there.

- **A Change In Content Too.** Excel modeling is not merely a new medium, but an opportunity to cover some unique content items which require computer support to be feasible. For example, the Portfolio Optimization chapter uses 10 years of monthly returns for individual stocks, U.S. Fama-French portfolios, and country ETFs to estimate the (unconstrained) Risky Opportunity Set and the (unconstrained) Complete Opportunity Set. The

---

[1] I have made one exception. The Constrained Portfolio Optimization spreadsheet uses a macro to repeatedly call Solver to map out the Constrained Risky Opportunity Set and the Constrained Complete Opportunity Set.

same data is used by Solver to numerically solve for the Constrained Risky Opportunity Set and the Constrained Complete Opportunity Set. The same data is used to estimate the Static CAPM using the Fama-MacBeth method and to estimate the APT or Intertemporal CAPM using the Fama-MacBeth method. The Market Microstructure chapter uses current Trade and Quote (TAQ) data to compute the National Best Bid and Offer (NBBO), the quoted spread, the effective spread, and to determine which exchange has the lowest cost of trading The Excel model in US Yield Curve Dynamics shows 40 years of monthly US yield curve history in just a few minutes. Real call and put prices are fed into the Black-Scholes Option Pricing model and Excel's Solver is used to back-solve for the implied volatilities. Then the "smile" pattern (or more like a "scowl" pattern) of implied volatilities is graphed. As a practical matter, all of these sophisticated applications require Excel.

Conventions Used In This Book

This book uses a number of conventions.

- **Time Goes Across The Columns And Variables Go Down The Rows.** When something happens over time, I let each column represent a period of time. For example, in life-cycle financial planning, date 0 is in column B, date 1 is in column C, date 2 is in column D, etc. Each row represents a different variable, which is usually labeled in column A. This manner of organizing Excel models is so common because it is how financial statements are organized.

- **Color Coding.** A standard color scheme is used to clarify the structure of the Excel models. The Ready-To-Build spreadsheets on CD uses: (1) yellow shading for input values, (2) no shading (i.e. white) for throughput formulas, and (3) green shading for final results ("the bottom line"). A few Excel models include choice variables. Choice variables use blue shading. The Constrained Portfolio Optimization spreadsheet includes constraints. Constaints use pink-purple shading.

- **The Time Line Technique.** The most natural technique for discounting cash flows in an Excel model is the time line technique, where each column corresponds to a period of time. As an example, see the section labeled "Bond Price using a Timeline" in the figure below.

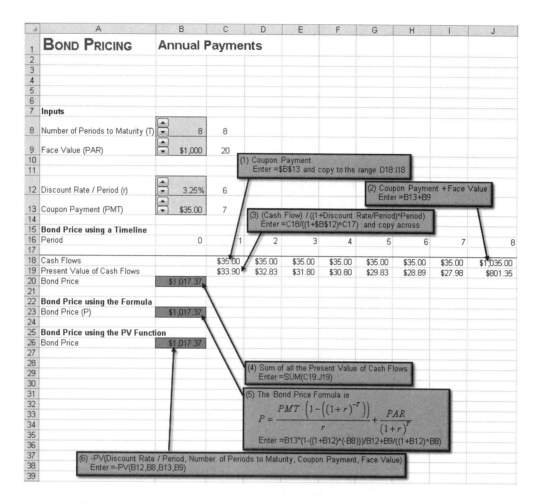

- **Using As Many Different Techniques As Possible.** In the figure above, the bond price is calculated using as many different techniques as possible. Specifically, it is calculated three ways: (1) discounting each cash flow on a time line, (2) using the closed-form formula, and (3) using Excel's PV function. This approach makes the point that all three techniques are equivalent. This approach also develops skill at double-checking these calculations, which is a very important method for avoiding errors in practice.

- **Symbolic Notation is Self-Contained.** Every spreadsheet that contains symbolic notation in the instruction boxes is self-contained (i.e., all symbolic notation is defined on the spreadsheet).

Craig's Challenge

I challenge the readers of this book to dramatically improve your finance education by personally constructing all of the Excel models in this book. This will take you about 10 – 20 hours hours depending on your current Excel modeling skills. Let me assure you that it will be an excellent investment. You will:

- gain a practical understanding of the core concepts of Investments,
- develop hands-on, Excel modeling skills, and
- build an entire suite of finance applications, which you fully understand.

When you complete this challenge, I invite you to send an e-mail to me at **cholden@indiana.edu** to share the good news. Please tell me your name, school, (prospective) graduation year, and which Excel modeling book you completed. I will add you to a web-based honor roll at:

http://www.excelmodeling.com/honor-roll.htm

We can celebrate together!

Excel® Modeling Books

This book is one of two **Excel Modeling** books by Craig W. Holden, published by Pearson / Prentice Hall. The other book is **Excel Modeling in Corporate Finance**. Both books teach value-added skills in constructing financial models in Excel. Complete information about my **Excel Modeling** books is available at my web site:

http://www.excelmodeling.com

If you have any suggestions or corrections, please e-mail them to me at **cholden@indiana.edu**. I will consider your suggestions and will implement any corrections in the next edition.

Suggestions for Faculty Members

There is no single best way to use **Excel Modeling in Investments**. There are as many different techniques as there are different styles and philosophies of teaching. You need to discover what works best for you. Let me highlight several possibilities:

1. **Out-of-class individual projects with help.** This is a technique that I have used and it works well. I require completion of several short Excel modeling projects of every individual student in the class. To provide help, I schedule special "help lab" sessions in a computer lab during which time myself and my graduate assistant are available to answer questions while students do each assignment in about an hour. Typically about half the questions are

Excel questions and half are finance questions. I have always graded such projects, but an alternative approach would be to treat them as ungraded homework.

2. **Out-of-class individual projects without help.** Another technique is to assign Excel modeling projects for individual students to do on their own out of class. One instructor assigns seven Excel modeling projects at the beginning of the semester and has individual students turn in all seven completed Excel models for grading at the end of the semester. At the end of each chapter are problems that can be assigned with or without help. Faculty members can download the completed Excel models and answers to end-of-chapter problems at **http://www.pearsonhighered.com/irc**. See your local Pearson representative to gain access.

3. **Out-of-class group projects.** A technique that I have used for the last fifteen years is to require students to do big Excel modeling projects in groups. I have students write a report to a hypothetical boss, which intuitively explains their method of analysis, key assumptions, and key results.

4. **In-class reinforcement of key concepts.** The class session is scheduled in a computer lab or equivalently students are required to bring their (required) laptop computers to a technology classroom, which has a data jack and a power outlet at every student station. I explain a key concept in words and equations. Then I turn to a 10-15 minute segment in which students open a Ready-To-Build spreadsheet and build the Excel model in real-time in the class. This provides real-time, hands-on reinforcement of a key concept. This technique can be done often throughout the semester.

5. **In-class demonstration of Excel modeling.** The instructor can perform an in-class demonstration of how to build Excel models. Typically, only a small portion of the total Excel model would be demonstrated.

6. **In-class demonstration of key relationships using Spin Buttons, Option Buttons, and Charts.** The instructor can dynamically illustrate comparative statics or dynamic properties over time using visual, interactive elements. For example, one spreadsheet provides a "movie" of 37 years of U.S. term structure dynamics. Another spreadsheet provides an interactive graph of the sensitivity of bond prices to changes in the coupon rate, yield-to-maturity, number of payments / year, and face value.

I'm sure I haven't exhausted the list of potential teaching techniques. Feel free to send an e-mail to **cholden@indiana.edu** to let me know novel ways in which you use this book.

Acknowledgements

I thank Tessa O'Brien, Mark Pfaltzgraff, David Alexander, Jackie Aaron, P.J. Boardman, Mickey Cox, Maureen Riopelle, and Paul Donnelly of Pearson for their vision, innovativeness, and encouragement of **Excel Modeling in Investments**. I thank Amy Foley, Nancy Fenton, Susan Abraham, Mary Kate

Murray, Ana Jankowski, Lori Braumberger, Holly Brown, Debbie Clare, Cheryl Clayton, Kevin Hancock, Josh McClary, Bill Minic, Melanie Olsen, Beth Ann Romph, Erika Rusnak, Gladys Soto, and Lauren Tarino of Pearson for many useful contributions. I thank Professors Alan Bailey (University of Texas at San Antonio), Zvi Bodie (Boston University), Jack Francis (Baruch College), David Griswold (Boston University), Carl Hudson (Auburn University), Robert Kleiman (Oakland University), Mindy Nitkin (Simmons College), Steve Rich (Baylor University), Tim Smaby (Penn State University), Charles Trzcinka (Indiana University), Sorin Tuluca (Fairleigh Dickinson University), Marilyn Wiley (Florida Atlantic University), and Chad Zutter (University of Pittsburgh) for many thoughtful comments. I thank my dad, Bill Holden, and my graduate students Sam Singhania, Harry Bramson, Brent Cherry, Scott Marolf, Heath Eckert, Ryan Brewer, Ruslan Goyenko, Wendy Liu, and Wannie Park for careful error-checking. I thank Jim Finnegan and many other students for providing helpful comments. I thank my family, Kathryn, Diana, and Jimmy, for their love and support.

About The Author

CRAIG W. HOLDEN

Craig W. Holden is a Professor of Finance at the Kelley School of Business at Indiana University. His M.B.A. and Ph.D. are from the Anderson School at UCLA. He is the winner of many teaching and research awards, including a Fama/DFA Prize. His research on security trading and market making ("market microstructure") has been published in leading academic journals. He has written **Excel Modeling in Investments** and **Excel Modeling in Corporate Finance**. The Fourth Editions in English are published by Pearson / Prentice Hall and there are International, Chinese, and Italian editions. He has chaired eighteen dissertations, been a member or chair of 51 dissertations, served on the program committee of the *Western Finance Association* for eleven years, and served as an associate editor of the *Journal of Financial Markets* for thirteen years. He chaired the finance department undergraduate committee for twelve years, chaired the finance department doctoral committee for four years, and chaired three different schoolwide committees for a combination of six years. He has led several major curriculum innovations in the finance department. More information is available at Craig's home page: **www.kelley.iu.edu/cholden**.

PART 1 BONDS / FIXED INCOME SECURITIES

Chapter 1 Bond Pricing

1.1 Annual Payments

Problem. On February 26, 2010, an 8 year Treasury Bond with a face value of $1,000.00, paying $35.00 in coupon payments per year had a discount rate per year (yield) of 3.25%. Consider a bond that paid a $35.00 coupon payment once per year. What is price of this annual payment bond?

FIGURE 1.1 Bond Pricing – Annual Payments.

	A	B	C	D	E	F	G	H	I	J
1	**BOND PRICING**	**Annual Payments**								
2										
3										
4										
5										
6										
7	Inputs									
8	Number of Periods to Maturity (T)	8	8							
9	Face Value (PAR)	$1,000	20							
10										
11										
12	Discount Rate / Period (r)	3.25%	6							
13	Coupon Payment (PMT)	$35.00	7							
14										
15	Bond Price using a Timeline									
16	Period		0	1	2	3	4	5	6	7	8
17										
18	Cash Flows			$35.00	$35.00	$35.00	$35.00	$35.00	$35.00	$35.00	$1,035.00
19	Present Value of Cash Flows			$33.90	$32.83	$31.80	$30.80	$29.83	$28.89	$27.98	$801.35
20	Bond Price	$1,017.37								
21										
22	Bond Price using the Formula									
23	Bond Price (P)	$1,017.37								
24										
25	Bond Price using the PV Function									
26	Bond Price	$1,017.37								
27										
28										
29										
30										
31										
32										
33										
34										
35										
36										
37										
38										
39										

(1) Coupon Payment
Enter =$B$13 and copy to the range D18:I18

(2) Coupon Payment + Face Value
Enter =B13+B9

(3) (Cash Flow) / ((1+Discount Rate/Period)^Period)
Enter =C18/((1+$B$12)^C17) and copy across

(4) Sum of all the Present Value of Cash Flows
Enter =SUM(C19:J19)

(5) The Bond Price Formula is

$$P = \frac{PMT \cdot \left(1 - \left((1+r)^{-T}\right)\right)}{r} + \frac{PAR}{(1+r)^{T}}$$

Enter =B13*(1-((1+B12)^(-B8)))/B12+B9/((1+B12)^B8)

(6) -PV(Discount Rate / Period, Number of Periods to Maturity, Coupon Payment, Face Value)
Enter =-PV(B12,B8,B13,B9)

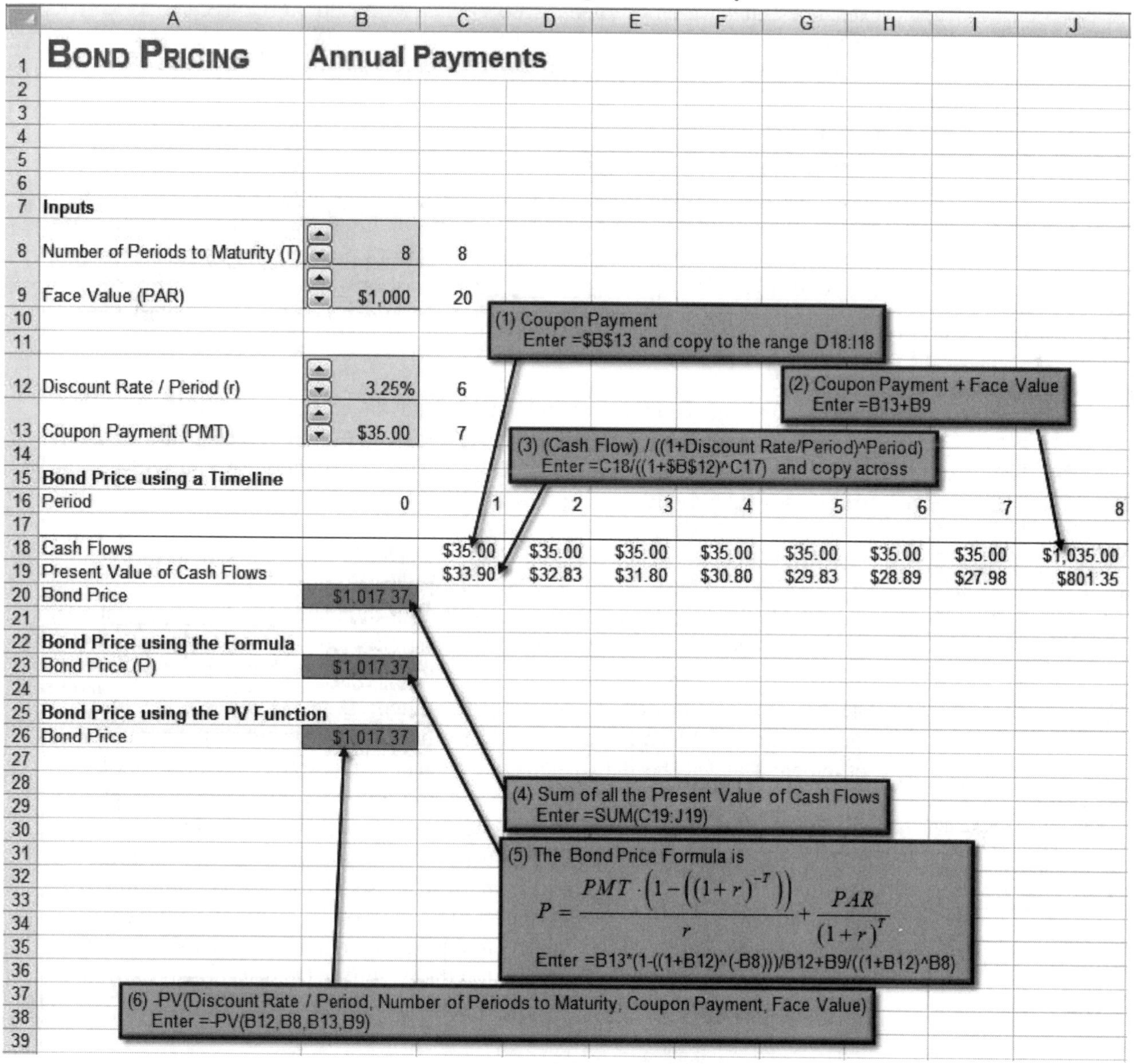

Solution Strategy. We calculate the bond price in three equivalent ways. First, we will calculate the bond price as the present value of the bond's cash flows. Second, we use a formula for the bond price. Third, we use Excel's PV function for a bond price.

The resulting annual bond price is $1,017.37. Notice you get the same answer all three ways: using the cash flows, using the formula, or using the PV function!

1.2 EAR, APR, and Foreign Currencies

Problem. On February 26, 2010, a 4 year Treasury Bond with a face value of $1,000 and an annual coupon rate of 4.00% had a yield to maturity of 1.74%. This bond makes 2 (semi-annual) coupon payments per year and thus has 8 periods until maturity. What is the price of this bond based on the Effective Annual Rate (EAR) convention? What is the price of this bond based on the Annual Percentage Rate (APR) convention? On the same date, the following exchanges rates were observed: $1.00 = ¥7.3790, $1.00 = €0.6805, and $1 = IDR 39.30. Under both the EAR and APR conventions, what is the price of the bond in Chinese Yuan (¥), European Euros (€), and in Indian Rupees (IDR)?

Solution Strategy. We will create an option button that can be used to select either the EAR or APR rate convention. The choice of rate convention will determine the discount rate / period. For a given discount rate / period, we will calculate the bond price in four equivalent ways. First, we will calculate the bond price as the present value of the bond's cash flows. Second, we use a formula for the bond price. Third, we use Excel's PV function for a bond price. Fourth, we use Excel's Analysis ToolPak Add-In **PRICE** function, which only works under the APR convention.

Excel's Analysis ToolPak contains several advanced bond functions, including the **PRICE** function which uses the APR convention. To access any of these functions, you need to install the Analysis ToolPak. Otherwise you will get the error message #NAME?.

To install the Analysis ToolPak, click on [File], click on Options, click on **Add-Ins**, highlight the **Analysis ToolPak** in the list of Inactive Applications, click on **Go**, check the **Analysis ToolPak**, and click on **OK**.

The bond price function is =PRICE(Settlement Date, Maturity Date, Annual Coupon Rate, Yield To Maturity, Redemption Value, Number of Payments). The Settlement Date is the date when you exchange money to purchase the bond. Specifying the exact day of settlement and maturity allows a very precise calculation. For our purpose, we simply want the difference between the two dates to equal the (8 Periods To Maturity) / (2 Payments / Year) = 4 Years To Maturity. This is easily accomplished by the use of the DATE function. The DATE Function has the format =DATE(Year, Month, Day). We will enter an arbitrary starting date of 1/1/2000 for the Settlement Date and then specify a formula for 1/1/2000 plus T / NOP for the Maturity Date. We also add an IF statement to test for the rate convention being used.

FIGURE 1.2 Bond Pricing – EAR, APR, & Foreign Currencies.

	A	B	C	D	E	F	G	H	I	J
1	**BOND PRICING**	**EAR, APR, & Foreign Currencies**					Currency: US Dollar		Exch Rate $1.00 =	$1.00
2										
3	**Inputs**									
4	Rate Convention	◯ EAR ⦿ APR	2	**Annual Percentage Rate**						
5	Annual Coupon Rate	4.00%	8	(1) If Rate Convention = EAR, Then (1+Yield To Maturity)^(1 / (Number of Payments / Year)) - 1 Else (Yield To Maturity) / Number of Payment / Year) Enter =IF(C4=1,((1+B6)^(1/B7))-1,B6/B7)						
6	Yield to Maturity (Annualized)	1.74%	3							
7	Number of Payments / Year	2		(2) Coupon Rate * Face Value / (Number of Payments / Year) Enter =B5*B9/B7						
8	Number of Periods to Maturity (T)	8	8							
9	Face Value (PAR)	$1,000		(3) Period / (Number of Payments / Year) Enter =B16/$B$7 and copy across						
10										
11	**Outputs**			(4) Copy the Timeline, Formula, and Function from the previous sheet Copy the range B18:J26 from the previous sheet to B18						
12	Discount Rate / Period (r)	0.9%								
13	Coupon Payment (PMT)	$20								
14										
15	**Bond Price using a Timeline**									
16	Period	0	1	2	3	4	5	6	7	8
17	Time (Years)	0.0	0.5	1.0	1.5	2.0	2.5	3.0	3.5	4.0
18	Cash Flows		$20.00	$20.00	$20.00	$20.00	$20.00	$20.00	$20.00	$1,020.00
19	Present Value of Cash Flows		$19.83	$19.66	$19.49	$19.32	$19.15	$18.99	$18.82	$951.71
20	Bond Price	$1,086.96								
21										
22	**Bond Price using a Formula**									
23	Bond Price	$1,086.96								
24										
25	**Bond Price using a Function**									
26	Bond Price	$1,086.96								
27										
28	**Bond Price using the PRICE Function (under APR)**									
29	Bond Price	$1,086.96								
30										
31		(5) If Rate Convention = EAR, Then Blank, Else =PRICE(DATE(2000,1,1),DATE(2000 + Number of Periods to Maturity / (Number of Payments / Year),1,1), Coupon Rate, Yield To Maturity, 100, (Number of Payments / Year)) * Number of Periods to Maturity / 100) Enter =IF(C4=1,"",PRICE(DATE(2000,1,1), DATE(2000+B8/B7,1,1),B5,B6,100,B7)*B9/100)								

Bond Price By Yield To Maturity

Bond Pricing by Calendar Time

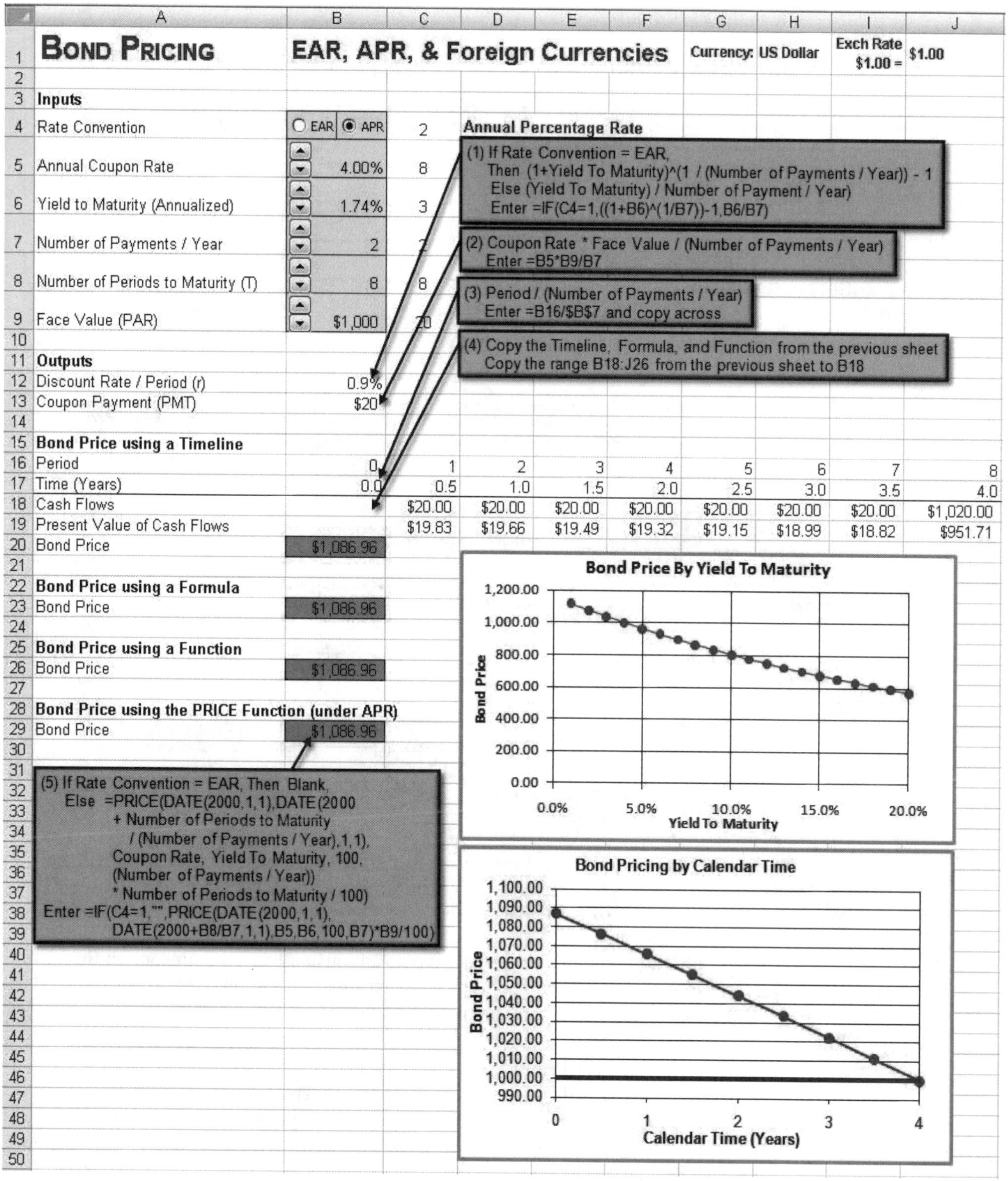

The resulting semi-annual bond price is $1,086.96 under APR and $1,087.26 under EAR. Notice you get the same answer all ways: using the cash flows, using the formula, using the PV function, or using the PRICE function under APR!

It is interesting to link two graphs: (1) bond pricing by yield to maturity and (2) bond pricing by calendar time. The former is done with a Data Table and the later with the PV formula.

FIGURE 1.3 Bond Pricing – EAR, APR, & Foreign Currencies.

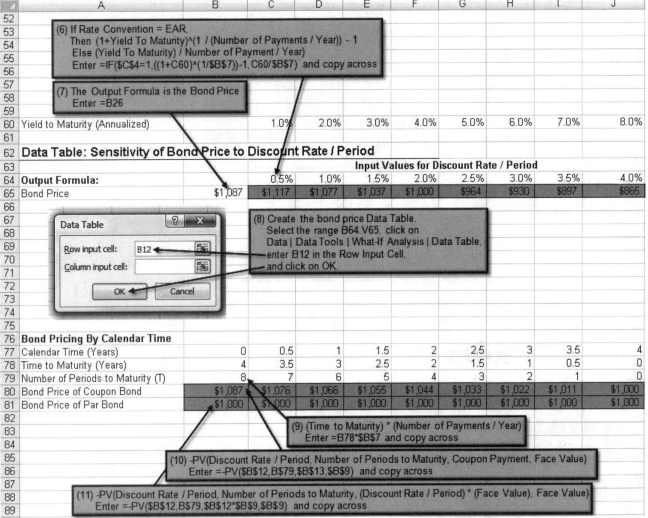

Excel 97-2003 Equivalent

To call up a Data Table in Excel 97-2003, click on **Data | Table**.

These graphs allow you to change the inputs and instantly see the impact on the bond price by yield to maturity and by calendar time. This allows you to perform instant experiments on the bond price, such as the following:

- What happens when the annual coupon rate is increased?
- What happens when the yield to maturity is increased?
- What happens when the number of payments / year is increased?
- What happens when the face value is increased?
- How does the price of coupon bond change over time when it is at a premium (above par) vs. at a discount (below par)?

What happens when the annual coupon rate is decreased to the point that it equals the yield to maturity? What happens when it is decreased further?

FIGURE 1.4 Bond Pricing – EAR, APR, & Foreign Currencies.

	G	H	I	J	K	L	M
1	Currency:	Chinese Yuan	Exch Rate $1.00 =	¥7.4			
2						Currency Number	1
3						(Select from below)	
4						1 = Chinese Yuan	¥ 7.3790
5	1 / (Number of Payments / Year)) - 1					2 = European Euro	€ 0.6805
6	mber of Payment / Year) 7))-1,B6/B7)					3 = Indian Rupee	IDR 39.30
7	(Number of Payments / Year)					4 = US Dollar	$1.00

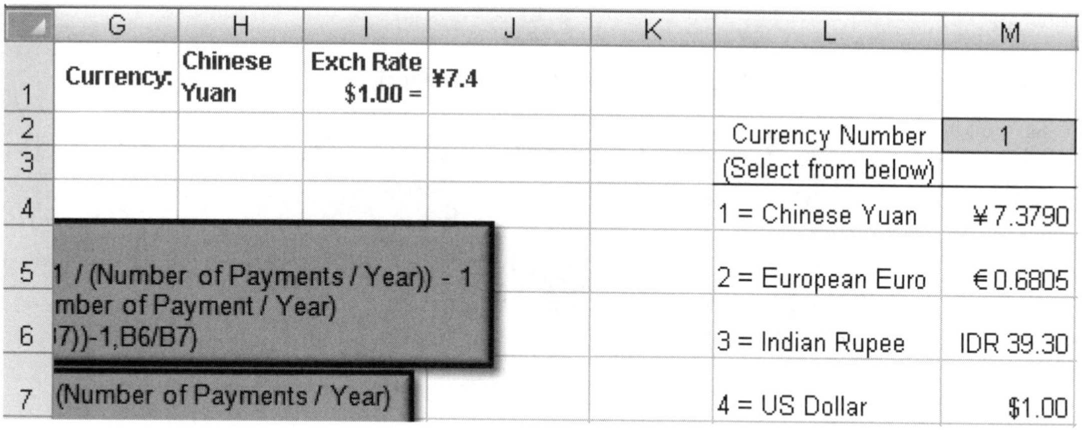

This spreadsheet has foreign currency conversion built into it. Cell **M2** is the currency selection cell. The default is currency 4, which is US Dollars. If you enter 1 in cell **M2**, then the spreadsheet converts to Chinese Yuan.

FIGURE 1.5 Bond Pricing – EAR, APR, & For. Cur. – in Chinese Yuan.

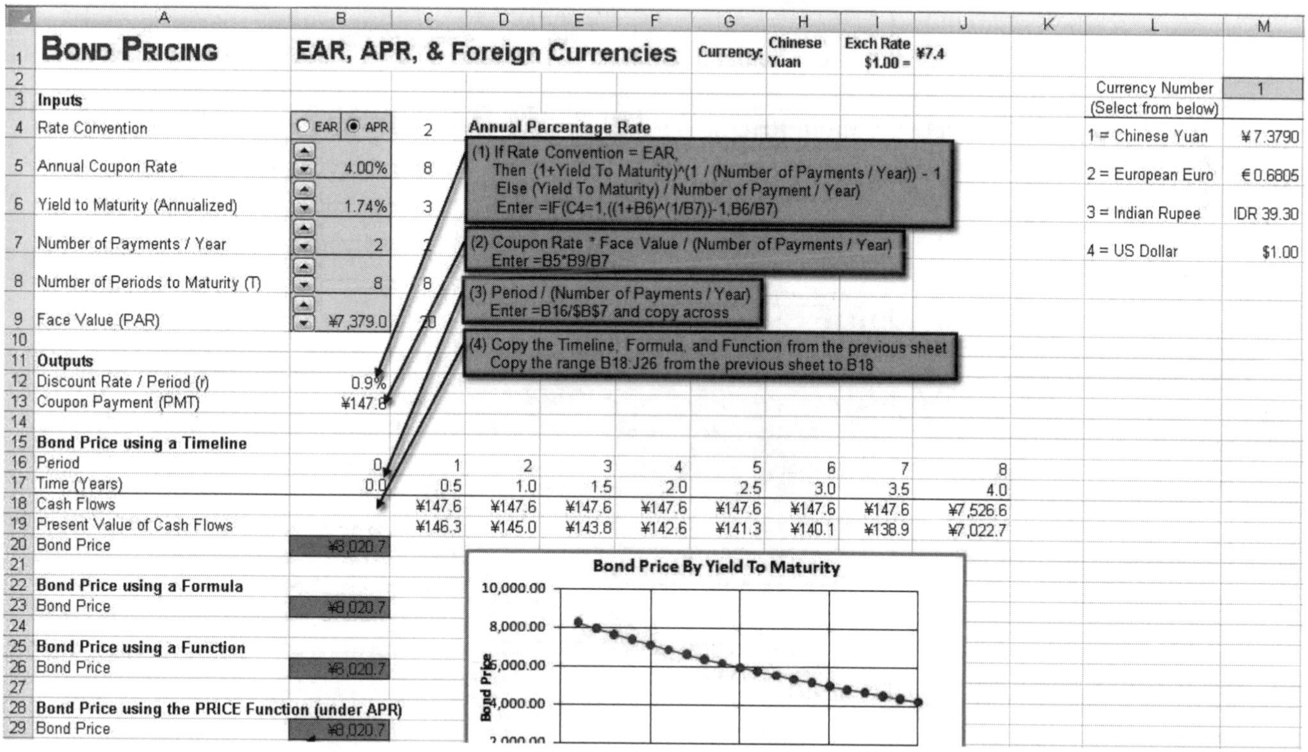

	A	B	C	D	E	F	G	H	I	J	K	L	M
1	**BOND PRICING**	**EAR, APR, & Foreign Currencies**					Currency:	Chinese Yuan	Exch Rate $1.00 =	¥7.4			
2												Currency Number	1
3	**Inputs**											(Select from below)	
4	Rate Convention	○ EAR ● APR	2	**Annual Percentage Rate**								1 = Chinese Yuan	¥ 7.3790
5	Annual Coupon Rate	4.00%	8	(1) If Rate Convention = EAR, Then (1+Yield To Maturity)^(1 / (Number of Payments / Year)) - 1 Else (Yield To Maturity) / Number of Payment / Year) Enter =IF(C4=1,((1+B6)^(1/B7))-1,B6/B7)								2 = European Euro	€ 0.6805
6	Yield to Maturity (Annualized)	1.74%	3									3 = Indian Rupee	IDR 39.30
7	Number of Payments / Year	2		(2) Coupon Rate * Face Value / (Number of Payments / Year) Enter =B5*B9/B7								4 = US Dollar	$1.00
8	Number of Periods to Maturity (T)	8	8	(3) Period / (Number of Payments / Year) Enter =B16/$B$7 and copy across									
9	Face Value (PAR)	¥7,379.0											
10				(4) Copy the Timeline, Formula, and Function from the previous sheet Copy the range B18:J26 from the previous sheet to B18									
11	**Outputs**												
12	Discount Rate / Period (r)	0.9%											
13	Coupon Payment (PMT)	¥147.6											
14													
15	**Bond Price using a Timeline**												
16	Period	0	1	2	3	4	5	6	7	8			
17	Time (Years)	0.0	0.5	1.0	1.5	2.0	2.5	3.0	3.5	4.0			
18	Cash Flows		¥147.6	¥147.6	¥147.6	¥147.6	¥147.6	¥147.6	¥147.6	¥7,526.6			
19	Present Value of Cash Flows		¥146.3	¥145.0	¥143.8	¥142.6	¥141.3	¥140.1	¥138.9	¥7,022.7			
20	Bond Price	¥8,020.7											
21													
22	**Bond Price using a Formula**												
23	Bond Price	¥8,020.7											
24													
25	**Bond Price using a Function**												
26	Bond Price	¥8,020.7											
27													
28	**Bond Price using the PRICE Function (under APR)**												
29	Bond Price	¥8,020.7											

Bond Price By Yield To Maturity

The selected exchange rate is displayed in cell **J1**, $1.00 = ¥7.3790 (rounded to ¥7.4). This exchange rate is multiplied by the $1,000 face value in cell B9 to get a ¥7,379 face value and this in turn spread throughout the spreadsheet. The resulting semi-annual bond price is ¥8,020.7 under APR and ¥8,022.9 under EAR. All of the dollar amount cells have conditional formatting rule to display ¥ for Chinese Yuan, € for European Euros, and IDR for Indian Rupees (see below).

FIGURE 1.6 Bond Pricing – EAR, APR, & For. Cur. – in European Euros.

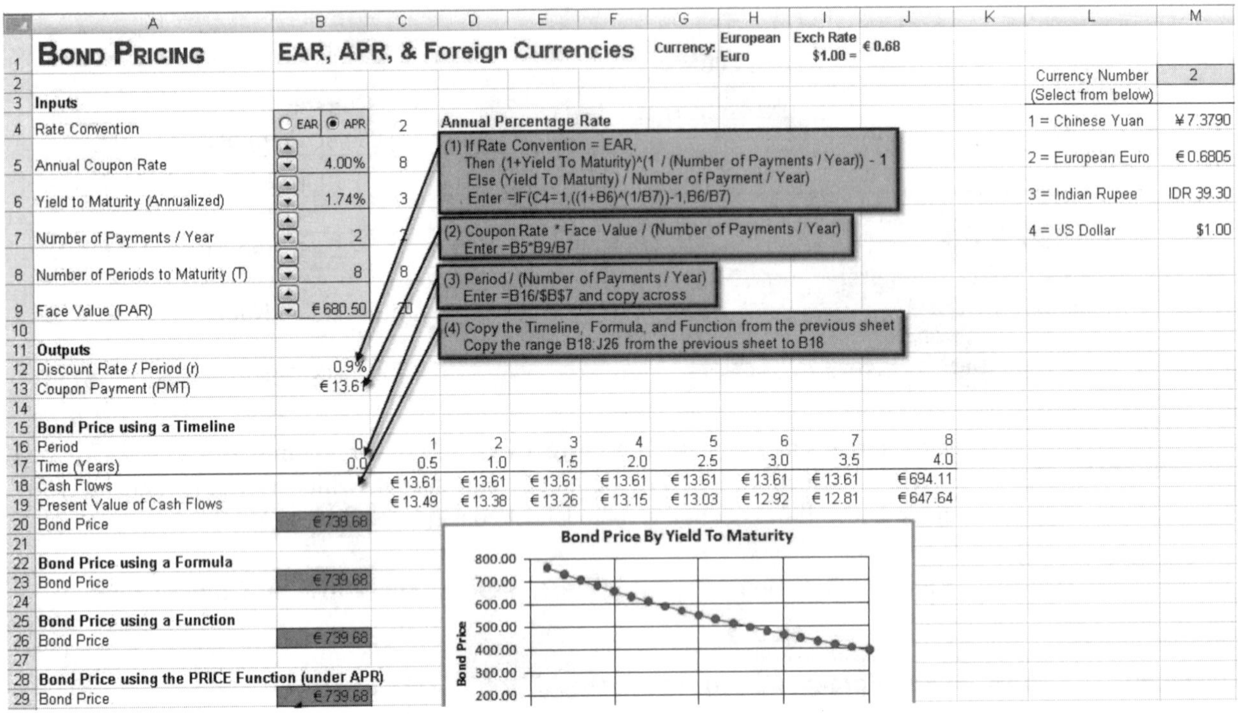

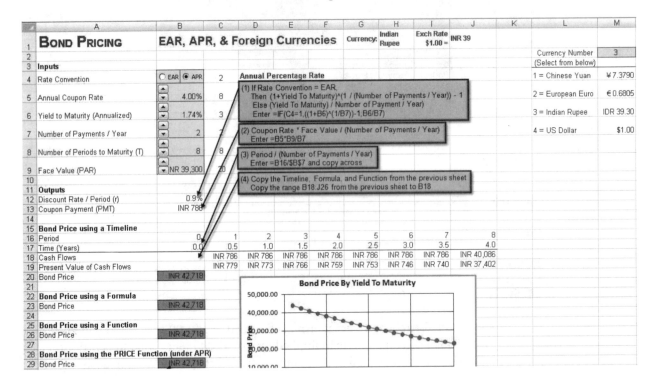

FIGURE 1.7 Bond Pricing – EAR, APR, & For. Cur. – in Indian Rupees.

1.3 Duration and Convexity

Problem. On February 26, 2010, a 4 year Treasury Bond with a face value of $1,000 and an annual coupon rate of 4.00% had a yield to maturity of 1.74%. This bond makes 2 (semi-annual) coupon payments per year and thus has 8 periods until maturity. What is the duration, modified duration, and convexity of this bond based on the Annual Percentage Rate (APR) convention? What is the duration, modified duration, and convexity of this bond based on the Effective Annual Rate (EAR) convention? What is the intuitive interpretation of duration?

Solution Strategy. The choice of either the EAR or APR rate convention will determine the discount rate / period. For a given the discount rate / period, we will calculate duration and modified duration three equivalent ways. First, we will calculate duration as the weighted-average time to the bond's cash flows. This method illustrates the intuitive interpretation of duration. Second, we use a formula for duration. In both cases, modified duration is a simple adjustment of regular duration (also called Macaulay's Duration). Third, we use Excel's Analysis ToolPak Add-In **DURATION** and **MDURATION** functions, which only work under the APR convention. We will calculate convexity two equivalent ways. First, we will calculate convexity as the weighted-average (time-squared plus time) to the bond's cash flows. Second, we use a formula for convexity.

FIGURE 1.8 Bond Pricing – Duration and Convexity.

	A	B	C	D	E	F	G	H	I	J
1	**BOND PRICING**	**Duration and Convexity**					Currency: US Dollar		Exch Rate $1.00 =	$1.00
2										
3	**Inputs**									
4	Rate Convention	○ EAR ● APR	2	Annual Percentage Rate						
5	Annual Coupon Rate	4.00%	8							
6	Yield to Maturity (Annualized)	1.74%	3							
7	Number of Payments / Year	2	2							
8	Number of Periods to Maturity (T)	8	8							
9	Face Value (PAR)	$1,000	20							
10										
11	**Outputs**									
12	Discount Rate / Period (r)	0.9%								
13	Coupon Payment (PMT)	$20								
14										
15	**Bond Duration using a Timeline**									
16	Period	0	1	2	3	4	5	6	7	8
17	Time (Years)	0.0	0.5	1.0	1.5	2.0	2.5	3.0	3.5	4.0
18	Cash Flows		$20.00	$20.00	$20.00	$20.00	$20.00	$20.00	$20.00	$1,020.00
19	Present Value of Cash Flows		$19.83	$19.66	$19.49	$19.32	$19.15	$18.99	$18.82	$951.71
20	Bond Price using a Timeline	$1,086.96								
21	Weight		1.8%	1.8%	1.8%	1.8%	1.8%	1.7%	1.7%	87.6%
22	Weight * Time		0.01	0.02	0.03	0.04	0.04	0.05	0.06	3.50
23	Duration using a Timeline	3.75								
24	Modified Duration using a Timeline	3.72								
25										
26	**Bond Duration using a Formula**									
27	Duration (D) using a Formula	3.75								
28	Modified Duration using a Formula	3.72								
29										
30	**Bond Duration using a Function (under APR)**									
31	Duration using a Function	3.75								
32	Modified Duration using a Function	3.72								
42	**Bond Convexity**									
43	Weight * (Time^2+Time)		0.01	0.04	0.07	0.11	0.15	0.21	0.27	17.51
44	Convexity using a Timeline	18.06								
45	Convexity using a Formula	18.06								

(1) Copy the Outputs & Timeline from the previous sheet
Copy the range B12:J20 from the previous sheet to B12

(2) PV of Cash Flow on Date t / Total PV of all Cash Flows
Enter =C19/$B$20 and copy across

(3) Weight * Time
Enter =C21*C17 and copy across

(4) Sum of all the Weight * Times
Enter =SUM(C22:J22)

(5) Duration / (1+(Discount Rate / Period))
Enter =B23/(1+$B$12) and copy to cell B28

(6) The Duration Formula is:
$$D = \frac{1+r}{r \cdot NOP} - \frac{1+r+T \cdot (CR/NOP-r)}{CR \cdot \left((1+r)^T - 1\right) + r \cdot NOP}$$

Enter =(1+B12)/(B12*B7)-(1+B12+B8*(B5/B7-B12))
/(B5*((1+B12)^B8-1)+B12*B7)

(7) DURATION (Settlement Date, Maturity Date, Annual
Coupon Rate, Yield to Maturity, Number of Periods)
Enter =IF($C$4=1,"",DURATION(DATE(2000,1,1),
DATE(2000+B8/B7,1,1),B5,B6,B7))

(8) MDURATION (Settlement Date, Maturity Date, Annual
Coupon Rate, Yield to Maturity, Number of Periods)
Enter =IF($C$4=1,"",MDURATION(DATE(2000,1,1),
DATE(2000+B8/B7,1,1),B5,B6,B7))

(9) Weight * (Time^2 + Time)
Enter =C21*(C17^2+C17) and copy across

(10) (Sum of Weight * (Time ^ 2 + Time))
/ ((1 + Yield to Maturity / Number of Payments) ^ 2)
Enter =SUM(C43:J43)/((1+B6/B7)^2)

(11) The Convexity Formula is:
$$\left(\begin{array}{l} CR \cdot (1+r)^{1+T} \cdot \left(r \cdot (NOP+1)+2\right) \\ -CR \cdot \left(r^2 \cdot (NOP+T+1) \cdot (T+1) + r \cdot (NOP+2 \cdot T+3)+2\right) + r^3 \cdot NOP \cdot T \cdot (NOP+T) \end{array} \right) \div \left((1+r)^2\right)$$
$$\overline{r^2 \cdot NOP^2 \cdot \left(CR \cdot (1+r)^T - CR + r \cdot NOP\right)}$$

Enter =((B5*((1+B12)^(1+B8))*(B12*(B7+1)+2)-B5*(B12^2*(B7+B8+1)*(B8+1)+B12*(B7+2*B8+3)+2)+B12^3*B7*B8*(B7+B8))
/(B12^2*B7^2*(B5*(1+B12)^B8-B5+B12*B7)))/((1+B12)^2))

The timeline method of calculation directly illustrates the key intuition that (Macaulay's) duration is the weighted-average of the time until cash flows are received. The weights are based on the ratio of the present value of each cash flow over the present value of the total bond.

Excel's Analysis ToolPak contains several advanced bond functions, including the **DURATION** and **MDURATION** functions, which use the APR convention. To install the Analysis ToolPak, click on [File], click on [Options] , click on **Add-Ins**, highlight the **Analysis ToolPak** in the list of Inactive Applications, click on **Go**, check the **Analysis ToolPak**, and click on **OK**.

The duration is 3.75 years and the modified duration is 3.72 years. Notice you get the same answer all three ways: using the cash flows, using the formula, or using the Analysis ToolPak Add-In function!

The value of bond convexity is 18.06. Again you get the same answer both ways: using the cash flows or using the formula!

1.4 Price Sensitivity

Bond duration is a measure of the price sensitivity of a bond to changes in interest rates. In other words, it is a measure of the bond's interest rate risk. Duration tells you approximately what percent change in bond price will result from a given change in yield to maturity.

Bond convexity complements bond duration in measuring of the price sensitivity of a bond to changes in interest rates. In other words, duration and convexity combined give you a better approximation of what percent change in bond price will result from a given change in yield to maturity than you can get from duration alone. To get the overall picture we will compare all three on a graph: the duration approximation, the duration and convexity approximation, and the actual percent change in the bond price.

Problem. On February 26, 2010, a 4 year Treasury Bond with a face value of $1,000 and an annual coupon rate of 4.00% had a yield to maturity of 1.74%. This bond makes 2 (semi-annual) coupon payments per year and thus has 8 periods until maturity. What is the price sensitivity of a bond to changes in yield and how does that compare to the duration approximation, and compare to the duration plus convexity approximation?

FIGURE 1.9 Bond Pricing – Price Sensitivity.

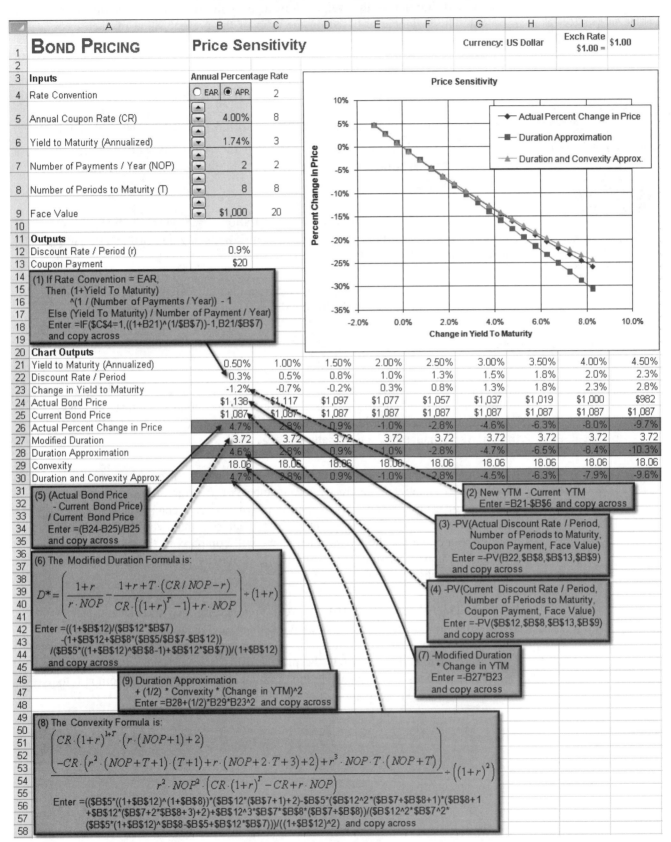

It is clear from the graph that duration does a very good job of approximating the price sensitivity of a bond. That is, the percent change in bond price from the duration approximation is very close to the actual percent change. This is especially true for relatively small changes in yield to maturity (say, plus or minus 3%). For larger changes in yield to maturity, there is a gap between the duration approximation and the actual percent change. The gap comes from the fact that the actual percent change is curved, whereas the duration approximation is a straight line.

One could do a better job of approximating the price sensitivity of a bond for larger changes in yield to maturity if one could account for the curvature. That is exactly what bond convexity does. The graph illustrates that duration and convexity approximation of the price sensitivity of a bond is better than the duration approximation alone. That is, the percent change in bond price from the duration and convexity approximation is very close to the actual percent change over a wide range of changes in yield to maturity (say, plus or minus 7%). Only for a very large change in yield to maturity is there any gap between the duration and convexity approximation and the actual percent change and the gap is pretty small.

In summary, duration alone does a good job of approximating the actual percent change using the slope only. Then convexity does a good job of adding the curvature. Together they do a great job of approximating the price sensitivity (i.e., interest rate risk) of a bond over a wide range of changes in yields.

1.5 Immunization

Problem. Suppose that an insurance company sells a guaranteed investment contract (GIC) to make a $4,000,000 lump-sum payment in 3 years. The company wishes to construct a portfolio of assets to cover this single liability, such that it is immunized against interest rate risk right now. The company is considering investing in two bonds: (1) a 2-year Treasury bond with a face value of $1,000 and an annual coupon rate of 1.50% and (2) a 4-year Treasury bond with a face value of $1,000 and an annual coupon rate of 2.00%. Both bonds make 2 (semi-annual) coupon payments per year. Thus they have 4 periods until maturity and 8 periods until maturity, respectively. The current yield on all bonds is 1.74%. How many 2-year and 4-year Treasury bonds should the insurance company buy in order to fully fund the liability and be immunized against interest rate risk right now?

Solution Strategy. To fully fund the liability, the present value of the assets must be equal to the present value of the liabilities. To be fully immunized right now, the duration of the assets must be equal to the duration of the liabilities. We will use Solver to find the number of 2-year and 4-year Treasury bonds that satisfy these requirements.

FIGURE 1.10 Bond Pricing – Immunization – A Single Liability.

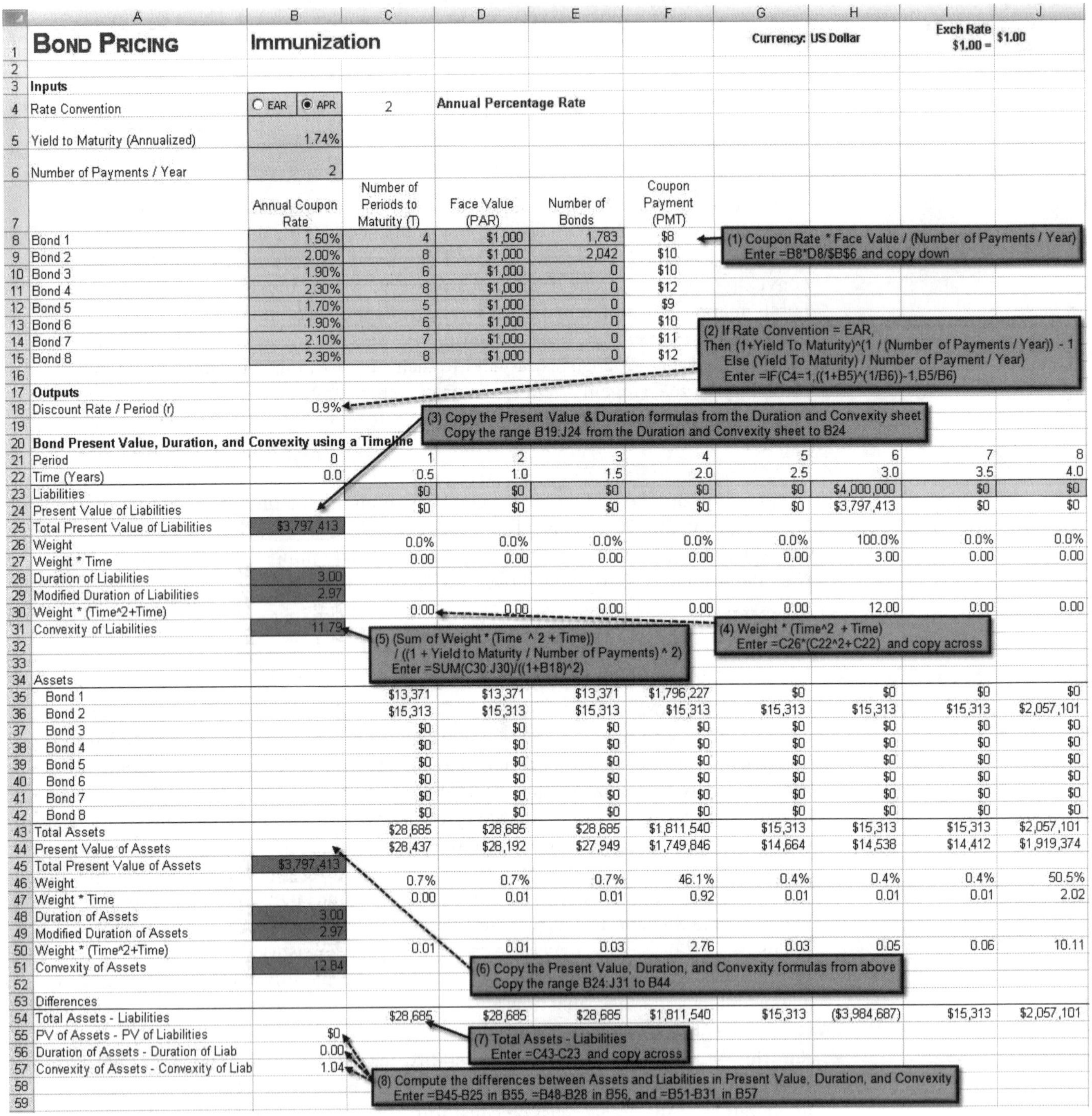

	A	B	C	D	E	F	G	H	I	J
1	**BOND PRICING**	**Immunization**					Currency: US Dollar		Exch Rate $1.00 =	$1.00
2										
3	**Inputs**									
4	Rate Convention	○ EAR ◉ APR	2	**Annual Percentage Rate**						
5	Yield to Maturity (Annualized)	1.74%								
6	Number of Payments / Year	2								
7		Annual Coupon Rate	Number of Periods to Maturity (T)	Face Value (PAR)	Number of Bonds	Coupon Payment (PMT)				
8	Bond 1	1.50%	4	$1,000	1,783	$8	(1) Coupon Rate * Face Value / (Number of Payments / Year) Enter =B8*D8/$B$6 and copy down			
9	Bond 2	2.00%	8	$1,000	2,042	$10				
10	Bond 3	1.90%	6	$1,000	0	$10				
11	Bond 4	2.30%	8	$1,000	0	$12				
12	Bond 5	1.70%	5	$1,000	0	$9				
13	Bond 6	1.90%	6	$1,000	0	$10	(2) If Rate Convention = EAR, Then (1+Yield To Maturity)^(1 / (Number of Payments / Year)) - 1 Else (Yield To Maturity) / Number of Payment / Year) Enter =IF(C4=1,((1+B5)^(1/B6))-1,B5/B6)			
14	Bond 7	2.10%	7	$1,000	0	$11				
15	Bond 8	2.30%	8	$1,000	0	$12				
16										
17	**Outputs**									
18	Discount Rate / Period (r)	0.9%								
19					(3) Copy the Present Value & Duration formulas from the Duration and Convexity sheet Copy the range B19:J24 from the Duration and Convexity sheet to B24					
20	**Bond Present Value, Duration, and Convexity using a Timeline**									
21	Period	0	1	2	3	4	5	6	7	8
22	Time (Years)	0.0	0.5	1.0	1.5	2.0	2.5	3.0	3.5	4.0
23	Liabilities		$0	$0	$0	$0	$0	$4,000,000	$0	$0
24	Present Value of Liabilities		$0	$0	$0	$0	$0	$3,797,413	$0	$0
25	Total Present Value of Liabilities	$3,797,413								
26	Weight		0.0%	0.0%	0.0%	0.0%	0.0%	100.0%	0.0%	0.0%
27	Weight * Time		0.00	0.00	0.00	0.00	0.00	3.00	0.00	0.00
28	Duration of Liabilities	3.00								
29	Modified Duration of Liabilities	2.97								
30	Weight * (Time^2+Time)		0.00	0.00	0.00	0.00	0.00	12.00	0.00	0.00
31	Convexity of Liabilities	11.73					(4) Weight * (Time^2 + Time) Enter =C26*(C22^2+C22) and copy across			
32			(5) (Sum of Weight * (Time ^ 2 + Time)) / ((1 + Yield to Maturity / Number of Payments) ^ 2) Enter =SUM(C30:J30)/((1+B18)^2)							
33										
34	**Assets**									
35	Bond 1		$13,371	$13,371	$13,371	$1,796,227	$0	$0	$0	$0
36	Bond 2		$15,313	$15,313	$15,313	$15,313	$15,313	$15,313	$15,313	$2,057,101
37	Bond 3		$0	$0	$0	$0	$0	$0	$0	$0
38	Bond 4		$0	$0	$0	$0	$0	$0	$0	$0
39	Bond 5		$0	$0	$0	$0	$0	$0	$0	$0
40	Bond 6		$0	$0	$0	$0	$0	$0	$0	$0
41	Bond 7		$0	$0	$0	$0	$0	$0	$0	$0
42	Bond 8		$0	$0	$0	$0	$0	$0	$0	$0
43	Total Assets		$28,685	$28,685	$28,685	$1,811,540	$15,313	$15,313	$15,313	$2,057,101
44	Present Value of Assets		$28,437	$28,192	$27,949	$1,749,846	$14,664	$14,538	$14,412	$1,919,374
45	Total Present Value of Assets	$3,797,413								
46	Weight		0.7%	0.7%	0.7%	46.1%	0.4%	0.4%	0.4%	50.5%
47	Weight * Time		0.00	0.01	0.01	0.92	0.01	0.01	0.01	2.02
48	Duration of Assets	3.00								
49	Modified Duration of Assets	2.97								
50	Weight * (Time^2+Time)		0.01	0.01	0.03	2.76	0.03	0.05	0.06	10.11
51	Convexity of Assets	12.84			(6) Copy the Present Value, Duration, and Convexity formulas from above Copy the range B24:J31 to B44					
52										
53	**Differences**									
54	Total Assets - Liabilities		$28,685	$28,685	$28,685	$1,811,540	$15,313	($3,984,687)	$15,313	$2,057,101
55	PV of Assets - PV of Liabilities	$0		(7) Total Assets - Liabilities Enter =C43-C23 and copy across						
56	Duration of Assets - Duration of Liab	0.00								
57	Convexity of Assets - Convexity of Liab	1.04								
58			(8) Compute the differences between Assets and Liabilities in Present Value, Duration, and Convexity Enter =B45-B25 in B55, =B48-B28 in B56, and =B51-B31 in B57							
59										

FIGURE 1.11 Bond Pricing – Immunization – A Single Liability.

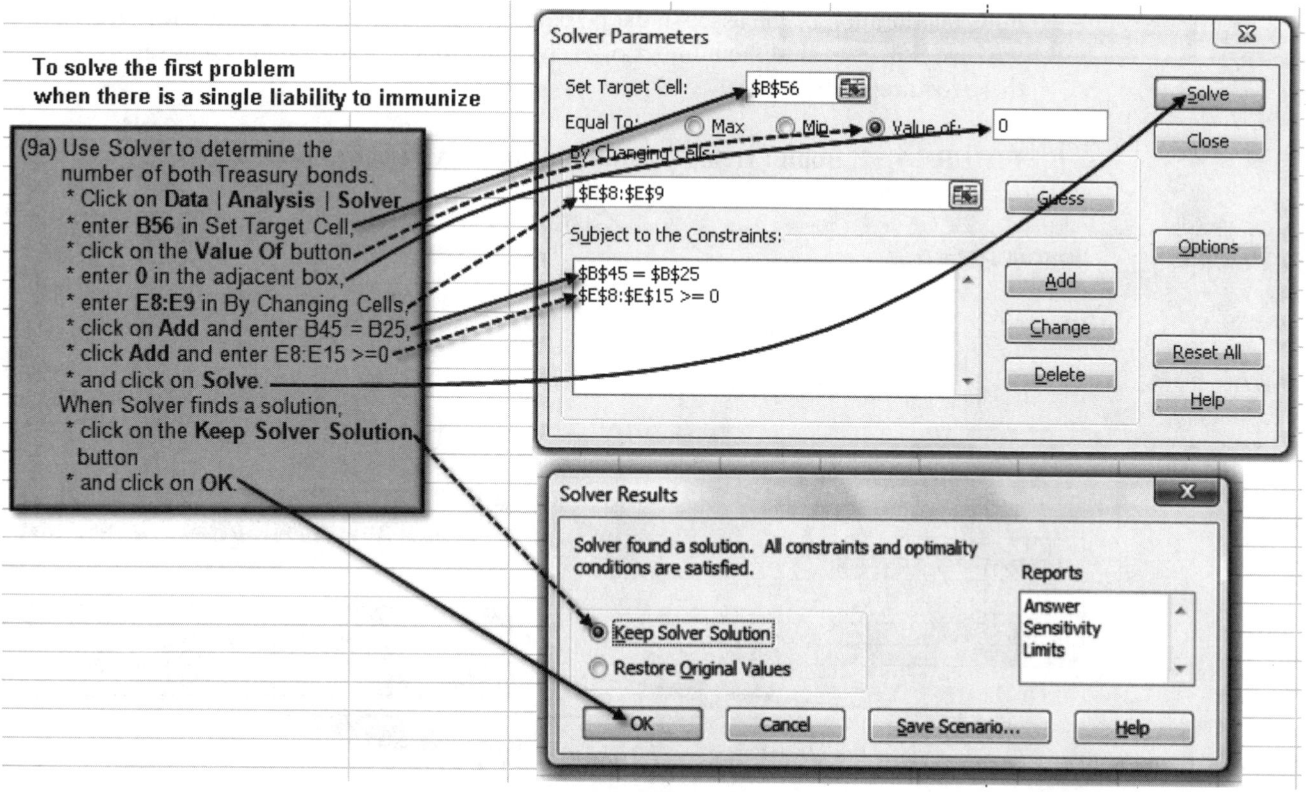

To solve the first problem when there is a single liability to immunize

(9a) Use Solver to determine the number of both Treasury bonds.
* Click on **Data | Analysis | Solver**
* enter **B56** in Set Target Cell,
* click on the **Value Of** button,
* enter **0** in the adjacent box,
* enter **E8:E9** in By Changing Cells,
* click on **Add** and enter **B45 = B25**,
* click **Add** and enter **E8:E15 >=0**
* and click on **Solve**.
When Solver finds a solution,
* click on the **Keep Solver Solution** button
* and click on **OK**.

Solver Parameters

Set Target Cell: $B$56
Equal To: Max Min Value of: 0
By Changing Cells:
$E$8:$E$9
Subject to the Constraints:
$B$45 = $B$25
$E$8:$E$15 >= 0

Solve / Close / Guess / Options / Add / Change / Delete / Reset All / Help

Solver Results

Solver found a solution. All constraints and optimality conditions are satisfied.

Reports: Answer / Sensitivity / Limits

Keep Solver Solution
Restore Original Values

OK / Cancel / Save Scenario... / Help

The answer is buy 1,783 2-year Treasury bonds and buy 2,042 4-year Treasury bonds. This portfolio of assets has a present value of $3,797,413, which equals the present value of the liability. This portfolio of assets has a duration of 3.00 years, which equals the duration of the liability. Thus, there is no interest rate risk at this moment. This portfolio of assets has a convexity of 12.84, which is greater than the liability convexity of 11.79. Thus, a change in yields will cause the portfolio to acquire interest rate risk in the future.

Problem 2. Suppose that a pension fund has a series of liabilities to be paid every six months to the pension plan beneficiaries: $2,000,000, $2,200,000, $2,500,000, $3,200,000, $3,700,000, $4,300,000, $4,700,000, and $5,100,000. The company wishes to construct a portfolio of assets to cover this series of liabilities, such that it is immunized against interest rate risk right now. The company is considering investing in four bonds: (1) a 1-year Treasury bond with a face value of $1,000 and an annual coupon rate of 0.90%, (2) a 2-year Treasury bond with a face value of $1,000 and an annual coupon rate of 1.50%, (3) a 3-year Treasury bond with a face value of $1,000 and an annual coupon rate of 1.90%, and (4) a 4-year Treasury bond with a face value of $1,000 and an annual coupon rate of 2.30%. All four bonds make 2 (semi-annual) coupon payments per year. Thus they have 2 periods, 4 periods, 6 periods, and 8 periods until maturity, respectively. The current yield on all bonds is 1.74%. How many of each of these four Treasury bonds should the pension fund buy in order to fully fund the liability and be immunized against interest rate risk right now?

Solution Strategy 2. To fully fund the liability, the present value of the assets must be equal to the present value of the liabilities. To be fully immunized right now, the duration of the assets must be equal to the duration of the liabilities. We will use Solver to find the number of each of the four Treasury bonds that satisfy these requirements.

FIGURE 1.12 Bond Pricing – Immunization – A Series of Liabilities.

	A	B	C	D	E	F	G	H	I	J
1	**BOND PRICING**	**Immunization**					Currency: US Dollar		Exch Rate $1.00 =	$1.00
2										
3	**Inputs**									
4	Rate Convention	○ EAR ◉ APR	2	**Annual Percentage Rate**						
5	Yield to Maturity (Annualized)	1.74%								
6	Number of Payments / Year	2								
7		Annual Coupon Rate	Number of Periods to Maturity (T)	Face Value (PAR)	Number of Bonds	Coupon Payment (PMT)				
8	Bond 1	0.90%	2	$1,000	6,038	$5	(1) Coupon Rate * Face Value / (Number of Payments / Year)			
9	Bond 2	1.50%	4	$1,000	5,937	$8	Enter =B8*D8/$B$6 and copy down			
10	Bond 3	1.90%	6	$1,000	7,017	$10				
11	Bond 4	2.30%	8	$1,000	8,068	$12				
12	Bond 5	1.70%	5	$1,000	0	$9				
13	Bond 6	1.90%	6	$1,000	0	$10	(2) If Rate Convention = EAR,			
14	Bond 7	2.10%	7	$1,000	0	$11	Then (1+Yield To Maturity)^(1 / (Number of Payments / Year)) - 1			
15	Bond 8	2.30%	8	$1,000	0	$12	Else (Yield To Maturity) / Number of Payment / Year)			
16							Enter =IF(C4=1,((1+B5)^(1/B6))-1,B5/B6)			
17	**Outputs**									
18	Discount Rate / Period (r)	0.9%								
19			(3) Copy the Present Value & Duration formulas from the Duration and Convexity sheet							
20	**Bond Present Value, Duration, and Convexity using a Timeline**		Copy the range B19:J24 from the Duration and Convexity sheet to B24							
21	Period	0	1	2	3	4	5	6	7	8
22	Time (Years)	0.0	0.5	1.0	1.5	2.0	2.5	3.0	3.5	4.0
23	Liabilities		$2,000,000	$2,200,000	$2,500,000	$3,200,000	$3,700,000	$4,300,000	$4,700,000	$5,100,000
24	Present Value of Liabilities		$1,982,750	$2,162,214	$2,435,869	$3,091,021	$3,543,167	$4,082,219	$4,423,476	$4,758,543
25	Total Present Value of Liabilities	$26,479,259								
26	Weight		7.5%	8.2%	9.2%	11.7%	13.4%	15.4%	16.7%	18.0%
27	Weight * Time		0.04	0.08	0.14	0.23	0.33	0.46	0.58	0.72
28	Duration of Liabilities	2.59								
29	Modified Duration of Liabilities	2.57								
30	Weight * (Time^2+Time)		0.06	0.16	0.34	0.70	1.17	1.85	2.63	3.59
31	Convexity of Liabilities	10.33								
32			(5) (Sum of Weight * (Time ^ 2 + Time))				(4) Weight * (Time^2 + Time)			
33			/ ((1 + Yield to Maturity / Number of Payments) ^ 2)				Enter =C26*(C22^2+C22) and copy across			
34	**Assets**		Enter =SUM(C30:J30)/((1+B18)^2)							
35	Bond 1		$27,171	$6,065,128	$0	$0	$0	$0	$0	$0
36	Bond 2		$26,715	$26,715	$26,715	$5,963,327	$0	$0	$0	$0
37	Bond 3		$31,575	$31,575	$31,575	$31,575	$31,575	$7,048,286	$0	$0
38	Bond 4		$36,306	$36,306	$36,306	$36,306	$36,306	$36,306	$36,306	$8,104,284
39	Bond 5		$0	$0	$0	$0	$0	$0	$0	$0
40	Bond 6		$0	$0	$0	$0	$0	$0	$0	$0
41	Bond 7		$0	$0	$0	$0	$0	$0	$0	$0
42	Bond 8		$0	$0	$0	$0	$0	$0	$0	$0
43	Total Assets		$121,767	$6,159,723	$94,596	$6,031,208	$67,881	$7,084,592	$36,306	$8,104,284
44	Present Value of Assets		$120,716	$6,053,927	$92,169	$5,825,809	$65,004	$6,725,781	$34,170	$7,561,683
45	Total Present Value of Assets	$26,479,259								
46	Weight		0.5%	22.9%	0.3%	22.0%	0.2%	25.4%	0.1%	28.6%
47	Weight * Time		0.00	0.23	0.01	0.44	0.01	0.76	0.00	1.14
48	Duration of Assets	2.59								
49	Modified Duration of Assets	2.57								
50	Weight * (Time^2+Time)		0.00	0.46	0.01	1.32	0.02	3.05	0.02	5.71
51	Convexity of Assets	10.41		(6) Copy the Present Value, Duration, and Convexity formulas from above						
52				Copy the range B24:J31 to B44						
53	**Differences**									
54	Total Assets - Liabilities		($1,878,233)	$3,959,723	($2,405,404)	$2,831,208	($3,632,119)	$2,784,592	($4,663,694)	$3,004,284
55	PV of Assets - PV of Liabilities	$0		(7) Total Assets - Liabilities						
56	Duration of Assets - Duration of Liab	0.00		Enter =C43-C23 and copy across						
57	Convexity of Assets - Convexity of Liab	0.08								
58			(8) Compute the differences between Assets and Liabilities in Present Value, Duration, and Convexity							
59			Enter =B45-B25 in B55, =B48-B28 in B56, and =B51-B31 in B57							

FIGURE 1.13 Bond Pricing – Immunization – A Series of Liabilities.

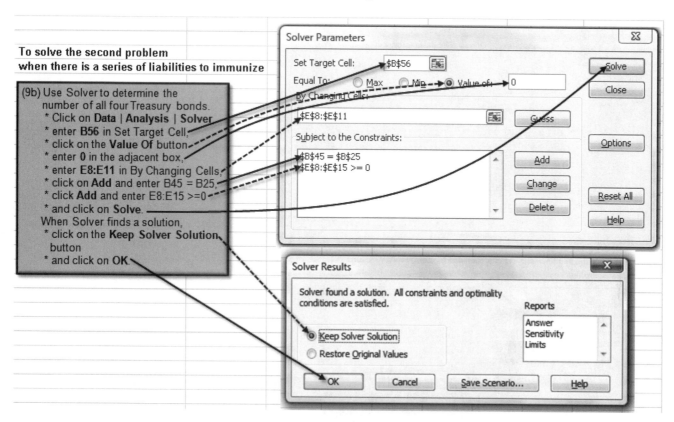

To solve the second problem
when there is a series of liabilities to immunize

(9b) Use Solver to determine the
number of all four Treasury bonds.
 * Click on **Data | Analysis | Solver**.
 * enter **B56** in Set Target Cell;
 * click on the **Value Of** button,
 * enter **0** in the adjacent box,
 * enter **E8:E11** in By Changing Cells;
 * click on **Add** and enter B45 = B25,
 * click **Add** and enter E8:E15 >=0
 * and click on **Solve**.
When Solver finds a solution,
 * click on the **Keep Solver Solution**
   button
 * and click on **OK**.

The answer is buy 6,038 1-year Treasury bonds, buy 5,937 2-year Treasury bonds, buy 7,017 3-year Treasury bonds, and buy 8,068 4-year Treasury bonds. This portfolio of assets has a present value of $26,479,259, which equals the present value of the liability. This portfolio of assets has a duration of 2.50 years, which equals the duration of the liability. Thus, there is no interest rate risk at this moment. This portfolio of assets has a convexity of 10.41, which is greater than the liability convexity of 10.33. Thus, a change in yields will cause the portfolio to acquire interest rate risk in the future.

Problem 3. Reconsider the same series of liabilities as in **Problem 2**. Suppose that the company wishes to construct a portfolio of assets to cover this series of liabilities, such that it is fully immunized against interest rate over the entire four year timeframe. Further suppose that the company has available eight Treasury Strips that mature in each of the eight periods. Treasury strips have no intermediate coupons (i.e., their annual coupon rate is 0.00%) and they just pay a single cash flow on the maturity date. The current yield on all bonds is 1.74%. How many of each of these eight Treasury strips should the pension fund buy in order to fully fund the liability and be fully immunized against interest rate risk over the entire four year timeframe?

FIGURE 1.14 Bond Pricing – Immunization – A Series of Liabilities.

	A	B	C	D	E	F	G	H	I	J
1	**BOND PRICING**	**Immunization**					Currency: US Dollar		Exch Rate $1.00 =	$1.00
2										
3	**Inputs**									
4	Rate Convention	○ EAR ◉ APR	2	Annual Percentage Rate						
5	Yield to Maturity (Annualized)	1.74%								
6	Number of Payments / Year	2								
7		Annual Coupon Rate	Number of Periods to Maturity (T)	Face Value (PAR)	Number of Bonds	Coupon Payment (PMT)				
8	Bond 1	0.00%	1	$1,000	2,000	$0	(1) Coupon Rate * Face Value / (Number of Payments / Year)			
9	Bond 2	0.00%	2	$1,000	2,200	$0	Enter =B8*D8/$B$6 and copy down			
10	Bond 3	0.00%	3	$1,000	2,500	$0				
11	Bond 4	0.00%	4	$1,000	3,200	$0				
12	Bond 5	0.00%	5	$1,000	3,700	$0				
13	Bond 6	0.00%	6	$1,000	4,300	$0	(2) If Rate Convention = EAR,			
14	Bond 7	0.00%	7	$1,000	4,700	$0	Then (1+Yield To Maturity)^(1 / (Number of Payments / Year)) - 1			
15	Bond 8	0.00%	8	$1,000	5,100	$0	Else (Yield To Maturity) / Number of Payment / Year)			
16							Enter =IF(C4=1,((1+B5)^(1/B6))-1,B5/B6)			
17	**Outputs**									
18	Discount Rate / Period (r)	0.9%								
19				(3) Copy the Present Value & Duration formulas from the Duration and Convexity sheet						
20	**Bond Present Value, Duration, and Convexity using a Timeline**			Copy the range B19:J24 from the Duration and Convexity sheet to B24						
21	Period	0	1	2	3	4	5	6	7	8
22	Time (Years)	0.0	0.5	1.0	1.5	2.0	2.5	3.0	3.5	4.0
23	Liabilities		$2,000,000	$2,200,000	$2,500,000	$3,200,000	$3,700,000	$4,300,000	$4,700,000	$5,100,000
24	Present Value of Liabilities		$1,982,750	$2,162,214	$2,435,869	$3,091,021	$3,543,167	$4,082,219	$4,423,476	$4,758,543
25	Total Present Value of Liabilities	$26,479,259								
26	Weight		7.5%	8.2%	9.2%	11.7%	13.4%	15.4%	16.7%	18.0%
27	Weight * Time		0.04	0.08	0.14	0.23	0.33	0.46	0.58	0.72
28	Duration of Liabilities	2.59								
29	Modified Duration of Liabilities	2.57								
30	Weight * (Time^2+Time)		0.06	0.16	0.34	0.70	1.17	1.85	2.63	3.59
31	Convexity of Liabilities	10.33	(5) (Sum of Weight * (Time ^ 2 + Time))			(4) Weight * (Time^2 + Time)				
32			/ ((1 + Yield to Maturity / Number of Payments) ^ 2)			Enter =C26*(C22^2+C22) and copy across				
33			Enter =SUM(C30:J30)/((1+B18)^2)							
34	**Assets**									
35	Bond 1		$2,000,000	$0	$0	$0	$0	$0	$0	$0
36	Bond 2		$0	$2,200,000	$0	$0	$0	$0	$0	$0
37	Bond 3		$0	$0	$2,500,000	$0	$0	$0	$0	$0
38	Bond 4		$0	$0	$0	$3,200,000	$0	$0	$0	$0
39	Bond 5		$0	$0	$0	$0	$3,700,000	$0	$0	$0
40	Bond 6		$0	$0	$0	$0	$0	$4,300,000	$0	$0
41	Bond 7		$0	$0	$0	$0	$0	$0	$4,700,000	$0
42	Bond 8		$0	$0	$0	$0	$0	$0	$0	$5,100,000
43	Total Assets		$2,000,000	$2,200,000	$2,500,000	$3,200,000	$3,700,000	$4,300,000	$4,700,000	$5,100,000
44	Present Value of Assets		$1,982,750	$2,162,214	$2,435,869	$3,091,021	$3,543,167	$4,082,219	$4,423,476	$4,758,543
45	Total Present Value of Assets	$26,479,259								
46	Weight		7.5%	8.2%	9.2%	11.7%	13.4%	15.4%	16.7%	18.0%
47	Weight * Time		0.04	0.08	0.14	0.23	0.33	0.46	0.58	0.72
48	Duration of Assets	2.59								
49	Modified Duration of Assets	2.57								
50	Weight * (Time^2+Time)		0.06	0.16	0.34	0.70	1.17	1.85	2.63	3.59
51	Convexity of Assets	10.33								
52			(6) Copy the Present Value, Duration, and Convexity formulas from above							
53	**Differences**		Copy the range B24:J31 to B44							
54	Total Assets - Liabilities		$0	$0	($0)	$0	$0	$0	$0	($0)
55	PV of Assets - PV of Liabilities	$0								
56	Duration of Assets - Duration of Liab	0.00	(7) Total Assets - Liabilities							
57	Convexity of Assets - Convexity of Liab	0.00	Enter =C43-C23 and copy across							
58			(8) Compute the differences between Assets and Liabilities in Present Value, Duration, and Convexity							
59			Enter =B45-B25 in B55, =B48-B28 in B56, and =B51-B31 in B57							

FIGURE 1.15 Bond Pricing – Immunization – A Series of Liabilities.

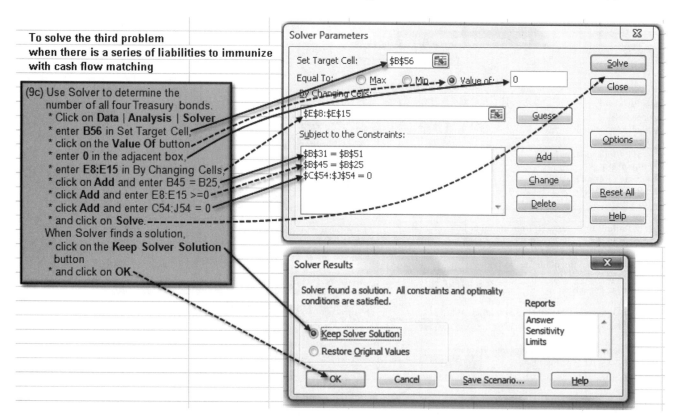

1.6 System of Five Bond Variables

Problem. There is a system of five bond variables: (1) Number of Periods to Maturity (T), (2) Face Value (PAR), (3) Discount Rate / Period (r), (4) Coupon Payments (PMT), and (5) Bond Price (P). Given any four of these variables, show how the fifth variable can be found by using Excel functions (and in some cases by formulas).

FIGURE 1.16 Bond Pricing - System of Five Bond Variables.

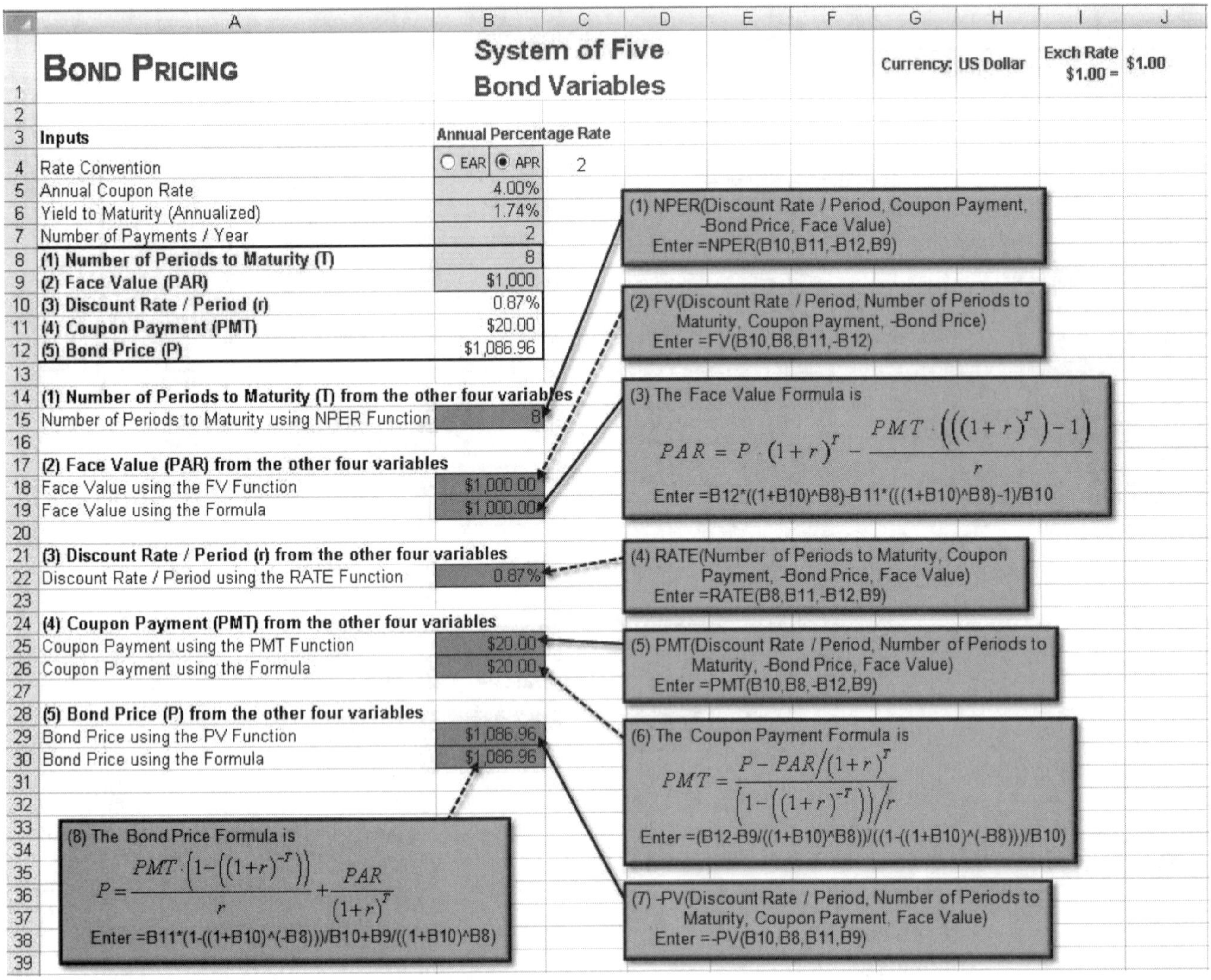

We see that the system of five bond variables is internally consistent. The five outputs in rows **15** through **30** (T=8, PAR=$1000.00, r=0.87%, PMT=$20.00, P=$1,086.96) are identical to the five inputs in rows **8** through **12**. Thus, any of the five bond variables can be calculated from the other four in a fully consistent manner.

Problems

1. An annual bond has a face value of $1,000.00, makes an annual coupon payment of $12.00 per year, has a discount rate per year of 4.37%, and has 8 years to maturity. What is price of this bond?

2. A 4 year Treasury Bond with a face value of $1,000 and an annual coupon rate of 6.50% had a yield to maturity of 3.15%. This bond makes 2 (semi-annual) coupon payments per year and thus has 8 periods until maturity. What is price of this bond based on the Effective Annual Rate (EAR)

convention? What is price of this bond based on the Annual Percentage Rate (APR) convention? On the same date, the following exchanges rates were observed: $1.00 = ¥9.5350, $1.00 = €0.4206, and $1 = IDR 52.75. Under both the EAR and APR conventions, what is the price of the bond in Chinese Yuan (¥), European Euros (€), and in Indian Rupees (IDR)?

3. Perform instant experiments on whether changing various inputs causes an increase or decrease in the Bond Price and by how much.

    (a.) What happens when the annual coupon rate is increased?
    (b.) What happens when the yield to maturity is increased?
    (c.) What happens when the number of payments / year is increased?
    (d.) What happens when the face value is increased?
    (e.) What is the relationship between the price of a par bond and time to maturity?
    (f.) What happens when the annual coupon rate is increased to the point that it equals the yield to maturity? What happens when it is increased further?

4. A 4 year Treasury Bond with a face value of $1,000 and an annual coupon rate of 3.20% had a yield to maturity of 2.53%. This bond makes 2 (semi-annual) coupon payments per year and thus has 8 periods until maturity. What is the duration, modified duration, and convexity of this bond based on the Annual Percentage Rate (APR) convention? What is the duration, modified duration, and convexity of this bond based on the Effective Annual Rate (EAR) convention? What is the intuitive interpretation of duration?

5. A 4 year Treasury Bond with a face value of $1,000 and an annual coupon rate of 5.80% had a yield to maturity of 4.29%. This bond makes 2 (semi-annual) coupon payments per year and thus has 8 periods until maturity. What is the price sensitivity of a bond to changes in yield and how does that compare to the duration approximation, and compare to the duration plus convexity approximation?

6. Suppose that an insurance company sells a guaranteed investment contract (GIC) to make a $7,300,000 lump-sum payment in 3 years. The company wishes to construct a portfolio of assets to cover this single liability, such that it is immunized against interest rate risk right now. The company is considering investing in two bonds: (1) a 2-year Treasury bond with a face value of $1,000 and an annual coupon rate of 3.25% and (2) a 4-year Treasury bond with a face value of $1,000 and an annual coupon rate of 4.25%.Both bonds make 2 (semi-annual) coupon payments per year. Thus they have 4 periods until maturity and 8 periods until maturity, respectively. The current yield on all bonds is 3.17%. How many 2-year and 4-year Treasury bonds should the insurance company buy in order to fully fund the liability and be immunized against interest rate risk right now?

7. Suppose that a pension fund has a series of liabilities to be paid every six months to the pension plan beneficiaries: $4,500,000, $5,100,000, $5,600,000, $6,300,000, $6,800,000, $7,200,000, $7,900,000, and $8,600,000. The company wishes to construct a portfolio of assets to cover

this series of liabilities, such that it is immunized against interest rate risk right now. The company is considering investing in four bonds: (1) a 1-year Treasury bond with a face value of $1,000 and an annual coupon rate of 1.50%, (2) a 2-year Treasury bond with a face value of $1,000 and an annual coupon rate of 2.70%, (3) a 3-year Treasury bond with a face value of $1,000 and an annual coupon rate of 2.90%, and (4) a 4-year Treasury bond with a face value of $1,000 and an annual coupon rate of 3.20%. All four bonds make 2 (semi-annual) coupon payments per year. Thus they have 2 periods, 4 periods, 6 periods, and 8 periods until maturity, respectively. The current yield on all bonds is 3.17%. How many of each of these four Treasury bonds should the pension fund buy in order to fully fund the liability and be immunized against interest rate risk right now?

8. Reconsider the same series of liabilities as in **Problem 7**. Suppose that the company wishes to construct a portfolio of assets to cover this series of liabilities, such that it is fully immunized against interest rate over the entire four year timeframe. Further suppose that the company has available eight Treasury Strips that mature in each of the eight periods. Treasury strips have no intermediate coupons (i.e., their annual coupon rate is 0.00%) and they just pay a single cash flow on the maturity date. The current yield on all bonds is 3.17%. How many of each of these eight Treasury strips should the pension fund buy in order to fully fund the liability and be fully immunized against interest rate risk over the entire four year timeframe?

9. Given four of the bond variables, determine the fifth bond variable.

   (a.) Given Number of Periods to Maturity is 10, Face Value is $1,000.00, Discount Rate / Period is 3.27%, and Coupon Payment is $40.00, determine the Bond Price.

   (b.) Given Number of Periods to Maturity is 8, Face Value is $1,000.00, Discount Rate / Period is 4.54%, and the Bond Price is $880.00, determine the Coupon Payment.

   (c.) Given Number of Periods to Maturity is 6, Face Value is $1,000.00, Coupon Payment is $30.00, and the Bond Price is $865.00, determine Discount Rate / Period.

   (d.) Given Number of Periods to Maturity is 8, Discount Rate / Period is 3.81%, Coupon Payment is $45.00, and the Bond Price is $872.00, determine Face Value.

   (e.) Given Face Value is $1,000.00, Discount Rate / Period is 4.38%, Coupon Payment is $37.00, and the Bond Price is $887.00, determine the Number of Periods to Maturity.

Chapter 2 The Yield Curve

2.1 Obtaining It From Treasury Bills and Strips

Problem. Given bond prices and yields as published by the financial press or other information sources, obtain the U.S. Treasury Yield Curve.

Solution Strategy. Collect maturity date and yield to maturity (e.g., the "ask yield") from the *Wall Street Journal Online* (wsj.com) for Treasury Bills and Treasury Strips of a variety of maturity dates. Compute the time to maturity. Graph the yield to maturity of these bonds against their time to maturity.

FIGURE 2.1 The Yield Curve – Obtaining It From Bond Listings.

	A	B	C	D	E
1	**THE YIELD CURVE**		Obtaining It From Treasury Bills and Strips		
2		Maturity	Time To	Yield To	Forward
3	**Yield Curve Inputs**	Date	Maturity	Maturity	Rates
4	Today's Date	3/11/2010			
5	One Month Treasury Bill	4/15/2010	0.09	0.101%	0.101%
6	Three Month Treasury Bill	6/10/2010	0.25	0.147%	0.175%
7	Six Month Treasury Bill	9/9/2010	0.49	0.211%	0.275%
8	One Year Treasury Strip	3/10/2011	1.00	0.349%	0.485%
9	Two Year Treasury Strip	2/15/2012	1.93	0.920%	1.536%
10	Three Year Treasury Strip	2/15/2013	2.93	1.430%	2.420%
11	Four Year Treasury Strip	2/15/2014	3.93	2.000%	3.687%
12	Five Year Treasury Strip	2/15/2015	4.93	2.470%	4.337%
13	Ten Year Treasury Strip	2/15/2020	9.93	4.070%	5.671%
14	Fifteen Year Treasury Bond	2/15/2025	14.93	4.750%	6.113%
15	Twenty Year Treasury Bond	2/15/2030	19.93	4.920%	5.429%
16	Twenty Five Year Treasury Bond	2/15/2035	24.93	4.940%	5.020%
17	Thirty Year Treasury Bond	2/15/2040	29.93	4.980%	5.180%
18					
19	(1) Maturity Date - Today's Date				
20	Enter =YEARFRAC($B$4,B5) and copy down				
21					

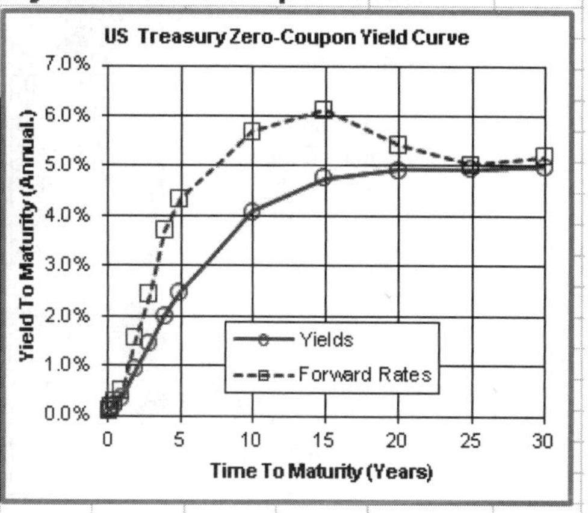

For a given bond, Time To Maturity = Maturity Date - Today's Date. We can calculate the fraction of a year between two calendar dates using the **YEARFRAC** function in Excel's Analysis ToolPak Add-In. Excel's Analysis ToolPak Add-In contains several advanced date functions that are useful in finance. To access any of these functions, you need to install the Analysis ToolPak. Otherwise you will get the error message #NAME?.

To install the Analysis ToolPak, click on [File], click on [Options], click on **Add-Ins**, highlight the **Analysis ToolPak** in the list of Inactive Applications, click on **Go**, check the **Analysis ToolPak**, and click on **OK**.

2.2 Using It To Price A Coupon Bond

Problem. Given the yield curve as published by the financial press, consider a coupon bond has a face value of $1,000, an annual coupon rate of 5.0%, makes 2 (semiannual) coupon payments per year, and 8 periods to maturity (or 4 years to maturity). What is price and yield to maturity of this coupon bond based on the Annual Percentage Rate (APR) convention? What is price and yield to maturity of this coupon bond based on the Effective Annual Rate (EAR) convention?

FIGURE 2.2 The Yield Curve – Using It To Price A Coupon Bond.

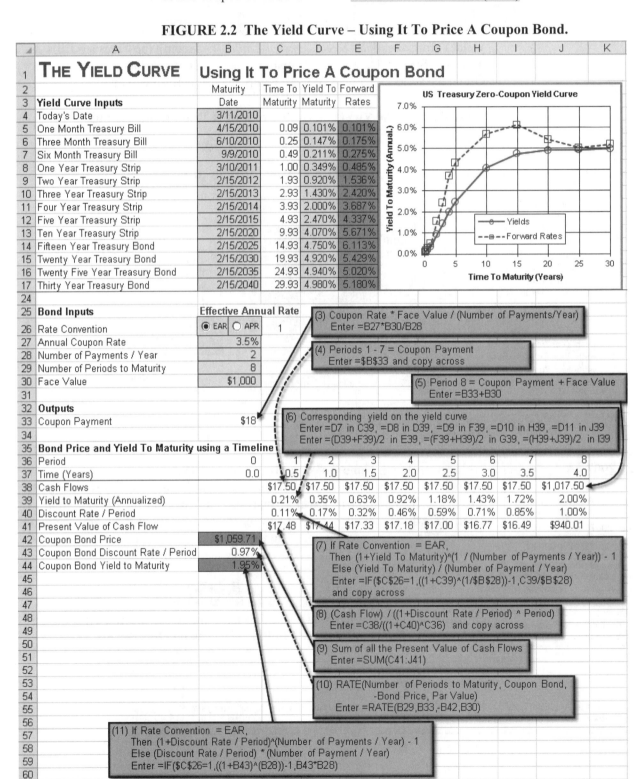

Solution Strategy. We will use the yield curve you entered in **The Yield Curve - Obtaining It From Bond Listings**. We will calculate the bond price as the present value of the bond's cash flows, where each cash flow is discounted based on the corresponding yield on the yield curve (e.g., a cash flow in year three will be discounted based on the yield curve's yield at year three). We will use Excel's **RATE** function to determine the yield to maturity of this coupon bond.

Results. The Coupon Bond's price is $1,059.71 and its Yield To Maturity is 1.95%. Note that this yield is not the same as four year yield or any other point on the yield curve. The yield of the coupon bond is a weighted average of the yields for each of the eight periods. Since the bond's biggest cash flow is on the maturity date, the biggest weight in the weighted average is on the maturity date. Thus the coupon bond's yield is closest to the yield of the maturity date, but it is not the same.

2.3 Using It To Determine Forward Rates

Problem. Given the yield curve as published by the financial press, calculate the implied forward rates at all maturities.

Solution Strategy. We will use the yield curve that you entered in an Excel model for **The Yield Curve - Obtaining It From Bond Listings**. We will calculate the forward rates implied by the yield curve and then graph our results.

FIGURE 2.3 The Yield Curve – Using It To Determine Forward Rates.

	A	B	C	D	E
1	THE YIELD CURVE	Using It To Determine Forward Rates			
2		Maturity	Time To	Yield To	Forward
3	**Yield Curve Inputs**	Date	Maturity	Maturity	Rates
4	Today's Date	3/11/2010			
5	One Month Treasury Bill	4/15/2010	0.09	0.101%	0.101%
6	Three Month Treasury Bill	6/10/2010	0.25	0.147%	0.175%
7	Six Month Treasury Bill	9/9/2010	0.49	0.211%	0.275%
8	One Year Treasury Strip	3/10/2011	1.00	0.349%	0.485%
9	Two Year Treasury Strip	2/15/2012	1.93	0.920%	1.536%
10	Three Year Treasury Strip	2/15/2013	2.93	1.430%	2.420%
11	Four Year Treasury Strip	2/15/2014	3.93	2.000%	3.687%
12	Five Year Treasury Strip	2/15/2015	4.93	2.470%	4.337%
13	Ten Year Treasury Strip	2/15/2020	9.93	4.070%	5.671%
14	Fifteen Year Treasury Bond	2/15/2025	14.93	4.750%	6.113%
15	Twenty Year Treasury Bond	2/15/2030	19.93	4.920%	5.429%
16	Twenty Five Year Treasury Bond	2/15/2035	24.93	4.940%	5.020%
17	Thirty Year Treasury Bond	2/15/2040	29.93	4.980%	5.180%

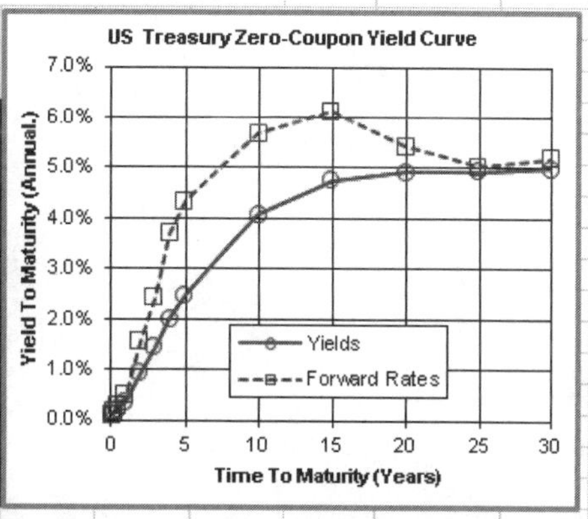

US Treasury Zero-Coupon Yield Curve — Yield To Maturity (Annual) vs Time To Maturity (Years): Yields, Forward Rates

Notation:
t = an earlier date
T = a later date
y_t = date t yield
y_T = date T yield
$f_{t,T}$ = forward rate from date t to date T

(2) Forward Rate from date t to date T

$$f_{T-t} = \left((1+y_T)^T / (1+y_t)^t \right)^{1/(T-t)} - 1$$

Enter =(((1+D5)^C5)/((1+D4)^C4))^(1/(C5-C4))-1 and copy down

Forward rates are an approximate forecast of future interest rates. One difficulty with taking this interpretation literally has to do with market segmentation in the demand for treasury securities. There is significantly more demand for short-term bonds than bonds of other maturities, for their use in short-term cash management. There is also extra demand by institutional bond funds for the newly-issued, longest maturity treasury bond (the so-called, "on-the-run" bond). High demand means high prices, which means low yields. Thus, the yield curve often has lower yields at the short end and the long end due to this segmentation.

Problems

1. Given bond prices and yields as published by the financial press or other information sources, obtain the U.S. Treasury Yield Curve.

2. Given the yield curve as published by the financial press, consider a coupon bond has a face value of $2,000, an annual coupon rate of 4.2%, makes 2 (semiannual) coupon payments per year, and 8 periods to maturity (or 4 years to maturity). Determine the price and yield to maturity of this coupon bond based on the Effective Annual Rate (EAR) convention. Then use it to determine the price and yield to maturity of this coupon bond based on the Annual Percentage Rate (APR) convention.

3. Given the yield curve as published by the financial press, calculate the implied forward rates at all maturities.

Chapter 3 Affine Yield Curve Models

3.1 US Yield Curve Dynamics

How does the US yield curve change over time? What determines the volatility of changes in the yield curve? Are there differences in the volatility of short rates, medium rates, long rates, etc.? You can answer these questions and more using a *Dynamic Chart* of the yield curve, which is based on more than 37 years of monthly US zero-coupon, yield curve data. I update this Excel model each year with the latest yield curve data and make it available for free in the "Free Samples" section of www.excelmodeling.com.

FIGURE 3.1 Excel Model of US Yield Curve Dynamics – Dynamic Chart.

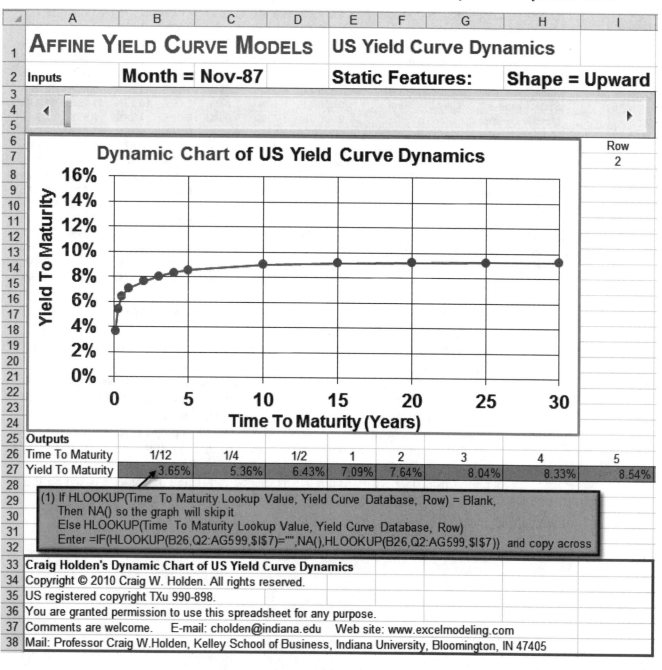

Time To Maturity	1/12	1/4	1/2	1	2	3	4	5
Yield To Maturity	3.65%	5.36%	6.43%	7.09%	7.64%	8.04%	8.33%	8.54%

(1) If HLOOKUP(Time To Maturity Lookup Value, Yield Curve Database, Row) = Blank,
   Then NA() so the graph will skip it
   Else HLOOKUP(Time To Maturity Lookup Value, Yield Curve Database, Row)
   Enter =IF(HLOOKUP(B26,Q2:AG599,$I$7)="",NA(),HLOOKUP(B26,Q2:AG599,$I$7)) and copy across

The dynamic chart uses a vertical scroll bar in rows **3** to **5**. Clicking on the right arrow of the scroll bar moves the yield curve forward by one month. Clicking on the left arrow moves back by one month. Clicking right of the position bar, moves the yield curve forward by one *year*. Clicking left of the position bar moves back by one *year*. This allows you to see a dynamic "movie" or animation of the yield curve over time. Thus, you can directly observe the volatility of the yield curve and other dynamic properties. For details of what to look for, see the discussion below on "using the Excel model."

FIGURE 3.2 Excel Model of the Yield Curve Database.

	P	Q	R	S	Time To Maturity	Time To Maturity	Time To Maturity	Time To Maturity	Time To Maturity	Time To Maturity
1					T	U	V	W	X	Y
2		Title 1	Title 2	Title 3	1/12	1/4	1/2	1	2	3
3		Static Features:	Shape = Upward	11/30/87	3.65%	5.36%	6.43%	7.09%	7.64%	8.04%
4		Static Features:	Shape = Downward	11/28/80	14.83%	14.60%	14.64%	14.17%	13.22%	12.75%
5		Static Features:	Shape = Flat	01/30/70	7.73%	8.00%	8.03%	7.98%	7.95%	7.94%
6		Static Features:	Shape = Hump	12/29/78	8.82%	9.48%	9.99%	10.18%	9.76%	9.40%
7		Static Features:	Level = Low	12/31/70	4.62%	4.91%	4.95%	5.02%	5.40%	5.69%
8		Static Features:	Level = High	10/30/81	12.65%	13.13%	13.53%	13.85%	14.01%	14.06%
9		Static Features:	Curvature = Little	12/29/72	4.93%	5.24%	5.44%	5.62%	5.86%	6.01%
10		Static Features:	Curvature = Lot	09/30/82	6.67%	7.87%	9.05%	10.29%	11.16%	11.43%
11		Monthly Dynamics		01/30/70	7.73%	8.00%	8.03%	7.98%	7.95%	7.94%
12		Monthly Dynamics		02/27/70	6.23%	6.99%	6.97%	6.96%	7.02%	7.04%
13		Monthly Dynamics		03/31/70	6.33%	6.44%	6.53%	6.67%	6.85%	6.95%
14		Monthly Dynamics		04/30/70	6.48%	7.03%	7.35%	7.50%	7.60%	7.67%
15		Monthly Dynamics		05/29/70	6.22%	7.03%	7.28%	7.45%	7.58%	7.63%
16		Monthly Dynamics		06/30/70	6.14%	6.47%	6.81%	7.17%	7.43%	7.53%
17		Monthly Dynamics		07/31/70	6.32%	6.38%	6.55%	6.87%	7.19%	7.31%
18		Monthly Dynamics		08/31/70	6.22%	6.38%	6.57%	6.83%	7.07%	7.18%
19		Monthly Dynamics		09/30/70	5.32%	6.04%	6.49%	6.63%	6.64%	6.77%
20		Monthly Dynamics		10/30/70	5.23%	5.91%	6.23%	6.33%	6.50%	6.69%
21		Monthly Dynamics		11/30/70	4.86%	5.05%	5.11%	5.10%	5.29%	5.59%
22		Monthly Dynamics		12/31/70	4.62%	4.91%	4.95%	5.02%	5.40%	5.69%

The yield curve database is located in columns **Q** to **AG**. Columns **Q**, **R**, and **S** contain three sets of titles for the dataset. Columns **T**, **U**, and **V** contain yield data for bond maturities of one month, three months, and six months (1/12, 1/4, and 1/2 years, respectively). Columns **W** through **AG** contain yield data for bond maturities of 1, 2, 3, 4, 5, 7, 10, 15, 20, 25, and 30 years. Rows **2** through **9** contain examples of static features of the yield curve that can be observed from actual data in a particular month. For example, the yield curve is sometimes upward sloping (as it was in Nov 87) or downward sloping (in Nov 80) or flat (in Jan 70) or hump shaped (in Dec 78). Rows **10** through **490** contain monthly US zero-coupon, yield curve data from January 1970 through January 2010. For the period from January 1970 through December 1991, the database is based on the

Bliss (1992) monthly estimates of the zero-coupon, yield curve.[2] For the period from January 1992 to July 2001, the yield curve is directly observed from Treasury Bills and Strips in the *Wall Street Journal*. For the period from August 2001 to January 2010, the data is from the St Louis Fed's free online economic database FRED II at research.stlouisfed.org/fred2.

Using The US Yield Curve Dynamic Chart.

To run the Dynamic Chart, click on the right arrow of the scroll bar. The movie / animation begins with some background on the yield curve's static features. In the 40-year database we observe:

- four different **shapes**: upward-sloping, downward-sloping, flat, and hump-shaped,
- the overall **level** of the yield curve ranges from low to high, and
- the amount of **curvature** at the short end ranges from a little to a lot.

Keep clicking on the right arrow of the scroll bar and you will get to the section of the Dynamic Chart covering 40 years of the US yield curve history. This section shows the yield curve on a month by month basis. For example, the figure below shows the US yield curve in January 1970.

FIGURE 3.3 The Yield Curve in January 1970.

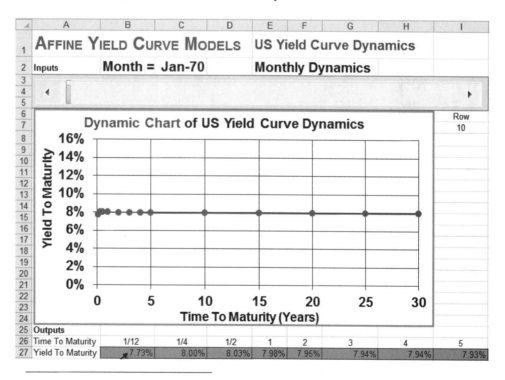

<hr />

[2] Bliss fits a parsimonious, nonlinear function that is capable of matching all of the empirically observed shapes of the zero-coupon, yield curve. For more details see Bliss, Robert, 1992, "Testing Term Structure Estimation Methods."

Keep clicking on the right arrow and you will see the yield curve move around over time. By observing this movie / animation, you should be able to recognize the following key **dynamic** properties of the yield curve:

- short rates (the 0 to 5 year piece of the yield curve) are more volatile than long rates (the 15 to 30 year piece),
- the overall volatility of the yield curve is higher when the level is higher (especially in the early 80's), and
- sometimes there are sharp reactions to government intervention.

As an example of the latter, consider what happened in 1980. The figure below shows the yield curve in January 1980.

FIGURE 3.4 The Yield Curve in January 1980.

	A	B	C	D	E	F	G	H	I
1	AFFINE YIELD CURVE MODELS				US Yield Curve Dynamics				
2	Inputs	Month = Jan-80			Monthly Dynamics				
3									
4	◄							►	
5									
6									Row
7	Dynamic Chart of US Yield Curve Dynamics								129

Dynamic Chart of US Yield Curve Dynamics

25	Outputs								
26	Time To Maturity	1/12	1/4	1/2	1	2	3	4	5
27	Yield To Maturity	11.69%	12.42%	12.31%	11.68%	11.16%	10.98%	10.89%	10.83%

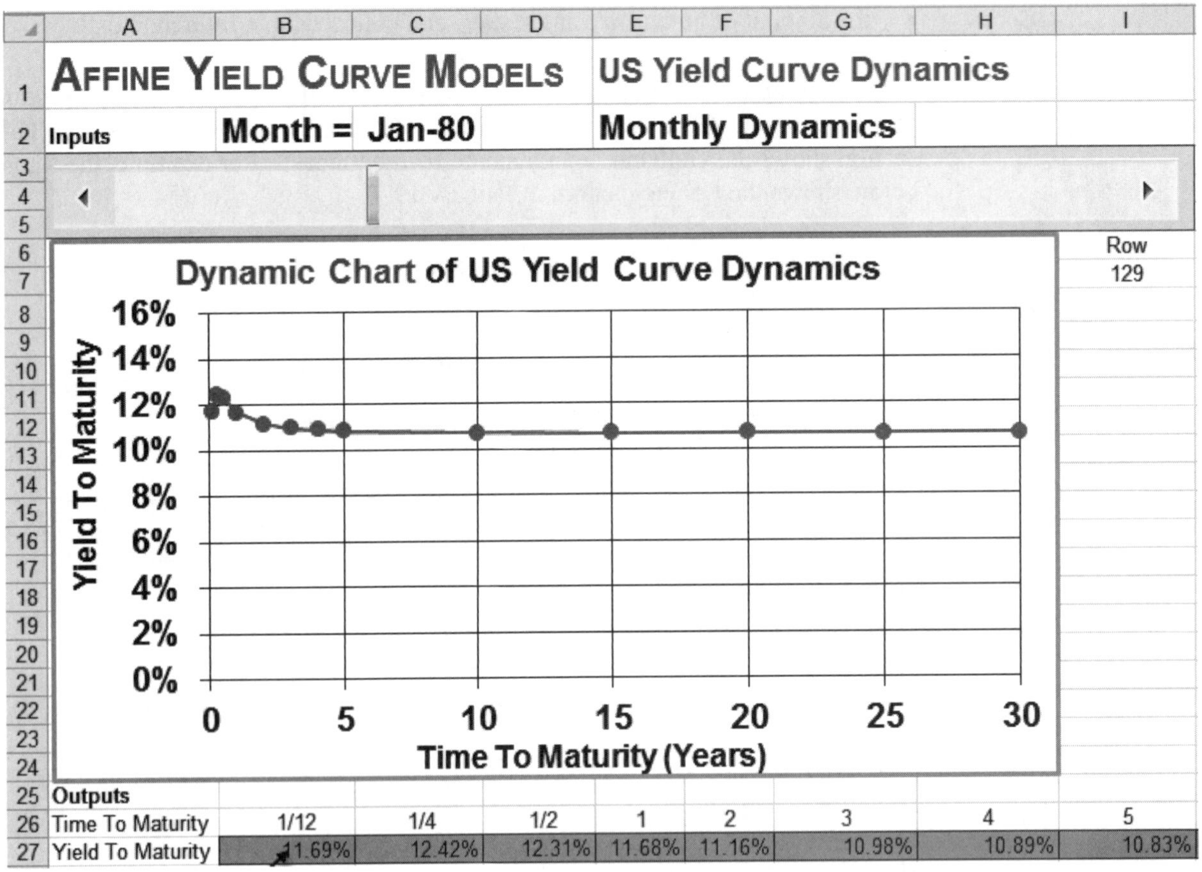

Short rates were around 12% and long rates were at 10.7%. President Jimmy Carter was running for re-election. He wished to manipulate the election year economy to make it better for his re-election bid. His strategy for doing this was to impose credit controls on the banking system. Click on the right arrow to see what the reaction of the financial market was.

FIGURE 3.5 The Yield Curve in March 1980.

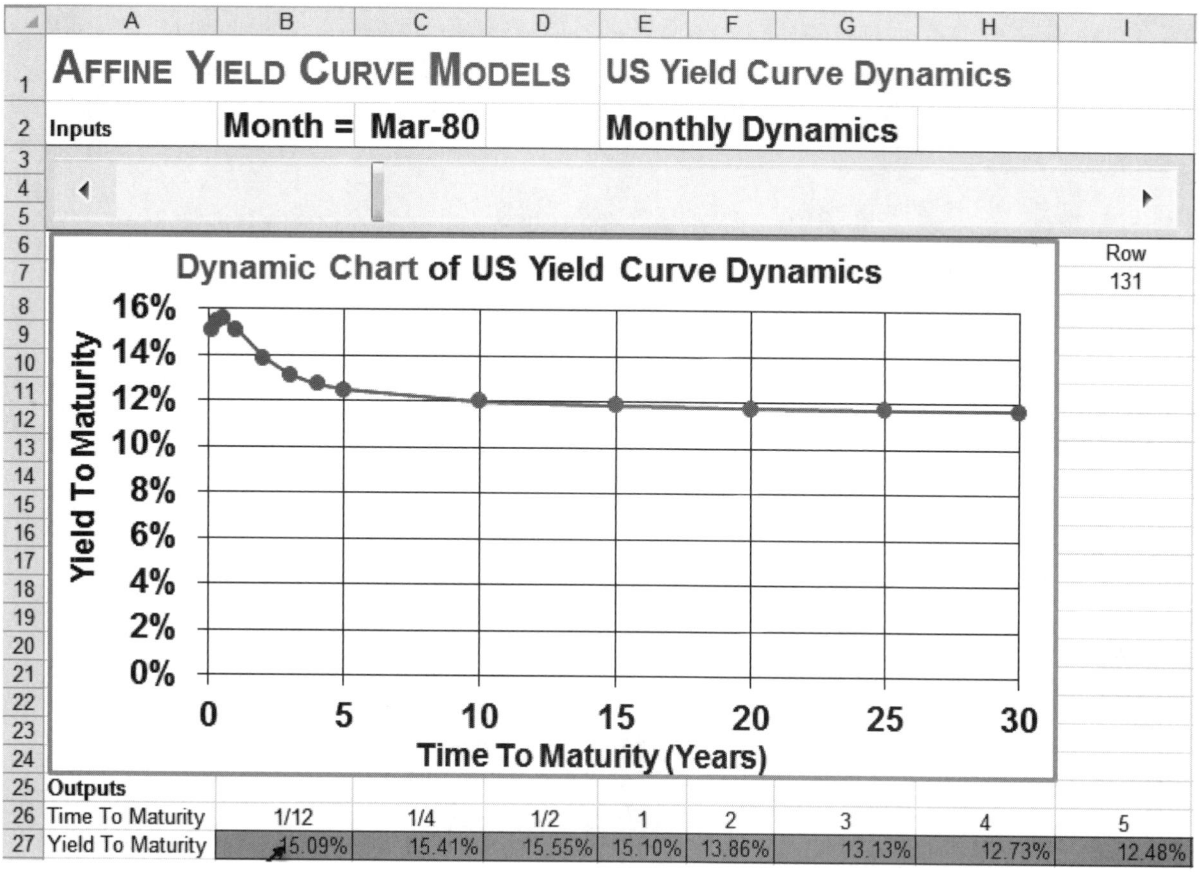

	A	B	C	D	E	F	G	H	I
1	**AFFINE YIELD CURVE MODELS**				**US Yield Curve Dynamics**				
2	Inputs	**Month = Mar-80**			**Monthly Dynamics**				
3									
4	◀								▶
5									
6									
7									Row 131

Dynamic Chart of US Yield Curve Dynamics

	A	B	C	D	E	F	G	H	I
25	Outputs								
26	Time To Maturity	1/12	1/4	1/2	1	2	3	4	5
27	Yield To Maturity	15.09%	15.41%	15.55%	15.10%	13.86%	13.13%	12.73%	12.48%

In two months, the short rate went up to 15.5%, an increase of 3.5%! What a disaster! This was the opposite of the reaction that Carter had intended. Notice that long rates went up to 11.7%, an increase of only 1%. Apparently, the market expected that this intervention would only be a short-lived phenomenon. Carter quickly realized what a big political mistake he had made and announced that the credit controls were being dropped. Click on the right arrow to see what the reaction of the financial market was.

FIGURE 3.6 The Yield Curve in April 1980.

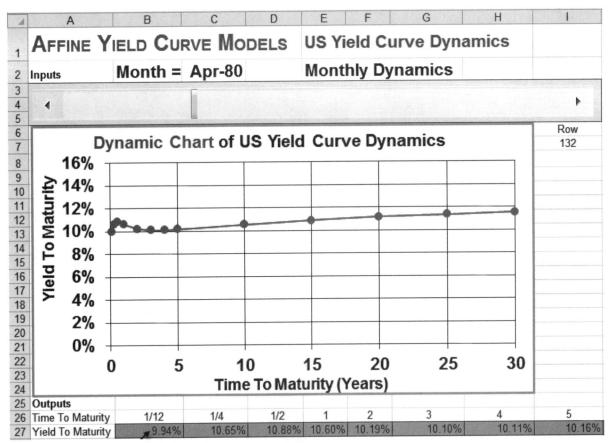

Short rates dropped to 10.9%! A drop of 4.6% in one month! The high interest rates went away, but the political damage was done. This is the single biggest one month change in the yield curve in 40 years.

3.2 The Vasicek Model

Problem. The current short rate is 3.5% per year. The short rate reverts to a long-run mean level of 5.0% at a speed of adjustment of 0.12 with a standard deviation of 2.00% per year. The market price of risk is 0.17% extra return per unit of interest rate risk. What is the price and yield to maturity of a six-month (0.5 year), pure discount bond?

FIGURE 3.7 Affine Yield Curve Models – The Vasicek Model

	A	B	C	D	E	F	G	H	I
1	AFFINE YIELD CURVE MODELS			The Vasicek Model					
2									
3	Inputs								
4	Time To Maturity (T)	0.50	5						
5	Short Rate (r)	2.50%	5						
6	Long-run Mean (μ)	5.00%	10						
7	Speed of Adjustment (κ)	0.12	11						
8	Standard Deviation (σ)	2.00%	10						
9	Market Price of Interest Rate Risk (λ)	1.00%	1						
10									
11									
12	Outputs								
13	Long Rate (R)	3.78%							
14	B	0.49							
15	A	-0.00075							
16	Bond Price (P)	0.987							
17	Yield To Maturity (Y)	2.58%							

Dynamic Chart of the Vasicek Model

$$^{(1)}\ R = \mu - \sigma^2 / \left(2\kappa^2\right) + \lambda\sigma/\kappa$$
Enter =B6-B8^2/(2*B7^2)+B9*B8/B7

$$^{(2)}\ B = \left(1 - e^{-\kappa T}\right)/\kappa$$
Enter =(1-EXP(-B7*B4))/B7

$$^{(3)}\ A = \left(B - T\right)R - \sigma^2 B^2 / \left(4\kappa\right)$$
Enter =(B14-B4)*B13-(B8^2*B14^2)/(4*B7)

$$^{(5)}\ Y = -A/T + \left(B/T\right)\cdot r$$
Enter =-B15/B4+(B14/B4)*B5

$$^{(4)}\ P = e^{A-Br}$$
Enter =EXP(B15-B14*B5)

(7) Enter the output formulas for the Long Rate and Yield To Maturity. Enter =B13 in cell B35 Enter =B17 in cell B36

(6) Enter the input values for Time To Maturity. Enter 1/12, 1/4, 1/2, 1, 2, etc. in the range C34:O34

	A	B	C	D	E	F	G	H	I
32	Data Table: Sensitivity of Yield To Maturity to Time To Maturity								
33								Input Values for Time To	
34	Output Formulas:		1/12	1/4	1/2	1	2	3	4
35	Long Rate (R)	3.78%	3.78%	3.78%	3.78%	3.78%	3.78%	3.78%	3.78%
36	Yield To Maturity (Y)	2.58%	2.51%	2.54%	2.58%	2.65%	2.77%	2.88%	2.97%

(8) Create the yield to maturity Data Table. Select the range B34:O36, click on Data | Data Tools | What-If Analysis | Data Table, enter B4 in the Row Input Cell, and click on OK.

Data Table

Row input cell: B4

Column input cell:

OK   Cancel

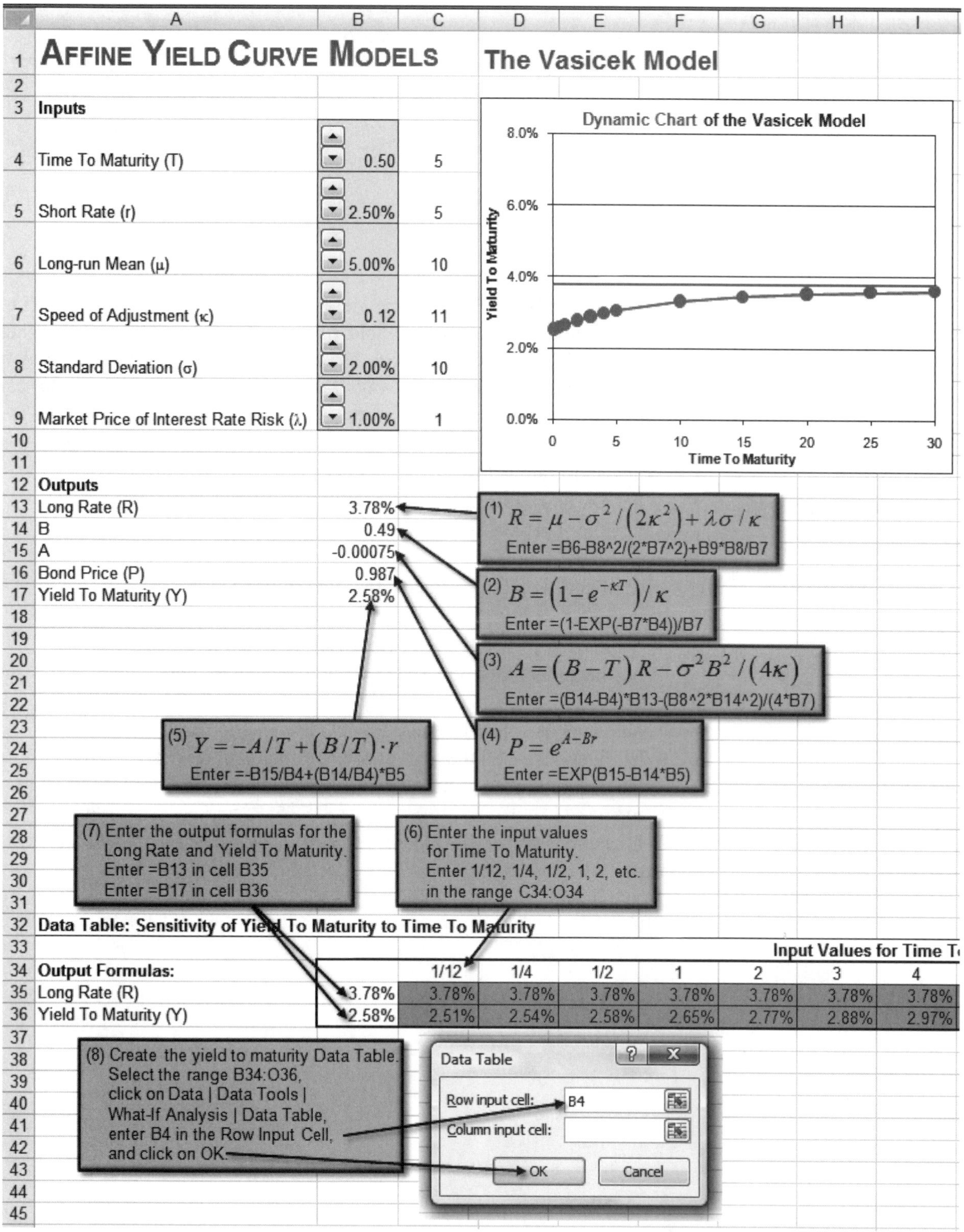

We see that a six-month, pure discount bond which pays $1 at maturity is predicted by the Vasicek model to have a current price of $0.987 and yield of 2.58%. On the graph, we see that the yield curve is upward slopping (i.e., bonds with longer time-to-maturity have a higher yield).

An interesting experiment is increase the short rate. Click on the Short Rate up-arrow spin button and notice what happens to the yield curve.

FIGURE 3.8 Short Rate is 4.00% and 6.00%

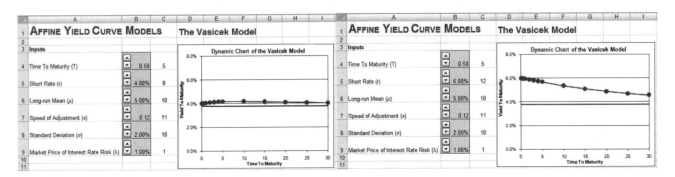

When the Short Rate is 4.00%, then the yield curve is slightly hump-shaped (i.e., as you increase time-to-maturity the yield first rises and then later falls). When the Short Rate is 6.00%, then the yield curve is downward sloping (i.e., as you increase time-to-maturity the yield always falls). Hence, the Vasicek model can generate three different shapes that we observe in the real world:

- When short rate is low, the yield curve is upward sloping.
- When the short rate is intermediate, the yield curve is hump shaped.
- When the short rate is high, the yield curve is downward sloping.

Here is a list of additional experiments that you might want to perform:

- What happens when the long-run mean level is increased?
- What happens when the speed of adjustment is increased over a large range?
- What happens when the standard deviation is increased?
- What happens when the market price of interest rate risk is increased?
- What happens when the standard deviation is decreased over a large range?
- What happens when the market price of interest rate risk is really close to zero?

3.3 The Cox-Ingersoll-Ross Model

Problem. The current short rate is 3.5% per year. The short rate reverts to a long-run mean level of 5.0% at a speed of adjustment of 0.12 with a standard deviation of 2.00% per year. The market price of risk is 0.17% extra return per unit of interest rate risk. What is the price and yield to maturity of a six-month (0.5 year), pure discount bond?

FIGURE 3.9 Affine Yield Curve Models – Cox-Ingersoll-Ross.

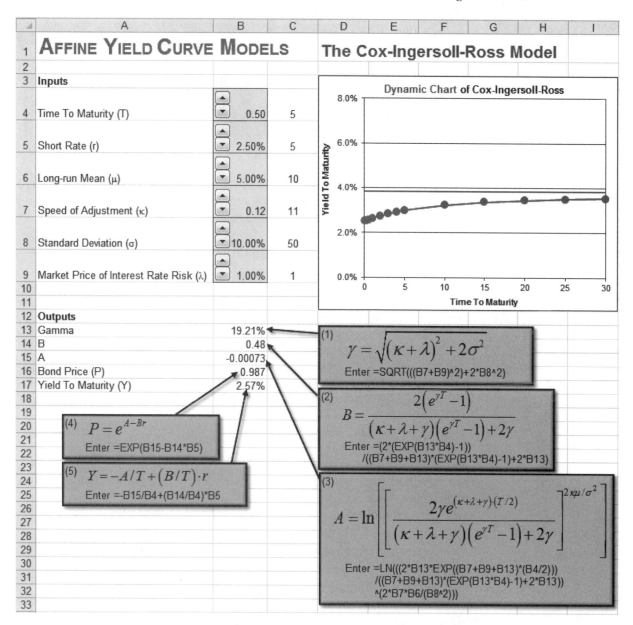

We see that a six-month, pure discount bond which pays $1 at maturity is predicted by the Vasicek model to have a current price of $0.982 and yield of 3.57%.

FIGURE 3.10 Affine Yield Curve - Cox-Ingersoll-Ross

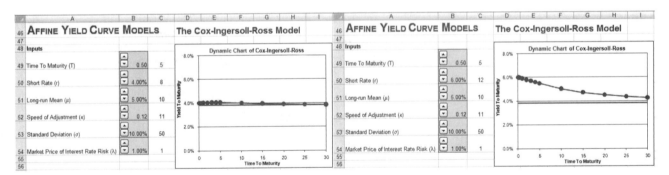

On the graph, we see that when the Short Rate is low, the yield curve is upward slopping. An interesting experiment is increase the short rate. Click on the Short Rate up-arrow spin button and notice what happens to the yield curve.

Excel 97-2003 Equivalent

To call up a Data Table in Excel 97-2003, click on **Data | Table**.

FIGURE 3.11 Short Rate is 4.00% and 6.00%

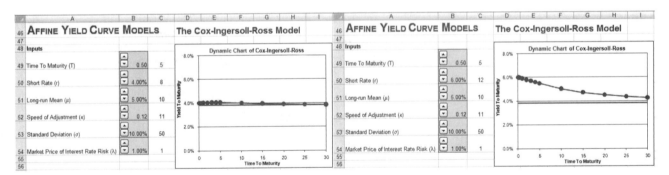

When the Short Rate is 4.00%, then the yield curve is slightly hump-shaped. When the Short Rate is 6.00%, then the yield curve is downward sloping. Just like the Vasicek model, the Cox-Ingersoll-Ross (CIR) model can generate the same three real-world shapes:

- When short rate is low, the yield curve is upward sloping.
- When the short rate is intermediate, the yield curve is hump shaped.
- When the short rate is high, the yield curve is downward sloping.

Here is a list of additional experiments that you might want to perform:
- What happens when the long-run mean level is increased?
- What happens when the speed of adjustment is increased over a large range?

- What happens when the standard deviation is increased?
- What happens when the market price of interest rate risk is increased?
- What happens when the standard deviation is decreased over a large range?
- What happens when the market price of interest rate risk is really close to zero?

Problems

1. How volatile are short rates versus medium rates versus long rates?
    a. Get a visual sense of the answer to this question by clicking on the right arrow of the scroll bar to run through all of the years of US Yield Curve history in the database.

    b. Calculate the variance of the time series of: (i) one-month yields, (ii) five-year yields, (iii) fifteen-year yields, and (iv) thirty-year yields. Use Excel's VAR function to calculate the variance of the yields in columns **T, AA, AD**, and **AG**.

2. Determine the relationship between the volatility of the yield curve and the level of the yield curve. Specifically, for each five year time period (70-74, 75-79, 80-84, etc.) calculate the variance and the average level of the time series of: (i) one-month yields, (ii) five-year yields, (iii) fifteen-year yields, and (iv) thirty-year yields. Use Excel's VAR and AVERAGE functions to calculate the variance and the average of five-year ranges of the yields in columns **T, AA, AD**, and **AG**. For example:
    a. The 70-74 time series of one-month yields is in the range **T11-T69**.
    b. The 75-79 time series of one-month yields is in the range **T70-T129**.
    c. The 80-84 time series of one-month yields is in the range **T130-T189**.
    d. And so on.
    Summarize what you have learned from this analysis.

3. The current short rate is 8.2% per year. The short rate reverts to a long-run mean level of 6.1% at a speed of adjustment of 0.18 with a standard deviation of 3.40% per year. The market price of risk is 0.11% extra return per unit of interest rate risk. Determine the price and yield to maturity of a nine-month (0.75 year), pure discount bond.

4. Perform instant experiments on what impact changing various inputs causes on the Vasicek and Cox-Ingersoll-Ross yield curve models.
    a. What happens when the short rate is increased?
    b. What happens when the long-run mean level is increased?
    c. What happens when the speed of adjustment is increased over a large range?
    d. What happens when the standard deviation is increased?
    e. What happens when the market price of interest rate risk is increased?
    f. What happens when the standard deviation is decreased over a large range?
    g. What happens when the market price of interest rate risk is really close to zero?

PART 2 PORTFOLIO MANAGEMENT

Chapter 4 Portfolio Optimization

4.1 Two Risky Assets and a Riskfree Asset

Problem. The one-month riskfree rate is 0.40%. Risky Asset 1 has a mean return / month of 1.50% and a standard deviation of 10.00%. Risky Asset 2 has a mean return / month of 0.80% and a standard deviation of 5.0%. The correlation between Risky Asset 1 and 2 is 40.0%. An individual investor with a simple mean and variance utility function has a risk aversion of 2.2. Graph the Risky Opportunity Set, the Optimal Risky Portfolio, the Capital Allocation Line, the investor's Indifference Curve, and the Optimal Complete Portfolio.

Solution Strategy. The two-asset Risky Opportunity Set involves varying the proportion in the first asset and calculating the portfolio's standard deviation and expected return. The Optimal Risky Portfolio is computed using a formula for the optimal proportion in the first asset. The Capital Allocation Line comes from any two weights in the Optimal Risky Portfolio. The Optimal Complete Portfolio is computed from a formula for the utility maximizing standard deviation. Then, the Indifference Curve through the Optimal Complete Portfolio is computed.

FIGURE 4.1 Excel Model of Portfolio Optimization - Two Assets

	A	B	C	D	E
1	PORTFOLIO OPTIMIZATION				Two Risky Assets and a Riskfree Asset
2					
3	Inputs	Display on the Graph			
4	Display on the Graph	○ Risky Opportunity Set ○ + Capital Allocation Line ◉ + Indifference Curve		3	
5		Expected	Standard	Exp Ret	
6		Return/Mon	Deviation	- Riskless	
7		$E(r_i)$	σ_i	$E_i=E(r_i)-r_f$	
8	Riskfree Rate (r_f)	0.40%	0.00%	0.00%	
9	Risky Asset 1	1.50%	10.00%	1.10%	
10	Risky Asset 2	0.80%	5.00%	0.40%	
11	Correlation (ρ)		40.0%		
12	Risk Aversion	2.2			
13		4			
14		15	100		
15		8	50		
16			14		
17		22			

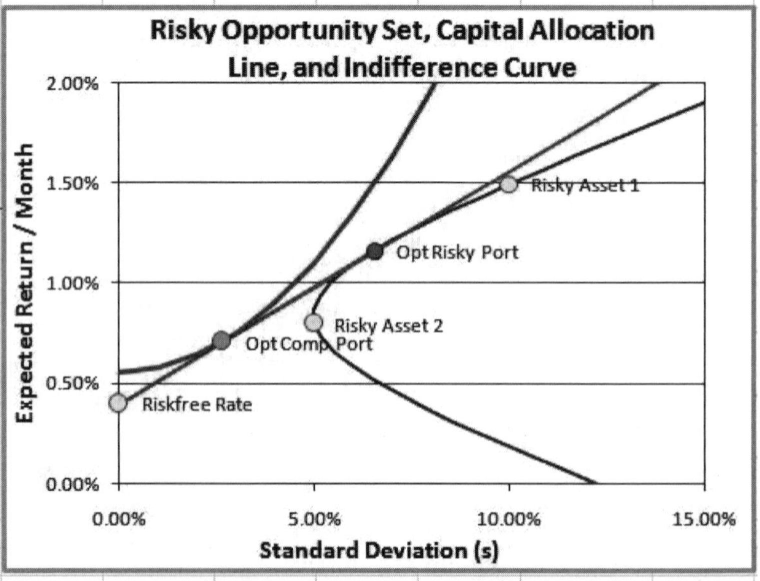

FIGURE 4.2 Excel Model of Portfolio Optimization - Two Assets

	A	B	C	D	E	F	G	H	I	J	K
19	**Outputs**			Risky Asset	Capital	Utility	Optimal				
20		Proportion		Opp Set	Allocation	Indifference	Complete				
21		in Risky	(x-axis)	Curve	Line	Curve	Portfolio				
22		Asset 1 or	Standard	Expected	Expected	Expected	Expected				
23		Opt Risky	Deviation	Ret / Mon	Ret / Mon	Ret / Mon	Ret / Mon				
24	Opp Set Curve	-500.0%	46.9%	-2.7%							
25	Opp Set Curve	-150.0%	15.2%	0.3%							
26	Opp Set Curve	-80.0%	9.3%	0.2%							
27	Opp Set Curve	-70.0%	8.6%	0.3%							
28	Opp Set Curve	-60.0%	7.8%	0.4%							
29	Opp Set Curve	-50.0%	7.2%	0.5%							
30	Opp Set Curve	-40.0%	6.5%	0.5%							
31	Opp Set Curve	-30.0%	6.0%	0.6%							
32	Opp Set Curve	-20.0%	5.5%	0.7%							
33	Opp Set Curve	-10.0%	5.2%	0.7%							
34	Opp Set Curve	0.0%	5.0%	0.8%							
35	Opp Set Curve	10.0%	5.0%	0.9%							
36	Opp Set Curve	20.0%	5.1%	0.9%							
37	Opp Set Curve	30.0%	5.4%	1.0%							
38	Opp Set Curve	40.0%	5.9%	1.1%							
39	Opp Set Curve	50.0%	6.4%	1.2%							
40	Opp Set Curve	60.0%	7.0%	1.2%							
41	Opp Set Curve	70.0%	7.7%	1.3%							
42	Opp Set Curve	80.0%	8.4%	1.4%							
43	Opp Set Curve	90.0%	9.2%	1.4%							
44	Opp Set Curve	100.0%	10.0%	1.5%							
45	Opp Set Curve	110.0%	10.8%	1.6%							
46	Opp Set Curve	120.0%	11.6%	1.6%							
47	Opp Set Curve	250.0%	23.0%	2.6%							
48	Opp Set Curve	750.0%	68.8%	6.1%							
49	Opt Risky Port	52.0%	6.5%		1.2%						
50	Cap Alloc Line	0.0%	0.0%		0.4%						
51	Cap Alloc Line	1000.0%	65.4%		8.0%						
52	Indifference Curve		0.0%			0.56%					
53	Indifference Curve		1.0%			0.58%					
54	Indifference Curve		2.0%			0.64%					
55	Indifference Curve		3.0%			0.75%					
56	Indifference Curve		4.0%			0.91%					
57	Indifference Curve		5.0%			1.11%					
58	Indifference Curve		6.0%			1.35%					
59	Indifference Curve		7.0%			1.63%					
60	Indifference Curve		8.0%			1.96%					
61	Indifference Curve		9.0%			2.34%					
62	Indifference Curve		10.0%			2.76%					
63	Indifference Curve		11.0%			3.22%					
64	Indifference Curve		12.0%			3.72%					
65	Indifference Curve		13.0%			4.27%					
66	Indifference Curve		14.0%			4.87%					
67	Indifference Curve		15.0%			5.51%					
68	Opt Comp Port		2.7%				0.7%				
69											
70	Constant Utility Value		0.0056								

(1) The portfolio's standard deviation formula is

$$\sigma = \sqrt{w^2 \sigma_1^2 + (1-w)^2 \sigma_2^2 + 2w(1-w)\rho\sigma_1\sigma_2}$$

Enter =SQRT(B24^2*$C$9^2+(1-B24)^2*$C$10^2
+2*B24*(1-B24)*$C$11*$C$9*$C$10)
and copy to the range C25:C49

(2) The portfolio's expected return formula is

$$E(r) = wE(r_1) + (1-w)E(r_2)$$

Enter =B24*$B$9+(1-B24)*$B$10
and copy to the range D25:D49.
Then **Cut** the cell D49 and **Paste** it to E49.

(3) The optimal proportion in the first asset formula is

$$w_1 = \left(E_1\sigma_2^2 - E_2\rho\sigma_1\sigma_2 \right)$$
$$/ \left(E_1\sigma_2^2 + E_2\sigma_1^2 - (E_1 + E_2)\rho\sigma_1\sigma_2 \right)$$

Enter =(D9*C10^2-D10*C11*C9*C10)
/(D9*C10^2+D10*C9^2-(D9+D10)*C11*C9*C10)

(4) (Portion in Opt Comb) * (Std Dev of Opt Comb)
Enter =B50*$C$49 and copy to cell C51

(5) If Display on Graph > Risky Opportunity Set
Then (Opt Comb Exp Ret) * (Portion in Opt Comb)
+ (Riskfree Rate) * (1 - Portion in Opt Comb)
Else -1
Enter =IF($D$4>1,$E$49*B50+$B$8*(1-B50),-1)
and copy to cell E51

(6) If Display on Graph = + Indifference Curve
Then Constant Utility Value
+ (Risk Aversion) * (Std Dev)^2
Else -1
Enter =IF($D$4=3,$C$70+$B$12*C52^2,-1)
and copy down

(7) (Exp Return of Optimal Risky Port - Riskfree Rate)
/ (2 * Risk Aversion * Std Dev of Opt Risky Port)
Enter =(E49-B8)/(2*B12*C49)

(8) If Display on Graph = + Indifference Curve
Then Riskfree Rate
+ ((Exp Ret of Optimal Risky Port - Riskfree Rate)
/ Std Dev of Optimal Risky Portfolio)
* (Std Dev of Optimal Complete Portfolio)
Else -1
Enter =IF($D$4=3,B8+((E49-B8)/C49)*C68,-1)

(9) Riskfree Rate + (1 / Risk Aversion) *
* ((Exp Ret of Opt Risky Port - Riskfree Rate)
/ (2 * Std Dev of Opt Risky Port)^2
Enter =B8+(1/B12)*((E49-B8)/(2*C49))^2

To focus on the two-asset Risky Opportunity Set, click on the **Risky Opportunity Set** option button. An interesting experiment is to click on the **Correlation** spin button to raise or lower the correlation.

FIGURE 4.3 Two Assets – Correlation of -20.0% and -100.0%

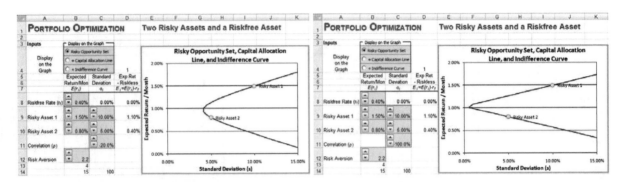

As the correlation is lowered, the Risky Opportunity Set shifts to the left permitting portfolios with lower standard deviations. At the extreme, a correlation of -100% permits a zero standard devivation (i.e., the Risky Opportunity Set should touch the y-axis). The graph would indeed touch y-axis if additional points in the vicinity were graphed.

FIGURE 4.4 Two Assets – Correlation of +70.0% and +100.0%

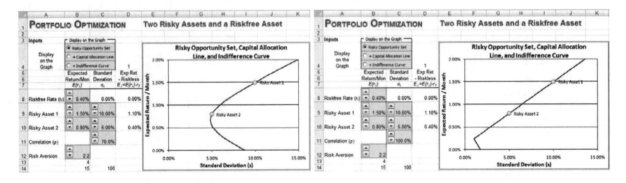

As the correlation is raised, the Risky Opportunity Set shifts to the right. At the other extreme, when the correlation is +100%, then the Risky Opportunity Set is a straight line.

Click on the **+Capital Allocation Line** option button to add the Capital Allocation Line and the Optimal Risky Portfolio. Click on the **+Indifference Curve** option button to add the Indifference Curve and the Optimal Complete Portfolio.

FIGURE 4.5 +Capital Allocation Line and +Indifference Curve

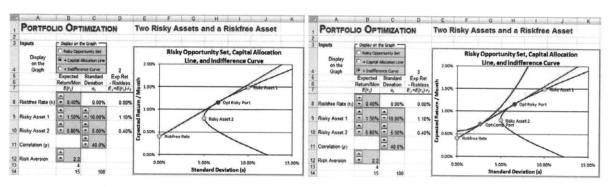

An interesting experiment is to click on the **Risk Aversion** down-arrow spin button to lower the investor's risk aversion.

FIGURE 4.6 Two Assets – Risk Aversion of 1.0 and 0.5

As risk aversion decreases, the Optimal Complete Portfolio slides up the Capital Allocation Line.

4.2 Descriptive Statistics

Mean-variance optimization is a very useful technique that can be used to find the optimal portfolio investment for any number of risky assets and any type of risky asset: stocks, corporate bonds, international bonds, real estate, commodities, etc. The key inputs required are the means, standard deviations, and correlations of the risky assets and the riskfree rate. Of course, these inputs must be estimated from historical data.

One approach to estimating the inputs is to use descriptive statistics. That is, use the sample means, sample standard deviations, and sample correlations. A serious limitation of this approach is that it assumes that past winners will be future winners and past losers will be future losers. Not surprisingly, the portfolio optimizer concludes that you should heavily buy past winners and heavily short-sell past losers. Given strong evidence that future returns are independent of past returns, then chasing past winners is a fruitless strategy.

A better approach is to estimate an asset pricing model (see the asset pricing chapter), use the estimated model to forecast the future expected return of each asset, and then use these forecasted means in the portfolio optimization. This has the significant advantage of eliminating past idiosyncratic realizations (both positive and negative) from future forecasts. It is especially advantageous to eliminate past idiosyncratic realizations at *all three levels*: firm-specific, industry/sector-specific, and country-specific. This approach is limited if the asset pricing model has poor forecast power (e.g., the static CAPM). It is desirable to use asset pricing models with higher forecast power (check the R^2 of each model in the asset pricing chapter).

A useful technique for greatly reducing the influence of past idiosyncratic realizations is to analyze portfolios. Therefore, we will use three asset types: individual stocks, broad U.S. portfolios, and country portfolios. The individual stocks include all idiosyncratic realizations. The broad U.S. portfolios have eliminated firm-specific realizations, but still have industry/sector-specific realizations and U.S.-specific realizations. The country portfolios have eliminated firm-specific realizations and mostly eliminated industry/sector-specific realizations, but each country portfolio still has own-country realizations.

The individual stocks are Barrick, IBM, KEP, Nokia, Telephonos, and YPF. They were picked using pre-sample information to avoid selection bias. The US portfolios are six Fama-French portfolios formed by size and by book/market. For example, Small-Growth is an equally-weighted portfolio created from all NYSE/AMEX/NASDAQ firms that have both a small market capitalization and a low book value / market value ratio. Similarly, Big-Value is an equally-weighted portfolio of firms that have both a big market capitalization and a high book value / market value ratio. The country portfolios, created by Fama and French, are broadly-diversified portfolios of firms in each country. The six country portfolios and there corresponding Exchange Traded Fund (ETF) symbols are Australia (EWA), Canada (EWC), Germany (EWG), Malaysia (EWM), Mexico (EWW), and Singapore (EWS). The monthly returns for all risky assets are computed from prices in US dollars that are adjusted for stock splits and dividends.

Problem. Given monthly returns for stocks, U.S. portfolios, and country portfolios, estimate the means, standard deviations, correlations, and variances/covariances among the risky assets. Given the U.S riskfree rate, compute the mean riskfree rate.

Solution Strategy. Monthly returns for 10 years are provided (see below). Each asset goes down a column. Use TRANSPOSE entered as an Excel matrix to transpose the monthly returns so that each asset goes across a row. This allows convenient computation of the correlation matrix. Specifically, you compute the correlation between one asset going down the column and another asset going across the row. The same approach works for the variance/covariance matrix. Compute the sample descriptive statistics using Excel's AVERAGE, STDEV, CORREL, and COVAR functions.

The starting point is the monthly returns for each asset.

FIGURE 4.7 Excel Model of Portfolio Optimization – Descriptive Statistics

	A	B	C	D	E	F	G	H	I
1	**PORTFOLIO OPTIMIZATION**					**Descriptive Statistics**			
2									
3									
4	**Returns**	Stock	Stock	Stock	Stock	Stock	Stock	US FF Port	US FF Port
5	Month	Barrick	IBM	KEP	Nokia	Telefonos	YPF	Small-Growth	Small-Neutral
6	Dec 2009	-7.75%	3.60%	5.98%	-3.09%	-3.18%	17.39%	8.58%	8.38%
7	Nov 2009	19.37%	5.22%	-1.15%	5.15%	8.07%	2.70%	1.60%	1.85%
8	Oct 2009	-5.20%	0.84%	-8.92%	-13.75%	-4.76%	-0.63%	-6.92%	-6.31%
9	Sep 2009	9.22%	1.32%	23.40%	4.35%	-5.25%	-2.41%	6.52%	5.63%
10	Aug 2009	-0.57%	0.57%	-7.63%	5.02%	17.58%	9.97%	0.90%	3.04%
11	Jul 2009	4.02%	12.94%	16.26%	-8.50%	-2.47%	16.20%	6.78%	10.11%
12	Jun 2009	-11.90%	-1.75%	0.17%	-4.71%	-1.38%	-10.93%	5.18%	1.04%
13	May 2009	31.55%	3.51%	7.49%	8.20%	3.81%	26.21%	3.78%	2.96%
14	Apr 2009	-10.24%	6.52%	16.72%	25.60%	6.38%	14.53%	15.52%	16.67%
15	Mar 2009	7.35%	5.28%	19.92%	24.68%	10.48%	-14.14%	9.14%	10.02%
16	Feb 2009	-19.45%	0.96%	-23.24%	-23.72%	-22.42%	-33.33%	-10.11%	-11.41%
17	Jan 2009	1.96%	8.90%	-14.38%	-21.35%	-15.43%	-5.43%	-7.44%	-10.45%

For computational convenience, transpose the monthly returns.

FIGURE 4.8 Excel Model of Portfolio Optimization – Descriptive Statistics

	AB	AC	AD	AE	AF	AG
1		(1) TRANSPOSE(Monthly Returns Matrix) - enter as an				
2		Excel matrix (i.e., using Shift-Control-Enter) Select the range AB5:ES24				
3		Type =TRANSPOSE(A4:T125)				
4		Hold down the Shift and Control buttons and then press Enter				
5	**Returns**	Month	Dec 2009	Nov 2009	Oct 2009	Sep 2009
6	Stock	Barrick	-7.75%	19.37%	-5.20%	9.22%
7	Stock	IBM	3.60%	5.22%	0.84%	1.32%
8	Stock	KEP	5.98%	-1.15%	-8.92%	23.40%
9	Stock	Nokia	-3.09%	5.15%	-13.75%	4.35%
10	Stock	Telefonos	-3.18%	8.07%	-4.76%	-5.25%
11	Stock	YPF	17.39%	2.70%	-0.63%	-2.41%
12	US FF Port	Small-Growth	8.58%	1.60%	-6.92%	6.52%
13	US FF Port	Small-Neutral	8.38%	1.85%	-6.31%	5.63%
14	US FF Port	Small-Value	8.66%	4.10%	-9.62%	7.85%
15	US FF Port	Big-Growth	1.87%	6.71%	-0.57%	3.55%
16	US FF Port	Big-Neutral	2.80%	4.80%	-2.74%	4.11%
17	US FF Port	Big-Value	3.22%	4.38%	-6.60%	5.39%
18	Country ETF	Australia (EWA)	0.54%	6.38%	-2.96%	11.49%
19	Country ETF	Canada (EWC)	2.55%	8.64%	-6.40%	7.15%
20	Country ETF	Germany (EWG)	-0.21%	7.14%	-5.36%	6.12%
21	Country ETF	Malaysia (EWM)	-0.90%	3.53%	3.45%	4.75%
22	Country ETF	Mexico (EWW)	3.08%	9.89%	-0.18%	2.95%
23	Country ETF	Singapore (EWS)	3.41%	8.40%	-2.51%	5.08%
24	US Riskfree	US Riskfree	0.00%	0.00%	0.00%	0.00%

Compute the sample average and sample standard deviation. Columns W to Y contain the forecasted expected return based on various asset pricing models (Static CAPM, Fama-French 3 Factor, and Macro 3 Factor). See the Asset Pricing chapter for details on how these forecasts were made.

FIGURE 4.9 Excel Model of Portfolio Optimization – Descriptive Statistics

⊿	T	U	V	W	X	Y	Z
1	(2) Average(Monthly Returns for Asset i) Enter =AVERAGE(AD6:ES6) and copy down					Second Pass	Second Pass
2				Second Pass	Fama-French	Macro	
3			Average	Static CAPM	3 Factor	3 Factor	
4	US Riskfree		Past	Expected	Expected	Expected	Standard
5	US Riskfree		Return	Return	Return	Return	Deviation
6	0.00%		1.33%	1.09%	1.55%	1.39%	10.65%
7	0.00%		0.60%	0.61%	1.32%	0.17%	8.56%
8	0.00%		0.55%	0.78%	1.43%	3.30%	9.91%
9	0.00%		-0.13%	0.37%	1.22%	-0.52%	12.50%
10	0.01%		1.07%	0.85%	1.47%	-0.01%	8.49%
11	0.01%		1.51%	0.75%	1.36%	5.82%	10.68%
12	0.00%		0.19%	0.03%	-0.14%	-3.34%	7.83%
13	0.00%		0.97%	0.00%	0.25%	-2.36%	5.77%
14	0.01%		1.13%	0.00%	0.23%	-3.07%	6.30%
15	0.01%		0.00%	-0.01%	0.15%	-1.26%	4.65%
16	0.01%		0.38%	-0.01%	0.15%	-0.78%	4.81%
17	0.00%		0.50%	-0.01%	0.16%	-1.90%	5.71%
18	0.09%		1.15%	1.01%	1.32%	1.43%	6.89%
19	0.02%		0.95%	1.01%	1.21%	1.66%	6.89%
20	0.08%		0.40%	1.08%	1.81%	1.66%	7.68%
21	0.15%		0.74%	0.92%	0.73%	1.18%	6.22%
22	0.12%		1.32%	1.04%	1.98%	1.84%	7.90%
23	0.15%		0.72%	0.99%	1.87%	1.76%	7.37%
24	0.17%		0.23%				
25	0.17%				(3) Standard Deviation(Monthly Returns of Asset i) Enter =STDEV(AD6:ES6) and copy down		
26	0.17%						
27	0.17%						

FIGURE 4.10 Excel Model of Portfolio Optimization – Descriptive Statistics

⊿	AB	AC	AD	AE	AF	AG	AH
27				(4) CORREL(Returns for asset i, Returns for asset j) Enter =CORREL(B$6:B$125,$AD6:$ES6) and copy to the range AD33:AU50			
28							
29							
30							
31			Stock	Stock	Stock	Stock	Stock
32		**Correlations**	Barrick	IBM	KEP	Nokia	Telefonos
33	Stock	Barrick	100.00%	2.35%	31.15%	18.37%	20.53%
34	Stock	IBM	2.35%	100.00%	30.21%	39.29%	34.21%
35	Stock	KEP	31.15%	30.21%	100.00%	34.83%	35.29%
36	Stock	Nokia	18.37%	39.29%	34.83%	100.00%	34.97%
37	Stock	Telefonos	20.53%	34.21%	35.29%	34.97%	100.00%
38	Stock	YPF	19.00%	25.14%	22.13%	22.46%	30.42%
39	US FF Port	Small-Growth	11.31%	51.52%	47.44%	48.78%	59.64%
40	US FF Port	Small-Neutral	16.10%	42.93%	50.81%	46.48%	57.85%
41	US FF Port	Small-Value	16.34%	38.64%	55.21%	44.26%	55.91%
42	US FF Port	Big-Growth	13.46%	69.47%	57.50%	59.20%	52.65%
43	US FF Port	Big-Neutral	24.98%	49.62%	55.24%	52.89%	41.26%
44	US FF Port	Big-Value	21.90%	43.98%	52.71%	49.14%	41.83%
45	Country ETF	Australia (EWA)	38.97%	44.35%	63.60%	49.52%	47.55%
46	Country ETF	Canada (EWC)	45.08%	52.64%	58.22%	49.40%	42.19%
47	Country ETF	Germany (EWG)	22.94%	49.21%	53.54%	54.88%	52.59%
48	Country ETF	Malaysia (EWM)	22.27%	30.58%	33.44%	22.29%	27.90%
49	Country ETF	Mexico (EWW)	28.93%	50.63%	58.18%	46.44%	75.56%
50	Country ETF	Singapore (EWS)	32.35%	43.75%	60.93%	37.97%	45.68%

FIGURE 4.11 Excel Model of Portfolio Optimization – Descriptive Statistics

	AB	AC	AD	AE	AF	AG	AH
53							
54				(5) COVAR(Returns for asset i, Returns for asset j)			
55				Enter =COVAR(B$6:B$125,$AD6:$E$6)			
56				and copy to the range AD59:AU76			
57			Stock	Stock	Stock	Stock	Stock
58		**Covariances**	Barrick	IBM	KEP	Nokia	Telefonos
59	Stock	Barrick	1.13%	0.02%	0.33%	0.24%	0.18%
60	Stock	IBM	0.02%	0.73%	0.25%	0.42%	0.25%
61	Stock	KEP	0.33%	0.25%	0.97%	0.43%	0.29%
62	Stock	Nokia	0.24%	0.42%	0.43%	1.55%	0.37%
63	Stock	Telefonos	0.18%	0.25%	0.29%	0.37%	0.71%
64	Stock	YPF	0.21%	0.23%	0.23%	0.30%	0.27%
65	US FF Port	Small-Growth	0.09%	0.34%	0.37%	0.47%	0.39%
66	US FF Port	Small-Neutral	0.10%	0.21%	0.29%	0.33%	0.28%
67	US FF Port	Small-Value	0.11%	0.21%	0.34%	0.35%	0.30%
68	US FF Port	Big-Growth	0.07%	0.27%	0.26%	0.34%	0.21%
69	US FF Port	Big-Neutral	0.13%	0.20%	0.26%	0.32%	0.17%
70	US FF Port	Big-Value	0.13%	0.21%	0.30%	0.35%	0.20%
71	Country ETF	Australia (EWA)	0.28%	0.26%	0.43%	0.42%	0.28%
72	Country ETF	Canada (EWC)	0.33%	0.31%	0.39%	0.42%	0.24%
73	Country ETF	Germany (EWG)	0.19%	0.32%	0.40%	0.52%	0.34%
74	Country ETF	Malaysia (EWM)	0.15%	0.16%	0.20%	0.17%	0.15%
75	Country ETF	Mexico (EWW)	0.24%	0.34%	0.45%	0.45%	0.50%
76	Country ETF	Singapore (EWS)	0.25%	0.27%	0.44%	0.35%	0.28%

4.3 Many Risky Assets and a Riskfree Asset

Problem. An individual investor with a simple mean and variance utility function has a risk aversion of 2.8. This investor is considering investing in the given individual stocks, US portfolios, or country portfolios. This investor considers four methods to forecast expected returns: average past return, Static CAPM, Fama-French 3 Factor, or Macro 3 Factor. Determine the Portfolio Weights of the Optimal Risky Portfolio and the Optimal Complete Portfolio.

Solution Strategy. To compute the many-asset Risky Opportunity Set, vary the portfolio expected return from 0.00% in cell **D76** to 4.00% in cell **D106**. Then compute the corresponding portfolio's standard deviation on the Risky Opportunity Set using the analytic formula. The Optimal Risky Portfolio is computed using a many-asset formula. The Capital Allocation Line comes from any two weights in the Optimal Risky Portfolio. The Optimal Complete Portfolio is computed from a many-asset formula for utility maximization. Then, the Indifference Curve through the Optimal Complete Portfolio is computed.

FIGURE 4.12 Excel Model of Portfolio Optimization - Many Assets

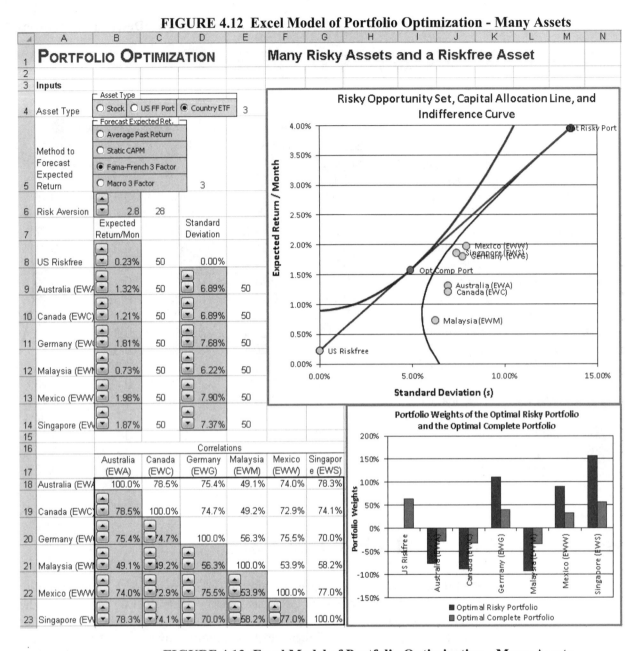

FIGURE 4.13 Excel Model of Portfolio Optimization - Many Assets

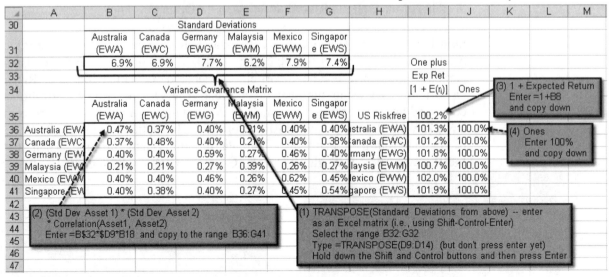

FIGURE 4.14 Excel Model Details of Portfolio Optimization - Many Assets.

(5) Enter A, B, C, Delta, and Gamma as Excel matrices (Shift-Control-Enter)
Type =MMULT(MMULT(TRANSPOSE(J36:J41),MINVERSE(B36:G41)),J36:J41)
Hold down the Shift and Control buttons and then press Enter

(6) Type =MMULT(MMULT(TRANSPOSE(J36:J41),MINVERSE(B36:G41)),I36:I41)
Hold down the Shift and Control buttons and then press Enter

(7) Type =MMULT(MMULT(TRANSPOSE(I36:I41),MINVERSE(B36:G41)),I36:I41)
Hold down the Shift and Control buttons and then press Enter

(8) A*C - B^2
Type =B58*B60-(B59^2)
Hold down the Shift and Control buttons and press Enter

(9) 1 / (B - A*(1 + Riskfree))
Type =1/(B59-B58*I35)
Hold down the Shift and Control buttons and then press Enter

Outputs

A	329.32746
B	332.10029
C	334.95949
Delta	2.1E+01
Gamma	0.4937623

	Proportion in Optimal Risky Port	Standard Deviation	Risky Asst Opp Set Curve Expected Ret / Mon	Capital Allocation Line Expected Ret / Mon	Individual Asset Expected Ret / Mon	Optimal Risky (Tangent) Portfolio Weights	Indifference Curve Expected Ret / Mon	Optimal Complete Portfolio Expected Ret / Mon	Optimal Complete Portfolio Weights
US Riskfree									63.8%
Australia (EWA)		6.9%			1.3%	-76.8%			-27.8%
Canada (EWC)		6.9%			1.2%	-87.6%			-31.7%
Germany (EWG)		7.7%			1.8%	110.4%			39.9%
Malaysia (EWM)		6.2%			0.7%	-92.3%			-33.4%
Mexico (EWW)		7.9%			2.0%	89.9%			32.5%
Singapore (EWS)		7.4%			1.9%	156.4%			56.6%
Opp Set Curve		6.45%	0.00%						
Opp Set Curve		6.19%	0.13%						
Opp Set Curve		5.97%	0.27%						
Opp Set Curve		5.78%	0.40%						
Opp Set Curve		5.65%	0.53%						
Opp Set Curve		5.55%	0.67%						
Opp Set Curve		5.51%	0.80%						
Opp Set Curve		5.52%	0.93%						
Opp Set Curve		5.58%	1.07%						
Opp Set Curve		5.69%	1.20%						
Opp Set Curve		5.85%	1.33%						
Opp Set Curve		6.05%	1.47%						
Opp Set Curve		6.28%	1.60%						
Opp Set Curve		6.56%	1.73%						
Opp Set Curve		6.86%	1.87%						
Opp Set Curve		7.19%	2.00%						
Opp Set Curve		7.54%	2.13%						
Opp Set Curve		7.91%	2.27%						
Opp Set Curve		8.30%	2.40%						

(10) Expected Return of Asset i
Enter =B9 and copy down

(11) Enter the Optimal Risky (Tangent) Port Weights as an Excel matrix
Select G70:G75
Type =B62*MMULT(MINVERSE(B36:G41),(I36:I41-I35*J36:J41))
Hold down the Shift and Control buttons and then press Enter

(12) Enter the Optimal Complete Portfolio Weights as an Excel matrix
Select J70:J75
Type =((E107-B8)/(2*B6*C107^2))*G70:G75
Hold down the Shift and Control buttons and then press Enter
US Riskfree Weight = 1 - Sum of the Risky Weights
Enter =1-SUM(J70:J75) in cell J69

(13) [A*(1+Expected Return)^2 - (2*B*(1+Expected Return)) + C) / (A*C - B^2)]^(1/2)
Enter =((\$B\$58*(1+D76)^2-(2*\$B\$59*(1+D76))+\$B\$60)
/(\$B\$58*\$B\$60-(\$B\$59^2)))^(1/2)
and copy to the range C77:C106

Hyperbola Coefficients. In a Mean vs. Standard Deviation graph, the Risky Opportunity Set is a hyperbola. The exact location of the hyperbola is uniquely determined by three coefficients, usually called A, B, and C. The derivation of the formulas can be found in Merton (1972).[3]

---

[3] See Robert C. Merton, "An Analytic Derivation of the Efficient Portfolio Frontier," *Journal of Financial and Quantitative Analysis*, September 1972, pp. 1851-72. His article uses slightly different notation.

FIGURE 4.15 Excel Model Details of Portfolio Optimization - Many Assets.

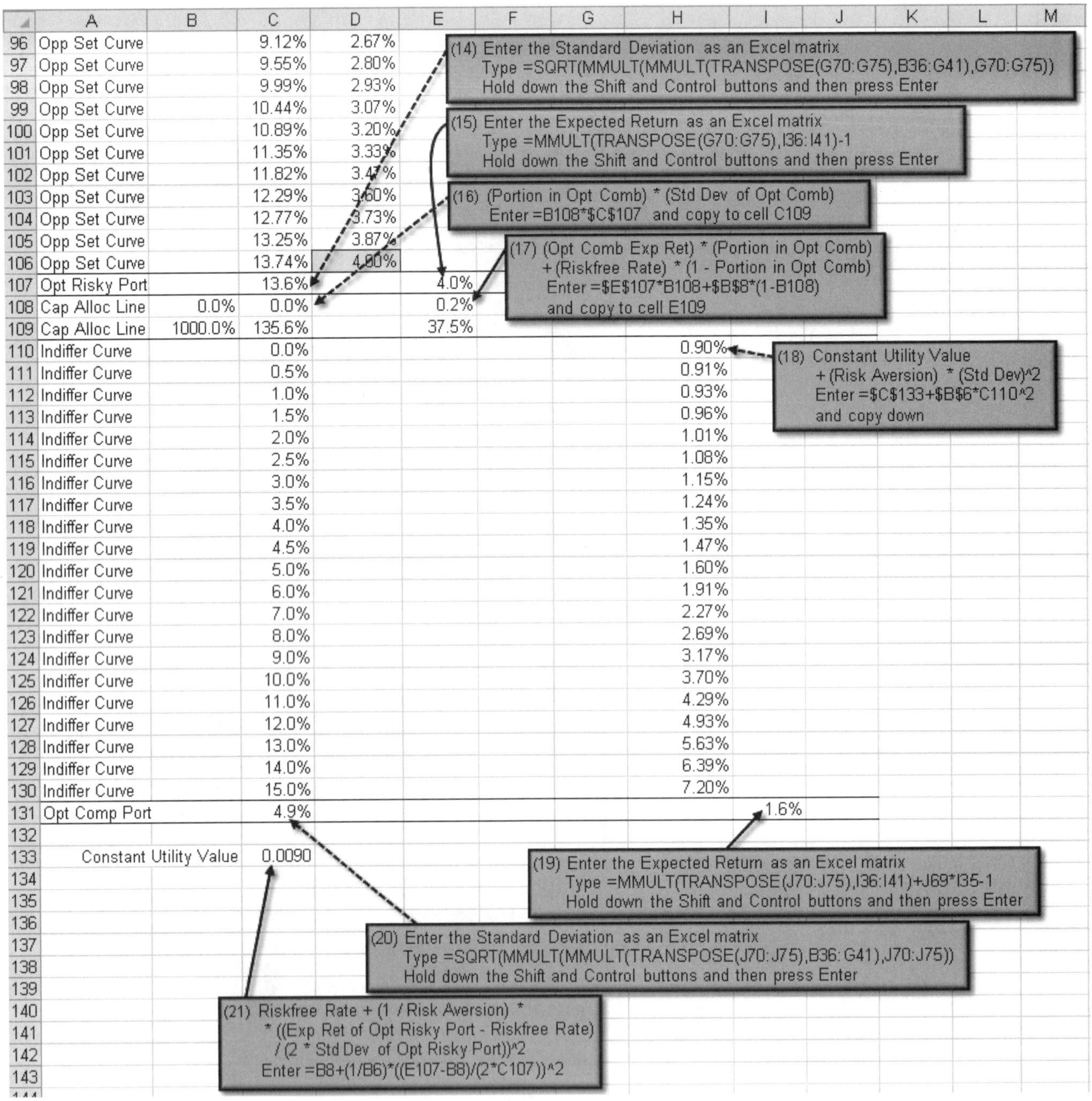

#	A	B	C	D	E	F	G	H	I	J	K	L	M
96	Opp Set Curve		9.12%	2.67%									
97	Opp Set Curve		9.55%	2.80%									
98	Opp Set Curve		9.99%	2.93%									
99	Opp Set Curve		10.44%	3.07%									
100	Opp Set Curve		10.89%	3.20%									
101	Opp Set Curve		11.35%	3.33%									
102	Opp Set Curve		11.82%	3.47%									
103	Opp Set Curve		12.29%	3.60%									
104	Opp Set Curve		12.77%	3.73%									
105	Opp Set Curve		13.25%	3.87%									
106	Opp Set Curve		13.74%	4.00%									
107	Opt Risky Port		13.6%		4.0%								
108	Cap Alloc Line	0.0%	0.0%		0.2%								
109	Cap Alloc Line	1000.0%	135.6%		37.5%								
110	Indiffer Curve		0.0%					0.90%					
111	Indiffer Curve		0.5%					0.91%					
112	Indiffer Curve		1.0%					0.93%					
113	Indiffer Curve		1.5%					0.96%					
114	Indiffer Curve		2.0%					1.01%					
115	Indiffer Curve		2.5%					1.08%					
116	Indiffer Curve		3.0%					1.15%					
117	Indiffer Curve		3.5%					1.24%					
118	Indiffer Curve		4.0%					1.35%					
119	Indiffer Curve		4.5%					1.47%					
120	Indiffer Curve		5.0%					1.60%					
121	Indiffer Curve		6.0%					1.91%					
122	Indiffer Curve		7.0%					2.27%					
123	Indiffer Curve		8.0%					2.69%					
124	Indiffer Curve		9.0%					3.17%					
125	Indiffer Curve		10.0%					3.70%					
126	Indiffer Curve		11.0%					4.29%					
127	Indiffer Curve		12.0%					4.93%					
128	Indiffer Curve		13.0%					5.63%					
129	Indiffer Curve		14.0%					6.39%					
130	Indiffer Curve		15.0%					7.20%					
131	Opt Comp Port		4.9%							1.6%			
132													
133	Constant Utility Value		0.0090										
134													
135													
136													
137													
138													
139													
140													
141													
142													
143													

(14) Enter the Standard Deviation as an Excel matrix
Type =SQRT(MMULT(MMULT(TRANSPOSE(G70:G75),B36:G41),G70:G75))
Hold down the Shift and Control buttons and then press Enter

(15) Enter the Expected Return as an Excel matrix
Type =MMULT(TRANSPOSE(G70:G75),I36:I41)-1
Hold down the Shift and Control buttons and then press Enter

(16) (Portion in Opt Comb) * (Std Dev of Opt Comb)
Enter =B108*$C$107 and copy to cell C109

(17) (Opt Comb Exp Ret) * (Portion in Opt Comb)
+ (Riskfree Rate) * (1 - Portion in Opt Comb)
Enter =$E$107*B108+$B$8*(1-B108)
and copy to cell E109

(18) Constant Utility Value
+ (Risk Aversion) * (Std Dev)^2
Enter =$C$133+$B$6*C110^2
and copy down

(19) Enter the Expected Return as an Excel matrix
Type =MMULT(TRANSPOSE(J70:J75),I36:I41)+J69*I35-1
Hold down the Shift and Control buttons and then press Enter

(20) Enter the Standard Deviation as an Excel matrix
Type =SQRT(MMULT(MMULT(TRANSPOSE(J70:J75),B36:G41),J70:J75))
Hold down the Shift and Control buttons and then press Enter

(21) Riskfree Rate + (1 / Risk Aversion) *
* ((Exp Ret of Opt Risky Port - Riskfree Rate)
/ (2 * Std Dev of Opt Risky Port))^2
Enter =B8+(1/B6)*((E107-B8)/(2*C107))^2

The graphs show several interesting things. First, click on **Country ETF** and click on various option buttons for the **Method to Forecast Expected Return**.

FIGURE 4.16 Average Past Returns and Static CAPM

FIGURE 4.17 Fama-French 3 Factor and Macro 3 Factor

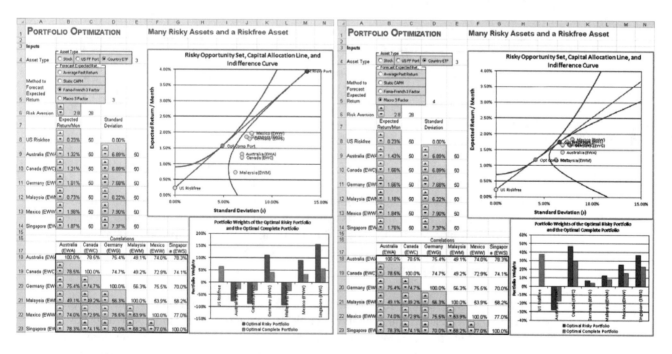

Germany had a relatively low average return from 2000 – 2000, so the Average Past Return method results in a negative portfolio weight on Germany in the Optimal Risky and Complete Portfolios. However, the three methods based on asset pricing models forecast much higher returns for Germany and thus, all three asset pricing based methods result in positive portfolio weights on Germany in the Optimal Risky and Complete Portfolios. This demonstrates that asset pricing based methods eliminate past realizations, which are not generally predictive of future returns.

Another point is that the **Method to Forecast Expected Return** matters a great deal. The four methods produce very different portfolio weights for the Optimal Risky and Complete Portfolios.

An interesting experiment is to click on the **Risk Aversion** down-arrow spin button to lower the investor's risk aversion.

FIGURE 4.18 Risk Aversion of 1.0 and 0.6

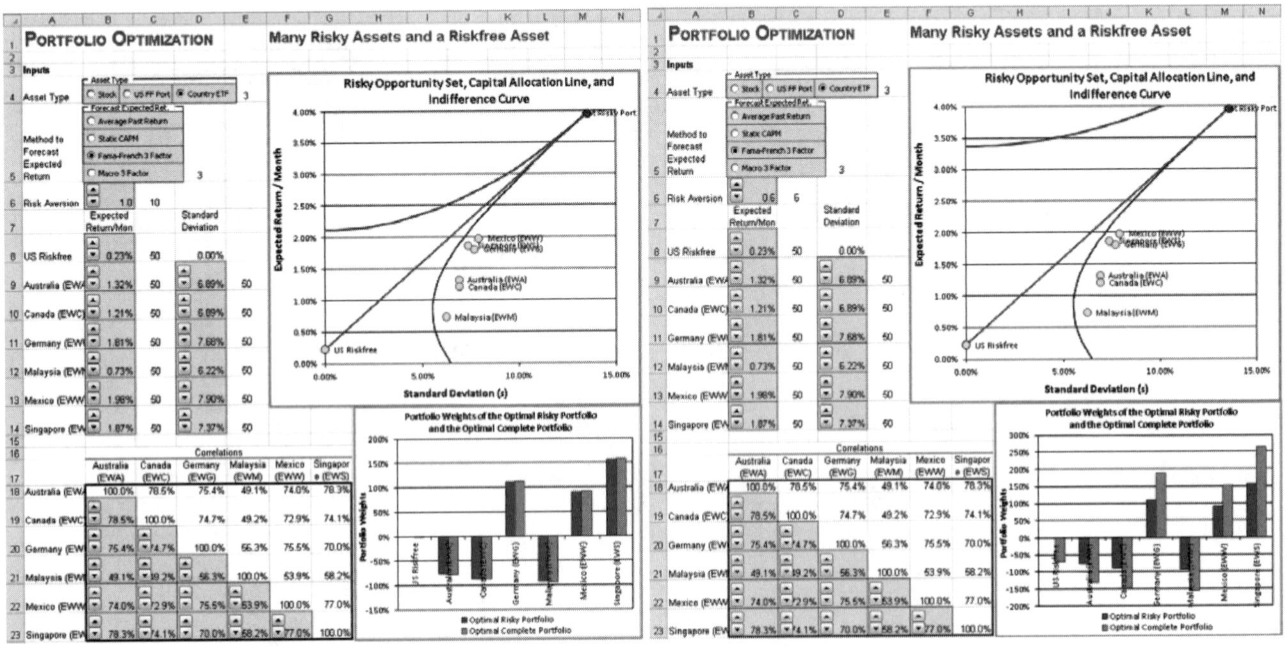

As risk aversion decreases, the Optimal Complete Portfolio slides up the Capital Allocation Line. When it reaches the Optimal Risky Portfolio, then the Optimal Complete Portfolio involves putting 0% in the riskfree asset and 100% in the Optimal Risky Portfolio. As risk aversion decreases further, it slides above the Optimal Risky Portfolio, then the Optimal Complete Portfolio involves a negative weigh in the riskfree asset (e.g., borrowing) and "more than 100%" in the Optimal Risky Portfolio.

Return risk aversion to 2.8 and imagine that you did security analysis on Germany. Click on the **Germany (EWG) Expected Return/Month** up-arrow spin button to raise expected return/month to 2.25% (e.g., Germany is underpriced). Then try the opposite experiment by clicking on the **Germany (EWG) Expected Return/Month** down-arrow spin button to lower expected return/month to 1.09% (e.g., Germany is overpriced).

FIGURE 4.19 Germany's Expected Return/Month of 2.25% and 1.09%

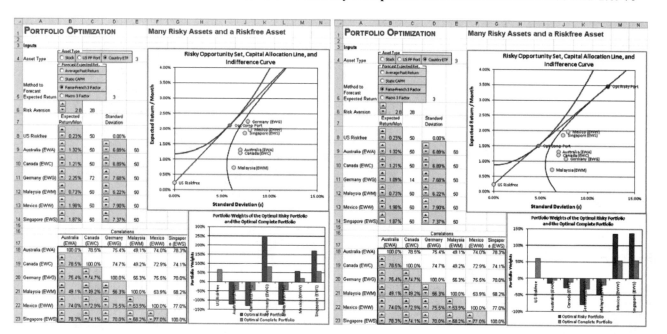

When Germany's Expected Return/Month increases to 2.25%, the Optimal Risky Portfolio weight in Germany rises dramatically (to 245.3%) to exploit this higher return. But also notice that the Optimal Risky Portfolio does NOT put 100% in Germany even though it has the highest expected return of all assets considered. The Optimal Risky Portfolio maintains an investment in all six risky assets in order to lower the portfolio standard deviation by diversification. Thus, the Optimal Risky Portfolio is always a trade-off between putting a higher weight in assets with higher returns vs. spreading out the investment to lower portfolio risk.

When Germany's Expected Return/Month decreases to 1.09%, the Optimal Risky Portfolio weight in Germany declines so far that it even goes negative (to -79.4%) to exploit this low return. A negative portfolio weight means short-selling. Putting a -79.4% in low return asset raises the overall portfolio return by allowing 179.4% to be invested in high return assets.

Return Barrick's Expected Return/Month to 1.81% and consider changes in Standard Deviation. Click on the **Canada (EWC) Standard Deviation** down-arrow spin button to lower the standard deviation to 4.89%. Then try the opposite experiment by clicking on the **Canada (EWC) Standard Deviation** up-arrow spin button to raise the standard deviation to 10.89%.

FIGURE 4.20 Canada (EWC) Standard Deviation of 4.89% and 10.89%

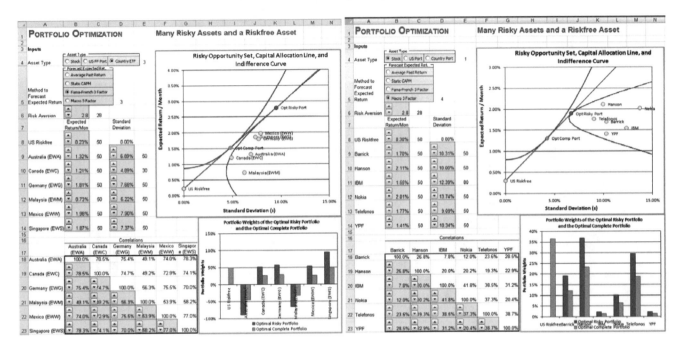

When Canada's Standard Deviation falls to 4.89%, the Optimal Risky Portfolio weight in Canada rises dramatically (to 51.7%) to exploit this low risk. But also notice that the Optimal Risky Portfolio does NOT put 100% in Canada even though it has the lowest standard deviation. It still pays to maintain some investment in all six risk assets in order lower the portfolio standard deviation by diversification. When Canada's Standard Deviation rises to 10.89%, the Optimal Risky Portfolio weight in Canada falls dramatically (to -83.4%) to avoid this high risk.

Return Canada's Standard Deviation to 6.89% and consider changes in Correlation. Click on the **Mexico/Singapore Correlation** down-arrow spin button (in cell **F23**) to lower the correlation to 57.0%. Then try the opposite experiment by clicking on the **Mexico/Singapore Correlation** up-arrow spin button to raise the correlation to 87.0%.

FIGURE 4.21 Mexico/Singapore Correlation of 57.0% and 87.0%

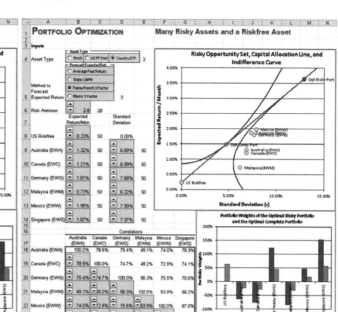

When Mexico/Singapore's Correlation falls to 57.0%, the Optimal Risky Portfolio weight in both Mexico and Singapore rises dramatically (Mexico to 223.5% and Singapore to 282.2%) to exploit this low correlation. When Mexico/Singapore's Correlation rises to 87.0%, the Optimal Risky Portfolio weight in both Mexico and Singapore falls dramatically (Mexico to 46.0% and Singapore to 153.0%) to avoid this high correlation.

Return Mexico/Singapore's Correlation to 77.0% and consider changes in the Riskfree Rate. Click on the **US Riskfree Expected Return/Month** up-arrow spin button to raise the Riskfree Rate to 0.73%. Then try the opposite experiment by clicking on the **US Riskfree Expected Return/Month** down-arrow spin button to lower the Riskfree Rate to 0.01%.

FIGURE 4.22 US Riskfree Rate of 0.73% and 0.01%

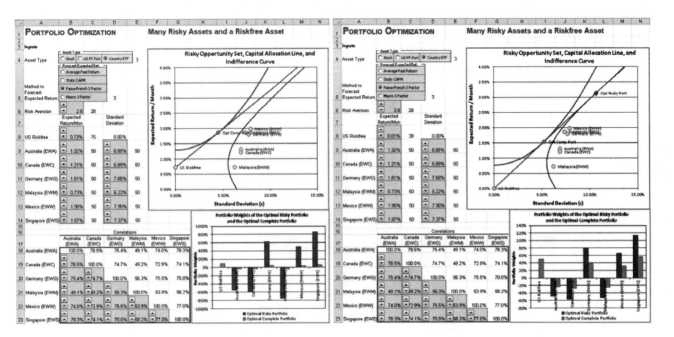

When the US Riskfree Rate increases to 0.73%, the Risky Opportunity Set (the blue curve) stays the same and Capital Allocation Line (the red line) slides up it, such that the Optimal Risky Portfolio (the purple dot) slides up the Risky Opportunity Set. This higher position means that Optimal Risky Portfolio increases the weights on high expected return assets like Mexico. When the US Riskfree Rate decreases to 0.01%, Capital Allocation Line slides down the Risky Opportunity Set, such that the Optimal Risky Portfolio slides down the Risky Opportunity Set. This lower position means that Optimal Risky Portfolio spreads its weights more evenly across all six assets.

Return the US Riskfree Rate to 0.23% and consider portfolios. Click on **Stock.** Next, click on **US Fama-French Portfolios**.

FIGURE 4.23 Stock and US Fama-French Portfolios

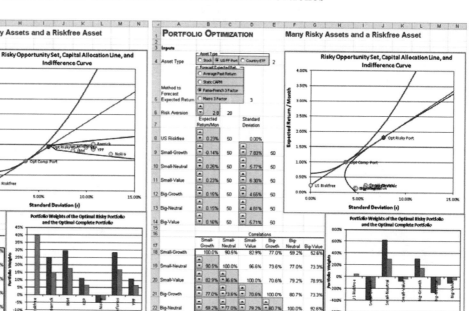

Notice that the Risky Opportunity Set shifts far to the right. This is because the standard deviations for individual Stocks are much smaller than US Fama-French Portfolios and County Portfolios. Roughly, the individual standard deviations are twice as big as the portfolio stock standard deviations. This demonstrates the impact of portfolio diversification in eliminating firm-specific risk.

Again, using portfolios matters a great deal. The US Portfolios and County Portfolios produce very different portfolio weights for the Optimal Risky and Complete Portfolios than the Individual Stocks.

4.4 Any Number of Risky Assets

Problem. An individual investor with a simple mean and variance utility function has a risk aversion of 14.5. This investor is considering investing in a riskfree asset and any number of risky assets up to a max of 20. The investor has forecasted the expected return of the risky assets. Determine the Portfolio Weights of the Optimal Risky Portfolio and the Optimal Complete Portfolio.

Solution Strategy. The number of risky assets is given in cell **B4**. Use Excel's OFFSET function to compute the portfolio calculations for any number of risky assets up to a maximum of 20. This spreadsheet does not explicitly address how the expected returns are computed (such as, average past return, static CAPM, Fama-French 3 Factor, or Macro 3 Factor). It is left to the user to supply the expected returns. See discussion in the prior section about how the forecast method affects the portfolio optimization results. Compute the many-asset Risky Opportunity Set while varying the portfolio expected return from -1.00% to 3.00%. Then compute the Optimal Risky Portfolio, Capital Allocation Line, Optimal Complete Portfolio, and Indifference Curve from many-asset formulas.

FIGURE 4.24 Portfolio Optimization – Any Number of Risky Assets

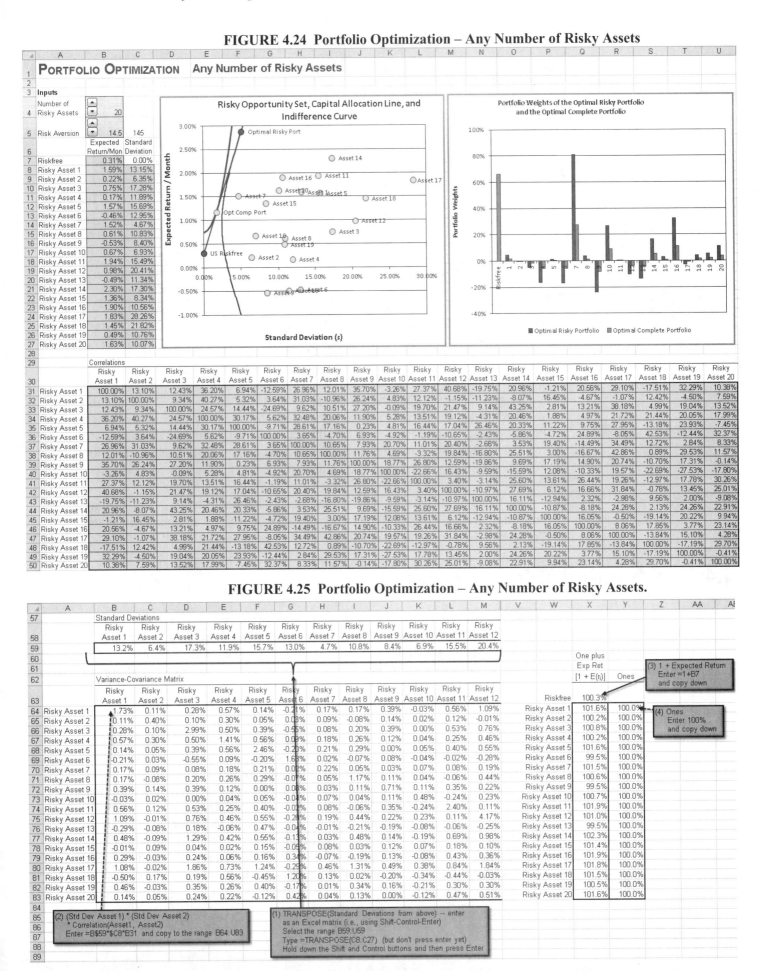

FIGURE 4.25 Portfolio Optimization – Any Number of Risky Assets.

FIGURE 4.26 Portfolio Optimization – Any Number of Risky Assets.

	A	B	C	D	E	F	G	H	I	J
90										
91										
92										
93										
94										
95										
96										
97										
98										
99	**Outputs**									
100	A	1662.0958								
101	B	1677.0455								
102	C	1692.3234								
103	Delta	3.2E+02								
104	Gamma	0.1020702								
105										
106				Risky Asst	Capital		Optimal		Optimal	
107				Opp Set	Allocation	Individual	Risky	ndifference	Complete	Optimal
108		Proportion		Curve	Line	Asset	(Tangent)	Curve	Portfolio	Complete
109		in Optimal	Standard	Expected	Expected	Expected	Portfolio	Expected	Expected	Portfolio
110		Risky Port	Deviation	Ret / Mon	Ret / Mon	Ret / Mon	Weights	Ret / Mon	Ret / Mon	Weights
111	Riskfree									66.2%
112	1		13.2%			1.6%	4.6%			1.5%
113	2		6.4%			0.2%	-0.3%			-0.1%
114	3		17.3%			0.8%	-4.8%			-1.6%
115	4		11.9%			0.2%	-16.5%			-5.6%
116	5		15.7%			1.6%	1.1%			0.4%
117	6		13.0%			-0.5%	-17.0%			-5.7%
118	7		4.7%			1.5%	81.0%			27.4%
119	8		10.8%			0.6%	3.5%			1.2%
120	9		8.4%			-0.5%	-23.9%			-8.1%
121	10		6.9%			0.7%	26.5%			9.0%
122	11		15.5%			1.9%	0.3%			0.1%
123	12		20.4%			1.0%	-10.4%			-3.5%
124	13		11.3%			-0.5%	-13.5%			-4.6%
125	14		17.3%			2.3%	16.3%			5.5%
126	15		8.3%			1.4%	2.8%			0.9%
127	16		10.6%			1.9%	32.6%			11.0%
128	17		28.3%			1.8%	-3.1%			-1.0%
129	18		21.8%			1.5%	4.3%			1.4%
130	19		10.8%			0.5%	5.4%			1.8%
131	20		10.1%			1.6%	11.0%			3.7%
132	Opp Set Curve		4.96%	-1.00%						
133	Opp Set Curve		4.89%	-0.96%						
134	Opp Set Curve		4.81%	-0.92%						
135	Opp Set Curve		4.73%	-0.88%						
136	Opp Set Curve		4.65%	-0.84%						
137	Opp Set Curve		4.57%	-0.80%						
138	Opp Set Curve		4.50%	-0.76%						
139	Opp Set Curve		4.42%	-0.72%						
140	Opp Set Curve		4.35%	-0.68%						
141	Opp Set Curve		4.27%	-0.64%						
142	Opp Set Curve		4.20%	-0.60%						
143	Opp Set Curve		4.12%	-0.56%						
144	Opp Set Curve		4.05%	-0.52%						
145	Opp Set Curve		3.98%	-0.48%						
146	Opp Set Curve		3.91%	-0.44%						
147	Opp Set Curve		3.84%	-0.40%						
148	Opp Set Curve		3.77%	-0.36%						
149	Opp Set Curve		3.70%	-0.32%						
150	Opp Set Curve		3.63%	-0.28%						
151	Opp Set Curve		3.57%	-0.24%						
152	Opp Set Curve		3.50%	-0.20%						
153	Opp Set Curve		3.44%	-0.16%						
154	Opp Set Curve		3.37%	-0.12%						

(5) Enter A, B, C, Delta, and Gamma as Excel matrices (Shift-Control-Enter)
Type =MMULT(MMULT(TRANSPOSE(Y64:OFFSET(Y64,$B$4-1,0))
,MINVERSE(B64:OFFSET(B64,$B$4-1,$B$4-1))),Y64:OFFSET(Y64,$B$4-1,0))
Hold down the Shift and Control buttons and then press Enter

(6) Type =MMULT(MMULT(TRANSPOSE(Y64:OFFSET(Y64,$B$4-1,0))
,MINVERSE(B64:OFFSET(B64,$B$4-1,$B$4-1))),X64:OFFSET(X64,$B$4-1,0))
Hold down the Shift and Control buttons and then press Enter

(7) Type =MMULT(MMULT(TRANSPOSE(X64:OFFSET(X64,$B$4-1,0))
,MINVERSE(B64:OFFSET(B64,$B$4-1,$B$4-1))),X64:OFFSET(X64,$B$4-1,0))
Hold down the Shift and Control buttons and then press Enter

(8) A*C - B^2
Type =B100*B102-(B101^2) Hold down the Shift and Control buttons and press Enter

(9) 1 / (B - A*(1 + Riskfree))
Type =1/(B101-B100*X63) Hold down the Shift and Control buttons and then press Enter

(10) IF Number of Assets >= Asset Number
Then Expected Return of Asset i
Else Not Applicable
Enter =IF($B$4>=A112,B8,NA())
and copy down

(11) Enter the Optimal Risky (Tangent) Port Weights as an Excel matrix
Select G112:G131
Type =B104*MMULT(MINVERSE(B64:OFFSET(B64,$B$4-1,$B$4-1))
,(X64:OFFSET(X64,$B$4-1,0)-X63*Y64:OFFSET(Y64,$B$4-1,0)))
Hold down the Shift and Control buttons and then press Enter

(12) Enter the Optimal Complete Portfolio Weights as an Excel matrix
Select J112:J131
Type =((E233-B7)/(2*B5*C233^2))*G112:OFFSET(G112,$B$4-1,0)
Hold down the Shift and Control buttons and then press Enter
US Riskfree Weight = 1 - Sum of the Risky Weights
Enter =1-SUM(J112:OFFSET(J112,$B$4-1,0)) in cell J111

(13) [A*(1+Expected Return)^2 - (2*B*(1+Expected Return)) + C)
/ (A*C - B^2)]^(1/2)
Enter =(($B$100*(1+D132)^2-(2*$B$101*(1+D132))+$B$102)
/($B$100*$B$102-($B$101^2)))^(1/2)
and copy to the range C133:C232

Hyperbola Coefficients. Again in a Mean vs. Standard Deviation graph, the Risky Opportunity Set is a hyperbola. The exact location of the hyperbola is uniquely determined by the three coefficients: A, B, and C.

FIGURE 4.27 Portfolio Optimization – Any Number of Risky Assets.

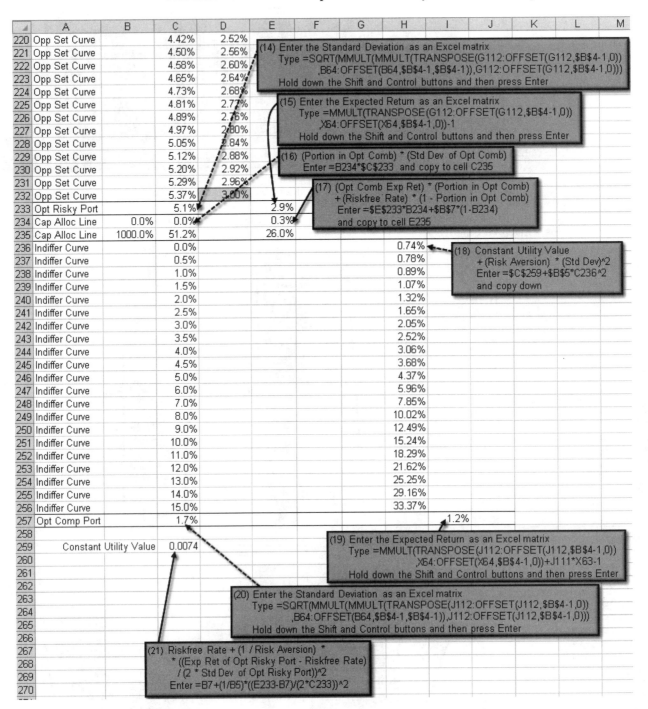

See what happens as you increase the number of risky assets.

FIGURE 4.28 Number of Risky Assets is Two

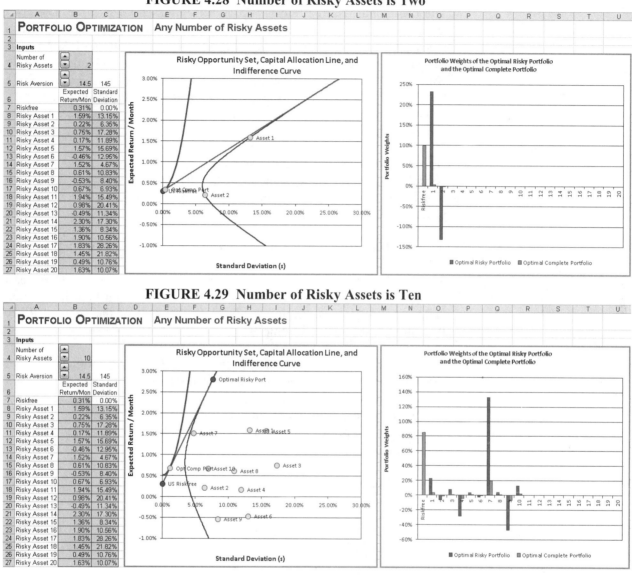

FIGURE 4.29 Number of Risky Assets is Ten

FIGURE 4.30 Number of Risky Assets is Twenty

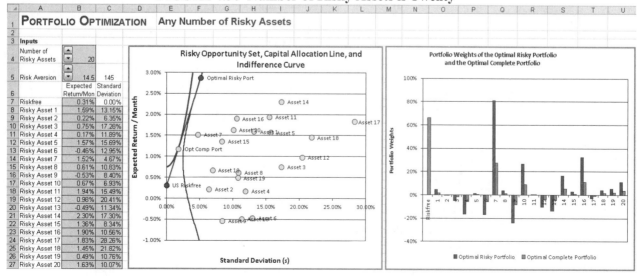

Problems

1. The one-month riskfree rate is 0.23%. Risky Asset 1 has a mean return / month of 2.10% and a standard deviation of 13.00%. Risky Asset 2 has a mean return / month of 1.30% and a standard deviation of 8.0%. The correlation between Risky Asset 1 and 2 is 20.0%. An individual investor with a simple mean and variance utility function has a risk aversion of 2.0. Graph the Risky Opportunity Set, the Optimal Risky Portfolio, the Capital Allocation Line, the investor's Indifference Curve, and the Optimal Complete Portfolio.

2. Download 10 years of monthly returns for stocks, U.S. portfolios, or country portfolios of your choice and estimate the means, standard deviations, correlations, and variances/covariances among the risky assets. Download 10 years of the U.S riskfree rate, compute the mean riskfree rate.

3. An individual investor with a simple mean and variance utility function has a risk aversion of 1.5. This investor is considering investing in the assets you downloaded for problem 2. This investor considers four methods to forecast expected returns: average past return, Static CAPM, Fama-French 3 Factor, or Macro 3 Factor. Determine the Portfolio Weights of the Optimal Risky Portfolio and the Optimal Complete Portfolio.

4. An individual investor with a simple mean and variance utility function has a risk aversion of 8.1. This investor is considering investing in a riskfree asset and any number of risky assets up to a max of 20. The investor has forecasted the expected return of the risky assets. Determine the Portfolio Weights of the Optimal Risky Portfolio and the Optimal Complete Portfolio.

Chapter 5 Constrained Portfolio Optimization

5.1 No Short Sales, No Borrowing, and Other Constraints

Problem. An individual investor with a simple mean and variance utility function has a risk aversion of 2.9. This investor is considering investing in the given individual stocks, US portfolios, or country portfolios. This investor considers four methods to forecast expected returns: average past return, Static CAPM, Fama-French 3 Factor, or Macro 3 Factor. The investor wishes to impose no short sales, no borrowing, and no portfolio weights great than 100%. Determine the Portfolio Weights of the Optimal Risky Portfolio and the Optimal Complete Portfolio.

Solution Strategy. There is no analytical solution, so the Constrained Risky Opportunity Set and the Constrained Complete Opportunity Set are found numerically using Excel **Solver**. Click on the Run Macro button

Click Here to Run Macro in the range **E2:G3** to run a macro which calls Solver 202 times. The "RepeatedlyRunSolver" macro takes about 2 minutes to run. With each call, Solver finds the portfolio weights which minimize the portfolio variance, subject to setting the portfolio expected return equal to a constant value and satisfying all constraints, (e.g., no short sales). When the weight in the Riskfree Asset *is constrained* to be exactly 0.00%, then you get the Constrained *Risky* Opportunity Set. When the weight in the Riskfree Asset is *not constrained*, then you get the Constrained *Complete* Opportunity Set. Computing the utility of each portfolio in the Constrained Complete Opportunity Set and rank ordering the utility values, identifies the *Optimal Complete* Portfolio. Zeroing out the weight in the riskfree asset and scaling up the weights in the risky assets determines the *Optimal Risky* Portfolio.

FIGURE 5.1 No Short Sales, No Borrowing, and Other Constraints

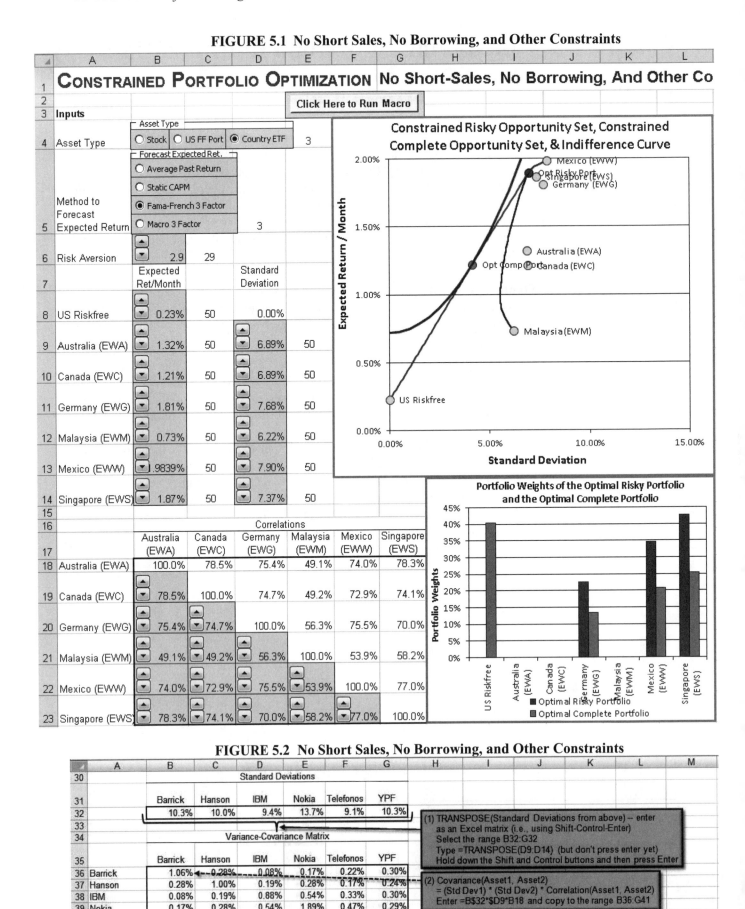

FIGURE 5.2 No Short Sales, No Borrowing, and Other Constraints

	A	B	C	D	E	F	G
30				Standard Deviations			
31		Barrick	Hanson	IBM	Nokia	Telefonos	YPF
32		10.3%	10.0%	9.4%	13.7%	9.1%	10.3%
33							
34				Variance-Covariance Matrix			
35		Barrick	Hanson	IBM	Nokia	Telefonos	YPF
36	Barrick	1.06%	0.28%	0.08%	0.17%	0.22%	0.30%
37	Hanson	0.28%	1.00%	0.19%	0.28%	0.17%	0.24%
38	IBM	0.08%	0.19%	0.88%	0.54%	0.33%	0.30%
39	Nokia	0.17%	0.28%	0.54%	1.89%	0.47%	0.29%
40	Telefonos	0.22%	0.17%	0.33%	0.47%	0.83%	0.36%
41	YPF	0.30%	0.24%	0.30%	0.29%	0.36%	1.07%

(1) TRANSPOSE(Standard Deviations from above) -- enter
as an Excel matrix (i.e., using Shift-Control-Enter)
Select the range B32:G32
Type =TRANSPOSE(D9:D14) (but don't press enter yet)
Hold down the Shift and Control buttons and then press Enter

(2) Covariance(Asset1, Asset2)
= (Std Dev1) * (Std Dev2) * Correlation(Asset1, Asset2)
Enter =B$32*$D9*B18 and copy to the range B36:G41

FIGURE 5.3 No Short Sales, No Borrowing, and Other Constraints

(3) Sum(Portfolio Weights)
Enter =SUM(R48:X48)

(4) Matrix Multiply(Port Weights, Expected Returns)
– enter as an Excel matrix (Shift-Control-Enter)
Type =MMULT(R48:X48,$B$8:$B$14)
Hold down the Shift and Control buttons and then press Enter

(5) Square Root(MMULT(MMULT(Risky Port Weights, Variance-Covariance Matrix),
TRANSPOSE(Risk Port Weights))) -- enter as an Excel matrix (Shift-Control-Enter)
Type =SQRT(MMULT(MMULT(S48:X48,$B$36:$G$41),TRANSPOSE(S48:X48)))
Hold down the Shift and Control buttons and then press Enter

Solver Analysis Area

	Sum of Portfolio Weights	Portfolio Expected Ret/Mon	Portfolio Standard Deviation	Solver Solution Code	Portfolio Weights						
					US Riskfree	Australia (EWA)	Canada (EWC)	Germany (EWG)	Malaysia (EWM)	Mexico (EWW)	Singapore (EWS)
48	100.00%	1.98%	7.90%	5	0.00%	0.00%	0.00%	0.00%	0.00%	100.00%	0.00%

Table of Problems and Solutions

	Sum of Portfolio Weights	Portfolio Expected Ret/Mon	Portfolio Standard Deviation	Solver Solution Code	Portfolio Weights						
					US Riskfree	Australia (EWA)	Canada (EWC)	Germany (EWG)	Malaysia (EWM)	Mexico (EWW)	Singapore (EWS)
55	100.00%	0.73%	6.22%	5	0.00%	0.00%	0.00%	0.00%	100.00%	0.00%	0.00%
56	100.00%	0.73%	6.22%	5	0.00%	0.00%	0.00%	0.00%	100.00%	0.00%	0.00%
57	100.00%	0.73%	6.22%	5	0.00%	0.00%	0.00%	0.00%	100.00%	0.00%	0.00%
58	100.00%	0.73%	6.22%	5	0.00%	0.00%	0.00%	0.00%	100.00%	0.00%	0.00%
89	100.00%	0.73%	6.22%	5	0.00%	0.00%	0.00%	0.00%	100.00%	0.00%	0.00%
90	100.00%	0.73%	6.22%	5	0.00%	0.00%	0.00%	0.00%	100.00%	0.00%	0.00%
91	100.00%	0.73%	6.22%	5	0.00%	0.00%	0.00%	0.00%	100.00%	0.00%	0.00%
92	100.00%	0.74%	6.16%	0	0.00%	0.00%	1.91%	0.00%	98.09%	0.00%	0.00%
93	100.00%	0.76%	6.06%	0	0.00%	0.00%	6.05%	0.00%	93.95%	0.00%	0.00%
94	100.00%	0.78%	5.96%	0	0.00%	0.00%	10.24%	0.00%	89.76%	0.00%	0.00%
95	100.00%	0.80%	5.87%	0	0.00%	0.00%	14.42%	0.00%	85.58%	0.00%	0.00%
96	100.00%	0.82%	5.80%	0	0.00%	0.00%	18.59%	0.00%	81.41%	0.00%	0.00%
97	100.00%	0.84%	5.74%	0	0.00%	2.34%	19.88%	0.00%	77.78%	0.00%	0.00%
98	100.00%	0.86%	5.68%	0	0.00%	5.42%	20.26%	0.00%	74.32%	0.00%	0.00%
99	100.00%	0.88%	5.64%	0	0.00%	8.51%	20.64%	0.00%	70.85%	0.00%	0.00%
100	100.00%	0.90%	5.60%	0	0.00%	11.59%	21.02%	0.00%	67.39%	0.00%	0.00%
101	100.00%	0.92%	5.57%	0	0.00%	14.67%	21.40%	0.00%	63.93%	0.00%	0.00%
102	100.00%	0.94%	5.55%	0	0.00%	17.75%	21.79%	0.00%	60.46%	0.00%	0.00%
103	100.00%	0.96%	5.54%	0	0.00%	20.83%	22.17%	0.00%	57.00%	0.00%	0.00%

Rows 55 to 256 contain 202 problems for Solver to solve. Columns R through X contain the portfolio weights, which are the *choice variables* for each problem. Columns Y through AN contain the *constraint constants* (for the sum of portfolio weights, target expected return, minimum portfolio weight, maximum portfolio weight) for each problem. Notice that the minimum portfolio weight for the risky assets (columns AB – AG) are 0.00%, which rules out negative weights (i.e., short-selling). The minimum portfolio weight for the riskfree asset (column AA) is 0.00%, which rules out a negative weight (i.e., borrowing). The maximum portfolio weight for the risky assets (columns AH – AN) are 100.00%, which rules out the most extremely undiversified positions.

Rows 55 to 155 contain 101 problems in which the weight in the Riskfree Asset is constrained to be exactly 0.00%. This is accomplished by setting minimum weight for the Riskfree Asset (column AA) to 0.00% and the maximum weight for the Riskfree Asset (column AH) to 0.00%. The solution to these problems yield the Constrained *Risky* Opportunity Set.

Rows 156 to 256 contain 101 problems in which the weight in the Riskfree Asset is NOT constrained to be exactly 0.00%. The maximum weight for the Riskfree Asset (column AH) is set to 100.00%. The solutions to these problems yield the Constrained Complete Opportunity Set.

FIGURE 5.4 No Short Sales, No Borrowing, and Other Constraints

	Y	Z	AA	AB	AC	AD	AE	AF	AG	AH	AI	AJ	AK	AL	AM	AN
	Sum of	Target				Minimum Portfolio Weights							Maximum Portfolio Weights			
46	Portfolio	Expected		Australia	Canada	Germany	Malaysia	Mexico	Singapore		Australia	Canada	Germany	Malaysia	Mexico	Singapore
47	Weights	Ret/Mon	US Riskfree	(EWA)	(EWC)	(EWG)	(EWM)	(EWW)	(EWS)	US Riskfree	(EWA)	(EWC)	(EWG)	(EWM)	(EWW)	(EWS)
48	100.00%	2.00%	0.00%	0.00%	0.00%	0.00%	0.00%	0.00%	0.00%	100.00%	100.00%	100.00%	100.00%	100.00%	100.00%	100.00%
49																
50																
51																
52									Constraints							
	Sum of	Target				Minimum Portfolio Weights							Maximum Portfolio Weights			
53	Portfolio	Expected		Australia	Canada	Germany	Malaysia	Mexico	Singapore		Australia	Canada	Germany	Malaysia	Mexico	Singapore
54	Weights	Ret/Mon	US Riskfree	(EWA)	(EWC)	(EWG)	(EWM)	(EWW)	(EWS)	US Riskfree	(EWA)	(EWC)	(EWG)	(EWM)	(EWW)	(EWS)
55	100.00%	0.00%	0.00%	0.00%	0.00%	0.00%	0.00%	0.00%	0.00%	0.00%	100.00%	100.00%	100.00%	100.00%	100.00%	100.00%
56	100.00%	0.02%	0.00%	0.00%	0.00%	0.00%	0.00%	0.00%	0.00%	0.00%	100.00%	100.00%	100.00%	100.00%	100.00%	100.00%
57	100.00%	0.04%	0.00%	0.00%	0.00%	0.00%	0.00%	0.00%	0.00%	0.00%	100.00%	100.00%	100.00%	100.00%	100.00%	100.00%
58	100.00%	0.06%	0.00%	0.00%	0.00%	0.00%	0.00%	0.00%	0.00%	0.00%	100.00%	100.00%	100.00%	100.00%	100.00%	100.00%
59	100.00%	0.08%	0.00%	0.00%	0.00%	0.00%	0.00%	0.00%	0.00%	0.00%	100.00%	100.00%	100.00%	100.00%	100.00%	100.00%
60	100.00%	0.10%	0.00%	0.00%	0.00%	0.00%	0.00%	0.00%	0.00%	0.00%	100.00%	100.00%	100.00%	100.00%	100.00%	100.00%
61	100.00%	0.12%	0.00%	0.00%	0.00%	0.00%	0.00%	0.00%	0.00%	0.00%	100.00%	100.00%	100.00%	100.00%	100.00%	100.00%
62	100.00%	0.14%	0.00%	0.00%	0.00%	0.00%	0.00%	0.00%	0.00%	0.00%	100.00%	100.00%	100.00%	100.00%	100.00%	100.00%
63	100.00%	0.16%	0.00%	0.00%	0.00%	0.00%	0.00%	0.00%	0.00%	0.00%	100.00%	100.00%	100.00%	100.00%	100.00%	100.00%

FIGURE 5.5 No Short Sales, No Borrowing, and Other Constraints

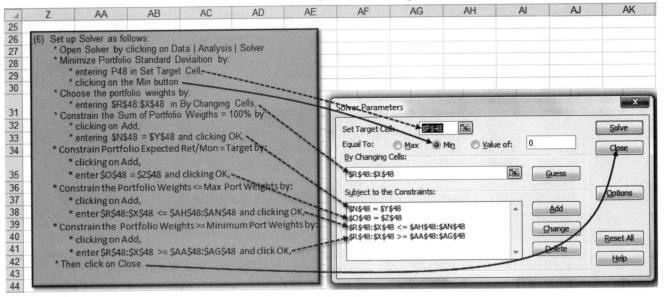

	Z	AA	AB	AC	AD	AE	AF	AG	AH	AI	AJ	AK
25												
26	(6) Set up Solver as follows:											
27	* Open Solver by clicking on Data	Analysis	Solver									
28	* Minimize Portfolio Standard Deviation by:											
29	* entering P48 in Set Target Cell,											
30	* clicking on the Min button											
31	* Choose the portfolio weights by:											
	* entering $R$48:$X$48 in By Changing Cells,											
32	* Constrain the Sum of Portfolio Weigths = 100% by:											
33	* clicking on Add,											
34	* entering $N$48 = $Y$48 and clicking OK,											
	* Constrain Portfolio Expected Ret/Mon = Target by:											
35	* clicking on Add,											
36	* enter $O$48 = $Z$48 and clicking OK,											
37	* Constrain the Portfolio Weights <=Max Port Weights by:											
38	* clicking on Add,											
39	* enter $R$48:$X$48 <= $AH$48:$AN$48 and clicking OK,											
40	* Constrain the Portfolio Weights >=Minimum Port Weights by:											
41	* clicking on Add,											
42	* enter $R$48:$X$48 >= $AA$48:$AG$48 and click OK,											
43	* Then click on Close.											
44												

Solver Parameters

Set Target Cell: $P$48

Equal To: ○ Max ● Min ○ Value of: 0

By Changing Cells:

$R$48:$X$48

Subject to the Constraints:

$N$48 = $Y$48
$O$48 = $Z$48
$R$48:$X$48 <= $AH$48:$AN$48
$R$48:$X$48 >= $AA$48:$AG$48

Solve
Close
Guess
Options
Add
Change
Delete
Reset All
Help

Excel 97-2003 Equivalent

To open Solver in Excel 97-2003, click on **Tools | Solver**.

Below we see rows 146 to 236, which contain the second set of 91 problems in which the weight in the Riskfree Asset is not constrained to be exactly 0.00%.

FIGURE 5.6 No Short Sales, No Borrowing, and Other Constraints

	H	I	J	K	L	M	N	O	P	Q
40	(7) If Solver Solution Code = 0 (Solver found a solution)									
41	Then Port Exp Return - (Risk Aversion) * (Port Std Dev)^2									
42	Else -1									
43	Enter =IF(Q55=0,O55-$B$6*P55^2,-1) and copy to the range L56:L256									
44										
45	Optimal	Optimal	Optimal				**Solver Analysis Area**			
46	Complete	Risky	Complete				Sum of	Portfolio	Portfolio	Solver
	Expected	Portfolio	Portfolio	Vlookup			Portfolio	Expected	Standard	Solution
47	Ret/Mon	Weights	Weights	Column			Weights	Ret/Mon	Deviation	Code
48			40.5%	6			100.00%	1.98%	7.90%	5
49		0.0%	0.0%	7						
50		0.0%	0.0%	8						
51		22.5%	13.4%	9						
52		0.0%	0.0%	10			**Table of Problems and Solutions**			
53		34.7%	20.7%	11			Sum of	Portfolio	Portfolio	Solver
					Investor	Portfolio	Portfolio	Expected	Standard	Solution
54		42.8%	25.5%	12	Utility	Ranking	Weights	Ret/Mon	Deviation	Code
55					-100.000%		100.00%	0.73%	6.22%	5
56					-100.000%		100.00%	0.73%	6.22%	5
57					-100.000%		100.00%	0.73%	6.22%	5
92					-0.362%		100.00%	0.74%	6.16%	0
93					-0.304%		100.00%	0.76%	6.06%	0
94					-0.250%		100.00%	0.78%	5.96%	0

FIGURE 5.7 No Short Sales, No Borrowing, and Other Constraints

	F	G	H	I	J	K	L	M	N	O	P	Q
53				34.7%	20.7%	11			Sum of	Portfolio	Portfolio	Solver
							Investor	Portfolio	Portfolio	Expected	Standard	Solution
54				42.8%	25.5%	12	Utility	Ranking	Weights	Ret/Mon	Deviation	Code
152	(8) RANK(Investor Utility from port i, Investor Utility from all portfolios)						0.402%		100.00%	1.94%	7.28%	0
153	Enter =RANK(L156,$L$156:$L$256) and copy down						0.325%		100.00%	1.96%	7.51%	0
154							0.263%		100.00%	1.98%	7.83%	0
155							-100.000%		100.00%	1.98%	7.90%	5
156							-100.000%	89	100.00%	0.23%	0.00%	5
157							-100.000%	89	100.00%	0.23%	0.00%	5
158							-100.000%	89	100.00%	0.23%	0.00%	5
213							0.718%	8	100.00%	1.14%	3.82%	0
214							0.719%	6	100.00%	1.16%	3.90%	0
215							0.720%	4	100.00%	1.18%	3.98%	0
216							0.721%	2	100.00%	1.20%	4.07%	0
217							0.721%	1	100.00%	1.22%	4.15%	0
218							0.720%	3	100.00%	1.24%	4.23%	0
219							0.720%	5	100.00%	1.26%	4.32%	0
220							0.718%	7	100.00%	1.28%	4.40%	0

Column L contains the utility of each portfolio in the Constrained Complete Opportunity Set and column M contains rank ordering of these utility values. In this case, the portfolio in row 217 yields the highest utility value and is thus the *Optimal Complete* Portfolio.

Column J in the figure below shows the portfolio weights of the Optimal Complete Portfolio. In column I in the figure below, the portfolio weight in the riskfree asset is zeroed out and the portfolio weights of the risky assets are scaled up proportionally so that they add up to 100%. This yields the portfolio weights of the Optimal Risky Portfolio.

FIGURE 5.8 No Short Sales, No Borrowing, and Other Constraints

	A	B	C	D	E	F	G	H	I	J	K
44			Constrd	Constrained							
45			Risky	Complete	Individual	Indiffer	Optimal	Optimal	Optimal	Optimal	
46			Opp Set	Opp Set	Asset	Curve	Risky	Complete	Risky	Complete	Vlookup
47		Standard Deviation	Expected Ret/Mon	Expected Ret/Mon	Expected Ret/Mon	Expected Ret/Mon	Expected Ret/Mon	Expected Ret/Mon	Portfolio Weights	Portfolio Weights	Column
48	US Riskfree	0.0%			0.2%					40.5%	6
49	Australia (EWA)	6.9%			1.3%				0.0%	0.0%	7
50	Canada (EWC)	6.9%			1.2%				0.0%	0.0%	8
51	Germany (EWG)	7.7%			1.8%				22.5%	13.4%	9
52	Malaysia (EWM)	6.2%			0.7%				0.0%	0.0%	10
53	Mexico (EWW)	7.9%			2.0%				34.7%	20.7%	11
54	Singapore (EWS)	7.4%			1.9%				42.8%	25.5%	12
55	Constrd Risky	#N/A	0.00%								
56	Constrd Risky	#N/A	0.02%								
57	Constrd Risky	#N/A	0.04%								
58	Constrd Risky	#N/A	0.06%								
59	Constrd Risky	#N/A	0.08%								
60	Constrd Risky	#N/A	0.10%								
61	Constrd Risky	#N/A	0.12%								
62	Constrd Risky	#N/A	0.14%								
63	Constrd Risky	#N/A	0.16%								
64	Constrd Risky	#N/A	0.18%								
65	Constrd Risky	#N/A	0.20%								
66	Constrd Risky	#N/A	0.22%								
67	Constrd Risky	#N/A	0.24%								
68	Constrd Risky	#N/A	0.26%								
69	Constrd Risky	#N/A	0.28%								
92	Constrd Risky	6.16%	0.74%								
93	Constrd Risky	6.06%	0.76%								
94	Constrd Risky	5.96%	0.78%								

(9) Expected Return of Asset i
Enter =B8 and copy down

(10) (Risky Weight i) / (Sum of the Risky Weights)
Type =J49/(SUM($J$49:$J$54))
and copy down

(11) VLOOKUP(#1 Utility Ranking, Complete Portfolio Range,Column,FALSE)
Enter =VLOOKUP(1,$M$156:$X$256,K48,FALSE)
and copy down

(12) If Solver Solution Code = 0 (Solver found a solution)
Then Port Std Dev
Else #N/A Error Code so it won't show up on the graph
Enter =IF(Q55=0,P55,NA()) and copy to the range B56:B236

FIGURE 5.9 No Short Sales, No Borrowing, and Other Constraints

	A	B	C	D	E	F	G	H	I	J	K
249	Constrd Compl	6.82%		1.86%							
250	Constrd Compl	6.91%		1.88%							
251	Constrd Compl	6.99%		1.90%							
252	Constrd Compl	7.11%		1.92%							
253	Constrd Compl	7.28%		1.94%							
254	Constrd Compl	7.51%		1.96%							
255	Constrd Compl	7.83%		1.98%							
256	Constrd Compl	#N/A		2.00%							
257	Opt Risky Port	6.97%				1.89%					
258	Opt Comp Port	4.2%						1.22%			
259	Indiffer Curve	0.0%				0.72%					
260	Indiffer Curve	0.5%				0.73%					
261	Indiffer Curve	1.0%				0.75%					
262	Indiffer Curve	1.5%				0.79%					
263	Indiffer Curve	2.0%				0.84%					
264	Indiffer Curve	2.5%				0.90%					
265	Indiffer Curve	3.0%				0.98%					
266	Indiffer Curve	3.5%				1.08%					
267	Indiffer Curve	4.0%				1.18%					
268	Indiffer Curve	4.5%				1.31%					
269	Indiffer Curve	5.0%				1.45%					
270	Indiffer Curve	6.0%				1.76%					
271	Indiffer Curve	7.0%				2.14%					
272	Indiffer Curve	8.0%				2.58%					
273	Indiffer Curve	9.0%				3.07%					
274	Indiffer Curve	10.0%				3.62%					
275	Indiffer Curve	11.0%				4.23%					
276	Indiffer Curve	12.0%				4.90%					
277	Indiffer Curve	13.0%				5.62%					
278	Indiffer Curve	14.0%				6.40%					
279	Indiffer Curve	15.0%				7.25%					
280											
281	Constant Utility Value		0.0072								

(13) Enter the Standard Deviation as an Excel matrix
Type =SQRT(MMULT(MMULT(TRANSPOSE(I49:I54),$B$36:$G$41),I49:I54))
Hold down the Shift and Control buttons and then press Enter

(14) Enter the Expected Return as an Excel matrix
Type =MMULT(TRANSPOSE(I49:I54),$B$9:$B$14)
Hold down the Shift and Control buttons and then press Enter

(16) Constant Utility Value
+ (Risk Aversion) * (Std Dev)^2
Enter =$C$281+$B$6*B259^2
and copy down

(15) VLOOKUP(#1 Utility Ranking,
Complete Portfolio Range, Column,FALSE)
Enter =VLOOKUP(1,M156:P256,4,FALSE) in cell B258
Enter =VLOOKUP(1,M156:P256,3,FALSE) in cell H258

(17) Exp Ret of Opt Complete Portfolio
- (Risk Aversion) * (Std Dev of Opt Complete Port)^2
Enter =H258-B6*B258^2

Excel 2007 Equivalent

To view the macro in Excel 2007, click on the **Office** button , click on the **Excel Options** button, check the **Show Developer tab in the Ribbon** checkbox, and click **OK**.

Excel 97-2003 Equivalent

To view the macro in Excel 97-2003, click on **Tools | Macro | Visual Basic Editor**

Once you have built the spreadsheet, you are ready to run the macro by clicking

on the Run Macro button | Click Here to Run Macro | in the range **E2:G3**. This button runs the macro "**RepeatedlyRunSolver**."

To view the macro, click on **Developer | Code | Visual Basic** (see below). If the

Developer tab is not visible, you can display it by click on | File |, click on

 Options , click on **Customize Ribbon**, check the Developer checkbox, and click **OK**.

FIGURE 5.10 Excel Model of Constrained Portfolio Optimization – No Short Sales, No Borrowing, and Other Constraints

This opens the Visual Basic Development Environment. In the main window, you see the code for the "**RepeatedlyRunSolver**" macro. The macro is very straight-forward. It runs a big loop that solves each of the 202 problems from Rows 55 to 256. First, it copies the starting values in the range R32:X32 to R48:X48 to initialize the portfolio weights. Then, the macro starts on row 55 and copies the constraint constants Y55:AN55 to Y48:AN48. Row 48 is the **Solver Analysis Area**. Then it calls Solver and asks it solve the problem on Row 48:

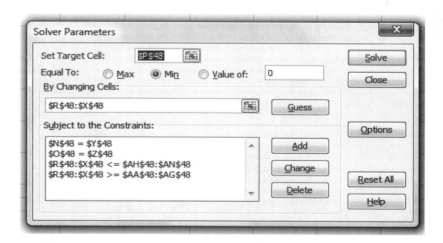

Then it copies the results from N48:X48 (namely, the sum of port weights, portfolio expected return, portfolio standard deviation, Solver solution code, and portfolio weights) and pastes the result values to N55:X55. Then it repeats this process for Row 56, for Row 57, for Row 58, etc.

FIGURE 5.11 No Short Sales, No Borrowing, and Other Constraints

The macro code itself is in blue and black. The comments in green explain how macro works.

Now let's experiment with various inputs. First, click on **Country ETF**, click on various option buttons for the **Method to Forecast Expected Return**, and then click the Recalculation button [Click Here to Run Macro]. See the results below.

FIGURE 5.12 Average Past Returns and Static CAPM

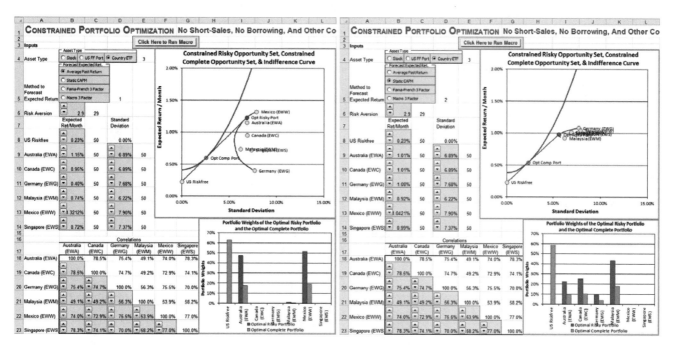

FIGURE 5.13 Fama-French 3 Factor and Macro 3 Factor

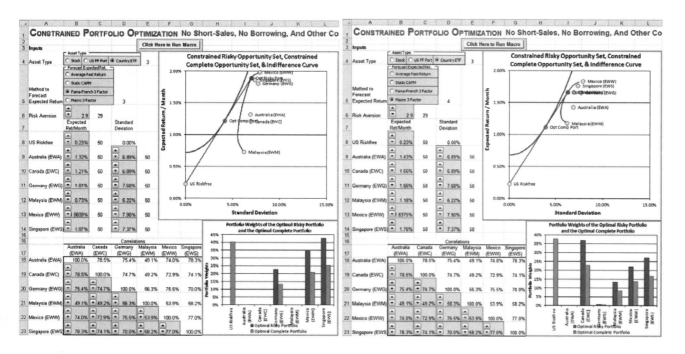

Again we see that the **Method to Forecast Expected Return** matters a great deal. The four methods produce very different portfolio weights for the Optimal Risky and Complete Portfolios.

An interesting experiment is to click on the **Risk Aversion** down-arrow spin button to lower the investor's risk aversion and then click the Run Macro button

Click Here to Run Macro .

FIGURE 5.14 Risk Aversion of 16 and 0.4

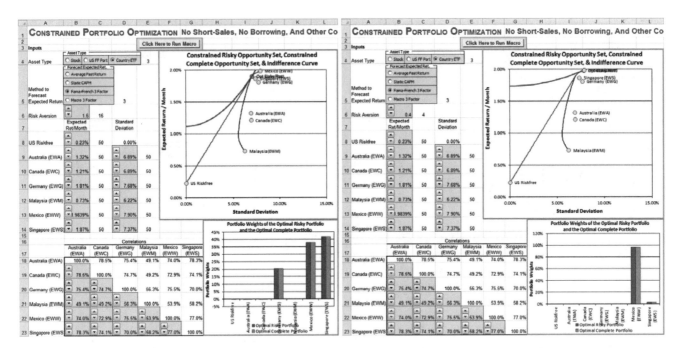

As risk aversion decreases, the Optimal Complete Portfolio slides up the Constrained Complete Opportunity Set. When it reaches the Optimal Risky Portfolio, then the Optimal Complete Portfolio involves putting 0% in the riskfree asset and 100% in the Optimal Risky Portfolio. As risk aversion decreases further, the Optimal Complete Portfolio follows the upper curve of the Constrained Risky Opportunity Set, because borrowing at the riskfree rate is not allowed. For a very low risk aversion level, the Optimal Complete Portfolio involves putting 100% in a single country ETF, Mexico (EWW), because it has the highest expected return.

Now consider portfolios. Click on **Stock** and then click the Run Macro button

Click Here to Run Macro . Then **US Fama-French Portfolio** and then click the Run Macro button.

FIGURE 5.15 US Portfolios and Country Portfolios

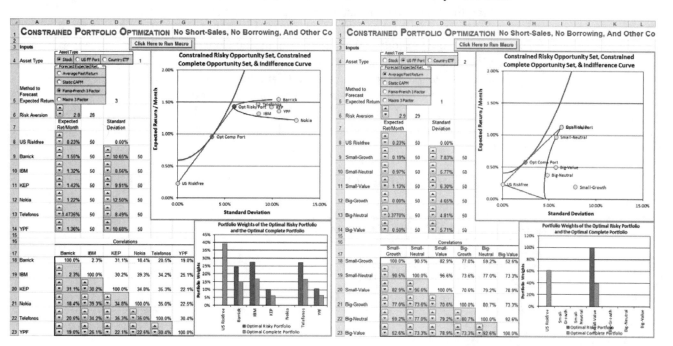

Again, we see that using portfolios matters a great deal. With individual stocks, the Risky Opportunity Set shifts far to the right, because firm-specific risk is not diversified away. The Stocks and US Fama-French Portfolios produce very different portfolio weights for the Optimal Risky and Complete Portfolios than the Country ETFs.

5.2 Any Number of Risky Assets

Problem. An individual investor with a simple mean and variance utility function has a risk aversion of 9.8. This investor is considering investing in a riskfree asset and any number of risky assets up to a max of 20. The investor has forecasted the expected return of the risky assets. The investor wishes to impose no short sales, no borrowing, and no portfolio weights great than 100%. Determine the Portfolio Weights of the Optimal Risky Portfolio and the Optimal Complete Portfolio.

Solution Strategy. The number of risky assets is given in cell **B4**. Use Excel's OFFSET function to compute the portfolio calculations for any number of risky assets up to a maximum of 20. This spreadsheet does not explicitly address how the expected returns are computed. See discussion in the prior section about how the forecast method affects the portfolio optimization results. There is no analytical solution, so the Constrained Risky Opportunity Set and the Constrained Complete Opportunity Set are found numerically using Excel

Solver. Click on the Run Macro button [Click Here to Run Macro] in the range **E2:G3** to run a macro which calls Solver 202 times. The "RepeatedlyRunSolver2" macro takes about 2 minutes to run. With each call,

Solver finds the portfolio weights which minimize the portfolio variance, subject to setting the portfolio expected return equal to a constant value and satisfying all constraints, (e.g., no short sales). When the weight in the Riskfree Asset *is constrained* to be exactly 0.00%, then you get the Constrained *Risky* Opportunity Set. When the weight in the Riskfree Asset is *not constrained*, then you get the Constrained *Complete* Opportunity Set. Computing the utility of each portfolio in the Constrained Complete Opportunity Set and rank ordering the utility values, identifies the *Optimal Complete* Portfolio. Zeroing out the weight in the riskfree asset and scaling up the weights in the risky assets determines the *Optimal Risky* Portfolio.

FIGURE 5.16 Constrained Port Optimization -Any Number of Risky Assets

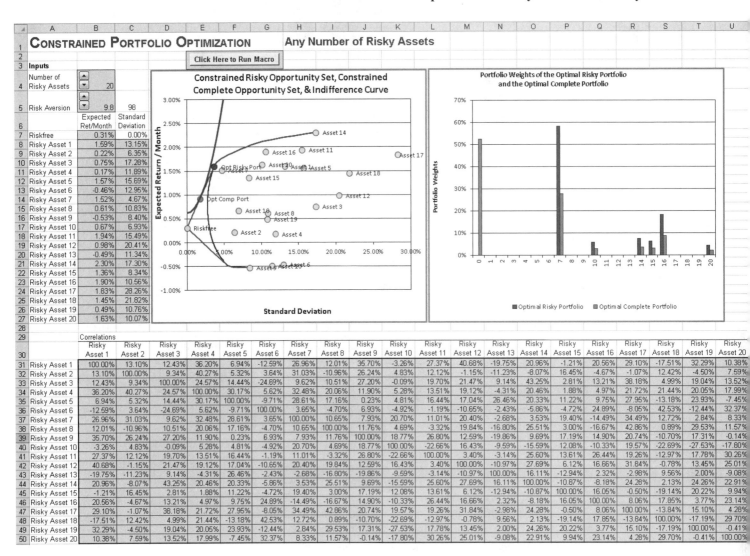

CONSTRAINED PORTFOLIO OPTIMIZATION — Any Number of Risky Assets

Inputs

Number of Risky Assets: 20

Risk Aversion: 9.8 | 98

	Expected Ret/Month	Standard Deviation
Riskfree	0.31%	0.00%
Risky Asset 1	1.59%	13.15%
Risky Asset 2	0.22%	6.35%
Risky Asset 3	0.75%	17.28%
Risky Asset 4	0.17%	11.89%
Risky Asset 5	1.57%	15.69%
Risky Asset 6	-0.46%	12.95%
Risky Asset 7	1.52%	4.67%
Risky Asset 8	0.61%	10.83%
Risky Asset 9	-0.53%	8.40%
Risky Asset 10	0.67%	6.93%
Risky Asset 11	1.94%	15.49%
Risky Asset 12	0.98%	20.41%
Risky Asset 13	-0.49%	11.34%
Risky Asset 14	2.30%	17.30%
Risky Asset 15	1.36%	8.34%
Risky Asset 16	1.90%	10.56%
Risky Asset 17	1.83%	28.26%
Risky Asset 18	1.45%	21.82%
Risky Asset 19	0.49%	10.76%
Risky Asset 20	1.63%	10.07%

Correlations

	Risky Asset 1	Risky Asset 2	Risky Asset 3	Risky Asset 4	Risky Asset 5	Risky Asset 6	Risky Asset 7	Risky Asset 8	Risky Asset 9	Risky Asset 10	Risky Asset 11	Risky Asset 12	Risky Asset 13	Risky Asset 14	Risky Asset 15	Risky Asset 16	Risky Asset 17	Risky Asset 18	Risky Asset 19	Risky Asset 20
Risky Asset 1	100.00%	13.10%	12.43%	36.20%	6.94%	-12.59%	26.96%	12.01%	35.70%	-3.26%	27.37%	40.68%	-19.75%	20.96%	-1.21%	20.56%	29.10%	-17.51%	32.29%	10.38%
Risky Asset 2	13.10%	100.00%	9.34%	40.27%	5.32%	3.64%	31.03%	-10.96%	26.24%	4.83%	12.12%	-1.15%	-11.23%	-8.07%	16.45%	-4.67%	-1.07%	12.42%	-4.50%	7.59%
Risky Asset 3	12.43%	9.34%	100.00%	24.57%	14.44%	-24.69%	9.62%	10.51%	27.20%	-0.09%	19.70%	21.47%	9.14%	43.25%	2.81%	13.21%	38.18%	4.99%	19.04%	13.52%
Risky Asset 4	36.20%	40.27%	24.57%	100.00%	30.17%	5.62%	32.48%	20.06%	11.90%	5.28%	13.51%	19.12%	-4.31%	20.46%	1.88%	4.97%	21.72%	21.44%	20.05%	17.99%
Risky Asset 5	6.94%	5.32%	14.44%	30.17%	100.00%	-9.71%	28.61%	17.16%	0.23%	4.81%	16.44%	17.04%	26.46%	20.33%	11.22%	9.75%	27.95%	-13.18%	23.93%	-7.45%
Risky Asset 6	-12.59%	3.64%	-24.69%	5.62%	-9.71%	100.00%	3.65%	-4.70%	6.93%	-4.92%	-1.19%	-10.65%	-2.43%	-5.86%	-4.72%	24.89%	-8.05%	42.53%	-12.44%	32.37%
Risky Asset 7	26.96%	31.03%	9.62%	32.48%	28.61%	3.65%	100.00%	10.65%	7.93%	20.70%	11.01%	20.40%	3.53%	3.53%	19.40%	-14.49%	34.49%	12.72%	2.84%	8.33%
Risky Asset 8	12.01%	-10.96%	10.51%	20.06%	17.16%	-4.70%	10.65%	100.00%	11.76%	4.69%	-3.32%	19.84%	-16.80%	25.51%	3.00%	-16.67%	42.86%	0.89%	29.53%	11.57%
Risky Asset 9	35.70%	26.24%	27.20%	11.90%	0.23%	6.93%	7.93%	11.76%	100.00%	18.77%	26.80%	12.59%	-19.86%	9.69%	17.19%	14.90%	20.74%	-10.70%	17.31%	-0.14%
Risky Asset 10	-3.26%	4.83%	-0.09%	5.28%	4.81%	-4.92%	20.70%	4.69%	18.77%	100.00%	-22.66%	16.43%	-9.59%	-15.59%	12.08%	-10.33%	19.57%	-22.69%	-27.53%	-17.80%
Risky Asset 11	27.37%	12.12%	19.70%	13.51%	16.44%	-1.19%	11.01%	-3.32%	26.80%	-22.66%	100.00%	3.40%	-3.14%	25.60%	13.61%	26.44%	19.26%	-12.97%	17.78%	30.26%
Risky Asset 12	40.68%	-1.15%	21.47%	19.12%	17.04%	-10.65%	20.40%	19.84%	12.59%	16.43%	3.40%	100.00%	-10.97%	27.69%	6.12%	16.66%	31.84%	-0.78%	13.45%	25.01%
Risky Asset 13	-19.75%	-11.23%	9.14%	-4.31%	26.46%	-2.43%	3.53%	-16.80%	-19.86%	-9.59%	-3.14%	-10.97%	100.00%	16.11%	-12.94%	16.05%	-2.98%	9.56%	2.00%	-9.08%
Risky Asset 14	20.96%	-8.07%	43.25%	20.46%	20.33%	-5.86%	3.53%	25.51%	9.69%	-15.59%	25.60%	27.69%	16.11%	100.00%	-10.87%	-8.18%	24.28%	2.13%	24.26%	22.91%
Risky Asset 15	-1.21%	16.45%	2.81%	1.88%	11.22%	-4.72%	19.40%	3.00%	17.19%	12.08%	13.61%	6.12%	-12.94%	-10.87%	100.00%	16.05%	-0.50%	-19.14%	20.22%	9.94%
Risky Asset 16	20.56%	-4.67%	13.21%	4.97%	9.75%	24.89%	-14.49%	-16.67%	14.90%	-10.33%	26.44%	16.66%	2.32%	-8.18%	16.05%	100.00%	8.06%	17.85%	3.77%	23.14%
Risky Asset 17	29.10%	-1.07%	38.18%	21.72%	27.95%	-8.05%	34.49%	42.86%	20.74%	19.57%	19.26%	31.84%	-2.98%	24.28%	-0.50%	8.06%	100.00%	-13.84%	15.10%	4.28%
Risky Asset 18	-17.51%	12.42%	4.99%	21.44%	-13.18%	42.53%	12.72%	0.89%	-10.70%	-22.69%	-12.97%	-0.78%	9.56%	2.13%	-19.14%	17.85%	-13.84%	100.00%	-17.19%	29.70%
Risky Asset 19	32.29%	-4.50%	19.04%	20.05%	23.93%	-12.44%	2.84%	29.53%	17.31%	-27.53%	17.78%	13.45%	2.00%	24.26%	20.22%	3.77%	15.10%	-17.19%	100.00%	-0.41%
Risky Asset 20	10.38%	7.59%	13.52%	17.99%	-7.45%	32.37%	8.33%	11.57%	-0.14%	-17.80%	30.26%	25.01%	-9.08%	22.91%	9.94%	23.14%	4.28%	29.70%	-0.41%	100.00%

FIGURE 5.17 Constrained Port Optimization -Any Number of Risky Assets

	A	B	C	D	E	F	G	H	I	J	K	L	M
52		Standard Deviations											
53		Risky Asset 1	Risky Asset 2	Risky Asset 3	Risky Asset 4	Risky Asset 5	Risky Asset 6	Risky Asset 7	Risky Asset 8	Risky Asset 9	Risky Asset 10	Risky Asset 11	Risky Asset 12
54		13.2%	6.4%	17.3%	11.9%	15.7%	13.0%	0.046693	0.108325	0.08399	0.069329	0.1548937	0.204128
55													
56		Variance-Covariance Matrix											
57		Risky Asset 1	Risky Asset 2	Risky Asset 3	Risky Asset 4	Risky Asset 5	Risky Asset 6	Risky Asset 7	Risky Asset 8	Risky Asset 9	Risky Asset 10	Risky Asset 11	Risky Asset 12
58	Risky Asset 1	1.73%	0.11%	0.28%	0.57%	0.14%	-0.21%	0.17%	0.17%	0.39%	-0.03%	0.56%	1.09%
59	Risky Asset 2	0.11%	0.40%	0.10%	0.30%	0.05%	0.03%	0.09%	-0.08%	0.14%	0.02%	0.12%	-0.01%
60	Risky Asset 3	0.28%	0.10%	2.99%	0.50%	0.39%	-0.55%	0.08%	0.20%	0.39%	0.00%	0.53%	0.76%
61	Risky Asset 4	0.57%	0.30%	0.50%	1.41%	0.56%	0.09%	0.18%	0.26%	0.12%	0.04%	0.25%	0.46%
62	Risky Asset 5	0.14%	0.05%	0.39%	0.56%	2.46%	-0.20%	0.21%	0.29%	0.00%	0.05%	0.40%	0.55%
63	Risky Asset 6	-0.21%	0.03%	-0.55%	0.09%	-0.20%	1.68%	0.02%	-0.07%	0.08%	-0.04%	-0.02%	-0.28%
64	Risky Asset 7	0.17%	0.09%	0.08%	0.18%	0.21%	0.02%	0.22%	0.05%	0.03%	0.07%	0.08%	0.19%
65	Risky Asset 8	0.17%	-0.08%	0.20%	0.26%	0.29%	-0.07%	0.05%	1.17%	0.11%	0.04%	-0.06%	0.44%
66	Risky Asset 9	0.39%	0.14%	0.39%	0.12%	0.00%	0.08%	0.03%	0.11%	0.71%	0.11%	0.35%	0.22%
67	Risky Asset 10	-0.03%	0.02%	0.00%	0.04%	0.05%	-0.04%	0.07%	0.04%	0.11%	0.48%	-0.24%	0.23%
68	Risky Asset 11	0.56%	0.12%	0.53%	0.25%	0.40%	-0.02%	0.08%	-0.06%	0.35%	-0.24%	2.40%	0.11%
69	Risky Asset 12	1.09%	-0.01%	0.76%	0.46%	0.55%	-0.28%	0.19%	0.44%	0.22%	0.23%	0.11%	4.17%
70	Risky Asset 13	-0.29%	-0.08%	0.18%	-0.06%	0.47%	-0.04%	-0.01%	-0.21%	-0.19%	-0.08%	-0.06%	-0.25%
71	Risky Asset 14	0.48%	-0.09%	1.29%	0.42%	0.55%	-0.13%	0.03%	0.48%	0.14%	-0.19%	0.69%	0.98%
72	Risky Asset 15	-0.01%	0.09%	0.04%	0.02%	0.15%	-0.05%	0.08%	0.03%	0.12%	0.07%	0.18%	0.10%
73	Risky Asset 16	0.29%	-0.03%	0.24%	0.06%	0.16%	0.34%	-0.07%	-0.19%	0.13%	-0.08%	0.43%	0.36%
74	Risky Asset 17	1.08%	-0.02%	1.86%	0.73%	1.24%	-0.29%	0.46%	1.31%	0.49%	0.38%	0.84%	1.84%
75	Risky Asset 18	-0.50%	0.17%	0.19%	0.56%	-0.45%	1.20%	0.13%	0.02%	-0.20%	-0.34%	-0.44%	-0.03%
76	Risky Asset 19	0.46%	-0.03%	0.35%	0.26%	0.40%	-0.17%	0.01%	0.34%	0.16%	-0.21%	0.30%	0.30%
77	Risky Asset 20	0.14%	0.05%	0.24%	0.22%	-0.12%	0.42%	0.04%	0.13%	0.00%	-0.12%	0.47%	0.51%

(2) Covariance(Asset1, Asset2)
= (Std Dev1) * (Std Dev2) * Correlation(Asset1, Asset2)
Enter =B$54*$C8*B31 and copy to the range B58:U77

(1) TRANSPOSE(Standard Deviations from above) -- enter as an Excel matrix (i.e., using Shift-Control-Enter)
Select the range B54:U54
Type =TRANSPOSE(C8:C27) (but don't press enter yet)
Hold down the Shift and Control buttons and then press Enter

FIGURE 5.18 Constrained Port Optimization -Any Number of Risky Assets

	L	M	N	O	P	Q	R	S	T	U	V	W	X	Y	Z	AA	AB	AC
87			Solver Analysis Area															
88			Sum of Portfolio Weights	Portfolio Expected Ret/Mon	Portfolio Standard Deviation	Solver Solution Code										Portfolio Weights		
89							Riskfree	Risky Asset 1	Risky Asset 2	Risky Asset 3	Risky Asset 4	Risky Asset 5	Risky Asset 6	Risky Asset 7	Risky Asset 8	Risky Asset 9	Risky Asset 10	Risky Asset 11
90			100.00%	2.30%	17.30%	5	0.00%	0.00%	0.00%	0.00%	0.00%	0.00%	0.00%	0.00%	0.00%	0.00%	0.00%	0.00%
91																		

(3) Sum(Portfolio Weights)
Enter =SUM(R90:OFFSET(R90,0,B4))

(5) Square Root(MMULT(MMULT(Risky Port Weights, Variance-Covariance Matrix), TRANSPOSE(Risk Port Weights))) -- enter as an Excel matrix (Shift-Control-Enter)
Type =SQRT(MMULT(MMULT(S90:OFFSET(S90,0,B4-1),B58:OFFSET(B58,B4-1,B4-1)),TRANSPOSE(S90:OFFSET(S90,0,B4-1))))
Hold down the Shift and Control buttons and then press Enter

(4) Matrix Multiply(Port Weights, Expected Returns)
-- enter as an Excel matrix (Shift-Control-Enter)
Type =MMULT(R90:OFFSET(R90,0,B4),B7:OFFSET(B7,B4,0))
Hold down the Shift and Control buttons and then press Enter

	L	M	N	O	P	Q	R	S	T	U	V	W	X	Y	Z	AA	AB	AC
101							Riskfree	1	2	3	4	5	6	7	8	9	10	11
102							0.00%	5.00%	5.00%	5.00%	5.00%	5.00%	5.00%	5.00%	5.00%	5.00%	5.00%	5.00%

Starting Values for Solver

(7) If Solver Solution Code = 0 (Solver found a solution)
Then Port Exp Return - (Risk Aversion) * (Port Std Dev)^2
Else -1
Enter =IF(Q111=0,O111-$B$5*P111^2,-1) and copy to the range L112:L312

Table of Problems and Solutions

	L Investor Utility	M Portfolio Ranking	N Portfolio Weights	O Portfolio Expected Ret/Mon	P Portfolio Standard Deviation	Q Solver Solution Code	R Riskfree	S Risky Asset 1	T Risky Asset 2	U Risky Asset 3	V Risky Asset 4	W Risky Asset 5	X Risky Asset 6	Y Risky Asset 7	Z Risky Asset 8	AA Risky Asset 9	AB Risky Asset 10	AC Risky Asset 11
109			Sum of	Portfolio	Portfolio	Solver										Portfolio Weights		
111	-100.000%		100.00%	-0.53%	8.40%	5	0.00%	0.00%	0.00%	0.00%	0.00%	0.00%	0.00%	0.00%	0.00%	100.00%	0.00%	0.00%
112	-100.000%		100.00%	-0.53%	8.40%	5	0.00%	0.00%	0.00%	0.00%	0.00%	0.00%	0.00%	0.00%	0.00%	100.00%	0.00%	0.00%
113	-100.000%		100.00%	-0.53%	8.40%	5	0.00%	0.00%	0.00%	0.00%	0.00%	0.00%	0.00%	0.00%	0.00%	100.00%	0.00%	0.00%
114	-100.000%		100.00%	-0.53%	8.40%	5	0.00%	0.00%	0.00%	0.00%	0.00%	0.00%	0.00%	0.00%	0.00%	100.00%	0.00%	0.00%
115	-100.000%		100.00%	-0.53%	8.40%	5	0.00%	0.00%	0.00%	0.00%	0.00%	0.00%	0.00%	0.00%	0.00%	100.00%	0.00%	0.00%
116	-100.000%		100.00%	-0.53%	8.40%	5	0.00%	0.00%	0.00%	0.00%	0.00%	0.00%	0.00%	0.00%	0.00%	100.00%	0.00%	0.00%
117	-100.000%		100.00%	-0.53%	8.40%	5	0.00%	0.00%	0.00%	0.00%	0.00%	0.00%	0.00%	0.00%	0.00%	100.00%	0.00%	0.00%
118	-100.000%		100.00%	-0.53%	8.40%	5	0.00%	0.00%	0.00%	0.00%	0.00%	0.00%	0.00%	0.00%	0.00%	100.00%	0.00%	0.00%
119	-100.000%		100.00%	-0.53%	8.40%	5	0.00%	0.00%	0.00%	0.00%	0.00%	0.00%	0.00%	0.00%	0.00%	100.00%	0.00%	0.00%
120	-100.000%		100.00%	-0.53%	8.40%	5	0.00%	0.00%	0.00%	0.00%	0.00%	0.00%	0.00%	0.00%	0.00%	100.00%	0.00%	0.00%
121	-100.000%		100.00%	-0.53%	8.40%	5	0.00%	0.00%	0.00%	0.00%	0.00%	0.00%	0.00%	0.00%	0.00%	100.00%	0.00%	0.00%
122	-7.446%		100.00%	-0.53%	8.40%	0	0.00%	0.00%	0.00%	0.00%	0.00%	0.00%	0.00%	0.00%	0.00%	100.00%	0.00%	0.00%
123	-4.172%		100.00%	-0.52%	6.10%	0	0.00%	0.00%	0.00%	0.00%	0.00%	0.00%	2.41%	0.00%	0.00%	69.80%	0.00%	0.00%
124	-3.337%		100.00%	-0.48%	5.40%	0	0.00%	0.00%	2.96%	0.00%	1.05%	0.00%	15.39%	0.00%	0.00%	49.67%	0.00%	0.00%

Rows 55 to 256 contain 202 problems for Solver to solve. Columns R through AL contain the portfolio weights, which are the *choice variables* for each problem. Columns AM through CD contain the *constraint constants* (for the sum of portfolio weights, target expected return, minimum portfolio weight, maximum portfolio weight) for each problem. Notice that the minimum portfolio weight for the risky assets (columns AP – BI) are 0.00%, which rules out negative weights (i.e., short-selling). The minimum portfolio weight for the riskfree asset (column AO) is 0.00%, which rules out a negative weight (i.e., borrowing). The maximum portfolio weight for the risky assets (columns BK – CD) are 100.00%, which rules out the most extremely undiversified positions.

Rows 55 to 155 contain 101 problems in which the weight in the Riskfree Asset is constrained to be exactly 0.00%. This is accomplished by setting minimum weight for the Riskfree Asset (column AO) to 0.00% and the maximum weight for the Riskfree Asset (column BJ) to 0.00%. The solution to these problems yield the Constrained *Risky* Opportunity Set.

Rows 156 to 256 contain 101 problems in which the weight in the Riskfree Asset is NOT constrained to be exactly 0.00%. The maximum weight for the Riskfree Asset (column BJ) is set to 100.00%. The solutions to these problems yield the Constrained Complete Opportunity Set.

FIGURE 5.19 Constrained Port Optimization -Any Number of Risky Assets

FIGURE 5.20 Constrained Port Optimization -Any Number of Risky Assets

FIGURE 5.21 Constrained Port Optimization -Any Number of Risky Assets

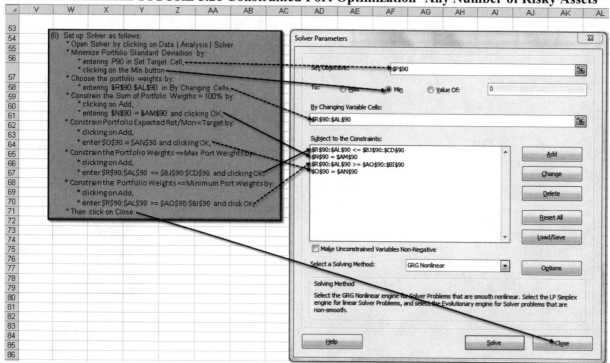

FIGURE 5.22 Constrained Port Optimization -Any Number of Risky Assets

	E	F	G	H	I	J	K	L	M	N	O	P	Q	R	S	Y
108	1.5%				0.0%	0.0%	24			**Table of Problems and Solutions**						
109	0.5%				0.0%	0.0%	25			Sum of	Portfolio	Portfolio	Solver			
110	1.6%				4.2%	2.0%	26	Investor Utility	Portfolio Ranking	Portfolio Weights	Expected Ret/Mon	Standard Deviation	Solution Code	Riskfree	Risky Asset 1	Risky Asset 7
208								-100.000%		100.00%	2.30%	17.30%	5	0.00%	0.00%	0.00%
209								-100.000%		100.00%	2.30%	17.30%	5	0.00%	0.00%	0.00%
210								-100.000%		100.00%	2.30%	17.30%	5	0.00%	0.00%	0.00%
211								-100.000%		100.00%	2.30%	17.30%	5	0.00%	0.00%	0.00%
212								-100.000%	74	100.00%	-0.53%	8.40%	5	0.00%	0.00%	0.00%
213								-100.000%	74	100.00%	-0.53%	8.40%	5	0.00%	0.00%	0.00%
214								-100.000%	74	100.00%	-0.53%	8.40%	5	0.00%	0.00%	0.00%
258								0.616%	5	100.00%	0.84%	1.51%	0	58.68%	0.00%	24.01%
259								0.621%	3	100.00%	0.88%	1.63%	0	55.56%	0.00%	25.82%
260								0.623%	1	100.00%	0.92%	1.74%	0	52.44%	0.00%	27.64%
261								0.623%	2	100.00%	0.96%	1.85%	0	49.32%	0.00%	29.45%
262								0.621%	4	100.00%	1.00%	1.97%	0	46.20%	0.00%	31.26%
263								0.615%	6	100.00%	1.04%	2.08%	0	43.09%	0.00%	33.07%

(8) RANK(Investor Utility from port i, Investor Utility from all portfolios)
Enter =RANK(L212,$L$212:$L$312) and copy down

Column L contains the utility of each portfolio in the Constrained Complete Opportunity Set and column M contains rank ordering of these utility values. In this case, the portfolio in row 260 yields the highest utility value and is thus the *Optimal Complete* Portfolio.

Column J in the figure below shows the portfolio weights of the Optimal Complete Portfolio. In column I in the figure below, the portfolio weight in the riskfree asset is zeroed out and the portfolio weights of the risky assets are scaled up proportionally so that they add up to 100%. This yields the portfolio weights of the Optimal Risky Portfolio.

FIGURE 5.23 Constrained Port Optimization -Any Number of Risky Assets

	A	B	C	D	E	F	G	H	I	J	K
86			Constrd	Constrained							
87			Risky	Complete	Individual	Indiffer	Optimal	Optimal	Optimal	Optimal	
88			Opp Set	Opp Set	Asset	Curve	Risky	Complete	Risky	Complete	Vlookup
89		Standard Deviation	Expected Ret/Mon	Expected Ret/Mon	Expected Ret/Mon	Expected Ret/Mon	Expected Ret/Mon	Expected Ret/Mon	Portfolio Weights	Portfolio Weights	Column
90	0	0.0%			0.3%					52.4%	6
91	1	13.2%			1.6%				0.0%	0.0%	7
92	2	6.4%			0.2%				0.0%	0.0%	8
93	3	17.3%			0.8%				0.0%	0.0%	9
94	4	11.9%			0.2%				0.0%	0.0%	10
95	5	15.7%			1.6%				0.0%	0.0%	11
96	6	13.0%			-0.5%				0.0%	0.0%	12
97	7	4.7%			1.5%				58.1%	27.6%	13
98	8	10.8%			0.6%				0.0%	0.0%	14
99	9	8.4%			-0.5%				0.0%	0.0%	15
100	10	6.9%			0.7%				5.7%	2.7%	16
101	11	15.5%			1.9%				0.0%	0.0%	17
102	12	20.4%			1.0%				0.0%	0.0%	18
103	13	11.3%			-0.5%				0.0%	0.0%	19
104	14	17.3%			2.3%				7.4%	3.5%	20
105	15	8.3%			1.4%				6.3%	3.0%	21
106	16	10.6%			1.9%				18.3%	8.7%	22
107	17	28.3%			1.8%				0.0%	0.0%	23
108	18	21.8%			1.5%				0.0%	0.0%	24
109	19	10.8%			0.5%				0.0%	0.0%	25
110	20	10.1%			1.6%				4.2%	2.0%	26
111	Constrd Risky	#N/A	-1.00%								
112	Constrd Risky	#N/A	-0.96%								
113	Constrd Risky	#N/A	-0.92%								
114	Constrd Risky	#N/A	-0.88%								
115	Constrd Risky	#N/A	-0.84%								
116	Constrd Risky	#N/A	-0.80%								
117	Constrd Risky	#N/A	-0.76%								
118	Constrd Risky	#N/A	-0.72%								
119	Constrd Risky	#N/A	-0.68%								
120	Constrd Risky	#N/A	-0.64%								
121	Constrd Risky	#N/A	-0.60%								
122	Constrd Risky	8.40%	-0.53%								
123	Constrd Risky	6.10%	-0.52%								
124	Constrd Risky	5.40%	-0.48%								
125	Constrd Risky	5.17%	-0.44%								

(9) Expected Return of Asset i
  Enter =IF($B$4>=A90,B7,NA()) and copy down

(10) (Risky Weight i) / (Sum of the Risky Weights)
  Type =IF($B$4>=A91,J91/(SUM($J$91:OFFSET($J$91,$B$4-1,0))),NA())
  and copy down

(11) VLOOKUP(#1 Utility Ranking, Complete Portfolio Range,Column,FALSE)
  Enter =IF($B$4>=A90,VLOOKUP(1,$M$212:$AL$312,K90,FALSE),NA())
  and copy down

(12) If Solver Solution Code = 0 (Solver found a solution)
  Then Port Std Dev
  Else #N/A Error Code so it won't show up on the graph
  Enter =IF(Q111=0,P111,NA()) and copy to the range B112:B312

FIGURE 5.24 Constrained Port Optimization -Any Number of Risky Assets

	A	B	C	D	E	F	G	H	I	J	K	L	M
303	Constrd Compl	#N/A		2.64%								100.000%	
304	Constrd Compl	#N/A		2.68%								000%	
305	Constrd Compl	#N/A		2.72%								000%	
306	Constrd Compl	#N/A		2.76%								000%	
307	Constrd Compl	#N/A		2.80%								000%	
308	Constrd Compl	#N/A		2.84%								000%	
309	Constrd Compl	#N/A		2.88%								-100.000%	
310	Constrd Compl	#N/A		2.92%								-100.000%	
311	Constrd Compl	#N/A		2.96%								-100.000%	
312	Constrd Compl	#N/A		3.00%								-100.000%	
313	Opt Risky Port	3.66%					1.59%					-100.000%	
314	Opt Comp Port	1.7%						0.92%					
315	Indiffer Curve	0.0%				0.62%							
316	Indiffer Curve	0.5%				0.65%							
317	Indiffer Curve	1.0%				0.72%							
318	Indiffer Curve	1.5%				0.84%							
319	Indiffer Curve	2.0%				1.02%							
320	Indiffer Curve	2.5%				1.24%							
321	Indiffer Curve	3.0%				1.51%							
322	Indiffer Curve	3.5%				1.82%							
323	Indiffer Curve	4.0%				2.19%							
324	Indiffer Curve	4.5%				2.61%							
325	Indiffer Curve	5.0%				3.07%							
326	Indiffer Curve	6.0%				4.15%							
327	Indiffer Curve	7.0%				5.43%							
328	Indiffer Curve	8.0%				6.90%							
329	Indiffer Curve	9.0%				8.56%							
330	Indiffer Curve	10.0%				10.42%							
331	Indiffer Curve	11.0%				12.48%							
332	Indiffer Curve	12.0%				14.74%							
333	Indiffer Curve	13.0%				17.19%							
334	Indiffer Curve	14.0%				19.83%							
335	Indiffer Curve	15.0%				22.67%							
336													
337	Constant Utility Value		0.0062										

(13) Enter the Standard Deviation as an Excel matrix
Type =SQRT(MMULT(MMULT(TRANSPOSE(I91:OFFSET(I91,$B$4-1,0))
,$B$58:OFFSET($B$58,$B$4-1,$B$4-1)),I91:OFFSET(I91,$B$4-1,0)))
Hold down the Shift and Control buttons and then press Enter

(14) Enter the Expected Return as an Excel matrix
Type =MMULT(TRANSPOSE(I91:OFFSET(I91,$B$4-1,0))
,$B$8:OFFSET($B$8,$B$4-1,0))
Hold down the Shift and Control buttons and then press Enter

(16) Constant Utility Value
+ (Risk Aversion) * (Std Dev)^2
Enter =$C$337+$B$5*B315^2
and copy down

(15) VLOOKUP(#1 Utility Ranking,
Complete Portfolio Range, Column,FALSE)
Enter =VLOOKUP(1,M212:P312,4,FALSE) in cell B314
Enter =VLOOKUP(1,M212:P312,3,FALSE) in cell H314

(17) Exp Ret of Opt Complete Portfolio
- (Risk Aversion) * (Std Dev of Opt Complete Port)^2
Enter =H314-B5*B314^2

Excel 2007 Equivalent

To view the macro in Excel 2007, click on the **Office** button, click on the **Excel Options** button, check the **Show Developer tab in the Ribbon** checkbox, and click **OK**.

Excel 97-2003 Equivalent

To view the macro in Excel 97-2003, click on **Tools | Macro | Visual Basic Editor**.

Once you have built the spreadsheet, you are ready to run the macro by clicking on the Run Macro button **Click Here to Run Macro** in the range **E2:G3**. This button runs the macro "**RepeatedlyRunSolver2**."

To view the macro, click on **Developer | Code | Visual Basic** (see below). If the Developer tab is not visible, you can display it by clicking on **File**, click on **Options**, click on **Customize Ribbon**, check the **Developer** checkbox, and click **OK**.

FIGURE 5.25 Constrained Port Optimization -Any Number of Risky Assets

This opens the Visual Basic Development Environment. In the main window, you see the code for the "**RepeatedlyRunSolver2**" macro. The macro is analogous to the macro in the prior section.

FIGURE 5.26 Constrained Port Optimization -Any Number of Risky Assets

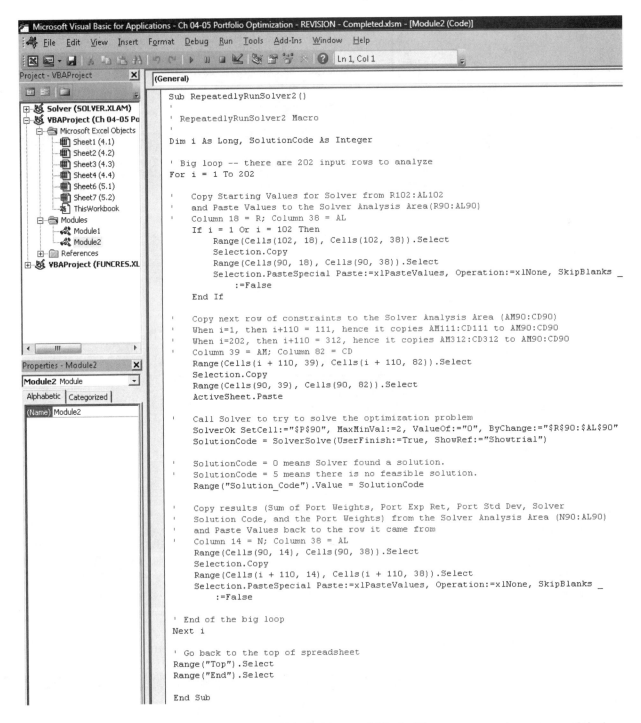

The macro code itself is in blue and black. The comments in green explain how macro works.

See what happens as you increase the number of risky assets.

FIGURE 5.27 Number of Risky Assets is Two

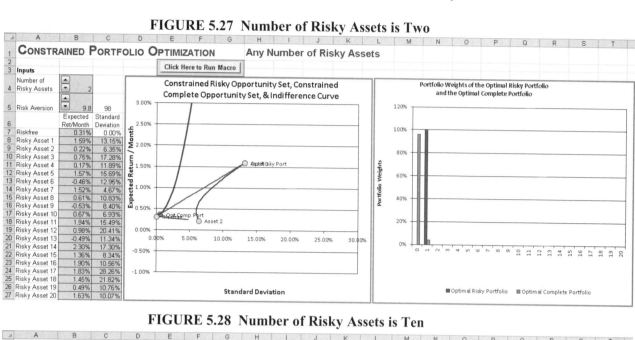

FIGURE 5.28 Number of Risky Assets is Ten

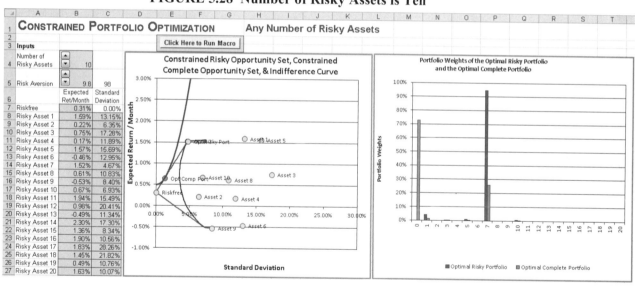

FIGURE 5.29 Number of Risky Assets is Twenty

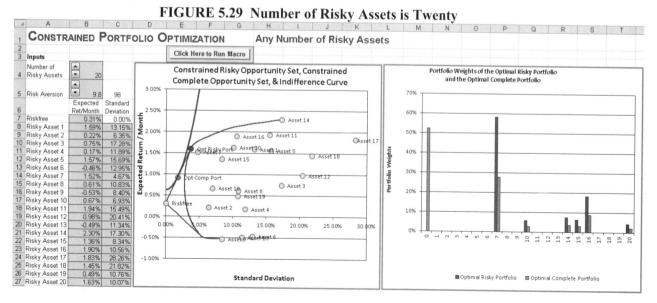

Problems

1. An individual investor with a simple mean and variance utility function has a risk aversion of 0.7. This investor is considering investing in the assets you downloaded for problem 2 of the prior chapter. This investor considers four methods to forecast expected returns: average past return, Static CAPM, Fama-French 3 Factor, or Macro 3 Factor. The investor wishes to impose no short sales, no borrowing, and no portfolio weights great than 100%. Determine the Portfolio Weights of the Optimal Risky Portfolio and the Optimal Complete Portfolio.

2. An individual investor with a simple mean and variance utility function has a risk aversion of 4.3. This investor is considering investing in a riskfree asset and any number of risky assets up to a max of 20. The investor has forecasted the expected return of the risky assets. The investor wishes to impose no short sales, no borrowing, and no portfolio weights great than 100%. Determine the Portfolio Weights of the Optimal Risky Portfolio and the Optimal Complete Portfolio.

Chapter 6 Portfolio Diversification Lowers Risk

6.1 Basics

Problem. For simplicity, suppose that all risky assets have a standard deviation of 30% and all pairs of risky assets have a correlation coefficient of 40%. In this simple setting, consider a portfolio diversification strategy of investing in equally-weighted portfolios (e.g., put an equal amount in each risky asset). As you increase the number of assets in your portfolio (that you are diversifying across), how much does this lower the risk of your portfolio?

Solution Strategy. Calculate the portfolio standard deviation of an equally-weighted portfolio as the number of assets increases. As a benchmark, compare with the portfolio standard deviation in the limiting case as the number of assets goes to infinity.

FIGURE 6.1 Excel Model of Portfolio Diversification Lowers Risk - Basics.

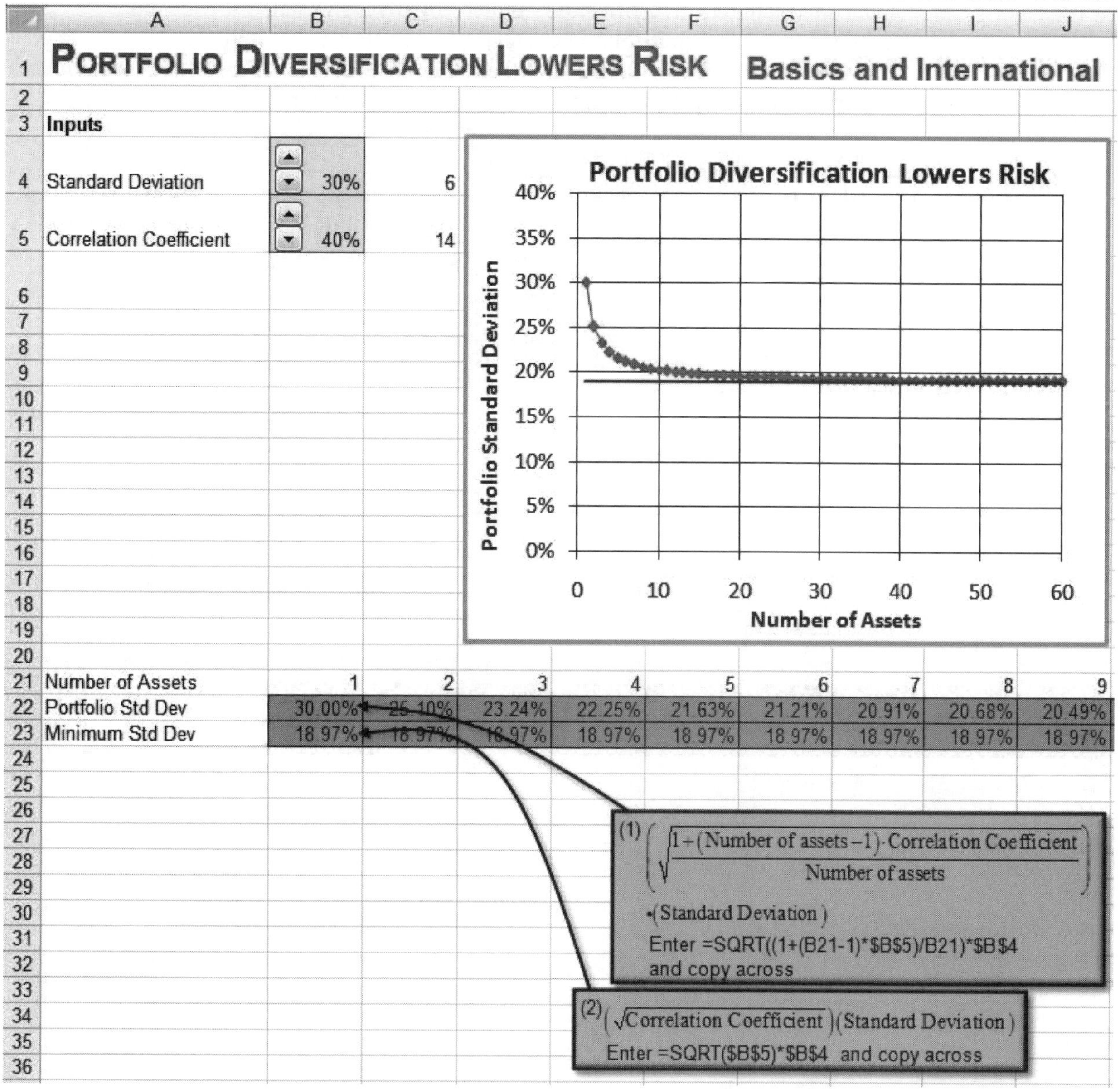

	A	B	C	D	E	F	G	H	I	J
21	Number of Assets	1	2	3	4	5	6	7	8	9
22	Portfolio Std Dev	30.00%	25.10%	23.24%	22.25%	21.63%	21.21%	20.91%	20.68%	20.49%
23	Minimum Std Dev	18.97%	18.97%	18.97%	18.97%	18.97%	18.97%	18.97%	18.97%	18.97%

(1)
$$\left(\sqrt{\frac{1+(\text{Number of assets}-1)\cdot\text{Correlation Coefficient}}{\text{Number of assets}}}\right)$$
$$\cdot(\text{Standard Deviation})$$
Enter =SQRT((1+(B21-1)*$B$5)/B21)*$B$4 and copy across

(2)
$$\left(\sqrt{\text{Correlation Coefficient}}\right)(\text{Standard Deviation})$$
Enter =SQRT($B$5)*$B$4 and copy across

This graph shows how diversifying across many assets can reduce risk from 30% to as low as 18.97%. Most of the risk reduction is accomplished with a relatively small number of assets. Increasing the number of assets from one to ten accomplishes more that 85% of the potential risk reduction. Increasing to thirty assets accomplishes more than 95% of the potential risk reduction. In summary, very significant risk reduction can be accomplished by diversifying across thirty assets, but relatively little risk reduction is accomplished by increasing the number of assets further.

6.2 International

Problem. There is a lot of evidence that international correlation coefficients are dramatically lower than local (same country) correlation coefficients. We can explore the benefits of international diversification by extending the Basics example. Suppose there are two countries and all risky assets in both countries have a standard deviation of 30%. All pairs of risky assets *within* the same country have a local correlation coefficient of 40%, but all pairs of risky assets *between* countries have an international correlation coefficient of 10%. Consider an international diversification strategy of investing half of your money in an equally-weighted portfolio in country 1 and the other half in an equally-weighted portfolio in country 2. As you increase the number of assets in your total portfolio, how much does this lower the risk of your portfolio?

Solution Strategy. Calculate the portfolio standard deviation of the internationally diversified portfolio as the number of assets increases. As a benchmark, compare with the international portfolio standard deviation in the limiting case as the number of assets goes to infinity.

FIGURE 6.2 Excel Model of Portfolio Diversification Lowers Risk - International.

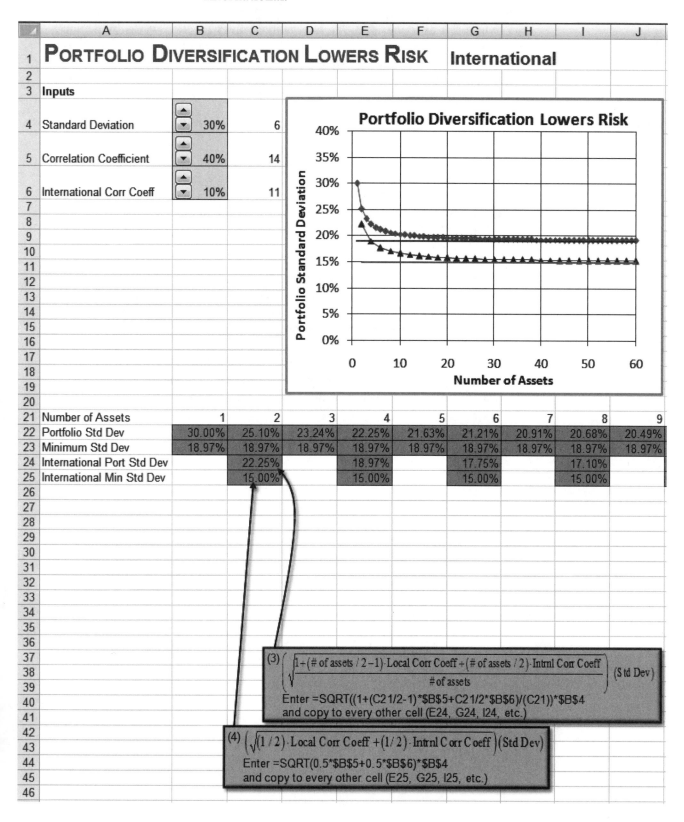

This graph shows how international diversification can significantly reduce risk beyond local (one country) diversification. In this example, local diversification reduces risk from 30.00% to as low as 18.97%, but international diversification can reduce risk as low as 15.00%. International diversification works by getting rid of some country-specific sources of risk. Again, most of the risk reduction is accomplished with a relatively small number of assets. Beyond 30 assets (15 in each country), there is not much risk reduction potential left.

Problems

1. All risky assets have a standard deviation of 50% and all pairs of risky assets have a correlation coefficient of 60%. Consider a portfolio diversification strategy of investing in equally-weighted portfolios (e.g., put an equal amount in each risky asset). As you increase the number of assets in your portfolio (that you are diversifying across), how much does this lower the risk of your portfolio?

2. There are two countries and all risky assets in both countries have a standard deviation of 50%. All pairs of risky assets within the same country have a local correlation coefficient of 60%, but all pairs of risky assets between countries have an international correlation coefficient of 20%. Consider an international diversification strategy of investing half of your money in an equally-weighted portfolio in country 1 and the other half in an equally-weighted portfolio in country 2. As you increase the number of assets in your total portfolio, how much does this lower the risk of your portfolio?

PART 3 SECURITY ANALYSIS

Chapter 7 Stock Valuation

7.1 Dividend Discount Model

Problem. Currently a stock pays a dividend per share of $6.64. A security analyst projects the future dividend growth rate over the next five years to be 12.0%, 11.0%, 10.0%, 9.0%, 8.0% and then 7.0% each year thereafter to infinity. The levered cost of equity capital for the firm is 12.0% per year. What is the stock's value?

Solution Strategy. Construct a two-stage discounted dividend model. In stage one, explicitly forecast the firm's dividend over a five-year horizon. In stage two, forecast the firm's dividend from year six to infinity and calculate its continuation value as the present value of this infinitely growing annuity. Then, discount the future dividends and the date 5 continuation value back to the present to get the stock's value.

FIGURE 7.1 Excel Model for Stock Valuation – Dividend Discount Model.

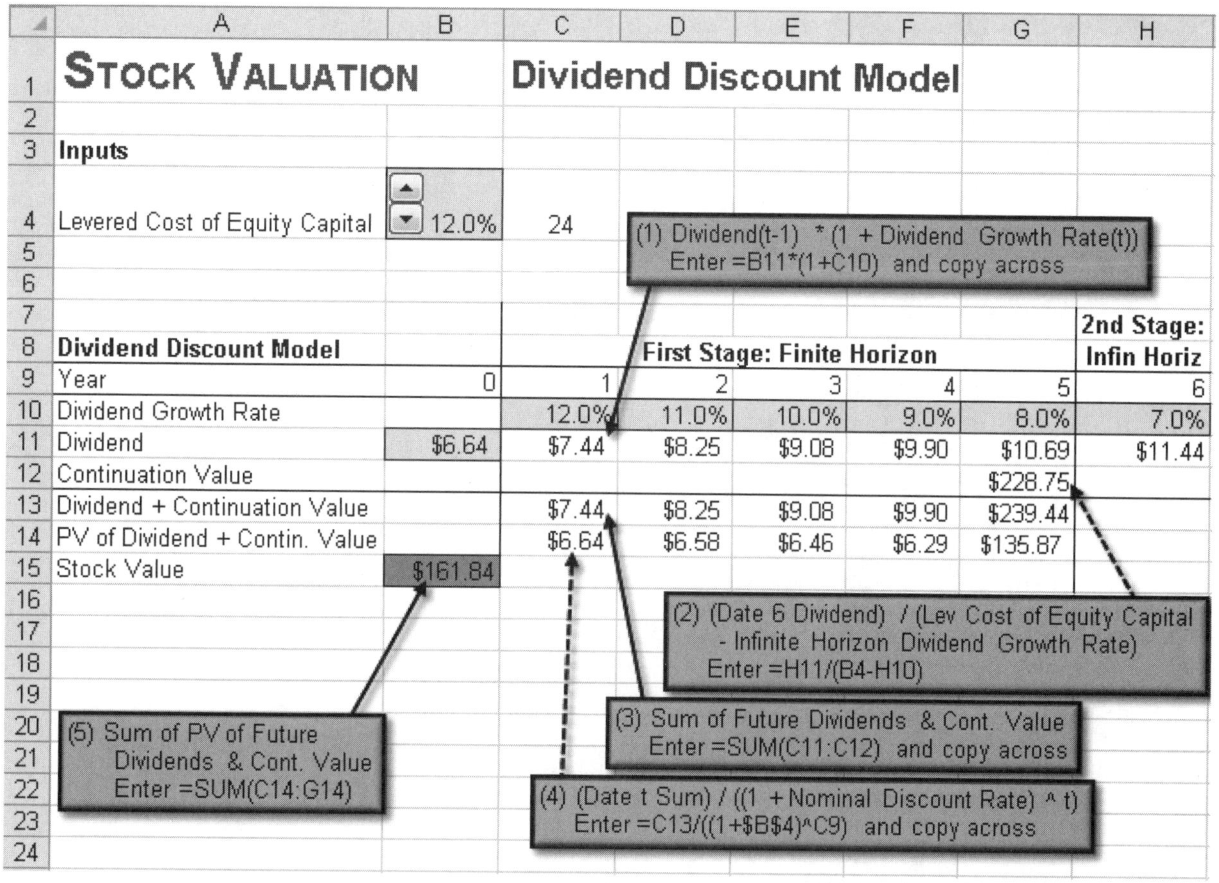

The stock value is estimated to be $161.84.

Problems

1. Currently a stock pays a dividend per share of $43.37. A security analyst projects the future dividend growth rate over the next five years to be 21.0%, 18.0%, 15.0%, 13.5%, 11.5% and then 11.0% each year thereafter to infinity. The levered cost of equity capital for the firm is 13.4% per year. What is the stock's value?

Chapter 8 Du Pont System Of Ratio Analysis

8.1 Basics

Problem. A company's Net Profit is $170, Pretax Profit is $260, EBIT is $470, Sales is $4,600, Assets is $4,200, and Equity is $4,300. Calculate the company's ROE and decompose the ROE into its components using the Du Pont System.

FIGURE 8.1   Excel Model of Du Pont System of Ratio Analysis - Basics.

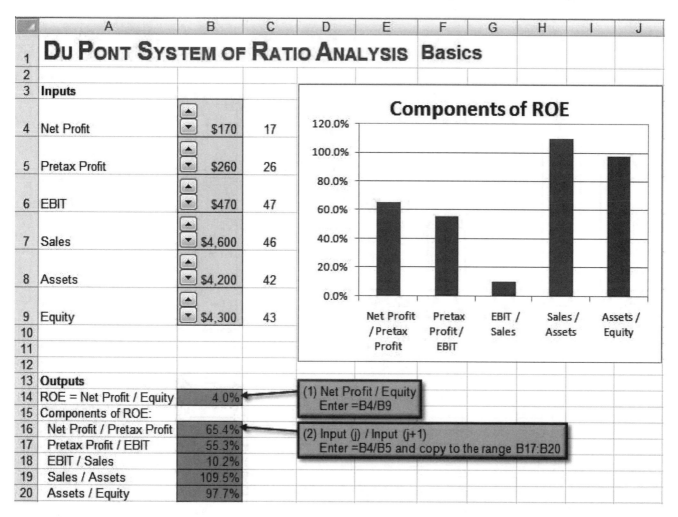

The ROE = 4.0%. The decomposition helps us see where this comes from. Here is an intuitive interpretation of the components:

- Net Profit / Pretax = 65.4% is a tax-burden ratio.
- Pretax Profits / EBIT = 55.3% is an interest-burden ratio.
- EBIT / Sales = 10.2% is the profit margin.
- Sales / Assets = 109.5% is the asset turnover.
- Asset / Equity = 97.7% is the leverage ratio.

Problems

1. A company's Net Profit is $82, Pretax Profit is $153, EBIT is $583, Sales is $3,740, Assets is $5,460, and Equity is $7,230. Calculate the company's ROE and decompose the ROE into its components using the Du Pont System.

2. A company's Net Profit is $265, Pretax Profit is $832, EBIT is $1,045, Sales is $5,680, Assets is $7,620, and Equity is $9,730. Calculate the company's ROE and decompose the ROE into its components using the Du Pont System.

PART 4 STOCKS

Chapter 9 Asset Pricing

9.1 Static CAPM Using Fama-MacBeth Method

Problem. Given monthly total return data on individual stocks, US portfolios, and country portfolios, estimate the Static CAPM under three market portfolio benchmarks (SPDR "Spider" Exchange Traded Fund, CRSP Value-Weighted Market Return, and Dow Jones World Stock Index) and using the standard Fama-MacBeth methodology. Then use the Static CAPM estimates from Jan 2000 – Dec 2009 data to forecast each asset's expected return over the next month (Jan 2010), or equivalently, each asset's cost of equity capital. Finally, determine how much variation of individual stocks, US portfolios, or country portfolios is explained by the Static CAPM.

Solution Strategy. First compute the monthly excess return of each asset. Then stage one of the Fama-MacBeth method is estimating the CAPM beta of an asset by doing a five-year, time-series regression of the asset's excess return on the excess return of a market portfolio benchmark. Repeat this time-series regression for many five-year windows and compute the average of the estimated CAPM betas. Then stage two of the Fama-Beth method is estimating the CAPM risk premium and intercept by doing a cross-sectional regression of the excess returns across assets in the following month on the CAPM beta from the immediately prior five-year window. Repeat this cross-sectional regression for many following months and compute the average of the estimated CAPM risk premium and intercept. Then use the estimated CAPM risk premium and intercept to forecast each asset's expected return, or equivalently, each asset's cost of equity capital. Finally, compute the R^2 ("explained variation") of both regressions.

FIGURE 9.1 Asset Pricing – Static CAPM Using Fama-MacBeth Method.

	A	B	C	D	E	F	G
1	**ASSET PRICING**		**Static CAPM Using Fama-MacBeth Method**				
2							
3	**Inputs**						
4	Market Portfolio Benchmark	Market Portfolio Benchmark: ○ SPDR ETF ○ CRSP VWMR ◉ DJ World Stock			3		
5	Asset Type	Asset Type: ○ Stock ○ US FF Port ◉ Country ETF			3		
6							
7		Stock	Stock	Stock	Stock	Stock	Stock
8		Barrick	IBM	KEP	Nokia	Telefonos	YPF
130							
131			(1) Monthly Return(Asset i, Month t) - Riskfree Rate(Month t) Enter =B10-$AC10 and copy to B133:V252				
132	**Monthly Excess Returns**						
133	Dec 2009	-7.75%	3.60%	5.98%	-3.09%	-3.18%	17.39%
134	Nov 2009	19.37%	5.22%	-1.15%	5.15%	8.07%	2.70%
135	Oct 2009	-5.20%	0.84%	-8.92%	-13.75%	-4.76%	-0.63%
136	Sep 2009	9.22%	1.32%	23.40%	4.35%	-5.25%	-2.41%
137	Aug 2009	-0.58%	0.56%	-7.64%	5.01%	17.57%	9.96%
138	Jul 2009	4.01%	12.93%	16.25%	-8.51%	-2.48%	16.19%
139	Jun 2009	-11.90%	-1.75%	0.17%	-4.71%	-1.38%	-10.93%

FIGURE 9.2 Asset Pricing – Static CAPM Using Fama-MacBeth Method.

	A	B	C	D	E	F	G	H	I	J	K
1	**ASSET PRICING**		**Static CAPM Using Fama-MacBeth Method**								
2											
3	**Inputs**										
4	Market Portfolio Benchmark	Market Portfolio Benchmark: ○ SPDR ETF ○ CRSP VWMR ◉ DJ World Stock			3						
5	Asset Type	Asset Type: ○ Stock ○ US FF Port ◉ Country ETF			3						
6											
7		Stock	Stock	Stock	Stock	Stock	Stock	US FF Port	US FF Port	US FF Port	US FF Port
8		Barrick	IBM	KEP	Nokia	Telefonos	YPF	Small-Growth	Small-Neutral	Small-Value	Big-Growth
253											
254					(2) LINEST(Asset Excess Returns over 5 Years, Market Port Benchmark Excess Returns over 5 Yrs) INDEX(LINEST(...), 1, 1) selects the slope coefficient ("Beta") of the regression above Enter =INDEX(LINEST(B134:B193,OFFSET($T134,0,($E$4-1)):OFFSET($T193,0,$E$4-1)),1,1) and copy to B259:S318						
255	**CAPM Beta from the First Pass, Time-Series Regression**										
256											
257	5 Yr Estimation Per:										
258	Beg Mon - End Mon	Barrick	IBM	KEP	Nokia	Telefonos	YPF	Small-Growth	Small-Neutral	Small-Value	Big-Growth
259	Dec 2004 - Nov 2009	0.81	0.67	1.38	1.32	0.98	0.82	1.03	0.98	1.11	0.74
260	Nov 2004 - Oct 2009	0.79	0.67	1.42	1.32	0.96	0.83	1.04	0.99	1.12	0.73
261	Oct 2004 - Sep 2009	0.79	0.68	1.42	1.31	0.96	0.83	1.04	0.98	1.11	0.73
262	Sep 2004 - Aug 2009	0.78	0.68	1.38	1.33	0.99	0.85	1.04	0.99	1.10	0.73
263	Aug 2004 - Jul 2009	0.79	0.69	1.41	1.33	0.96	0.83	1.04	0.99	1.09	0.73
264	Jul 2004 - Jun 2009	0.82	0.65	1.38	1.48	1.04	0.77	1.07	0.98	1.07	0.73
265	Jun 2004 - May 2009	0.80	0.65	1.38	1.49	1.03	0.77	1.07	0.99	1.07	0.73

FIGURE 9.3 Asset Pricing – Static CAPM Using Fama-MacBeth Method.

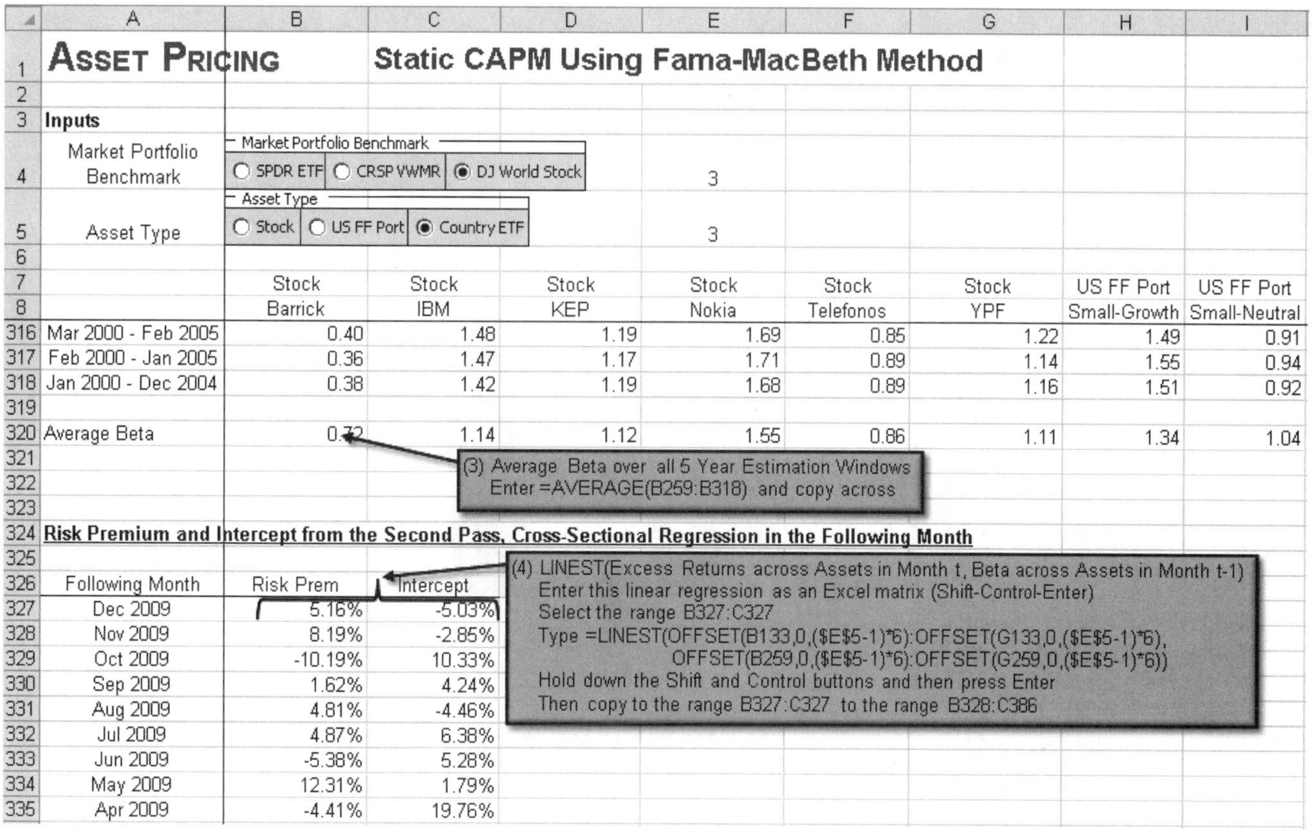

	A	B	C	D	E	F	G	H	I
1	**ASSET PRICING**		**Static CAPM Using Fama-MacBeth Method**						
2									
3	**Inputs**								
4	Market Portfolio Benchmark	Market Portfolio Benchmark ○ SPDR ETF ○ CRSP VWMR ⦿ DJ World Stock			3				
5	Asset Type	Asset Type ○ Stock ○ US FF Port ⦿ Country ETF			3				
6									
7		Stock	Stock	Stock	Stock	Stock	Stock	US FF Port	US FF Port
8		Barrick	IBM	KEP	Nokia	Telefonos	YPF	Small-Growth	Small-Neutral
316	Mar 2000 - Feb 2005	0.40	1.48	1.19	1.69	0.85	1.22	1.49	0.91
317	Feb 2000 - Jan 2005	0.36	1.47	1.17	1.71	0.89	1.14	1.55	0.94
318	Jan 2000 - Dec 2004	0.38	1.42	1.19	1.68	0.89	1.16	1.51	0.92
319									
320	Average Beta	0.72	1.14	1.12	1.55	0.86	1.11	1.34	1.04
321									
322			(3) Average Beta over all 5 Year Estimation Windows Enter =AVERAGE(B259:B318) and copy across						
323									
324	**Risk Premium and Intercept from the Second Pass, Cross-Sectional Regression in the Following Month**								
325									
326	Following Month	Risk Prem	Intercept	(4) LINEST(Excess Returns across Assets in Month t, Beta across Assets in Month t-1) Enter this linear regression as an Excel matrix (Shift-Control-Enter) Select the range B327:C327					
327	Dec 2009	5.16%	-5.03%	Type =LINEST(OFFSET(B133,0,($E$5-1)*6):OFFSET(G133,0,($E$5-1)*6), OFFSET(B259,0,($E$5-1)*6):OFFSET(G259,0,($E$5-1)*6))					
328	Nov 2009	8.19%	-2.85%	Hold down the Shift and Control buttons and then press Enter					
329	Oct 2009	-10.19%	10.33%	Then copy to the range B327:C327 to the range B328:C386					
330	Sep 2009	1.62%	4.24%						
331	Aug 2009	4.81%	-4.46%						
332	Jul 2009	4.87%	6.38%						
333	Jun 2009	-5.38%	5.28%						
334	May 2009	12.31%	1.79%						
335	Apr 2009	-4.41%	19.76%						

FIGURE 9.4 Asset Pricing – Static CAPM Using Fama-MacBeth Method.

	A	B	C	D	E	F	G	H	I	J
1	**ASSET PRICING**		**Static CAPM Using Fama-MacBeth Method**							
2										
3	**Inputs**									
4	Market Portfolio Benchmark	Market Portfolio Benchmark ○ SPDR ETF ○ CRSP VWMR ◉ DJ World Stock			3					
5	Asset Type	Asset Type ○ Stock ○ US FF Port ◉ Country ETF			3					
6										
7		Stock	Stock	Stock	Stock	Stock	Stock	US FF Port	US FF Port	US FF Port
8		Barrick	IBM	KEP	Nokia	Telefonos	YPF	Small-Growth	Small-Neutral	Small-Value
371	Apr 2006	-0.12%	5.79%							
372	Mar 2006	1.77%	-0.45%							
373	Feb 2006	-1.31%	0.54%							
374	Jan 2006	2.15%	5.18%							
375	Dec 2005	3.69%	-0.54%							
376	Nov 2005	6.25%	-4.03%							
377	Oct 2005	-0.56%	-3.63%							
378	Sep 2005	2.46%	1.57%							
379	Aug 2005	5.87%	-5.95%							
380	Jul 2005	0.09%	5.97%							
381	Jun 2005	-1.00%	4.42%							
382	May 2005	7.17%	-5.73%							
383	Apr 2005	-7.30%	5.69%							
384	Mar 2005	1.33%	-5.25%							
385	Feb 2005	7.58%	-4.35%							
386	Jan 2005	-6.63%	5.86%							
387										
388		Risk Prem	Intercept							
389	Empirical Average	0.29%	0.78%	<== Bottom-line Static CAPM estimates						
390	vs. Theoretical Value	-0.09%	0.00%	<== vs. what they should be if the Static CAPM was true						
391										
392		Australia (EWA)	Canada (EWC)	Germany (EWG)	Malaysia (EWM)	Mexico (EWM)	Singapore (EWS)			
393	Jan 2010 Exp Return	1.04%	1.01%	1.08%	0.92%	1.04%	0.99%	<== Using Second Pass Static CAPM		
394	Jan 2010 Exp Return	-0.10%	-0.10%	-0.13%	-0.06%	-0.12%	-0.09%	<== Using Theoretical Intercept & Risk Premium and First Pass Beta		
395										
396	Jan 2010 Riskfree Ra	0.00%								

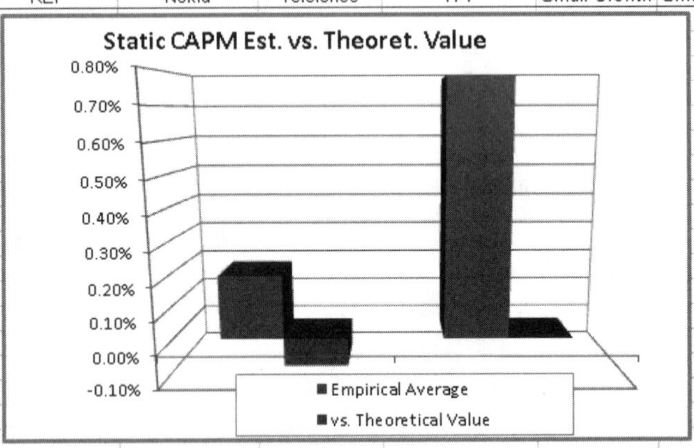

Static CAPM Est. vs. Theoret. Value

Empirical Average
vs. Theoretical Value

(5) Average Risk Prem over all Second Pass Estimates
Enter =AVERAGE(B327:B386) and copy across

(6) Average Market Portfolio Excess Return
Enter =AVERAGE(U133:U252)

(7) (Riskfree Rate) + (Second Pass Intercept)
+ (Second Pass Risk Prem) * (Average First Pass Beta)
Enter =$B$396+$C$389+$B$389*OFFSET(B320,0,($E$5-1)*6) and copy across

(8) (Riskfree Rate) + (Theoretical Intercept)
+ (Theoretical Risk Prem) * (Average First Pass Beta)
Enter =$B$396+$C$390+$B$390*OFFSET(B320,0,($E$5-1)*6) and copy across

Row 389 contains the empirical average of the CAPM risk premium and intercept from the second-pass, cross-sectional regressions. Row 390 contains the theoretical value of the CAPM risk premium and intercept based on the CAPM beta from the first-pass, time-series regressions.

With a lot of extra work it would be possible to compute the statistical significance of the Static CAPM estimates. However, it is much simpler to just compare the empirical average and the theoretical value on a graph. It is clear at a glance that the empirical average and the theoretical value don't match very well.

It is interesting to make the same comparison for different market portfolio benchmarks by clicking on the option buttons in row 4 and for different asset types by clicking on the option buttons in row 5. Often the empirical average CAPM risk premium is negative, which doesn't make any economic sense. Often the empirical average of the CAPM intercept is far away from zero, which doesn't make any economic sense.

Row 393 contains the Static CAPM forecast of each asset's expected return in the next month (Jan 2010), or equivalently, of each asset's cost of equity capital. This is a key output of this spreadsheet. However, given lack of economically sensible estimates for the Static CAPM, one should be very cautious about using the forecasts of each asset's expected return / cost of equity capital.

FIGURE 9.5 Asset Pricing – Static CAPM Using Fama-MacBeth Method.

	A	B	C	D	E	F	G	H	I
1	**ASSET PRICING**		**Static CAPM Using Fama-MacBeth Method**						
2									
3	Inputs								
4	Market Portfolio Benchmark	Market Portfolio Benchmark ○ SPDR ETF ○ CRSP VWMR ● DJ World Stock			3				
5	Asset Type	Asset Type ○ Stock ○ US FF Port ● Country ETF			3				
6									
7		Stock	Stock	Stock	Stock	Stock	Stock	US FF Port	US FF Port
8		Barrick	IBM	KEP	Nokia	Telefonos	YPF	Small-Growth	Small-Neutral
408									
409		(9) LINEST(Asset Excess Returns over 5 Years, Market Port Benchmark Excess Returns over 5 Yrs) INDEX(LINEST(...), 3, 1) selects the R² of the regression above Enter =INDEX(LINEST(B134:B193,OFFSET($T134,0,($E$4-1)):OFFSET($T193,0,$E$4-1),,TRUE),3,1) and copy to B417:S476							
413	R² (Explained Variation as a Percentage of Total Variation) from the First Pass, Time-Series Regression								
414									
415	5 Yr Estimation Per:								
416	Beg Mon - End Mon	Barrick	IBM	KEP	Nokia	Telefonos	YPF	Small-Growth	Small-Neutral
417	Dec 2004 - Nov 2009	12.1%	32.0%	49.9%	49.4%	29.8%	17.4%	78.6%	78.1%
418	Nov 2004 - Oct 2009	11.9%	32.2%	51.5%	49.3%	29.0%	17.8%	79.1%	78.5%
419	Oct 2004 - Sep 2009	11.9%	32.4%	51.6%	49.6%	29.0%	17.7%	79.7%	79.0%
420	Sep 2004 - Aug 2009	11.6%	32.6%	52.1%	48.8%	30.6%	18.4%	79.2%	78.6%

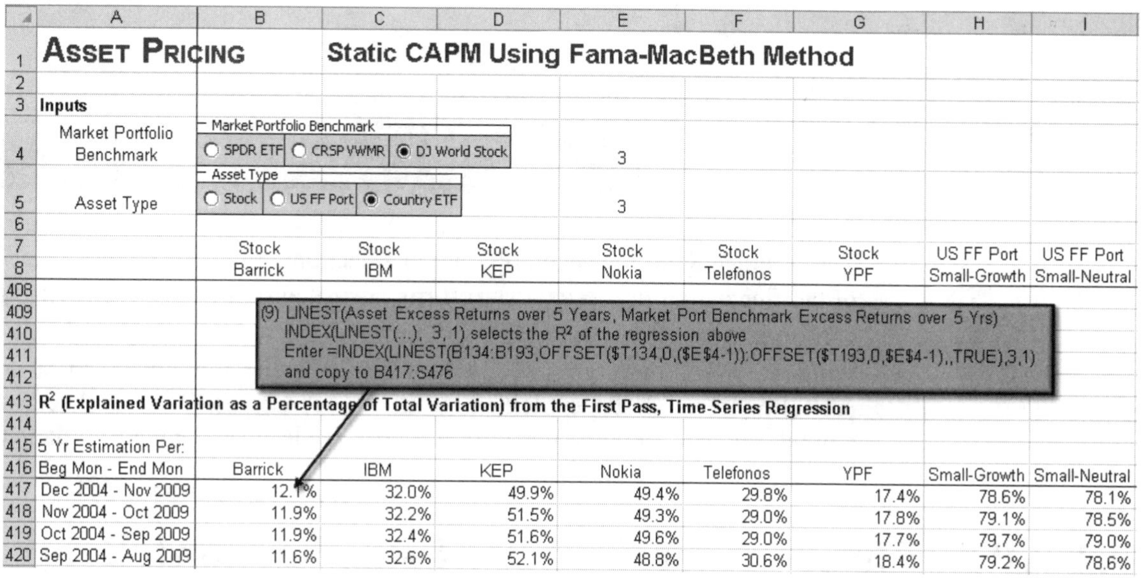

FIGURE 9.6 Asset Pricing – Static CAPM Using Fama-MacBeth Method.

	A	B	C	D	E	F	G	H	I
1	**ASSET PRICING**		**Static CAPM Using Fama-MacBeth Method**						
2									
3	Inputs								
4	Market Portfolio Benchmark	Market Portfolio Benchmark ○ SPDR ETF ○ CRSP VWMR ● DJ World Stock			3				
5	Asset Type	Asset Type ○ Stock ○ US FF Port ● Country ETF			3				
6									
7		Stock	Stock	Stock	Stock	Stock	Stock	US FF Port	US FF Port
8		Barrick	IBM	KEP	Nokia	Telefonos	YPF	Small-Growth	Small-Neutral
474	Mar 2000 - Feb 2005	4.3%	44.1%	33.9%	28.8%	34.3%	24.0%	66.3%	62.4%
475	Feb 2000 - Jan 2005	3.6%	42.8%	32.0%	28.9%	31.5%	23.6%	60.1%	59.5%
476	Jan 2000 - Dec 2004	4.0%	40.6%	33.6%	28.7%	32.1%	24.6%	58.4%	58.9%
477									
478	Average R²	9.5%	35.4%	30.1%	32.0%	26.4%	17.7%	73.7%	71.1%
479									
480		(10) Average R² over all 5 Year Estimation Windows Enter =AVERAGE(B417:B476) and copy across							
482		(11) LINEST(Excess Returns across Assets in Month t, Beta across Assets in Month t) INDEX(LINEST(...), 3, 1) selects the R² of the regression above Enter =INDEX(LINEST(OFFSET(B133,0,($E$5-1)*6):OFFSET(G133,0,($E$5-1)*6), OFFSET(B259,0,($E$5-1)*6):OFFSET(G259,0,($E$5-1)*6),,TRUE),3,1) and copy down							
489	R² (Explained Variation as a Percentage of Total Variation) from the Second Pass, Cross-sectional Regression in the Following Month								
490									
491	Following Month	R²							
492	Dec 2009	47.6%							
493	Nov 2009	76.6%							
494	Oct 2009	45.0%							
495	Sep 2009	1.7%							
496	Aug 2009	8.4%							
497	Jul 2009	23.8%							

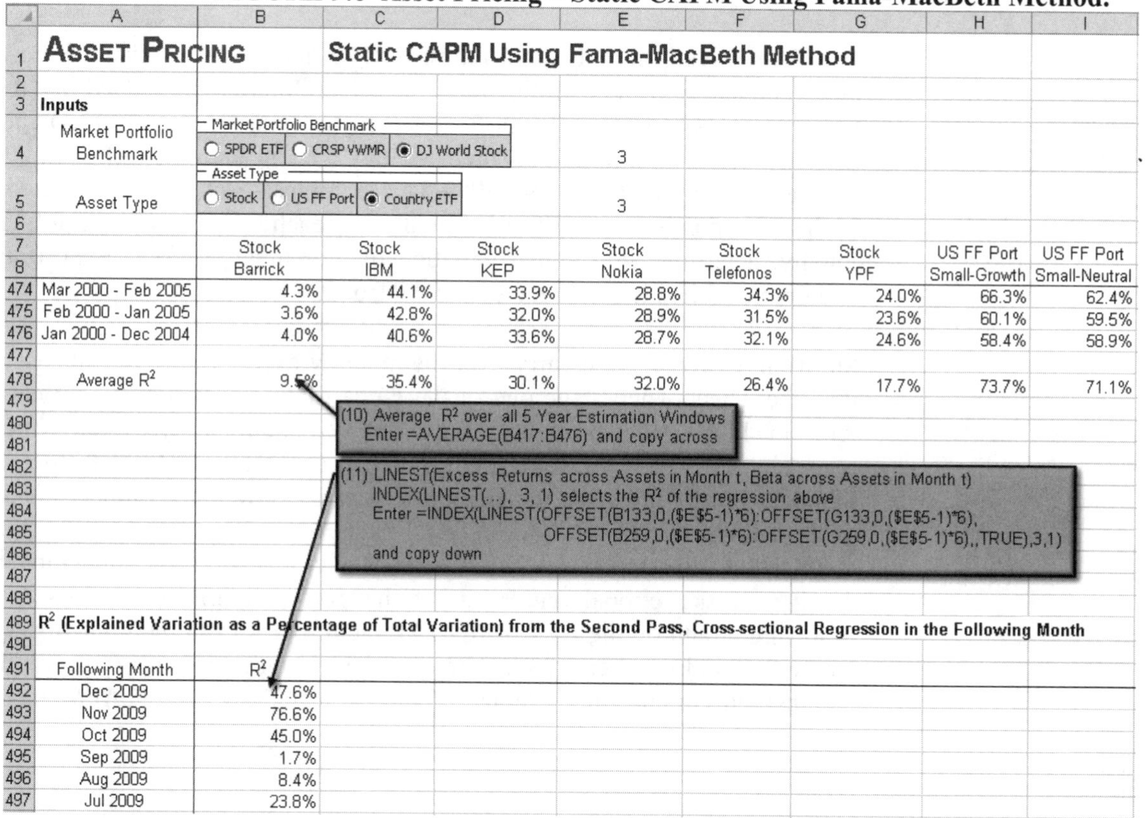

FIGURE 9.7 Asset Pricing – Static CAPM Using Fama-MacBeth Method.

▲	A	B	C	D	E	F	G
1	**ASSET PRICING**		**Static CAPM Using Fama-MacBeth Method**				
2							
3	**Inputs**						
4	Market Portfolio Benchmark	Market Portfolio Benchmark ○ SPDR ETF ○ CRSP VWMR ◉ DJ World Stock			3		
5	Asset Type	Asset Type ○ Stock ○ US FF Port ◉ Country ETF			3		
6							
7		Stock	Stock	Stock	Stock	Stock	Stock
8		Barrick	IBM	KEP	Nokia	Telefonos	YPF
550	Feb 2005	47.2%					
551	Jan 2005	45.3%					
552							
553	Average R²	25.3%					
554							
555			(12) Average R² over all Following Months in Second Pass Regressions Enter =AVERAGE(B492:B551)				
556							
557							

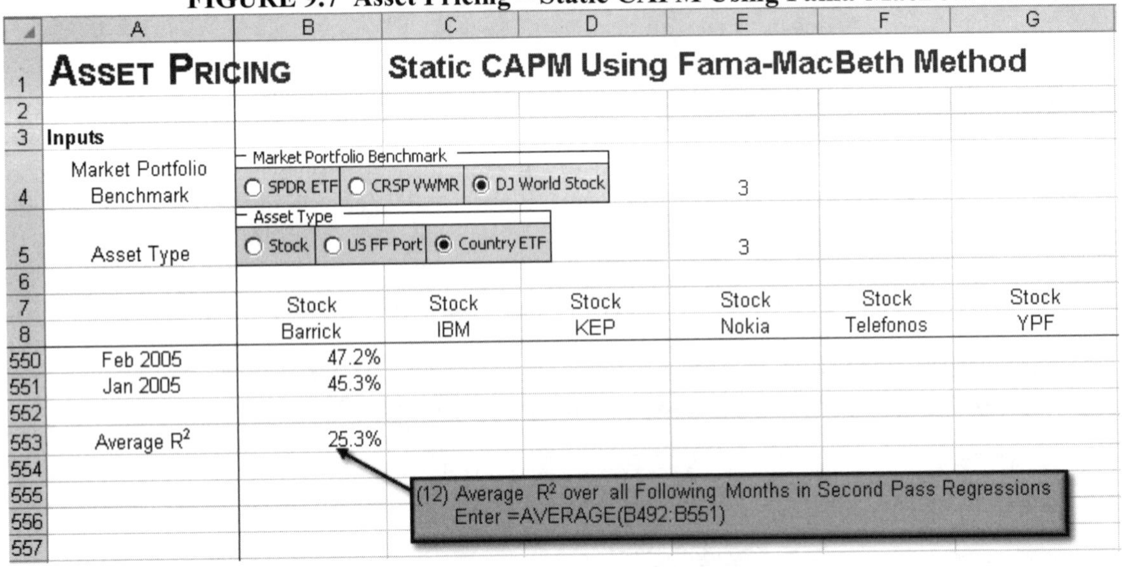

The Average R^2 of the second-pass, cross-sectional regression tells us how much of the fluctuation in the excess returns across assets in the following month can be explained by the CAPM beta from the immediately prior five-year window. With an Average R^2 of around 30%, the individual stocks and US portfolios are modestly explained by their CAPM betas. With an Average R^2 of around 25%, the country portfolio are very modestly explained by their CAPM betas.

9.2 APT or Intertemporal CAPM Using Fama-McBeth Method

Problem. Given monthly total return data on individual stocks, US portfolios, and country portfolios, estimate the APT or Intertemporal CAPM (ICAPM) under two sets of factors (Fama-French 3 factors and 3 macro factors) and using the standard Fama-MacBeth methodology. Then use the APT or ICAPM estimates from Jan 2000 – Dec 2009 data to forecast each asset's expected return in the next month (Jan 2010), or equivalently, each asset's cost of equity capital. Finally, determine how much variation of individual stocks, US portfolios, or country portfolios is explained by the APT or ICAPM.

Solution Strategy. First carry over the monthly excess return of each asset from the other sheet. Then stage one of the Fama-MacBeth method is estimating the APT or ICAPM factor betas of an asset by doing a five-year, time-series regression of the asset's excess return on sets of APT or ICAPM factors. Repeat this time-series regression for many five-year windows and compute the average of the estimated APT or ICAPM factor betas. Then stage two of the Fama-Beth method is estimating the APT or ICAPM factor risk premia and intercept by doing a cross-sectional regression of the excess returns across assets in the following month on the APT or ICAPM factor betas from the immediately prior five-year window. Repeat this cross-sectional regression for many following months and compute the average of the estimated APT or ICAPM factor risk premia and intercept. Then use the estimated APT or ICAPM factor risk premia and intercept to forecast each asset's expected return in the future (Jan 2010), or equivalently, each asset's cost of equity capital. Finally, compute the R^2 ("explained variation") of both regressions.

FIGURE 9.8 APT or Intertemporal CAPM Using Fama-MacBeth Method.

	A	B	C	D	E	F	G	H
1	**ASSET PRICING** APT or Intertemporal CAPM Using Fama-MacBeth Method							
2								
3	**Inputs**							
4	APT or ICAPM Factors	APT or ICAPM Factors: ⦿ Fama-French 3 Factors ○ 3 Macro Factors			1			
5	Asset Type	Asset Type: ⦿ Stock ○ US FF Port ○ Country ETF			1		(1) Monthly Return from Sheet 9.1 Enter =9.1'!B10 and copy to D10:AE129	
6								
7				Stock	Stock	Stock	Stock	Stock
8				Barrick	IBM	KEP	Nokia	Telefonos
9	**Monthly Returns**							
10	Dec 2009			-7.75%	3.60%	5.98%	-3.09%	-3.18%
11	Nov 2009			19.37%	5.22%	-1.15%	5.15%	8.07%
12	Oct 2009			-5.20%	0.84%	-8.92%	-13.75%	-4.76%
13	Sep 2009			9.22%	1.32%	23.40%	4.35%	-5.25%

FIGURE 9.9 APT or Intertemporal CAPM Using Fama-MacBeth Method.

	A	B	C	D	E	F	G	H
1	**ASSET PRICING** APT or Intertemporal CAPM Using Fama-MacBeth Method							
2								
3	**Inputs**							
4	APT or ICAPM Factors	APT or ICAPM Factors: ⦿ Fama-French 3 Factors ○ 3 Macro Factors			1			
5	Asset Type	Asset Type: ⦿ Stock ○ US FF Port ○ Country ETF			1			
6								
7				Stock	Stock	Stock	Stock	Stock
8				Barrick	IBM	KEP	Nokia	Telefonos
130	(2) LINEST(Asset Returns over 5 Years, 3 Factor Innovations over 5 Yrs)							
131	Enter this linear regression as an Excel matrix (Shift-Control-Enter)							
132	Select D143:D145							
133	Type =TRANSPOSE(LINEST(OFFSET(D$11,$B143,0):OFFSET(D$70,$B143,0),							
134	OFFSET($Y$11,$B143,($E$4-1)*3):OFFSET($AA$70,$B143,($E$4-1)*3)))							
135	Hold down the Shift and Control buttons and then press Enter							
136	Then copy to the range D143:D145 to the range E143:U145; Then copy the range D143:U145 to the range D146:U148;							
137	Then copy the doubled range D143:U148 to the range D149:U154; Keep doubling until row 322 is reached.							
138								
139	**Three Factor Betas from the First Pass, Time-Series Regression**							
140								
141	5 Yr Estimation Per:	Row						
142	Beg Mon - End Mon	Offset	Factors	Barrick	IBM	KEP	Nokia	Telefonos
143	Dec 2004 - Nov 2009	0	FF HML	-0.19	-0.51	0.20	0.23	0.69
144			FF SMB	-1.03	0.36	0.46	-0.32	0.04
145			FF Mkt-RF	0.93	0.84	1.30	1.40	0.93
146	Nov 2004 - Oct 2009	1	FF HML	-0.16	-0.51	0.19	0.22	0.68
147			FF SMB	-0.79	0.37	0.43	-0.39	0.00
148			FF Mkt-RF	0.86	0.83	1.37	1.43	0.92

FIGURE 9.10 APT or Intertemporal CAPM Using Fama-MacBeth Method.

	A	B	C	D	E	F	G	H
1	**ASSET PRICING** APT or Intertemporal CAPM Using Fama-MacBeth Method							
2								
3	**Inputs**							
4	APT or ICAPM Factors	APT or ICAPM Factors ⦿ Fama-French 3 Factors ◯ 3 Macro Factors			1			
5	Asset Type	Asset Type ⦿ Stock ◯ US FF Port ◯ Country ETF			1			
6								
7				Stock	Stock	Stock	Stock	Stock
8				Barrick	IBM	KEP	Nokia	Telefonos
317	Feb 2000 - Jan 2005	58	FF HML	0.86	-0.83	0.19	-0.41	-0.30
318			FF SMB	0.42	-0.77	-0.04	-0.37	0.55
319			FF Mkt-RF	0.50	1.27	1.13	1.53	0.58
320	Jan 2000 - Dec 2004	59	FF HML	0.86	-0.85	0.21	-0.41	-0.29
321			FF SMB	0.39	-0.75	-0.04	-0.35	0.53
322			FF Mkt-RF	0.51	1.22	1.17	1.52	0.60
323								
324			Average Factor Betas	Barrick	IBM	KEP	Nokia	Telefonos
325			FF HML	0.88	-0.80	0.47	-0.57	0.09
326			FF SMB	0.23	-0.20	0.21	-0.04	0.10
327			FF Mkt-RF	0.67	1.16	1.01	1.51	0.85
328								
329								
330	(3) LINEST(Returns across Assets in Month t, Factor Betas across Assets in Month t)							
331	Enter this linear regression as an Excel matrix (Shift-Control-Enter)							
332	Select the range D340:G340							
333	Type =LINEST(OFFSET(D10,0,($E$5-1)*6):OFFSET(I10,0,($E$5-1)*6), OFFSET($D$143,B340,($E$5-1)*6):OFFSET($I$145,B340,($E$5-1)*6))							
334	Hold down the Shift and Control buttons and then press Enter							
335	Then copy to the range D340:G340 to the range D341:G399							
336								
337	**Factor Risk Premia and Intercept from the Second Pass, Cross-Sectional Regression in the Following Month**							
338		Row						
339	Following Month	Offset		FF Mkt-RF	FF SMB	FF HML	Intercept	
340	Dec 2009	0		-14.80%	6.89%	7.07%	16.68%	
341	Nov 2009	3		-4.86%	-10.49%	-6.67%	11.44%	
342	Oct 2009	6		-16.23%	3.31%	-1.37%	12.24%	
343	Sep 2009	9		16.76%	1.01%	-5.87%	-11.16%	
344	Aug 2009	12		-9.85%	0.20%	7.71%	12.89%	

FIGURE 9.11 APT or Intertemporal CAPM Using Fama-MacBeth Method.

	A	B	C	D	E	F	G	H	I	J
1	ASSET PRICING APT or Intertemporal CAPM Using Fama-MacBeth Method									
2										
3	Inputs									
4	APT or ICAPM Factors	APT or ICAPM Factors ⦿ Fama-French 3 Factors ○ 3 Macro Factors			1					
5	Asset Type	Asset Type ⦿ Stock ○ US FF Port ○ Country ETF			1					
6										
7				Stock	Stock	Stock	Stock	Stock	Stock	US FF Port
8				Barrick	IBM	KEP	Nokia	Telefonos	YPF	Small-Growth
397	Mar 2005	171		-11.99%	-19.24%	5.28%	6.51%			
398	Feb 2005	174		20.67%	18.50%	7.96%	-11.37%			
399	Jan 2005	177		18.63%	12.77%	-0.66%	-20.79%			
400										
401				FF Mkt-RF	FF SMB	FF HML				
402	Factor Premia			Premium	Premium	Premium	Intercept			
403	Average			-0.36%	0.21%	-0.02%	1.76%	<= Bottom-line APT or Intertemporal		
404								CAPM estimates		
405	Expected Return using APT or ICAPM Est.			Barrick	IBM	KEP	Nokia	Telefonos	YPF	
406	Jan 2010	Fama-French 3 Factors		1.55%	1.32%	1.43%	1.22%	1.47%	1.36%	
407										
408		Jan 2010 Riskfree Rate		0.00%						
409						(4) Average Factor Risk Prem over all Second Pass Estimates				
410						Enter =AVERAGE(D340:D399) and copy across				
411										
412					(5) (Riskfree Rate) + (Second Pass Intercept)					
413					+ (Second Pass Factor 1 Risk Prem) * (First Pass Factor 1 Beta)					
414					+ (Second Pass Factor 2 Risk Prem) * (First Pass Factor 2 Beta)					
415					+ (Second Pass Factor 3 Risk Prem) * (First Pass Factor 3 Beta)					
416				Enter =$D$408+$G$403+$D$403*OFFSET(D327,0,($E$5-1)*6)						
417				+$E$403*OFFSET(D326,0,($E$5-1))						
418				+$F$403*OFFSET(D325,0,($E$5-1)*6) and copy across						

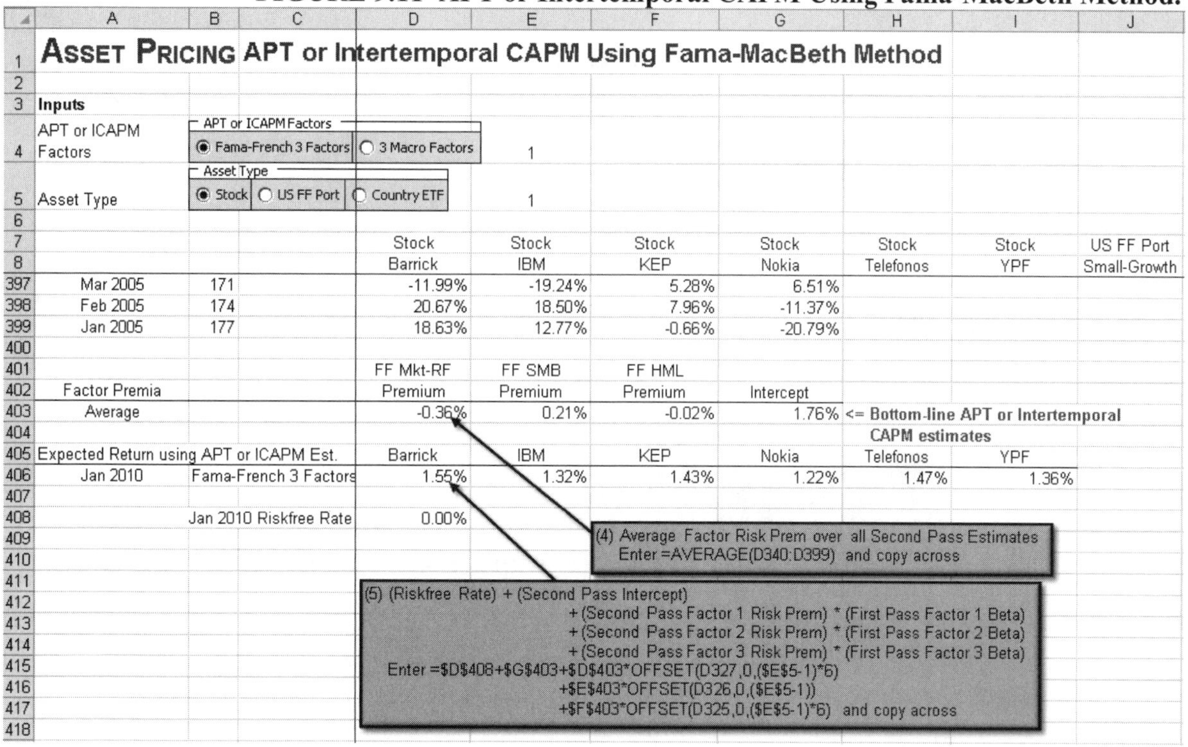

Row 403 contains the empirical average of the APT or ICAPM factor risk premia and intercept from the second-pass, cross-sectional regressions. Given the wide flexibility in specifying APT or ICAPM factors in terms of either long positions or short positions, it is legitimately possible that risk premia could be either positive or negative.

Row 406 contains the APT or ICAPM forecast of each asset's expected return in the next month (Jan 2010), or equivalently, of each asset's cost of equity capital. This is a key output of this spreadsheet.

FIGURE 9.12 APT or Intertemporal CAPM Using Fama-MacBeth Method.

	A	B	C	D	E	F	G	H
1	ASSET PRICING APT or Intertemporal CAPM Using Fama-MacBeth Method							
2								
3	Inputs							
4	APT or ICAPM Factors	APT or ICAPM Factors ⦿ Fama-French 3 Factors ○ 3 Macro Factors			1			
5	Asset Type	Asset Type ⦿ Stock ○ US FF Port ○ Country ETF			1			
6								
7				Stock	Stock	Stock	Stock	Stock
8				Barrick	IBM	KEP	Nokia	Telefonos
419								
420	(6) LINEST(Asset Returns over 5 Years, Three Factor Innovations over 5 Yrs)							
421	INDEX(LINEST(...), 3, 1) selects the R² of the regression above							
422	Enter =INDEX(LINEST(OFFSET(D$11,$B429,0):OFFSET(D$70,$B429,0),							
423	OFFSET($Y$11,$B429,($E$4-1)*3):OFFSET($AA$70,$B429,($E$4-1)*3),,TRUE),3,1)							
424	and copy to D429:U488							
425	R² (Explained Variation as a Percentage of Total Variation) from the First Pass, Time-Series Regression							
426								
427	5 Yr Estimation Per:	Row						
428	Beg Mon - End Mon	Offset		Barrick	IBM	KEP	Nokia	Telefonos
429	Dec 2004 - Nov 2009	0		41.4%	42.7%	48.0%	48.1%	35.7%
430	Nov 2004 - Oct 2009	1		9.3%	42.7%	50.2%	48.3%	34.8%
431	Oct 2004 - Sep 2009	2		9.9%	43.0%	49.6%	48.4%	34.3%
432	Sep 2004 - Aug 2009	3		9.6%	43.3%	49.5%	47.4%	36.3%

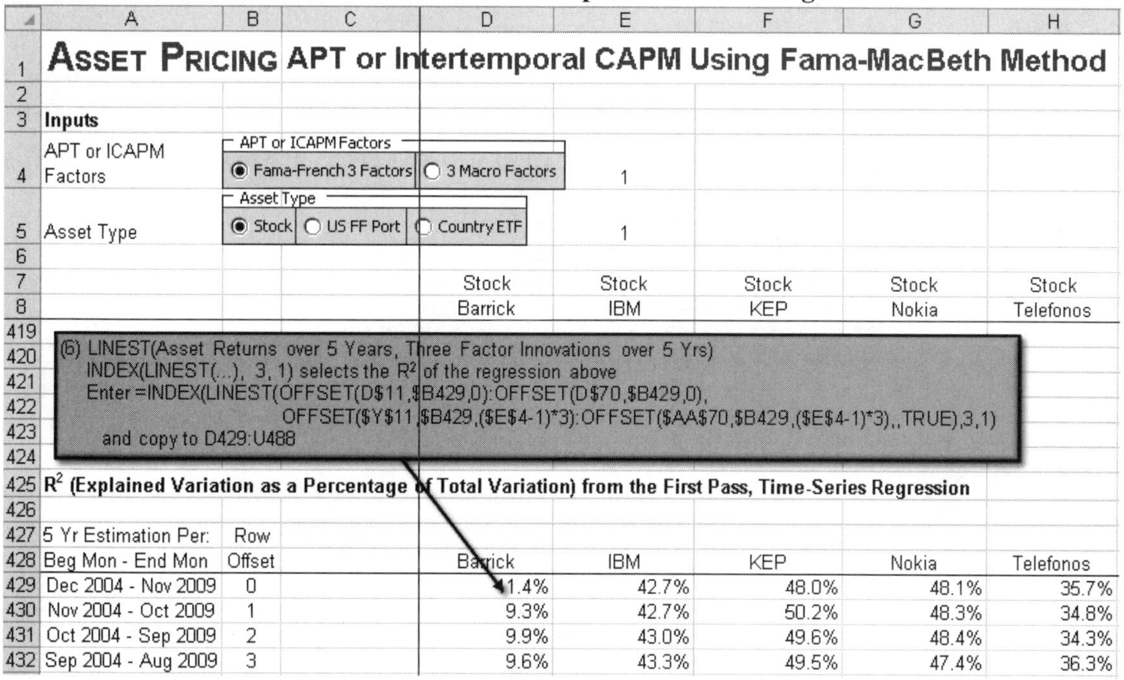

FIGURE 9.13 APT or Intertemporal CAPM Using Fama-MacBeth Method.

	A	B	C	D	E	F	G	H	I
1	**ASSET PRICING** APT or Intertemporal CAPM Using Fama-MacBeth Method								
2									
3	**Inputs**								
4	APT or ICAPM Factors	⊙ Fama-French 3 Factors ○ 3 Macro Factors			1				
5	Asset Type	⊙ Stock ○ US FF Port ○ Country ETF			1				
6									
7				Stock	Stock	Stock	Stock	Stock	Stock
8				Barrick	IBM	KEP	Nokia	Telefonos	YPF
486	Mar 2000 - Feb 2005	57		11.9%	58.4%	31.1%	31.6%	50.9%	23.7%
487	Feb 2000 - Jan 2005	58		11.4%	57.8%	29.7%	31.2%	57.9%	24.1%
488	Jan 2000 - Dec 2004	59		11.5%	56.0%	31.2%	31.1%	57.2%	25.1%
489									
490	Average R^2			15.9%	50.5%	27.1%	35.7%	31.3%	18.3%
491									
492		(7) Average R^2 over all 5 Year Estimation Windows							
493		Enter =AVERAGE(D429:D488) and copy across							
494									
495									
496		(8) LINEST(Returns across Assets in Month t, Factor Betas across Assets in Month t)							
497		INDEX(LINEST(...), 3, 1) selects the R^2 of the regression above							
498		Enter =INDEX(LINEST(OFFSET(D10,0,($E$5-1)*6):OFFSET(I10,0,($E$5-1)*6),							
499		OFFSET($D$143,B340,($E$5-1)*6):OFFSET($I$145,B340,($E$5-1)*6),,TRUE),3,1)							
500		and copy down							
501	**R^2 (Explained Variation as a Percentage of Total Variation) from the Second Pass, Cross-sectional Regression in the Following Month**								
502									
503	Following Month			R^2					
504	Dec 2009			49.0%					
505	Nov 2009			72.0%					
506	Oct 2009			98.9%					
507	Sep 2009			41.1%					

The Average R^2 of the first-pass, time-series regression tells us how much of the fluctuation in an asset's excess return can be explained by the APT or ICAPM factors. An R^2 of 0% means the two variables are unrelated vs. an R^2 of 100% means the two variables move together perfectly. With single-digit R^2s, the individual stocks are poorly explained. With an R^2 over 90%, the US portfolios are extremely well-explained by US-based APT or ICAPM factors. With an R^2 around 50%, country portfolios are somewhat-explained by US-based APT or ICAPM factors.

FIGURE 9.14 APT or Intertemporal CAPM Using Fama-MacBeth Method.

	A	B	C	D	E	F	G	H
1	**ASSET PRICING** APT or Intertemporal CAPM Using Fama-MacBeth Method							
2								
3	**Inputs**							
4	APT or ICAPM Factors	⊙ Fama-French 3 Factors ○ 3 Macro Factors			1			
5	Asset Type	⊙ Stock ○ US FF Port ○ Country ETF			1			
6								
7				Stock	Stock	Stock	Stock	Stock
8				Barrick	IBM	KEP	Nokia	Telefonos
561	Mar 2005			80.3%				
562	Feb 2005			48.1%				
563	Jan 2005			62.1%				
564								
565	Average R^2			59.6%				
566								
567			(9) Average R^2 over all Following Months in Second Pass Regressions					
568			Enter =AVERAGE(D504:D563)					
569								

The Average R^2 of the second-pass, cross-sectional regression tells us how much of the fluctuation in the excess returns across assets in the following month can be explained by the APT or ICAPM factor betas from the immediately prior five-year window. With an Average R^2 of 50% - 70%, the individual stocks, US portfolios, and country portfolios are pretty well-explained by their APT or ICAPM factors.[4]

Problems

1. Download ten years of monthly total return data for individual stocks, US portfolios, and country portfolios. Then use that data to estimate the Static CAPM under three market portfolio benchmarks (SPDR "Spider" Exchange Traded Fund, CRSP Value-Weighted Market Return, and Dow Jones World Stock Index) and using the standard Fama-MacBeth methodology. Then use the Static CAPM estimates to forecast each asset's expected return in the next future month, or equivalently, each asset's cost of equity capital. Finally, determine how much variation of individual stocks, US portfolios, or country portfolios is explained by the Static CAPM.

2. Download ten years of monthly total return data for individual stocks, US portfolios, and country portfolios. Then use that data to estimate the APT or Intertemporal CAPM (ICAPM) under two sets of factors (Fama-French 3 factors and 3 macro factors) and using the standard Fama-MacBeth methodology. Then use the APT or ICAPM estimates to forecast each asset's expected return in the next future month, or equivalently, each asset's cost of equity capital. Finally, determine how much variation of individual stocks, US portfolios, or country portfolios is explained by the APT or ICAPM.

---

[4] Lewellen, Nagel and Shaken (2010) suggest that apparently high cross-sectional R^2 provide quite weak support for an asset pricing model. They offer a number of suggestions for improving empirical asset pricing tests, including expanding the set of assets tested to include industry portfolios and using Generalized Least Squares (GLS) R^2, rather than regular regression (OLS) R^2. They test five popular asset pricing models, including the Static CAPM and the Fama-French 3 Factor model. They find that for an expanded set of assets which includes industry portfolios, the GLS R^2 is less than 10% for all asset pricing models. See Lewellen, J., S. Nagel, and J. Shaken, 2010, A Skeptical Appraisal of Asset-Pricing Tests, *Journal of Financial Economics* 96, 175-194.

Chapter 10 Market Microstructure

10.1 Effective Spread By Exchange Using TAQ Data

Select a Data Set:

Select an available datase
Help me find my data

Current Subscriptions

AuditAnalytics
BVD
BVD Trial
Bank Regulatory
Blockholders
CBOE Indexes
CISDM Hedge fund
COMPUSTAT
CRSP
CUSIP
DMEF Academic Data
Dow Jones
Eventus
FDIC
Fama French
Federal Reserve Bank
First Call
GSIOnline Trial
Global Insight
IBES
IRI
PHLX
Penn World Tables
Risk Metrics
SEC Order Execution
TAQ
TRACE
Thomson Reuters

Purpose

This is a quick project that can be done in approximately one hour per part. Its purpose is:

- To give you a feel for stock trading on a quote-by-quote and trade-by-trade basis.
- To provide hands-on experience calculating key concepts (e.g., BBO, Effective Spread, etc.)
- To analyze the execution performance of different exchanges.

There is nothing to turn in. Simply print out your results and come prepared to share your interpretation of the results in our next class. I will call on several people to provide their interpretations.

Your assignment is to download and analyze the TAQ data for one firm on one day. There are three parts of this project: download the data, organize the data, compute the BBO

Download The Data

The data we will use for this project is called Trade And Quote (TAQ) data. It is published monthly by the New York Stock Exchange based on publicly available data from the Intermarket Trading System (ITS). The data is delivered by a very convenient delivery vehicle called the Wharton Research Data Service (WRDS).

To access the TAQ data, open a web browser and go to http://wrds-web.wharton.upenn.edu/. Login to the class account created by your instructor using the username and password supplied by your instructor.

Now in the left-hand column, you get to see the larger majority of the datasets used in finance research. Feel free to explore any datasets that interest you. For this project, you will use the TAQ dataset.

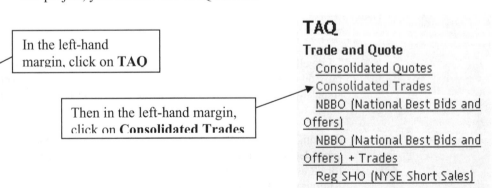

TAQ
Trade and Quote
  Consolidated Quotes
  Consolidated Trades
  NBBO (National Best Bids and Offers)
  NBBO (National Best Bids and Offers) + Trades
  Reg SHO (NYSE Short Sales)

In the left-hand margin, click on **TAQ**

Then in the left-hand margin, click on **Consolidated Trades**

• Do the following five steps to request trades data:

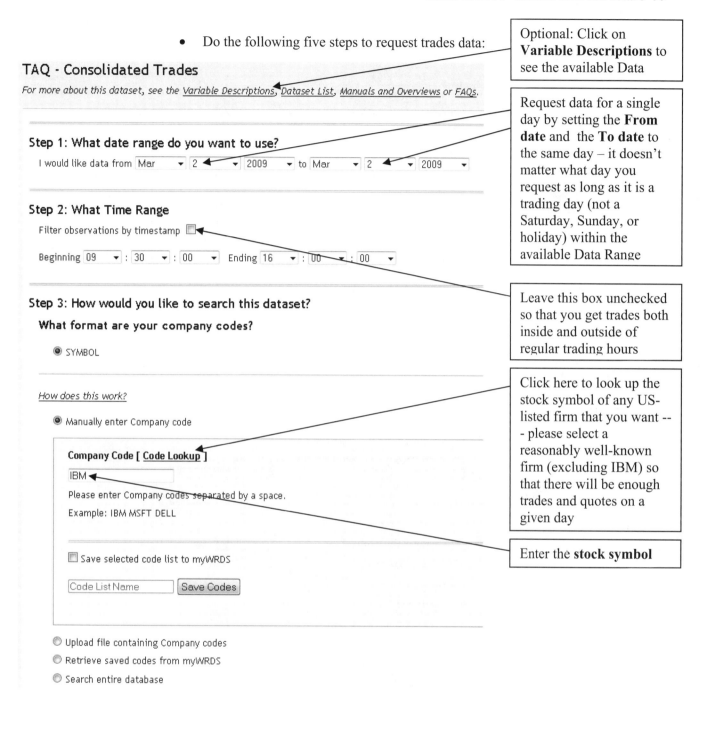

TAQ - Consolidated Trades

For more about this dataset, see the *Variable Descriptions, Dataset List, Manuals and Overviews* or *FAQs*.

Step 1: What date range do you want to use?

I would like data from | Mar ▼ | 2 ▼ | 2009 ▼ | to | Mar ▼ | 2 ▼ | 2009 ▼ |

Step 2: What Time Range

Filter observations by timestamp ☐

Beginning | 09 ▼ | : | 30 ▼ | : | 00 ▼ | Ending | 16 ▼ | : | 00 ▼ | : | 00 ▼ |

Step 3: How would you like to search this dataset?

What format are your company codes?

◉ SYMBOL

How does this work?

◉ Manually enter Company code

Company Code [Code Lookup]

| IBM |

Please enter Company codes separated by a space.

Example: IBM MSFT DELL

☐ Save selected code list to myWRDS

| Code List Name | [Save Codes]

○ Upload file containing Company codes

○ Retrieve saved codes from myWRDS

○ Search entire database

Optional: Click on **Variable Descriptions** to see the available Data

Request data for a single day by setting the **From date** and the **To date** to the same day – it doesn't matter what day you request as long as it is a trading day (not a Saturday, Sunday, or holiday) within the available Data Range

Leave this box unchecked so that you get trades both inside and outside of regular trading hours

Click here to look up the stock symbol of any US-listed firm that you want -- please select a reasonably well-known firm (excluding IBM) so that there will be enough trades and quotes on a given day

Enter the **stock symbol**

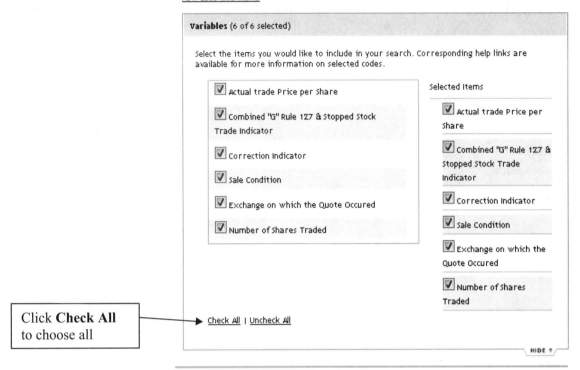

Step 4: What variables do you want in your query?

How does this work?

Variables (6 of 6 selected)

Select the items you would like to include in your search. Corresponding help links are available for more information on selected codes.

☑ Actual trade Price per Share

☑ Combined "G" Rule 127 & Stopped Stock Trade Indicator

☑ Correction Indicator

☑ Sale Condition

☑ Exchange on which the Quote Occured

☑ Number of Shares Traded

Selected Items

☑ Actual trade Price per Share

☑ Combined "G" Rule 127 & Stopped Stock Trade Indicator

☑ Correction Indicator

☑ Sale Condition

☑ Exchange on which the Quote Occured

☑ Number of Shares Traded

Check All | Uncheck All

HIDE ↑

Click **Check All** to choose all

Step 5: How would you like the query output?

Select the desired <u>format</u> of the output file. For large data requests, select a compression type to expedite downloads. If you enter your email address, you will receive an email that contains a URL to the output file when the data request is finished processing.

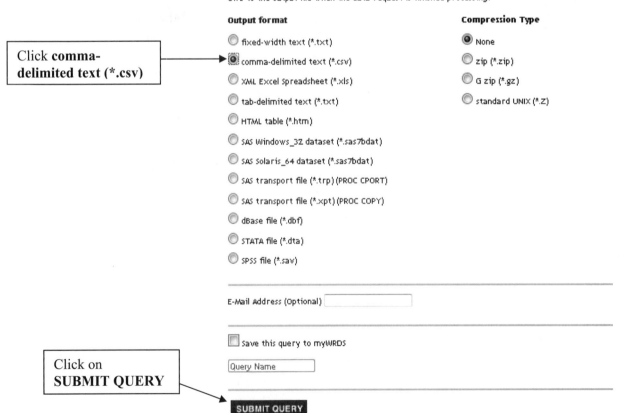

Output format

○ fixed-width text (*.txt)

◉ comma-delimited text (*.csv)

○ XML Excel Spreadsheet (*.xls)

○ tab-delimited text (*.txt)

○ HTML table (*.htm)

○ SAS Windows_32 dataset (*.sas7bdat)

○ SAS Solaris_64 dataset (*.sas7bdat)

○ SAS transport file (*.trp) (PROC CPORT)

○ SAS transport file (*.xpt) (PROC COPY)

○ dBase file (*.dbf)

○ STATA file (*.dta)

○ SPSS file (*.sav)

Compression Type

◉ None

○ zip (*.zip)

○ G zip (*.gz)

○ standard UNIX (*.Z)

E-Mail Address (Optional) [＿＿＿＿＿＿]

☐ Save this query to myWRDS

[Query Name]

SUBMIT QUERY

Click **comma-delimited text (*.csv)**

Click on **SUBMIT QUERY**

- A new tab/page will open up to track your request. It will automatically update every 10 seconds. After about a minute, it will say: "**Your output is complete. Click on the link below to open the output file.**"

Data Request Summary

Data Request ID	273802687
Libraries/Data Sets	taq/ct /
Frequency/Date Range	intraday / 02Mar2009 - 02Mar2009
Search Variable	SYMBOL
Input Codes 1 item(s)	IBM
Conditional Statements	n/a
Output format/Compression	csv /
Variables Selected	PRICE G127 CORR COND EX SIZE
Extra Variables and Parameters Selected	

As part of the WRDS Capacity Expansion Plans, this data query is being processed on a new g running this query, please contact <u>wrds-support@wharton.upenn.edu</u>.

Your output is complete. Click on the link below to open the output file.

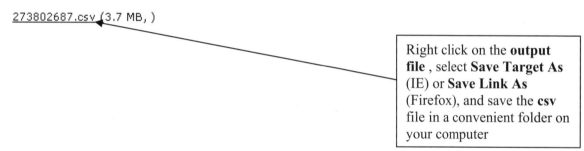

273802687.csv (3.7 MB,)

Right click on the **output file** , select **Save Target As** (IE) or **Save Link As** (Firefox), and save the **csv** file in a convenient folder on your computer

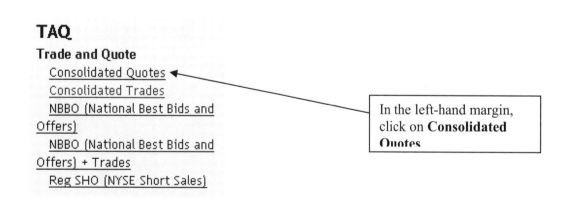

TAQ

Trade and Quote

   Consolidated Quotes

   Consolidated Trades

   NBBO (National Best Bids and Offers)

   NBBO (National Best Bids and Offers) + Trades

   Reg SHO (NYSE Short Sales)

In the left-hand margin, click on **Consolidated Quotes**

- Do the following five steps to request quote data:

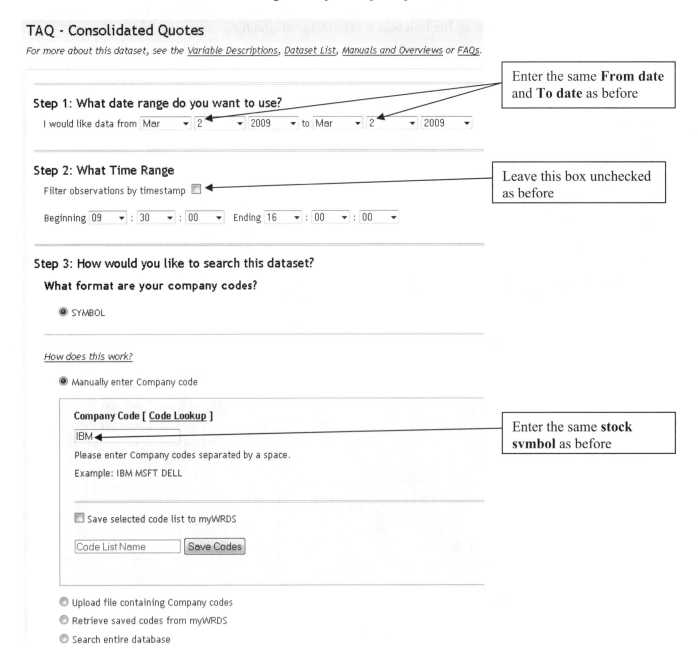

Step 4: What variables do you want in your query?

How does this work?

Variables (7 of 7 selected)

Select the items you would like to include in your search. Corresponding help links are available for more information on selected codes.

☑ Bid Price

☑ Offer Price

☑ Bid Size in Number of Round Lots

☑ Offer Size in Number of Round Lots

☑ Quote Condition

☑ Exchange on which the Quote Occured

☑ Nasdaq market marker for each NASD Quote

Selected Items

☑ Bid Price

☑ Offer Price

☑ Bid Size in Number of Round Lots

☑ Offer Size in Number of Round Lots

☑ Quote Condition

☑ Exchange on which the Quote Occured

☑ Nasdaq market marker for each NASD Quote

Check All | Uncheck All

HIDE ↑

Click **Check All** as before

Step 5: How would you like the query output?

Select the desired <u>format</u> of the output file. For large data requests, select a compression type to expedite downloads. If you enter your email address, you will receive an email that contains a URL to the output file when the data request is finished processing.

Output format

○ fixed-width text (*.txt)

◉ comma-delimited text (*.csv)

○ XML Excel Spreadsheet (*.xls)

○ tab-delimited text (*.txt)

○ HTML table (*.htm)

○ SAS Windows_32 dataset (*.sas7bdat)

○ SAS Solaris_64 dataset (*.sas7bdat)

○ SAS transport file (*.trp) (PROC CPORT)

○ SAS transport file (*.xpt) (PROC COPY)

○ dBase file (*.dbf)

○ STATA file (*.dta)

○ SPSS file (*.sav)

Compression Type

◉ None

○ zip (*.zip)

○ G zip (*.gz)

○ standard UNIX (*.Z)

Select **comma-delimited text (*.csv)** as before

E-Mail Address (Optional) [_____]

☐ Save this query to myWRDS

[Query Name]

SUBMIT QUERY

Click on **SUBMIT QUERY** as before

Again a new tab/page will open up to track your request. It will automatically update every 10 seconds. After about a minute, it will say: "**Your output is complete. Click on the link below to open the output file.**"

Data Request Summary

Data Request ID	273804757
Libraries/Data Sets	taq/cq /
Frequency/Date Range	intraday / 02Mar2009 - 02Mar2009
Search Variable	SYMBOL
Input Codes 1 item(s)	IBM
Conditional Statements	n/a
Output format/Compression	csv /
Variables Selected	BID OFR BIDSIZ OFRSIZ MODE EX MMID
Extra Variables and Parameters Selected	

As part of the **WRDS Capacity Expansion Plans, this data query is being processed on a new g** running this query, please contact **wrds-support@wharton.upenn.edu.**

Your output is complete. Click on the link below to open the output file.

273804757.csv (31.3 MB,)

> Right click on the **output file** , select **Save Target As** (IE) or **Save Link As** (Firefox), and save the **csv** file in a convenient folder on your computer

Copy The Data To The TAQ Project Format File

Launch Microsoft Excel and open the file **Ch 10 Market Microstructure.xlsx**. This file provides the organization for the calculations to follow. Open the two **csv** files that you just downloaded by clicking on [File] | **Open** | **All Files** [All Files (*.*)] (to see all types of files) and then open the **csv** files.

Excel 2007 Equivalent

To open csv files in Excel 2007, click on [icon], click on **Open**, click on **All Files**, and then open the **csv** files.

The Consolidated Trades **csv** file provides nine variables for every trade: Symbol, Date, Time, Price, Size, G127, Correction, Condition, and Exchange. Copy the data for the first 1,000 trades into the appropriate location in the **Ch 10 Market Microstructure** file. Specifically in the Consolidated Trades **csv** file, select the range **A3:I1000**, click **Copy**, in the **TAQ Project Format** file the cell **AW3**, and click **Paste**.

	AW	AX	AY	AZ	BA	BB	BC	BD	BE
1	Consolidated Trades Data								
2	SYMBOL	DATE	TIME	PRICE	SIZE	G127	CORR	COND	EX
21	IBM	20071211	9:30:23	109.39	700	0	0	E	P
22	IBM	20071211	9:30:23	109.39	100	0	0	E	P
23	IBM	20071211	9:30:23	109.39	100	0	0	E	P
24	IBM	20071211	9:30:23	109.39	100	0	0	F	P
25	IBM	20071211	9:30:23	109.39	200	0	0	F	P
26	IBM	20071211	9:30:24	109.39	100	0	0	E	P
27	IBM	20071211	9:30:24	109.39	100	0	0	F	P
28	IBM	20071211	9:30:24	108.9	138000	0	0	@	N
29	IBM	20071211	9:30:24	109.39	100	0	0	E	P
30	IBM	20071211	9:30:24	109.39	600	0	0	E	P

Now look down the Size column and you easily be able to pick out a trade that is *approximately 100 times larger* that most other trades. This is the opening trade of the regular trading session. It usually occurs a few seconds or minutes after 9:30:00. The opening call auction is very different than the continuous trading process. Given how large the open trade is might easily distort the rest of the analysis. So, **delete the row** containing the opening trade. In the example above, select cell **BA28** and click on **Home** tab, in the **Cell** group, click on the **Delete down arrow**, click on **Delete Sheet Rows**.

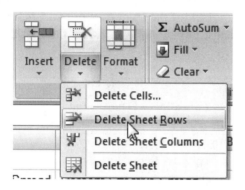

Next, note what time the 1000th trade of the day took place. In this example, the 1000th trade of the day took place at **9:38:02**.

	AW	AX	AY	AZ	BA	BB	BC	BD	BE
1	Consolidated Trades Data								
2	SYMBOL	DATE	TIME	PRICE	SIZE	G127	CORR	COND	EX
993	IBM	20071211	9:37:57	108.89	200	0	0	E	N
994	IBM	20071211	9:37:58	108.91	1000	0	0	E	N
995	IBM	20071211	9:37:59	108.96	200	0	0	E	N
996	IBM	20071211	9:38:02	108.91	100	0	0	E	N
997	IBM	20071211	9:38:02	108.91	100	0	0	F	N
998	IBM	20071211	9:38:02	108.88	100	0	0	F	T
999	IBM	20071211	9:38:02	108.88	100	0	0	F	T
1000	IBM	20071211	9:38:02	108.88	100	0	0	F	T

The Consolidated Quotes **csv** file provides ten variables for every quote: Symbol, Date, Time, Bid, Offer, Bid Size, Offer Size, Mode, Exchange, and Market Maker ID. Copy the data for the quotes up to the *same time* **9:38:02 (**which ends in row **13371** in this case) to the appropriate location in the **TAQ Project Format** file. Specifically in the Consolidated Quotes **csv** file, select the range **A2:J13371**, click **Copy**, in the **TAQ Project Format** file select the cell **A3**, and click **Paste**.

	A	B	C	D	E	F	G	H	I	J
1					**Consolidated Quotes Data**					
2	SYMBOL	DATE	TIME	BID	OFR	BIDSIZ	OFRSIZ	MODE	EX	MMID
13364	IBM	20071211	9:38:02	108.89	108.96	2	1	12	C	
13365	IBM	20071211	9:38:02	108.87	108.96	1	1	12	P	
13366	IBM	20071211	9:38:02	108.88	109	2	11	12	T	
13367	IBM	20071211	9:38:02	108.89	108.97	2	1	12	C	
13368	IBM	20071211	9:38:02	108.89	108.99	2	1	12	C	
13369	IBM	20071211	9:38:02	108.88	108.98	1	2	12	P	
13370	IBM	20071211	9:38:02	108.86	108.97	5	2	12	N	
13371	IBM	20071211	9:38:02	108.89	108.96	1	1	12	P	
13372	IBM	20071211	9:38:02	108.89	108.98	1	1	12	P	

Compute The BBO

Next calculate the Best Bid and Offer (BBO). The first step in computing the BBO is to keep track of the Currently Active Bid and Ask prices that are quoted by each exchange. For example, consider the first three quotes of the day shown below.

	A	B	C	D	E	F	G	H	I	J
1					**Consolidated Quotes Data**					
2	SYMBOL	DATE	TIME	BID	OFR	BIDSIZ	OFRSIZ	MODE	EX	MMID
3	IBM	20071211	4:12:49	109.1	109.8	2	5	12	P	
4	IBM	20071211	4:12:50	0	109.8	0	5	12	P	
5	IBM	20071211	4:12:50	109.1	109.8	6	5	12	P	

The first and third quotes were legitimate quotes for a Bid = $109.10 and an Ask = $109.80. The second quote was NOT legitimate, because the Bid = $0. The **EX** variable indicates what *exchange* updated its bid and ask. The exchange codes are: A = American, B = Boston, C = National, D = National Association of Securities Dealers (NASD), E = Market Independent (SIP – Generated), I = International Securities Exchange, J = DirectEdge A, K = DirectEdge X, M = Chicago, N = New York Stock Exchange (NYSE), P = NYSE ARCA, Q = NASD, S = Consolidated Tape System, T = NASD, X = Philadelphia, W = Chicago Board Options Exchange (CBOE), and Z = BATS. In the example above, all three quotes were by NYSE ARCA (exchange code = P). Now let's keep track of the Currently Active Bids in columns **L – AB** below

Currently Active Bids By Exchange

	L	M	N	O	P	Q	R	S	T	U	V	W	X	Y	Z	AA	AB
2	A	B	C	D	E	I	J	K	M	N	P	S	T	Q	W	X	Z
3	0.00	0.00	0.00	0.00	0.00	0.00	0.00	0.00	0.00	0.00	109.10	0.00	0.00	0.00	0.00	0.00	0.00
4	0.00	0.00	0.00	0.00	0.00	0.00	0.00	0.00	0.00	0.00	109.10	0.00	0.00	0.00	0.00	0.00	0.00
5	0.00	0.00	0.00	0.00	0.00	0.00	0.00	0.00	0.00	0.00	109.10	0.00	0.00	0.00	0.00	0.00	0.00

and the Currently Active Asks are in columns **AC – AS** below.

Currently Active Asks By Exchange

	AC	AD	AE	AF	AG	AH	AI	AJ	AK	AL	AM	AN	AO	AP	AQ	AR	AS
2	A	B	C	D	E	I	J	K	M	N	P	S	T	Q	W	X	Z
3	1000.00	1000.00	1000.00	1000.00	1000.00	1000.00	1000.00	1000.00	1000.00	1000.00	109.80	1000.00	1000.00	1000.00	1000.00	1000.00	1000.00
4	1000.00	1000.00	1000.00	1000.00	1000.00	1000.00	1000.00	1000.00	1000.00	1000.00	109.80	1000.00	1000.00	1000.00	1000.00	1000.00	1000.00
5	1000.00	1000.00	1000.00	1000.00	1000.00	1000.00	1000.00	1000.00	1000.00	1000.00	109.80	1000.00	1000.00	1000.00	1000.00	1000.00	1000.00

The Currently Active Bids and Asks for NYSE ARCA (exchange code = P) were updated in response to first three quotes. Specifically, the Currently Active Bids (in column **V**) were set to $109.10 and Currently Active Asks (in column **AM**) were set to $190.80. Since the second quote was NOT legitimate (because the bid was $0), then the Currently Active Bid in cell **V4** stayed the same ($109.10) as the Previous Active Bid in cell **V3** above it. The rest of the exchanges were assigned a default value for the Currently Active Bid = $0 and Currently Active Ask = $1000 until they supply a legitimate opening quote.

Consider what formula to enter in cell **L3** for the Currently Active Bid for exchange code "A."

Currently Active Bid for "A" =
    IF (EX variable = "A" and Bid > 0), THEN set it to Updated Bid,
    ELSE IF (This is the First Active Bid of the day for "A"),
        THEN set it to the default value $0,
    ELSE set it to the Previous Active Bid for "A"

Enter **=IF(AND($I3=L$2,$D3>0),$D3,IF(ISTEXT(L2),0,L2))** in cell **L3** and copy to the range **L3:AB13372**. Be sure to enter the $ symbols in the cell addresses in the same manner as above.

The formula for Currently Active Ask for exchange code "A" is analogous.

 Currently Active Ask for "A" =
    IF (EX variable = "A" and Ask > 0), THEN set it to Updated Ask,
     ELSE IF (This is the First Active Ask of the day for "A"),
        THEN set it to the default value $1000,
    ELSE set it to the Previous Active Ask for "A"

Enter **=IF(AND($I3=AC$2,$E3>0),$E3,IF(ISTEXT(AC2),1000,AC2))** in cell **AC3** and copy to the range **AC3:AS13372**. Again, enter the $ symbols in the cell addresses in the same manner as above.

⁍	AM	AN	AO	AP	AQ	AR	AS	AT	AU
1	e								**BBO**
2	P	S	T	Q	W	X	Z	Best Bid	Best Ask
3	109.80	1000.00	1000.00	1000.00	1000.00	1000.00	1000.00	109.10	109.80
4	109.80	1000.00	1000.00	1000.00	1000.00	1000.00	1000.00	109.10	109.80
5	109.80	1000.00	1000.00	1000.00	1000.00	1000.00	1000.00	109.10	109.80

The next step is to determine the Best Bid and Best Ask. The Best Bid is simply the *highest* Currently Active Bid by any exchange (in columns **L – AB**). Enter **=MAX(L3:AB3)** in cell **AT3** and copy it down the column. The easy way to do this is to hover the cursor over the fill handle ▬▮ (the square in the lower-right corner) of cell **AT3**, the cursor turns to a plus symbol ⊹ as shown below,

1	**BBO**	
2	Best Bid	Best Ask
3	109.10	
4		

and then double-click. This copies the formula in cell **AT3** as far down column **AT** as there are entries in neighboring column **AS** (i.e., down to row **13372**).

The Best Ask is simply the *lowest* Currently Active Ask by any exchange (in columns **AC – AS**). Enter **=MIN(AC3:AS3)** in cell **AU3** and copy it down the column by hovering the cursor over the fill handle ▬▮ and double-clicking.

Now you've computed the BBO!

Determine the BBO at trade time t – one second

For any given trade, we want to know what the BBO was at that moment the trade took place. It is possible for the quote to change a few milliseconds *after* the trade takes place, but still be reported as being occurring in the same second. Therefore, it is standard practice to refer to the BBO that was in effect one second *before* the trade takes place (that is, trade time t – one second).

⁍	AW	AX	AY	AZ	BA	BB	BC	BD	BE	BF	BG
1				**Consolidated Trades Data**						**BBO(t-1)**	
2	SYMBOL	DATE	TIME	PRICE	SIZE	G127	CORR	COND	EX	Best Bid(t-1)	Best Ask(t-1)
3	IBM	20071211	5:16:52	109.43	200	0	0		P	109.43	109.7
4	IBM	20071211	5:17:17	109.43	200	0	0		P	109.43	109.7
5	IBM	20071211	8:00:00	109.39	3000	0	0		D	109.43	109.9

This is done by using the **LOOKUP** command, which has three arguments: lookup value, lookup range, results range. We want the lookup value to be the trade time t – one second. For the trade in row **3** below, the trade time is **5:16.52**.

By convention, time in Excel is denoted in days. So one second is 1/24/60/60 of a day. After subtracting a second, our lookup value is **5:16.51.** The lookup range is the Consolidated Quote Time in Column **C**. The result range is the Best Bid in column **AT**. The **LOOKUP** command will find a time in column **C** that is equal to **5:16.51** (or the closest time less than it) and then find the corresponding Best Bid in column **AT**. Enter

$$=\text{LOOKUP}(\$AY3-1/24/60/60,\$C\$3:\$C\$13372,AT\$3:AT\$13372)$$

in cell **BF3**, copy it to cell **BG3**, and copy both cells down the column by selecting the range **BF3:BG3**, hovering the cursor over the fill handle ▬▪, and double-clicking. Notice that the formula above computes both the Best Bid(t-1) in column **BF** and the Best Ask(t-1) in column **BG**. This is because when the formula is copied to neighboring column **BG**, the result range becomes the neighboring column **AU** which contains the Best Ask.

Compute The Midpoint(t-1), Quoted Spread, and Effective Spread

The midpoint is a standard benchmark for the current value of the security. The Midpoint is simply the average of the Best Bid and Best Ask:

$$\text{Midpoint} = (\text{Best Bid} + \text{Best Ask}) / 2$$

Enter **=(BF3+BG3)/2** in cell **BH3** and copy down the column by hovering the cursor over the fill handle ▬▪ and double-clicking.

	AT	AU	AV	AW	AX	AY	AZ
1	BBO(t-1)						
2	Best Bid(t-1)	Best Ask(t-1)	Midpoint	Dollar Quoted Spread	Percent Quoted Spread	Dollar Effective Spread	Percent Effective Spread
3	109.43	109.7	$109.565	$0.27	0.25%	$0.27	0.25%
4	109.43	109.7	$109.565	$0.27	0.25%	$0.27	0.25%
5	109.43	109.9	$109.665	$0.47	0.43%	$0.55	0.50%

The dollar and percentage quoted spread are defined as follows:

$$\text{Dollar Quoted Spread} = \text{Best Ask} - \text{Best Bid}$$
$$\text{Percent Quoted Spread} = \text{Dollar Quoted Spread} / \text{Midpoint}$$

Enter **=BG3-BF3** in cell **BI3**, enter **=BI3/BH3** in cell **BJ3** and copy both cells down the column by selecting the range **BI3:BJ3**, hovering the cursor over the fill handle ▬▪, and double-clicking.

The dollar and percentage effective spread are defined as follows:

$$\text{Dollar Effective Spread} = |\text{Trade Price} - \text{Midpoint}| * 2$$
$$\text{Percent Effective Spread} = \text{Dollar Effective Spread} / \text{Midpoint}$$

Enter **=ABS(AZ3-BH3)*2** in cell **BK3**, enter **=BK3/BH3** in cell **BL3**, copy both cells down the column by selecting the range **BK3:BL3**, hovering the cursor over the fill handle ▬▪, and double-clicking.

Calculate Performance by Exchange

So far, we have calculated various measures of execution quality (i.e., Percent Quoted Spread and Percent Effective Spread) for each individual trade. But we would like to discover what kind of execution quality is provided by various exchanges on average over the 1,000 trades in your TAQ dataset. In other words, we want to calculate the *average* Percent Quoted Spread and the *average* Percent Effective Spread for each exchange.

The easiest way is to use a powerful feature of Excel called the PivotTable. Click on **Insert** tab, in the **Tables** group click on the **PivotTable down arrow**, click on **PivotTable**.

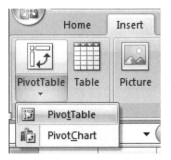

In the **Create PivotTable** dialog box, enter the range **$AW$2:$BL$1000** (which includes the Consolidate Trades Data, the BBO(t-1), and the Midpoint through Percent Effective Spread data) in the **Select a table or range** box, enter a cell location **$BN$3** in the **Location** box, and click **OK**.

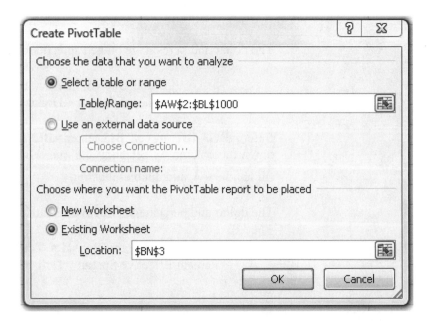

To create the report we are interested in, we will drag variables from the **PivotTable Field List** to one of the areas of the report. Check the box for **Ex** and it is automatically added to **Row Labels** area. You will immediately see rows for the various exchanges (C, D, I, etc.) and a grand total. Check the boxes for **Percent Quoted Spread**, **Percent Effective Spread**, and **Size**. They are automatically added to the **Values** area.

The figure above shows the result at this intermediate step. Excel guessed incorrectly that we wanted to calculate the **Sum** our variables. We are actually interested in calculating the Average of each of our variables. To change this, click on the orange **Sum of Perce..** button ⟨Sum of Perce... ▼⟩ in the **Values** area and then click on **Value Field Settings** on the pop-up menu.

In the Value Field Setting dialog box, select **Average** and click on **OK**.

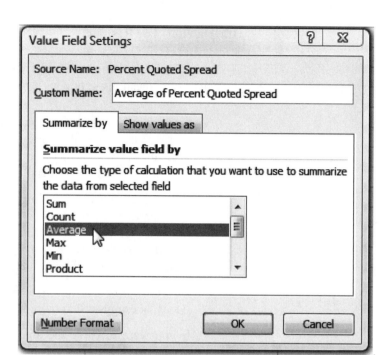

Repeat the procedure for the Percent Effective Spread and Size. That is, click the *second* orange **Sum of Perce..** button ▐ Sum of Perce... ▼ ▐, click on **Value Field Settings**, select **Average** and click on **OK**. Then click the orange **Sum of Size** button ▐ Sum of SIZE ▼ ▐, click on **Value Field Settings**, select **Average** and click on **OK**.

You can make the output a little easier to interpret with some formatting. Select the range **B05:BP11** and click on the **Home** tab, in the **Number** group click on the **Percent Style** ▐ % ▐ and click two times on **Increase Decimal** ▐ ← .0 / .00 ▐. Select the range **BQ6:BQ11** and click on the **Home** tab, in the **Number** group click five times on **Decrease Decimal** ▐ .00 / →.0 ▐. The final result will look like the figure below.

	BN	BO	BP	BQ
1				
2				
3		Values		
4	Row Labels ▼	Average of Percent Quoted Spread	Average of Percent Effective Spread	Average of SIZE
5	C	0.044%	0.044%	146.67
6	D	0.092%	0.266%	325.93
7	N	0.051%	0.085%	274.86
8	P	0.072%	0.115%	117.92
9	T	0.049%	0.074%	149.50
10	Grand Total	0.062%	0.118%	217.36

Now we have the results that we want and are ready to interpret!

Interpreting The Results

To help with interpreting the results you have generated for your particular firm, here are some questions to ponder:

- Do you notice a difference between the Average of Percent Quoted Spread and the Average of Percent Effective Spread for most exchanges? Which of these two measures of execution quality is most relevant for security traders?

- Which exchanges had the lowest Average of Percent Effective Spread for your particular firm? Which had the highest? Do you see any patterns in the Average of Percent Effective Spread for the Regionals vs. NYSE vs. NASDAQ? Why would anyone send an order to the exchange with the highest Average of Percent Effective Spread?

- Do you notice a difference in the Average of Size across exchanges? Does this suggest that there is any segmentation by Size? Explain.

- If you were to carry the analysis of your data further, what might you look at?

Chapter 11 Life-Cycle Financial Planning

11.1 Basics

Problem. Suppose that you are currently 30 years old and expect to earn a constant real salary of $80,000 starting next year. You are planning to retire at age 70. You currently have $0 in financial capital. You are limited to investing in the riskfree asset. The real riskfree rate is 2.8%. Develop a financial plan for real savings and real consumption over your lifetime.

Solution Strategy. Develop a financial plan on a year-by-year basis over an entire lifetime. During your working years, divide your salary each year between current consumption and savings to provide for consumption during your retirement years. Put savings in a retirement fund that is invested at the riskfree rate. During your retirement years, your salary is zero, but you are able to consume each year by withdrawing money from your retirement fund. Calculate a constant level of real consumption that can be sustained in both working years and retirement years. Since there is substantial uncertainty about how long you will actually live and since it's not a good idea to run out of money, calculate real consumption based on infinite annuity. This level of real consumption can be sustained indefinitely. Finally, analyze human capital, financial capital, and total wealth over your lifetime.

Life Expectancy. How long will you live? For the US in 2007, the average age of death ("life expectancy at birth") was 78. Also in 2007, the average age of death by those 65 or older ("life expectancy at 65") was 84. Life expectancy at birth and at age 65 have both increased by approximately 1 year over the prior 5 years due to medical and health progress. By simply extrapolating this trend into the future, the next 60 years would add 12 years to life expectancy. So life expectancy at birth would rise to 90 and life expectancy at 65 would rise to 96. So averaging between those two figures, today's typical 30 year old might expect to live to 93. This is a very conservative forecast in the sense that medical and health progress is likely to accelerate, rather than just maintain the current rate of improvement.

To determine your individual life expectancy, add to (or subtract from) 93 based on your individual health-conscious practices. Not smoking adds nine years. Aerobic exercising and getting seven to eight hours of sleep per night adds three years. A healthy diet and maintaining a desirable weight based on your height adds three years. A thorough annual medical exam to catch cancer and other health problems early adds two years. The following six items add one year each: (1) daily aspirin to reduce fatal heart attacks, (2) preventing high blood pressure, (3) avoiding accidents, (4) getting immunized against pneumonia and influenza, (5) avoiding suicide and AIDS, and (6) avoiding heavy alcohol consumption. For more information on the factors effecting longevity and the long-run impact of scientific and medical progress, visit George Webster's web site at: www.george-webster.com.

FIGURE 11.1 Excel Model of Life-Cycle Financial Planning - Basics.

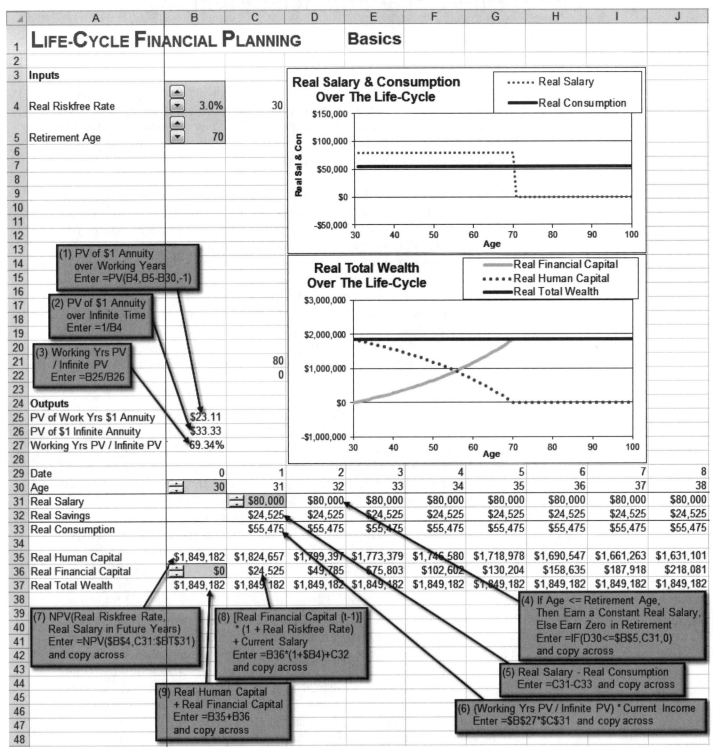

FIGURE 11.2 Transition from Working Years to Retirement Years.

	A	AN	AO	AP	AQ	AR
29	Date	38	39	40	41	42
30	Age	68	69	70	71	72
31	Real Salary	$80,000	$80,000	$80,000	$0	$0
32	Real Savings	$24,525	$24,525	$24,525	-$55,475	-$55,475
33	Real Consumption	$55,475	$55,475	$55,475	$55,475	$55,475
34						
35	Real Human Capital	$153,078	$77,670	$0	$0	$0
36	Real Financial Capital	$1,696,104	$1,771,512	$1,849,182	$1,849,182	$1,849,182
37	Real Total Wealth	$1,849,182	$1,849,182	$1,849,182	$1,849,182	$1,849,182

From the first graph, we see that your Real Salary from working years only is used to support a constant level of Real Consumption over an "infinite" lifetime. By using this approach, the same level of Real Consumption can be sustained even if you end up living much longer than originally anticipated. From the second graph, we see that Real Total Wealth is constant over a lifetime. At date 0, Real Total Wealth comes entirely from Real Human Capital, which is the present value of all future Real Salary. Over time Real Human Capital declines and Real Financial Capital builds up. After retirement, Real Total Wealth comes entirely from Real Financial Capital.

11.2 Full-Scale Estimation

Problem. Suppose that you are currently 30 years old and expect to earn a constant real salary of $80,000 starting next year. You are planning to retire at age 70. You currently have $0 in financial capital. You can invest in the riskfree asset or a broad stock portfolio. The inflation rate is 2.1% and the real riskfree rate is 2.8%. A broad stock portfolio offers an average real return of 6.0% and a standard deviation of 17.0%. Suppose that federal income taxes have six brackets with the following rates: 10.0%, 15.0%, 25.0%, 28.0%, 33.0%, and 35.0%. For current year, the upper cutoffs on the first five brackets are $7,550, $30,650, $74,200, $154,800, and $336,550 and these cutoffs are indexed to inflation. The state tax rate is 3.0%, federal FICA-SSI tax rate on salary up to $97,500 is 6.2%, and the federal FICA-Medicare tax rate on any level of salary is 1.45%. The current level of social security benefits is $34,368 per year and this is indexed to inflation. Develop a financial plan for real savings and real consumption over your lifetime.

Solution Strategy. The full-scale Excel model of life-cycle financial planning adds consideration of inflation, taxes, social security, and the opportunity to invest in a broad stock index. It is assumed that your savings are put in a tax-deferred retirement fund. You pay zero taxes on contributions to the retirement fund during your working years. But you have to pay taxes on withdrawals from the retirement fund during your retirement years. This Excel model includes several *choice variables*. You need to choose your Real Growth Rate in Salary. You need to choose your Taxable Income / Total Wealth. Specifying taxable income as a percentage of total wealth indirectly determines your consumption and savings as a percentage of total wealth. You also need to choose your Asset Allocation: Stock Portfolio %, that is, what percentage of your savings to invest in the broad stock portfolio. Investing in the broad stock portfolio will give you higher average returns than the riskfree asset, but also more risk. The balance of your savings will be invested in the riskfree asset and will grow at the riskfree rate.

FIGURE 11.3 Excel Model of Life-Cycle Fin Plan – Full-Scale Estimation.

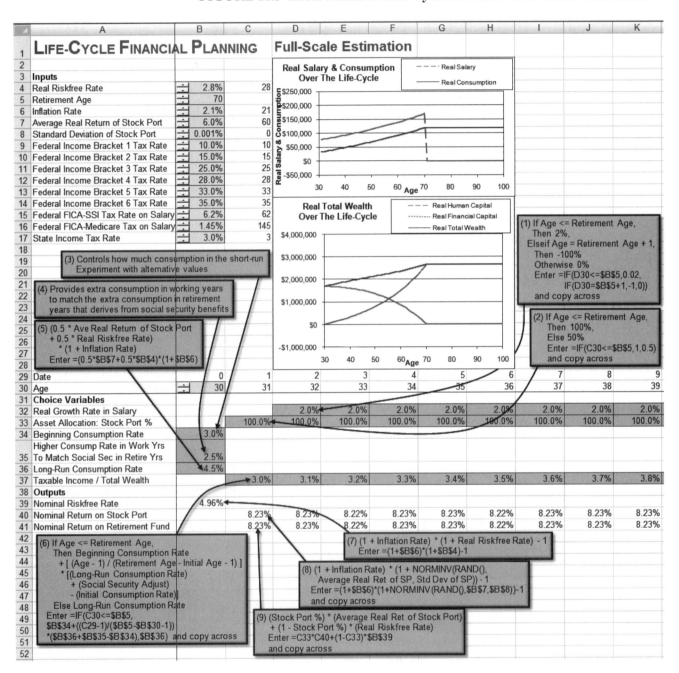

FIGURE 11.4 Excel Model of Life-Cycle Fin Plan – Full-Scale Estimation.

(13) = (Bracket 1 Tax Rate) * MIN(Taxable Income, Bracket 1 Cutoff)
+ (Bracket 2 Tax Rate) * MAX(MIN(Taxable Income, Bracket 2 Cutoff) - Bracket 1 Cutoff, 0)
+ (Bracket 3 Tax Rate) * MAX(MIN(Taxable Income, Bracket 3 Cutoff) - Bracket 2 Cutoff, 0)
+ (Bracket 4 Tax Rate) * MAX(MIN(Taxable Income, Bracket 5 Cutoff) - Bracket 3 Cutoff, 0)
+ (Bracket 5 Tax Rate) * MAX(MIN(Taxable Income, Bracket 5 Cutoff) - Bracket 4 Cutoff, 0)
+ (Bracket 6 Tax Rate) * MAX(Taxable Income - Bracket 5 Cutoff, 0)
+ (Federal FICA-SSI Tax Rate) * MIN(Salary, Federal FICA-SSI Wage Cap)
+ (Federal FICA-Medicare Tax Rate) * Salary
+ (State Income Tax Rate) * Taxable Income
Enter =$B$9*MIN(C74,C110)
+$B$10*MAX(MIN(C74,C111)-C110, 0)
+$B$11*MAX(MIN(C74,C112)-C111, 0)
+$B$12*MAX(MIN(C74,C113)-C112, 0)
+$B$13*MAX(MIN(C74,C114)-C113, 0)
+$B$14*MAX(C74-C114, 0)
+$B$15*MIN(C72,C115)
+$B$16*C72
+$B$17*C74 and copy across

(10) Salary (t-1) * (1 + Inflation Rate)
* (1 + Real Growth Rate in Salary (t))
Enter =C72*(1+$B$6)*(1+D32) and copy across

(11) Salary - Taxable Income
Enter =C72-C74 and copy across

(12) (Taxable Income / Total Wealth)
* Total Wealth (t-1)
Enter =C37*B101 and copy across

	A	B	C	D	E	F	G	H	I	J
71	Age	30	31	32	33	34	35	36	37	38
72	Salary		$80,000	$83,314	$86,764	$90,358	$94,101	$97,999	$102,058	$106,285
73	Retire. Fund Contribution (Withdrawal)		$29,254	$28,823	$28,554	$28,146	$27,700	$27,217	$26,698	$26,142
74	Taxable Income		$50,746	$54,391	$58,211	$62,212	$66,400	$70,781	$75,360	$80,143
75	Less Taxes		$16,814	$18,014	$19,273	$20,591	$21,971	$23,416	$24,927	$26,506
76	After-Tax Income		$33,932	$36,376	$38,938	$41,621	$44,429	$47,365	$50,433	$53,637
77	Plus Social Security Benefits		$0	$0	$0	$0	$0	$0	$0	$0
78	Consumption		$33,932	$36,376	$38,938	$41,621	$44,429	$47,365	$50,433	$53,637
79											
80	Savings / Salary (%)		36.6%	34.7%	32.9%	31.1%	29.4%	27.8%	26.2%	24.6%

(14) Taxable Income - Taxes
Enter =C74-C75 and copy across

(16) After-Tax Income + Social Security Benefits
Enter =C76+C77 and copy across

(15) To calculate Social Security Benefits
Enter =IF(C30>$B$5,C109,0) and copy across

(17) To calculate Savings / Salary
Enter =IF(C72>0,C73/C72,0) and copy across

FIGURE 11.5 Excel Model of Life-Cycle Fin Plan – Full-Scale Estimation.

(18) Net Present Value of Future Before-Tax Salary
* (1 - Federal Income Tax Rate - Federal FICA-SSI Tax Rate
- Federal FICA-Medicare Tax Rate - State Income Tax Rate)
Enter =NPV($B$39,C72:$BT$72)
*(1-$B$11-$B$15-$B$16-$B$17) and copy across

(19) Financial Capital (t-1)
* (1 + Nominal Return on Retirement Fund)
+ [Retirement Fund Contribution (Withdrawal)]
Enter =B100*(1+C41)+C73 and copy across

(20) Human Capital + Financial Capital
Enter =B99+B100 and copy across

(21) (Nominal Salary) / ((1 + Inflation Rate) ^ Number of periods)
Enter =C72/((1+$B$6)^C$29) and copy across

(22) (Nominal Consumption) / ((1 + Inflation Rate) ^ Number of periods)
Enter =C78/((1+$B$6)^C$29) and copy across

	A	B	C	D	E	F	G	H	I	J	K
88					0						
89					34.368						
90					7.550						
91					30.650						
92					74.200						
93					154.800						
94					336.550						
95					97.500						
96											
97											
98	Age		30	31	32	33	34	35	36	37	38	39
99	Human Capital		$1,691,539	$1,723,939	$1,755,813	$1,787,047	$1,817,518	$1,847,091	$1,875,623	$1,902,957	$1,928,926	$1,953,351
100	Financial Capital		$0	$29,254	$60,584	$94,121	$130,010	$168,407	$209,475	$253,404	$300,391	$350,650
101	Total Wealth		$1,691,539	$1,753,192	$1,816,397	$1,881,168	$1,947,528	$2,015,498	$2,085,098	$2,156,361	$2,229,317	$2,304,001
102												
103	Real Salary			$78,355	$79,922	$81,520	$83,150	$84,813	$86,510	$88,240	$90,005	$91,805
104	Real Consumption			$33,234	$34,895	$36,585	$38,301	$40,044	$41,812	$43,605	$45,421	$47,261
105	Real Human Capital		$1,691,539	$1,688,481	$1,684,328	$1,679,031	$1,672,537	$1,664,791	$1,655,736	$1,645,314	$1,633,465	$1,620,125
106	Real Financial Capital		$0	$28,652	$58,117	$88,432	$119,639	$151,786	$184,918	$219,096	$254,378	$290,832
107	Real Total Wealth		$1,691,539	$1,717,133	$1,742,446	$1,767,463	$1,792,176	$1,816,576	$1,840,653	$1,864,410	$1,887,843	$1,910,957
108												
109	Social Security Benefit Level		$34,368	$35,090	$35,827	$36,579	$37,347	$38,131	$38,932	$39,750	$40,584
110	Federal Income Tax Bracket 1 Cutoff	$7,550	$7,709	$7,870	$8,036	$8,204	$8,377	$8,553	$8,732	$8,916	$9,103
111	Federal Income Tax Bracket 2 Cutoff	$30,650	$31,294	$31,951	$32,622	$33,307	$34,006	$34,720	$35,450	$36,194	$36,954
112	Federal Income Tax Bracket 3 Cutoff	$74,200	$75,758	$77,349	$78,973	$80,632	$82,325	$84,054	$85,819	$87,621	$89,461
113	Federal Income Tax Bracket 4 Cutoff	$154,800	$158,051	$161,370	$164,759	$168,219	$171,751	$175,358	$179,040	$182,800	$186,639
114	Federal Income Tax Bracket 5 Cutoff	$336,550	$343,618	$350,834	$358,201	$365,723	$373,403	$381,245	$389,251	$397,425	$405,771
115	Federal FICA-SSI Wage Cap	$97,500	$99,548	$101,638	$103,772	$105,952	$108,177	$110,448	$112,768	$115,136	$117,554

(23) Real Variables = (Nominal Variables) / ((1 + Inflation Rate) ^ Number of periods)
Enter =B99/((1+$B$6)^B29) and copy to the range B105:BT107

(24) Nominal Variable (t-1) * (1 + Inflation Rate)
Enter =C109*(1+$B$6) and copy across.
Then copy it to the range C110:BT115.

FIGURE 11.6 Transition From Working To Retirement Years.

	A	AN	AO	AP	AQ	AR
29	Date	38	39	40	41	42
30	Age	68	69	70	71	72
31	**Choice Variables**					
32	Real Growth Rate in Salary	2.0%	2.0%	2.0%	-100.0%	0.0%
33	Asset Allocation: Stock Port %	100.0%	100.0%	100.0%	50.0%	50.0%
34	Beginning Consumption Rate					
35	Higher Consump Rate in Work Yrs To Match Social Sec in Retire Yrs					
36	Long-Run Consumption Rate					
37	Taxable Income / Total Wealth	6.8%	6.9%	7.0%	4.5%	4.5%
38	**Outputs**					
39	Nominal Riskfree Rate					
40	Nominal Return on Stock Port	8.23%	8.23%	8.23%	8.23%	8.22%
41	Nominal Return on Retirement Fund	8.23%	8.23%	8.23%	6.59%	6.59%
42						
70						
71	Age	68	69	70	71	72
72	Salary	$359,128	$374,003	$389,494	$0	$0
73	Retire. Fund Contribution (Withdrawl)	-$15,466	-$19,060	-$23,015	-$274,181	-$279,940
74	Taxable Income	$374,594	$393,063	$412,509	$274,181	$279,940
75	Less Taxes	$123,841	$130,364	$137,242	$71,706	$73,212
76	After-Tax Income	$250,753	$262,698	$275,267	$202,475	$206,727
77	Plus Social Security Benefits	$0	$0	$0	$78,919	$80,577
78	Consumption	$250,753	$262,698	$275,267	$281,395	$287,304
79						
80	Savings / Salary (%)	-4.3%	-5.1%	-5.9%	0.0%	0.0%
81						
97						
98	Age	68	69	70	71	72
99	Human Capital	$456,816	$238,798	$0	$0	$0
100	Financial Capital	$5,247,985	$5,660,592	$6,103,227	$6,231,408	$6,362,232
101	Total Wealth	$5,704,801	$5,899,390	$6,103,227	$6,231,408	$6,362,232
102						
103	Real Salary	$163,031	$166,292	$169,618	$0	$0
104	Real Consumption	$113,833	$116,803	$119,874	$120,022	$120,022
105	Real Human Capital	$207,378	$106,176	$0	$0	$0
106	Real Financial Capital	$2,382,398	$2,516,853	$2,657,846	$2,657,852	$2,657,837
107	Real Total Wealth	$2,589,777	$2,623,029	$2,657,846	$2,657,852	$2,657,837
108						
109	Social Security Benefit Level	$74,149	$75,706	$77,296	$78,919	$80,577
110	Federal Income Tax Bracket 1 Cutoff	$16,631	$16,981	$17,337	$17,701	$18,073
111	Federal Income Tax Bracket 2 Cutoff	$67,516	$68,934	$70,382	$71,860	$73,369
112	Federal Income Tax Bracket 3 Cutoff	$163,449	$166,881	$170,386	$173,964	$177,617
113	Federal Income Tax Bracket 4 Cutoff	$340,996	$348,157	$355,468	$362,933	$370,555
114	Federal Income Tax Bracket 5 Cutoff	$741,358	$756,926	$772,822	$789,051	$805,621
115	Federal FICA-SSI Wage Cap	$214,775	$219,285	$223,890	$228,591	$233,392

As you adapt this model to your own situation, it is not necessary to go from full-time work to zero work. You could consider retiring to part-time work and then gradually tapering off. For example, you could drop to half-time work by setting your Real Growth in Salary to **-50%** in your first retirement year and then set your Real Growth in Salary to **-100.0%** in the year that you stop working entirely.

It is assumed that the Real Return on Broad Stock Portfolio is normally distributed with the average return given in cell **B7** and the standard deviation given in cell **B8**. The Excel function **RAND()** generates a random variable with a uniform distribution over the interval from 0 to 1 (that is, with an equal chance of getting any number between 0 and 1). To transform this uniformly distributed random variable into a normally distributed one, just place **RAND()** inside the Excel function **NORMINV**.[5]

The Human Capital computation make a fairly rough adjustment for taxes, but the year-by-year cash flow analysis has a more sophisticated calculation of taxes. The reason for doing it this way (as opposed to present valuing the After-Tax Income row) is that this approach avoids generating circular references

It doesn't make any sense to live like a king in your working years and then live in poverty in your retirement years. Similarly, it doesn't make sense to live in poverty in your working years and live like a king in your retirement years. The key idea is that you want to have a smooth pattern of real consumption over the life-cycle. Setting Taxable Income as a percentage of Total Wealth does a good job of delivering a smooth pattern. The only tricky part is when social security kicks in. Looking at the graph of Real Consumption, you should see a smooth pattern with no jump up or down at your retirement date. Notice that Taxable Income / Total Wealth is 7.0% in cell **AP37** and 4.5% the next year in cell **AQ37**, which is an adjustment of 2.5%. In other words, the drop in Taxable Income is offset by addition of Social Security Benefits (which are NOT taxable). Notice that Real Consumption transitions smoothly from $119,874 in cell **AP104** to $120,022 in cell **AQ104**. The Higher Consumption in Working Years of 2.5% in cell **B35** works well for the default input values of this Excel model. When you change input values, you may need to change the adjustment. Manually adjust the value in cell **B35** in small increments until the graph of Real Consumption shows a smooth pattern with no jump at the retirement date.

---

[5] The "Transformation Method" for converting a uniform random variable x into some other random variable y based on a cumulative distribution F is $y(x) = F^{-1}(x)$. See Press, W., B. Flannery, S. Teukolsky, and W. Vetterling, 1987, *Numerical Recopies: The Art of Scientific Computing*, Cambridge University Press, chapter on Random Numbers, subsection on the Transformation Method, page 201.

Since the standard deviation (risk) in cell **B8** is virtually zero, the results we see in the two graphs are based on *average returns*. Starting with the second graph, we see that Real Human Capital starts at $1.7 million and declines smoothly to $0 at retirement. Real Financial Capital starts at $0, rises smoothly to $2.7 million at retirement, and then stays constant at that level. Turning to the first graph, Real Consumption starts at $33,234, rises smoothly to $120,022 at retirement, and then stays constant at that level.

How much saving does it take to reach such a comfortable lifestyle? Savings starts at 36.6% of salary at age 31 and gradually tapers off. Clearly, a lot of saving is required to live so well in retirement.

Now let's consider the risk involved. Change the standard deviation to a realistic figure. Enter **17.000%** in cell **B8**. The random variables in rows **40** and **41** spring to life and the graph of real consumption over the life-cycle reflect the high or low realizations of the broad stock portfolio. Press the function key **F9** and the Excel model is recalculated. You see a new realization of real consumption on the first graph. The three figures below show: (a) a low real consumption case due to low stock returns, (b) a medium real consumption case due to medium stock returns, and (c) a high real consumption case due to high stock returns.

FIGURE 11.7 Low Real Consumption Due To Low Stock Returns.

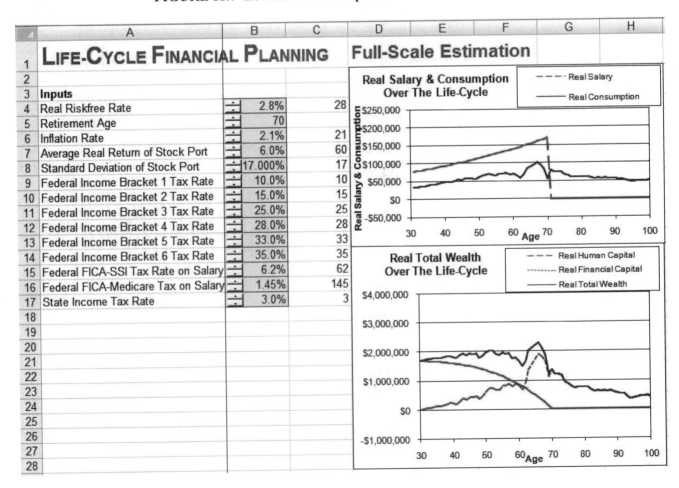

FIGURE 11.8 Medium Real Consumption Due To Medium Stock Returns.

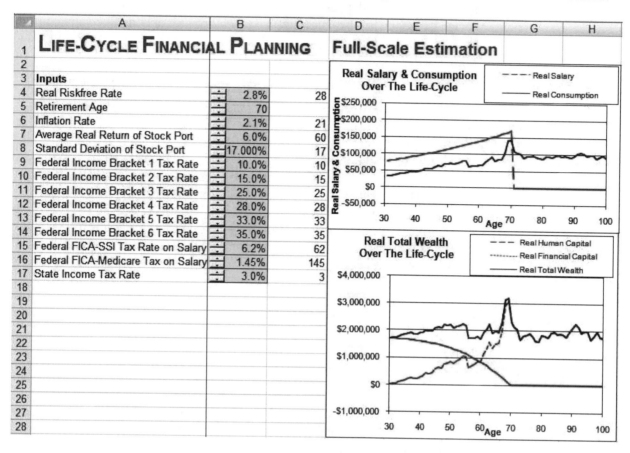

FIGURE 11.9 High Real Consumption Due To High Stock Returns.

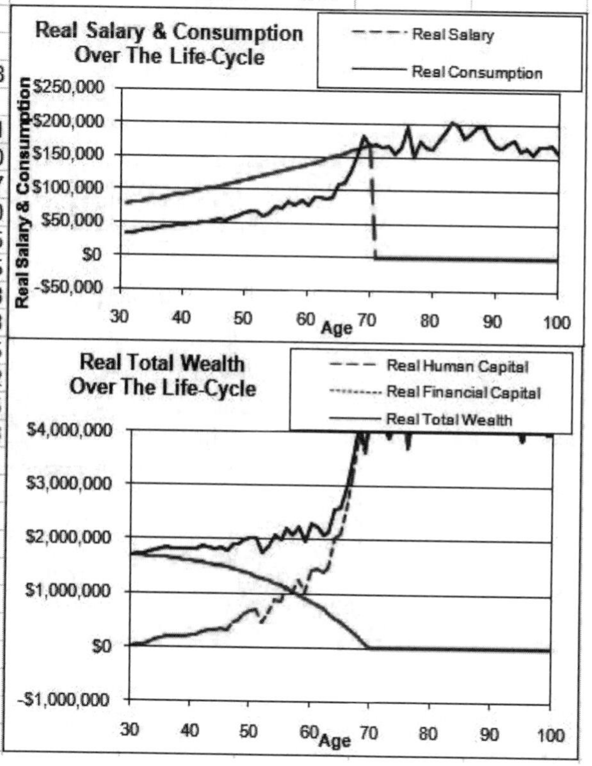

These three graphs are "representative" of the risk you face from being heavily invested in the broad stock portfolio. In the low case, real consumption drops to about $50,000. In the medium case, real consumption fluctuates around $100,000. In the high case, real consumption fluctuates between $150,000 and $200,000. Clearly, there is substantial risk from being so heavily exposed to the broad stock portfolio.

Now that we have completed the Excel model, it is time for you to explore. Click on the spin buttons to change the inputs and/or edit the values of the choice variables and see the implications for lifetime real consumption and real total wealth. For example, if you are uncomfortable with the amount of risk implied by the three figures above, consider more conservative strategies. Many investors reduce stock exposure in retirement years to little or nothing.

A key driver in the model is the Beginning Consumption Rate in cell **B34**. Raise this value and there will be more real consumption in early working years and less real consumption in retirement years. Lower this value and it will tilt in the opposite direction.

Play around with the choice variables and have fun exploring your lifetime opportunities. Enjoy!

Problems

1. Suppose that you are currently 28 years old and expect to earn a constant real salary of $64,000 starting next year. You are planning to work for 32 years and then retire. You currently have $0 in financial capital. You are limited to investing in the riskfree asset. The real riskfree rate is 2.8%. Develop a financial plan for real savings and real consumption over your lifetime.

2. Suppose that you are currently 32 years old and expect to earn a constant real salary of $85,000 starting next year. You are planning to work for 25 years and then retire. You currently have $10,000 in financial capital. You can invest in the riskfree asset or a broad stock portfolio. The inflation rate is 3.4% and the real riskfree rate is 2.5%. A broad stock portfolio offers an average real return of 7.3% and a standard deviation of 25.0%. Suppose that federal income taxes have six brackets with the following rates: 10.0%, 15.0%, 27.0%, 30.0%, 35.0%, and 38.6%. For current year, the upper cutoffs on the first five brackets are $6,000, $27,950, $67,700, $141,250, and $307,050 and these cutoffs are indexed to inflation. The state tax rate is 4.5%, federal FICA-SSI tax rate on salary up to $87,000 is 6.2%, and the federal FICA-Medicare tax rate on any level of salary is 1.45%. You will start receiving social security benefits at age 66. The current level of social security benefits is $24,204 per year and this is indexed to inflation. Develop a financial plan for real savings and real consumption over your lifetime.

PART 5 INTERNATIONAL INVESTMENTS

Chapter 12 International Parity

12.1 System of Four Parity Conditions

Problem. Suppose the Euro/Dollar Exchange Rate is €1 = $1.3640, the annual US riskfree rate is 4.47%, the US inflation rate is 2.69%, and the annual Eurozone riskfree rate is 4.27%. What is the one-year Forward Euro/Dollar Exchange Rate, the one-year ahead Expected Spot Euro/Dollar Exchange Rate, and Eurozone inflation rate? What is the Percent Difference in:

- the Eurozone Riskfree Rate vs. US Riskfree Rate,
- the Forward Euro/Dollar Exchange Rate vs. the Spot Rate,
- the Expected Spot Euro/Dollar Exchange Rate vs. the Spot Rate, and
- the Eurozone Inflation Rate vs. the US Inflation Rate?

Solution Strategy. Use Interest Rate Parity to determine the one-year Forward Euro/Dollar Exchange Rate. Then use the Expectations Theory of Exchange Rates to determine the one-year ahead Expected Spot Euro/Dollar Exchange Rate. Then use Purchase Power Parity to determine the Eurozone inflation rate. Finally, the International Fisher Effect to confirm the Eurozone riskfree rate. Compute the four percent differences. Under the four international parity condition, the four percent differences should be identical.

FIGURE 12.1 International Parity – System of Four Parity Conditions.

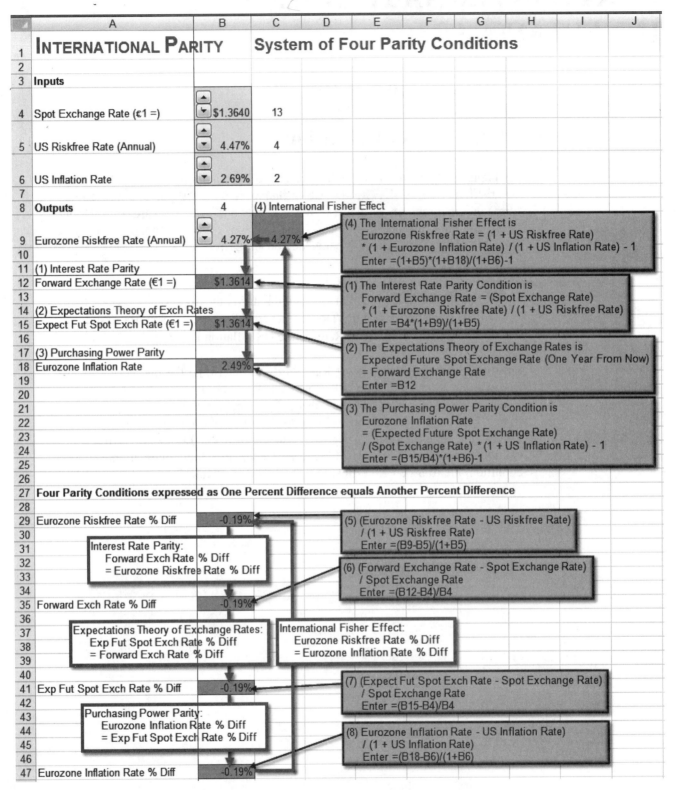

In theory, the four international parity conditions are tightly connected to each other.

12.2 Estimating Future Exchange Rates

Problem. Suppose the Euro/Dollar Exchange Rate is €1 = $1.3640, the annual US riskfree rate is 4.47%, the US inflation rate is 2.69%, the annual Eurozone riskfree rate is 4.27%, the Eurozone inflation rate is 1.90%, and the one-year Forward Euro/Dollar Exchange Rate is €1 = $1.3739. What will the Euro/Dollar Exchange Rate be in one-year, two-years, three-years, four-years, and five-years?

FIGURE 12.2 International Parity – Estimating Future Exchange Rates.

	A	B	C	D	E	F	G	H	I	J
50	**INTERNATIONAL PARITY**		**Estimating Future Exchange Rates**							
51										
52	**Inputs**									
53	Spot Exchange Rate (€1 =)	$1.3460								
54	US Riskfree Rate (Annual)	4.47%								
55	US Inflation Rate	2.69%								
56	Eurozone Riskfree Rate (Annual)	4.27%								
57	Eurozone Inflation Rate	1.90%								
58	Forward Exchange Rate (€1 =)	$1.3739								
59										
...										
79	**Outputs**									
80	Years	0	1	2	3	4	5			
81	Method 1 = Purchasing Power Parity									
82	Eurozone Inflation Rate % Diff	-0.77%								
83	Exp Fut Spot Exch Rates (€1 =)	$1.3460	$1.3356	$1.3254	$1.3152	$1.3051	$1.2950			
84										
85	Method 2 = Interest Rate Parity + Expectations Theory of Exchange Rates									
86	Eurozone Riskfree Rate % Diff	-0.19%								
87	Forward Exchange Rate (€1 =)	$1.3460	1.3434	1.3409	1.3383	1.3357	1.3332			
88	Exp Fut Spot Exch Rates (€1 =)	$1.3460	$1.3434	$1.3409	$1.3383	$1.3357	$1.3332			
89										
90	Method 3 = Expectations Theory of Exchange Rates									
91	Forward Exch Rate % Diff	2.07%								
92	Exp Fut Spot Exch Rates (€1 =)	$1.3460	$1.3739	$1.4024	$1.4314	$1.4611	$1.4914			

Chart title: **Estimating Future Exchange Rates**

Y-axis: $1.2500, $1.3000, $1.3500, $1.4000, $1.4500, $1.5000, $1.5500

X-axis: 0, 2, 4, 6

Legend:
- Method 1 = Purchasing Power Parity
- Method 2 = Interest Rate Parity + Expectations Theory of Exchange Rates
- Method 3 = Expectations Theory of Exchange Rates

Annotations:

(9) (Eurozone Inflation Rate - US Inflation Rate) / (1 + US Inflation Rate) Enter =(B57-B55)/(1+B55)

(10) Exp Fut Spot Exch Rate (t-1) * (1 + Eurozone Inflation Rate % Diff) Enter =B83*(1+$B$82) and copy across

(11) (Eurozone Riskfree Rate - US Riskfree Rate) / (1 + US Riskfree Rate) Enter =(B56-B54)/(1+B54)

(12) Exp Fut Spot Exch Rate (t-1) * (1 + Eurozone Riskfree Rate % Diff) Enter =B87*(1+$B$86) and copy across

(13) Expected Future Spot Exchange Rate (t) = Forward Exchange Rate for Year (t) Enter =C87 and copy across

(14) (Forward Exchange Rate - Spot Exchange Rate) / Spot Exchange Rate Enter =(B58-B53)/B53

(15) Exp Fut Spot Exch Rate (t-1) * (1 + Forward Exch Rate % Diff) Enter =B92*(1+$B$91) and copy across

Solution. Use three different methods for forecast future exchange rates: (1) Purchasing Power Parity, (2) Interest Rate Parity + Expectations Theory of Exchange Rates, (3) Only the Expectations Theory of Exchange Rates.

In practice, when you use real data, the various international parity conditions yield very different forecasts of future exchange rates.

Problems

1. Suppose the Euro/Dollar Exchange Rate is €1 = $1.283, the annual US riskfree rate is 3.61%, the US inflation rate is 2.69%, and the annual Eurozone riskfree rate is 5.39%. What is the one-year Forward Euro/Dollar Exchange Rate, the one-year ahead Expected Spot Euro/Dollar Exchange Rate, and Eurozone inflation rate? What is the Percent Difference in:
   - the Eurozone Riskfree Rate vs. US Riskfree Rate,
   - the Forward Euro/Dollar Exchange Rate vs. the Spot Rate,
   - the Expected Spot Euro/Dollar Exchange Rate vs. the Spot Rate, and
   - the Eurozone Inflation Rate vs. the US Inflation Rate?

2. Suppose the Euro/Dollar Exchange Rate is €1 = $1.7271, the annual US riskfree rate is 6.31%, the US inflation rate is 4.52%, the annual Eurozone riskfree rate is 3.15%, the Eurozone inflation rate is 3.15%, and the one-year Forward Euro/Dollar Exchange Rate is €1 = $1.8241. What will the Euro/Dollar Exchange Rate be in one-year, two-years, three-years, four-years, and five-years under three forecast methods: (1) purchasing power parity, (2) interest rate parity + expectations theory of exchange rates, and (3) using just the expectations theory of exchange rates?

Chapter 13 Swaps

13.1 Valuation of Interest Rate Swaps

Problem. A particular interest rate swap involves one party paying a fixed rate of 4.13% on a notional principal of $63 million to a second party and that party paying a floating rate LIBOR on the same notional amount. On the prior payment date, LIBOR was 3.27%. There is 0.41 years until the next payment date and over the remaining life of the swap an additional six payments will be made every six months thereafter. LIBOR rates with maturities corresponding to the seven remaining payment dates are: 3.32%, 3.42%, 3.49%, 3.55%, 3.61%, 3.67%, and 3.74%, respectively. What is the value of the interest rate swap to the party that receives the fixed-rate payment and pays the floating-rate payment? What is the value of the same interest rate swap to the party that receives floating and pays fixed?

Solution Strategy. There are two methods for valuing an interest rate swap. The first method values a fixed-rate bond, values a floating-rate bond, and then takes the difference. The second method treats the swap as a portfolio of forward rate agreements by computing the net interest payment on each date and then discounts them back to the present.

FIGURE 13.1 Excel Model for the Valuation of Interest Rate Swaps.

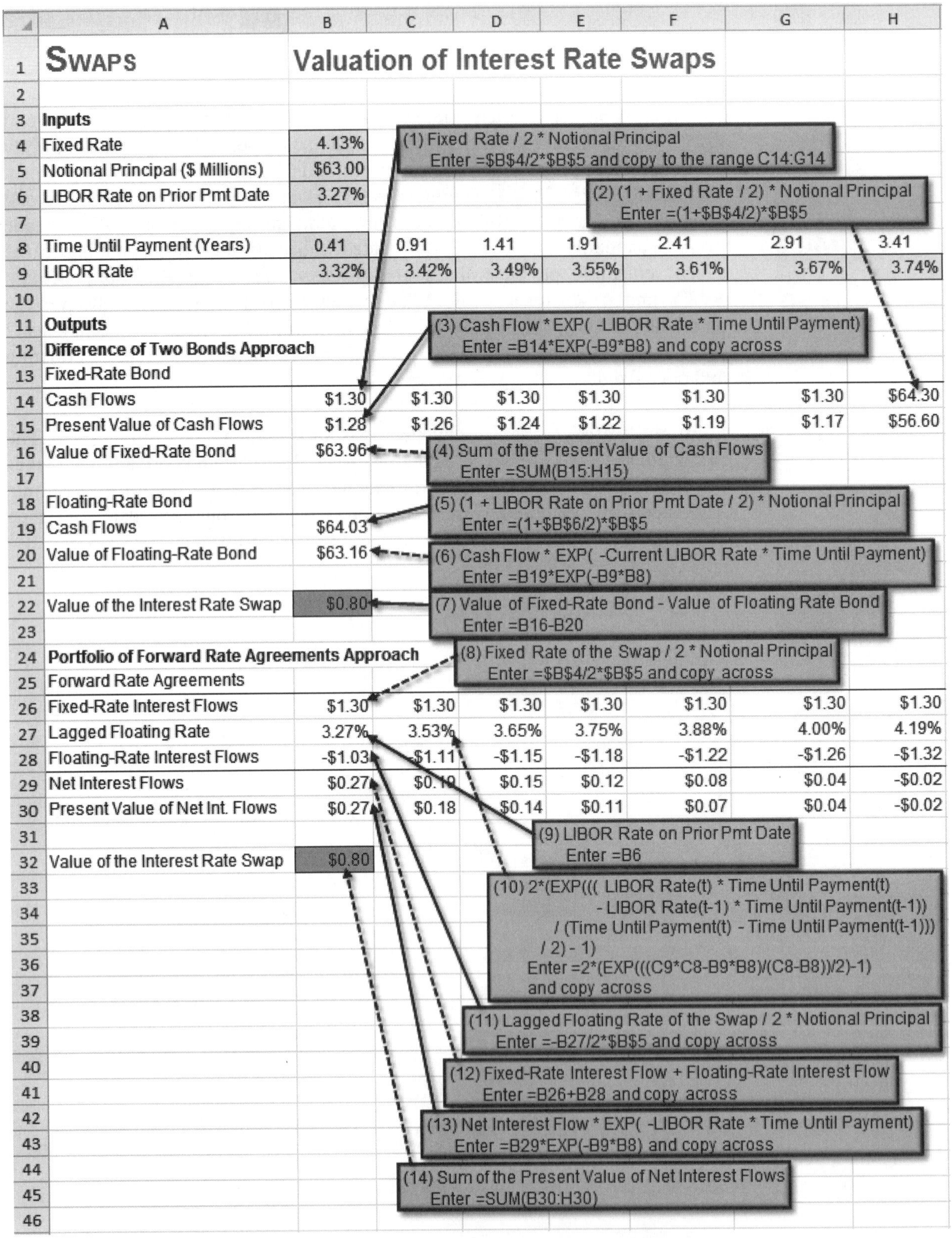

▲	A	B	C	D	E	F	G	H
1	SWAPS	Valuation of Interest Rate Swaps						
2								
3	**Inputs**							
4	Fixed Rate	4.13%						
5	Notional Principal ($ Millions)	$63.00						
6	LIBOR Rate on Prior Pmt Date	3.27%						
7								
8	Time Until Payment (Years)	0.41	0.91	1.41	1.91	2.41	2.91	3.41
9	LIBOR Rate	3.32%	3.42%	3.49%	3.55%	3.61%	3.67%	3.74%
10								
11	**Outputs**							
12	**Difference of Two Bonds Approach**							
13	Fixed-Rate Bond							
14	Cash Flows	$1.30	$1.30	$1.30	$1.30	$1.30	$1.30	$64.30
15	Present Value of Cash Flows	$1.28	$1.26	$1.24	$1.22	$1.19	$1.17	$56.60
16	Value of Fixed-Rate Bond	$63.96						
17								
18	Floating-Rate Bond							
19	Cash Flows	$64.03						
20	Value of Floating-Rate Bond	$63.16						
21								
22	Value of the Interest Rate Swap	$0.80						
23								
24	**Portfolio of Forward Rate Agreements Approach**							
25	Forward Rate Agreements							
26	Fixed-Rate Interest Flows	$1.30	$1.30	$1.30	$1.30	$1.30	$1.30	$1.30
27	Lagged Floating Rate	3.27%	3.53%	3.65%	3.75%	3.88%	4.00%	4.19%
28	Floating-Rate Interest Flows	-$1.03	-$1.11	-$1.15	-$1.18	-$1.22	-$1.26	-$1.32
29	Net Interest Flows	$0.27	$0.19	$0.15	$0.12	$0.08	$0.04	-$0.02
30	Present Value of Net Int. Flows	$0.27	$0.18	$0.14	$0.11	$0.07	$0.04	-$0.02
31								
32	Value of the Interest Rate Swap	$0.80						
33								
34								
35								
36								
37								
38								
39								
40								
41								
42								
43								
44								
45								
46								

Callout annotations:

(1) Fixed Rate / 2 * Notional Principal
Enter =$B$4/2*$B$5 and copy to the range C14:G14

(2) (1 + Fixed Rate / 2) * Notional Principal
Enter =(1+$B$4/2)*$B$5

(3) Cash Flow * EXP(-LIBOR Rate * Time Until Payment)
Enter =B14*EXP(-B9*B8) and copy across

(4) Sum of the Present Value of Cash Flows
Enter =SUM(B15:H15)

(5) (1 + LIBOR Rate on Prior Pmt Date / 2) * Notional Principal
Enter =(1+$B$6/2)*$B$5

(6) Cash Flow * EXP(-Current LIBOR Rate * Time Until Payment)
Enter =B19*EXP(-B9*B8)

(7) Value of Fixed-Rate Bond - Value of Floating Rate Bond
Enter =B16-B20

(8) Fixed Rate of the Swap / 2 * Notional Principal
Enter =$B$4/2*$B$5 and copy across

(9) LIBOR Rate on Prior Pmt Date
Enter =B6

(10) 2*(EXP(((LIBOR Rate(t) * Time Until Payment(t)
      - LIBOR Rate(t-1) * Time Until Payment(t-1))
      / (Time Until Payment(t) - Time Until Payment(t-1)))
      / 2) - 1)
Enter =2*(EXP(((C9*C8-B9*B8)/(C8-B8))/2)-1)
and copy across

(11) Lagged Floating Rate of the Swap / 2 * Notional Principal
Enter =-B27/2*$B$5 and copy across

(12) Fixed-Rate Interest Flow + Floating-Rate Interest Flow
Enter =B26+B28 and copy across

(13) Net Interest Flow * EXP(-LIBOR Rate * Time Until Payment)
Enter =B29*EXP(-B9*B8) and copy across

(14) Sum of the Present Value of Net Interest Flows
Enter =SUM(B30:H30)

Both methods value the interest rate swap to the party that receives fixed and pays floating at $0.80. Since it is a zero-sum game, the value of the same swap to the party that receives floating and pays fixed is -$0.80.

13.2 Valuation of Currency Swaps

Problem. A particular currency swap involves one party paying a domestic rate of 2.10% on a domestic notional principal of $30 million to a second party and that party paying a foreign rate 4.32% on a foreign notional principal of €21 million. The spot exchange rate is $1.2363 per euro. There is 0.87 years until the next payment date and over the remaining life of the currency swap an additional five payments will be made every 12 months thereafter. Domestic discount rates with maturities corresponding to the six remaining payment dates are: 4.31%, 4.38%, 4.45%, 4.51%, 4.56%, and 4.62% respectively. Foreign discount rates with maturities corresponding to the six remaining payment dates are: 6.53%, 6.59%, 6.66%, 6.72%, 6.79%, and 6.83% respectively. What is the value of the currency swap to the party that receives the foreign payment and pays the domestic payment? What is the value of the same currency swap to the party that receives domestic and pays foreign?

FIGURE 13.2 Excel Model for the Valuation of Currency Swaps.

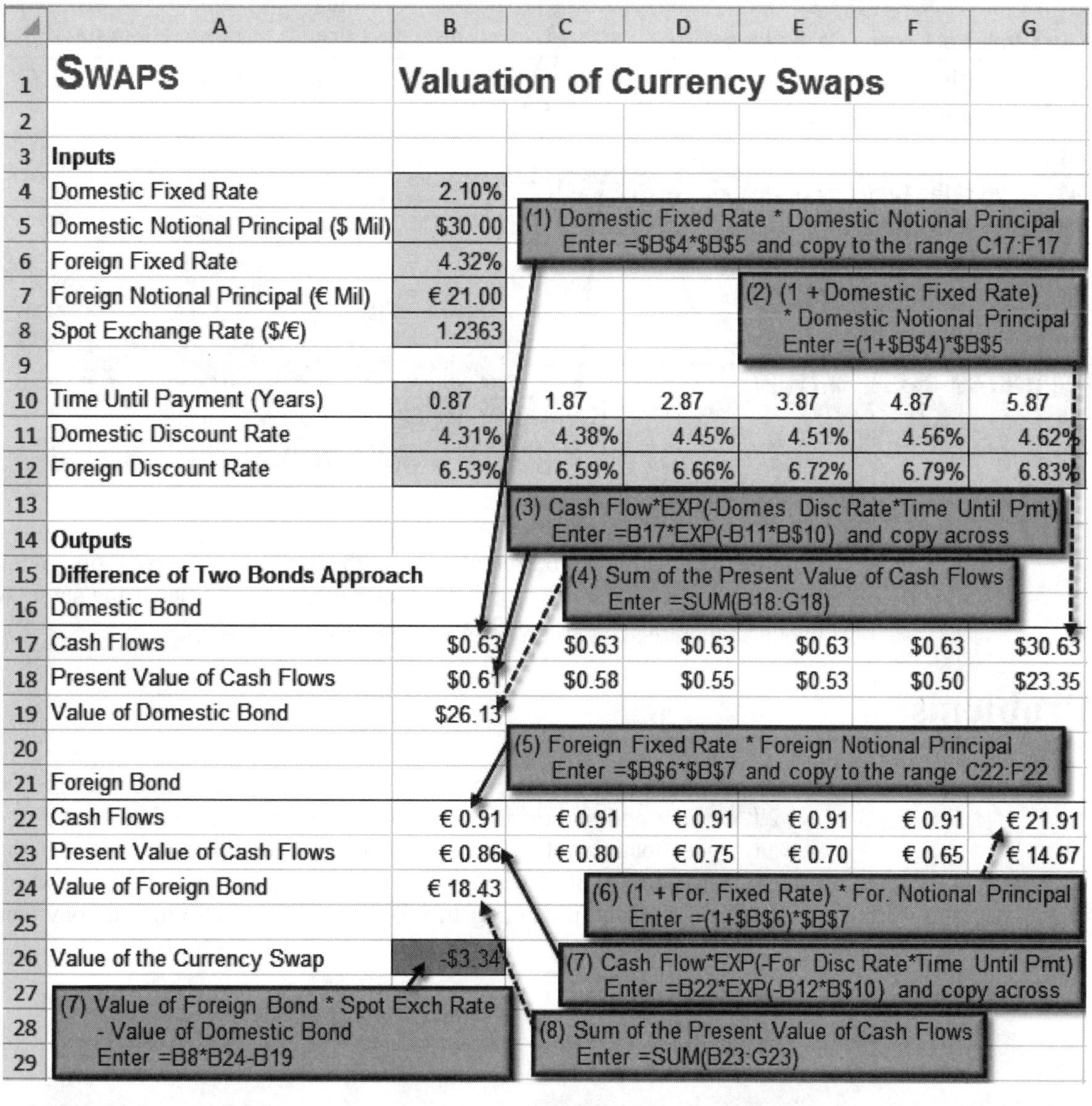

	A	B	C	D	E	F	G
1	**SWAPS**	**Valuation of Currency Swaps**					
2							
3	**Inputs**						
4	Domestic Fixed Rate	2.10%					
5	Domestic Notional Principal ($ Mil)	$30.00	(1) Domestic Fixed Rate * Domestic Notional Principal				
6	Foreign Fixed Rate	4.32%	Enter =$B$4*$B$5 and copy to the range C17:F17				
7	Foreign Notional Principal (€ Mil)	€ 21.00		(2) (1 + Domestic Fixed Rate)			
8	Spot Exchange Rate ($/€)	1.2363		* Domestic Notional Principal			
9				Enter =(1+$B$4)*$B$5			
10	Time Until Payment (Years)	0.87	1.87	2.87	3.87	4.87	5.87
11	Domestic Discount Rate	4.31%	4.38%	4.45%	4.51%	4.56%	4.62%
12	Foreign Discount Rate	6.53%	6.59%	6.66%	6.72%	6.79%	6.83%
13			(3) Cash Flow*EXP(-Domes Disc Rate*Time Until Pmt)				
14	**Outputs**		Enter =B17*EXP(-B11*B$10) and copy across				
15	**Difference of Two Bonds Approach**		(4) Sum of the Present Value of Cash Flows				
16	Domestic Bond		Enter =SUM(B18:G18)				
17	Cash Flows	$0.63	$0.63	$0.63	$0.63	$0.63	$30.63
18	Present Value of Cash Flows	$0.61	$0.58	$0.55	$0.53	$0.50	$23.35
19	Value of Domestic Bond	$26.13					
20			(5) Foreign Fixed Rate * Foreign Notional Principal				
21	Foreign Bond		Enter =$B$6*$B$7 and copy to the range C22:F22				
22	Cash Flows	€ 0.91	€ 0.91	€ 0.91	€ 0.91	€ 0.91	€ 21.91
23	Present Value of Cash Flows	€ 0.86	€ 0.80	€ 0.75	€ 0.70	€ 0.65	€ 14.67
24	Value of Foreign Bond	€ 18.43					
25				(6) (1 + For. Fixed Rate) * For. Notional Principal			
26	Value of the Currency Swap	-$3.34		Enter =(1+$B$6)*$B$7			
27	(7) Value of Foreign Bond * Spot Exch Rate		(7) Cash Flow*EXP(-For Disc Rate*Time Until Pmt)				
28	- Value of Domestic Bond		Enter =B22*EXP(-B12*B$10) and copy across				
29	Enter =B8*B24-B19		(8) Sum of the Present Value of Cash Flows				
			Enter =SUM(B23:G23)				

Solution Strategy. There are two methods for valuing a currency swap. The first method values a domestic bond, values a foreign bond, and then takes the difference in a common currency. The second method treats the swap as a portfolio of forwards by computing the net cash flows in a common currency on each date and then discounts them back to the present.

Note. The same two methods can be applied to value currency swaps involving domestic floating for foreign fixed, domestic fixed for foreign floating, and domestic floating for foreign floating.

FIGURE 13.3 Excel Model for the Valuation of Currency Swaps (Cont.).

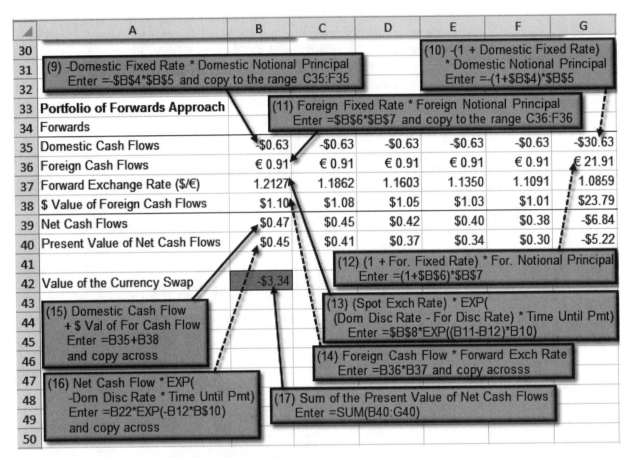

Both methods value the currency swap to the party that receives foreign and pays domestic at -$3.34. Since it is a zero-sum game, the value of the same swap to the party that receives domestic and pays foreign is $3.34.

Problems

1. A particular interest rate swap involves one party paying a fixed rate of 2.84% on a notional principal of $95 million to a second party and that party paying a floating rate LIBOR on the same notional amount. On the prior payment date, LIBOR was 2.16%. There is 0.34 years until the next payment date and over the remaining life of the swap an additional six payments will

be made every six months thereafter. LIBOR rates with maturities corresponding to the seven remaining payment dates are: 2.23%, 2.31%, 2.36%, 2.42%, 2.47%, 2.51%, and 2.56%, respectively. What is the value of the interest rate swap to the party that receives the fixed-rate payment and pays the floating-rate payment? What is the value of the same interest rate swap to the party that receives floating and pays fixed?

2. A particular currency swap involves one party paying a domestic rate of 3.45% on a domestic notional principal of $53 million to a second party and that party paying a foreign rate 5.79% on a foreign notional principal of €37 million. The spot exchange rate is $1.3842 per euro. There is 0.73 years until the next payment date and over the remaining life of the currency swap an additional five payments will be made every 12 months thereafter. Domestic discount rates with maturities corresponding to the six remaining payment dates are: 3.48%, 3.53%, 3.61%, 3.65%, 3.70 and 3.79% respectively. Foreign discount rates with maturities corresponding to the six remaining payment dates are: 5.83%, 5.88%, 5.93%, 5.96%, 6.04%, and 6.07% respectively. What is the value of the currency swap to the party that receives the foreign payment and pays the domestic payment? What is the value of the same currency swap to the party that receives domestic and pays foreign?

PART 6 OPTIONS, FUTURES, AND OTHER DERIVATIVES

Chapter 14 Option Payoffs and Profits

14.1 Basics

Problem. A call option has an exercise price of $40.00 and an option price of $5.00. A put option has the same exercise price and option price. Graph the option payoffs and profits for buying or selling a call option and for buying or selling a put option.

Solution Strategy. For a range of stock prices at maturity, calculate option payoffs and profits. Then graph it.

FIGURE 14.1 Excel Model of Option Payoffs and Profits - Basics.

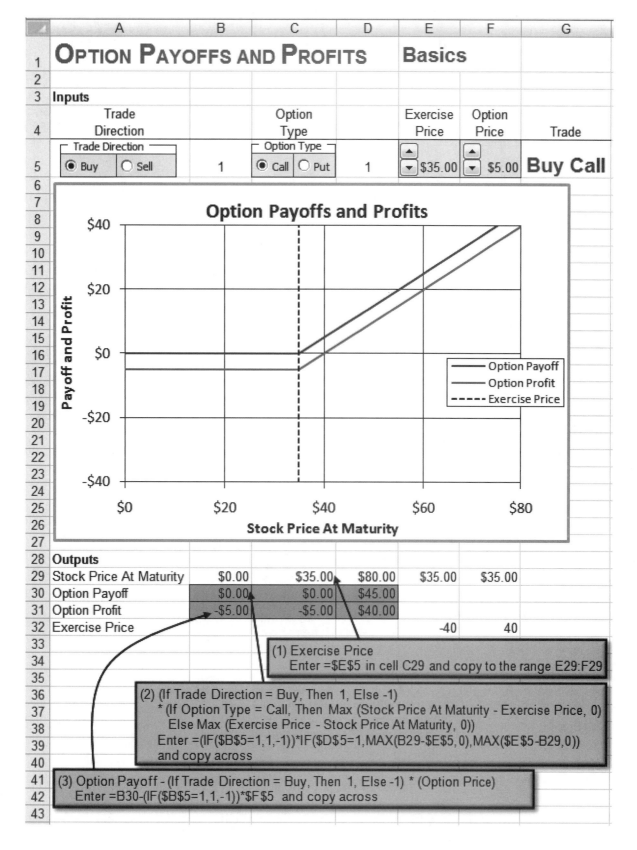

The graph displays the "hockey stick" payoffs and profits that characterize options. Click the option buttons to see all of possibilities.

FIGURE 14.2 Option Payoffs and Profits –Buy a Call and Sell a Call.

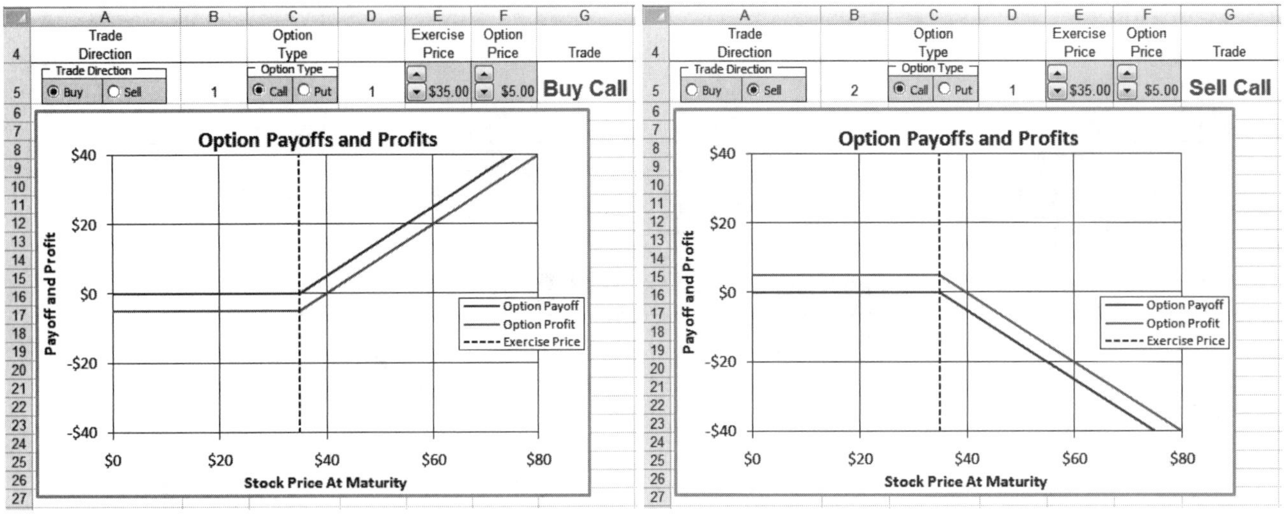

FIGURE 14.3 Option Payoffs and Profits –Buy a Put and Sell a Put.

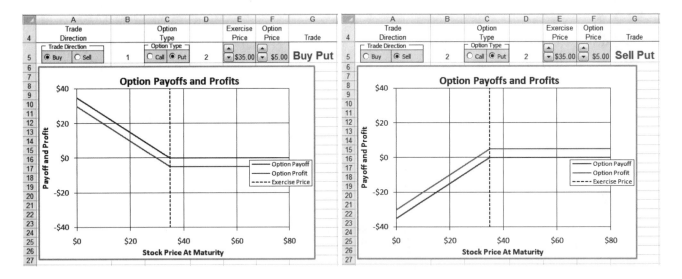

Problems

1. A call option has an exercise price of $32.54 and an option price of $4.71. A put option has the same exercise price and option price. Graph the option payoffs and profits for buying or selling a call option and for buying or selling a put option.

2. A call option has an exercise price of $18.23 and an option price of $2.96. A put option has the same exercise price and option price. Graph the option payoffs and profits for buying or selling a call option and for buying or selling a put option.

Chapter 15 Option Trading Strategies

15.1 Two Assets

Problem. There are three types of trading strategies involving options: (1) strategies involving a single option and a stock, (2) spreads involving options of one type (i.e., two or more calls or two or more puts), and (3) combinations involving both call(s) and put(s). Construct a chart that can show all of the trading strategies involving two assets.

FIGURE 15.1 Excel Model of Option Trading Strategies - Two Assets.

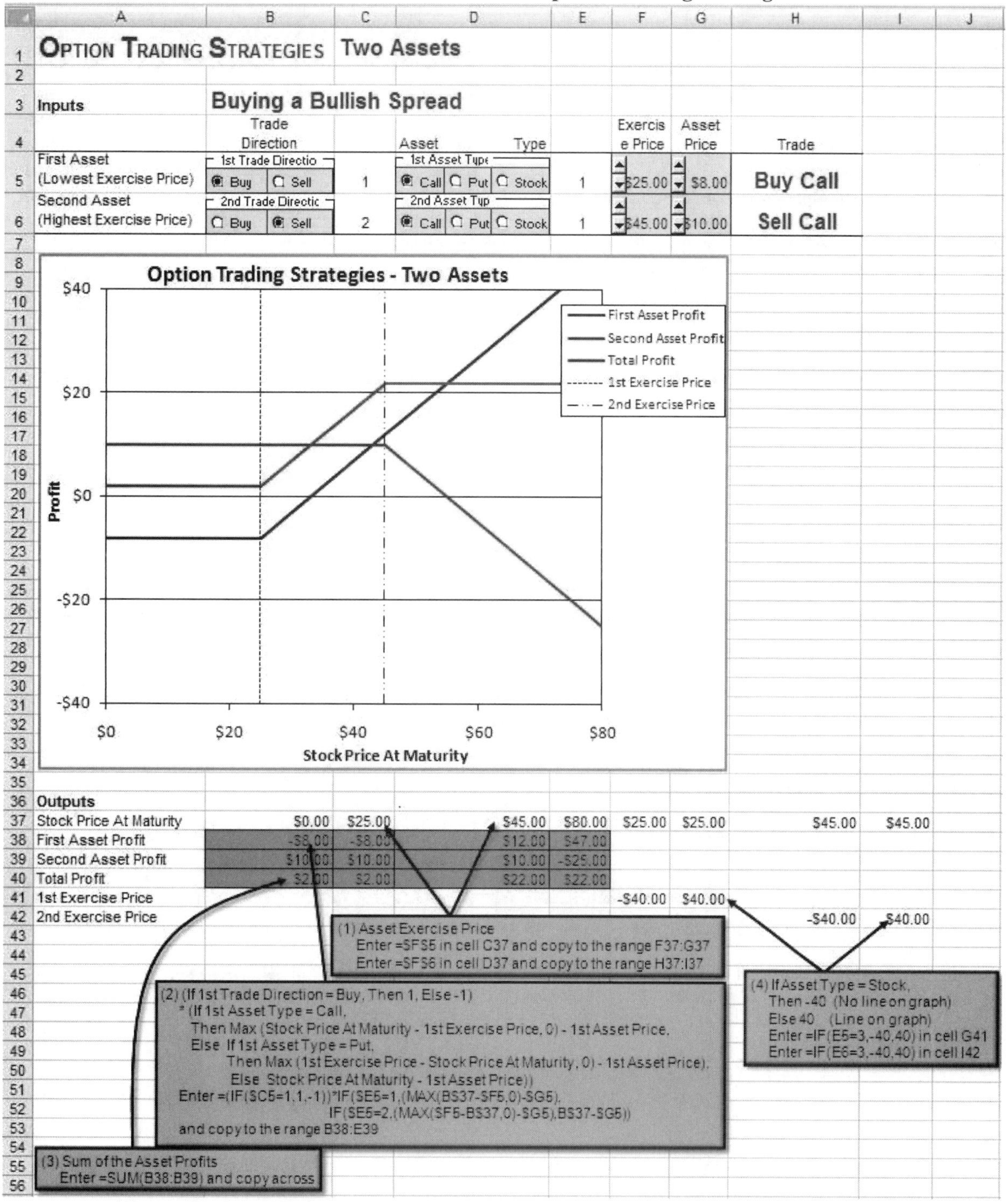

Solution Strategy. We will create ranges for first asset inputs and for second asset inputs. Then calculate first asset profit, second asset profit, total profit, exercise price lines, and graph them.

FIGURE 15.2 Table of Option Trading Strategies.

	J	K	L	M
4	Trades Listed From Asset 1 to Asset 2 (Lowest To Highest Exercise Price)			
5	Buy Call, Sell Call			
6				
7				
8	Test	Two-Asset Strategies	Description (Lowest To Highest Exercise Price)	Type
9	Yes	Buying a Bullish Spread	"Buy Call, Sell Call" or "Buy Put, Sell Put"	Spread
10	No	Buying a Bearish Spread	"Sell Call, Buy Call" or "Sell Put, Buy Put"	Spread
11	No	Buying a Straddle	"Buy Call, Buy Put" or "Buy Put, Buy Call" at the same exercise price	Combination
12	No	Writing a Straddle	"Sell Call, Sell Put" or "Sell Put, Sell Call" at the same exercise price	Combination
13	No	Buying a Strangle	"Buy Put, Buy Call"	Combination
14	No	Writing a Strangle	"Sell Put, Sell Call"	Combination
15	No	Buying a Covered Call	"Buy Stock, Sell Call" or "Sell Call, Buy Stock"	N.A.
16	No	Writing a Covered Call	"Sell Stock, Buy Call" or "Buy Call, Sell Stock"	N.A.
17	No	Buying a Protective Put	"Buy Stock, Buy Put" or "Buy Put, Buy Stock"	N.A.
18	No	Writing a Protective Put	"Sell Stock, Sell Put" or "Sell Put, Sell Stock"	N.A.
19	No	Other Strategies		
20				
21	Note: Writing a Bullish Spread = Buying a Bearish Spread			
22		Writing a Bearish Spread = Buying a Bullish Spread		

FIGURE 15.3 Buying a Bullish Spread using Calls and Buying a Bullish Spread using Puts.

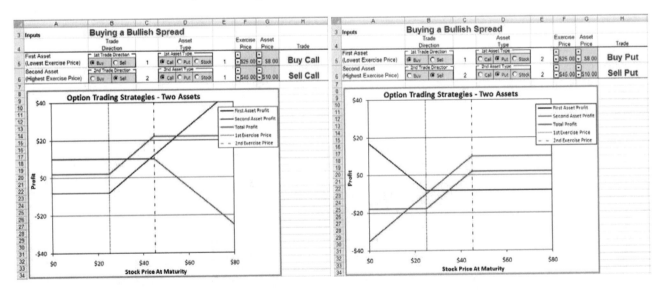

FIGURE 15.4 Buying a Bearish Spread using Calls and Buying a Bearish Spread using Puts.

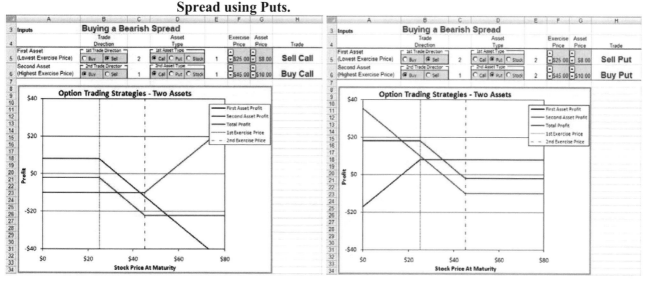

FIGURE 15.5 Buying a Straddle and Writing a Straddle.

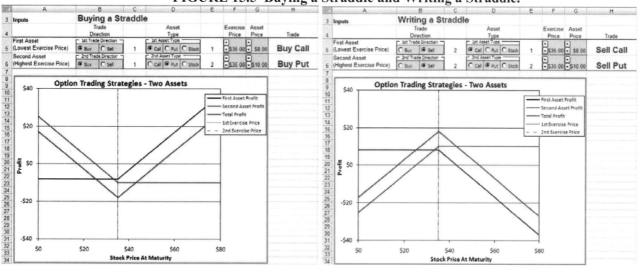

FIGURE 15.6 Buying a Strangle and Writing a Strangle.

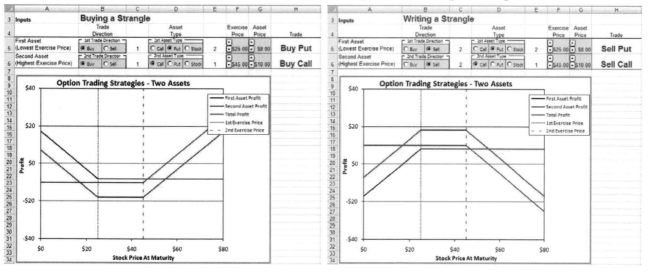

FIGURE 15.7 Buying a Covered Call and Writing a Covered Call.

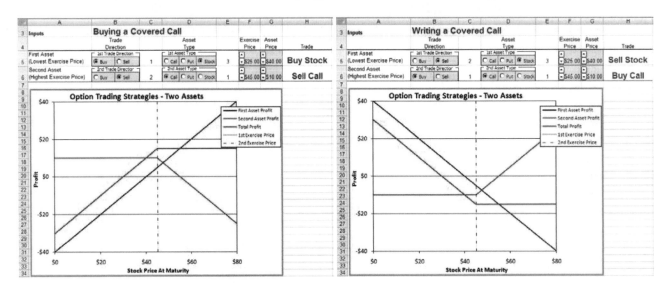

FIGURE 15.8 Buying a Protective Put and Writing a Protective Put.

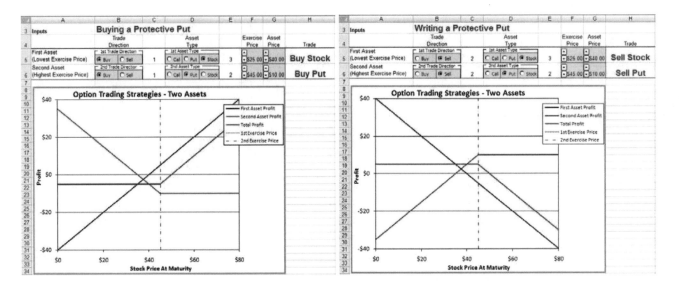

15.2 Four Assets

Problem. Construct a chart that can show the trading strategies which involve four assets.

Solution Strategy. We will expand the input ranges to include a place for third asset inputs and fourth asset inputs. Then expand the calculations to include third asset profit, fourth asset profit, total profit, exercise price lines, and graph them.

FIGURE 15.9 Excel Model of Option Trading Strategies - Four Assets.

	A	B	C	D	E	F	G	H
1	OPTION TRADING STRATEGIES Four Assets					Buying a Butterfly Spread		
2								
3	Inputs							
4		Trade Direction			Asset Type		Exercise Price	Asset Price	Trade
5	First Asset (Lowest Exercise Price)	1st Trade Direction ● Buy ○ Sell	1	1st Asset Type ● Call ○ Put ○ Stock	1	$25.00	$8.00	Buy Call
6	Second Asset (Med-Low Exercise Price)	2nd Trade Direction ○ Buy ● Sell	2	2nd Asset Type ● Call ○ Put ○ Stock	1	$35.00	$10.00	Sell Call
7	Third Asset (Med-High Exercise Price)	3rd Trade Direction ○ Buy ● Sell	2	3rd Asset Type ● Call ○ Put ○ Stock	1	$35.00	$4.00	Sell Call
8	Fourth Asset (Highest Exercise Price)	4th Trade Direction ● Buy ○ Sell	1	4th Asset Type ● Call ○ Put ○ Stock	1	$45.00	$10.00	Buy Call

Option Trading Strategies - Four Assets

Legend:
— First Asset Profit
— Second Asset Profit
— Third Asset Profit
— Fourth Asset Profit
— Total Profit
----- 1st Exercise Price
– – – 2nd Exercise Price
–·–· 3rd Exercise Price
–··– 4th Exercise Price

Y-axis: Profit ($40, $20, $0, -$20, -$40)
X-axis: Stock Price At Maturity ($0, $20, $40, $60, $80)

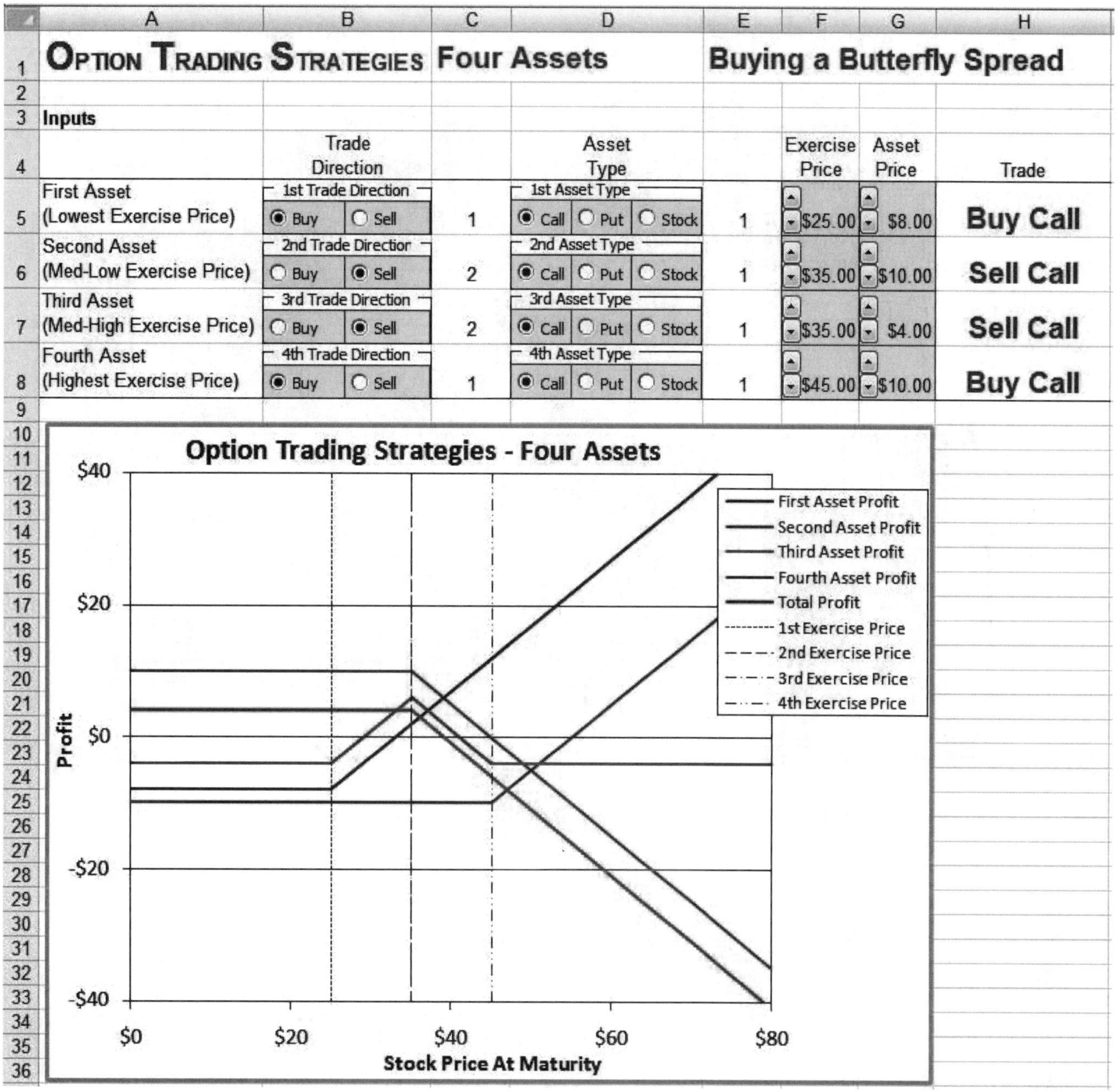

FIGURE 15.10 Excel Model of Option Trading Strategies - Four Assets.

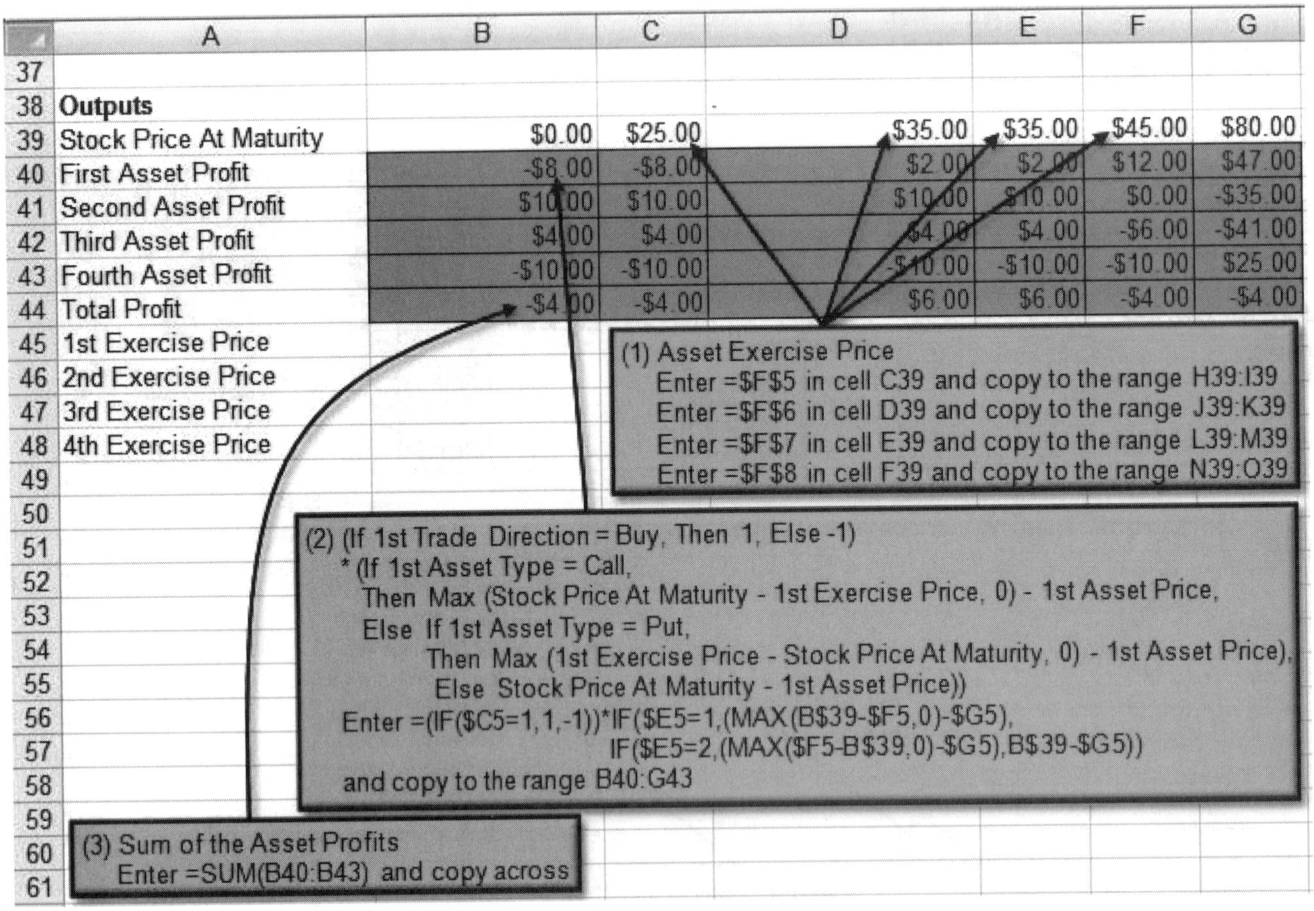

	A	B	C	D	E	F	G
37							
38	**Outputs**						
39	Stock Price At Maturity	$0.00	$25.00	$35.00	$35.00	$45.00	$80.00
40	First Asset Profit	-$8.00	-$8.00	$2.00	$2.00	$12.00	$47.00
41	Second Asset Profit	$10.00	$10.00	$10.00	$10.00	$0.00	-$35.00
42	Third Asset Profit	$4.00	$4.00	$4.00	$4.00	-$6.00	-$41.00
43	Fourth Asset Profit	-$10.00	-$10.00	-$10.00	-$10.00	-$10.00	$25.00
44	Total Profit	-$4.00	-$4.00	$6.00	$6.00	-$4.00	-$4.00
45	1st Exercise Price						
46	2nd Exercise Price						
47	3rd Exercise Price						
48	4th Exercise Price						
49							

(1) Asset Exercise Price
  Enter =$F$5 in cell C39 and copy to the range H39:I39
  Enter =$F$6 in cell D39 and copy to the range J39:K39
  Enter =$F$7 in cell E39 and copy to the range L39:M39
  Enter =$F$8 in cell F39 and copy to the range N39:O39

(2) (If 1st Trade Direction = Buy, Then 1, Else -1)
  * (If 1st Asset Type = Call,
    Then Max (Stock Price At Maturity - 1st Exercise Price, 0) - 1st Asset Price,
    Else If 1st Asset Type = Put,
      Then Max (1st Exercise Price - Stock Price At Maturity, 0) - 1st Asset Price),
      Else Stock Price At Maturity - 1st Asset Price))
  Enter =(IF($C5=1,1,-1))*IF($E5=1,(MAX(B$39-$F5,0)-$G5),
                    IF($E5=2,(MAX($F5-B$39,0)-$G5),B$39-$G5))
  and copy to the range B40:G43

(3) Sum of the Asset Profits
  Enter =SUM(B40:B43) and copy across

FIGURE 15.11 Excel Model of Option Trading Strategies - Four Assets.

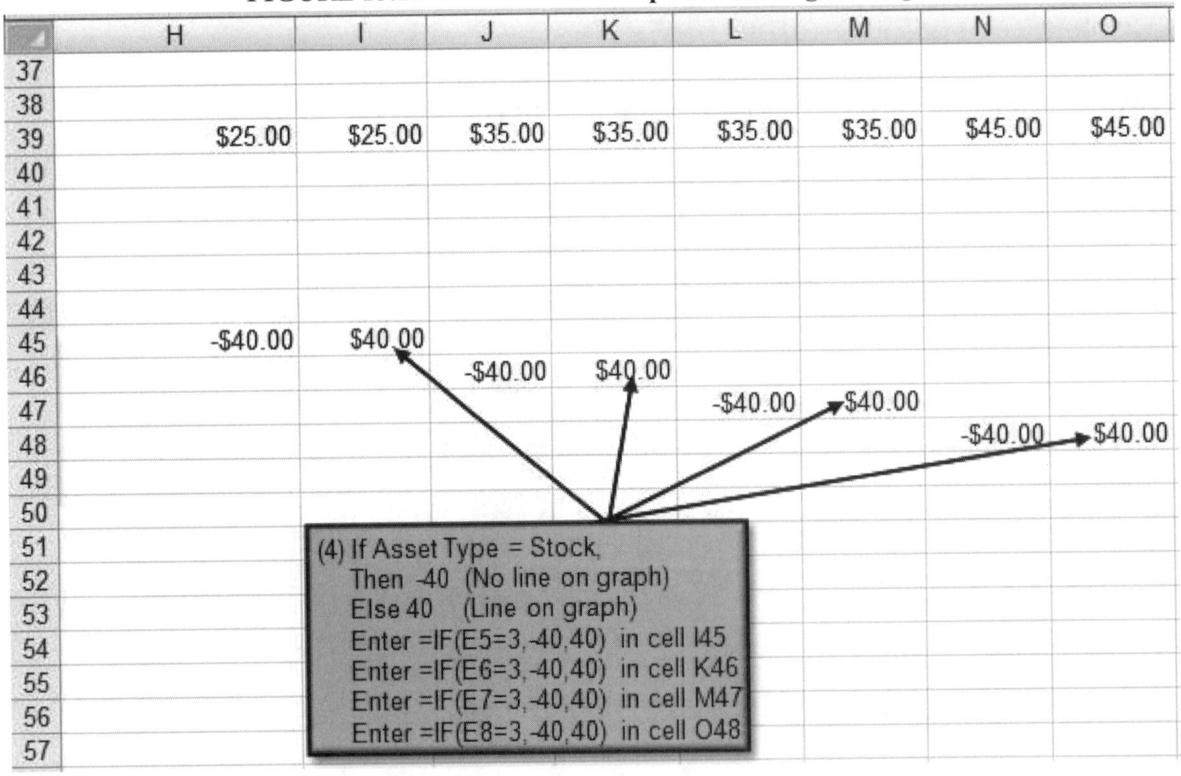

	H	I	J	K	L	M	N	O
37								
38								
39	$25.00	$25.00	$35.00	$35.00	$35.00	$35.00	$45.00	$45.00
40								
41								
42								
43								
44								
45	-$40.00	$40.00						
46			-$40.00	$40.00				
47					-$40.00	$40.00		
48							-$40.00	$40.00
49								
50								

(4) If Asset Type = Stock,
  Then -40 (No line on graph)
  Else 40 (Line on graph)
  Enter =IF(E5=3,-40,40) in cell I45
  Enter =IF(E6=3,-40,40) in cell K46
  Enter =IF(E7=3,-40,40) in cell M47
  Enter =IF(E8=3,-40,40) in cell O48

FIGURE 15.12 Table of Option Trading Strategies.

	J	K	L	M	N	O	P	Q	R	S	T	U	V
4	Trades Listed From Asset 1 to Asset 4 (Lowest To Highest Exercise Price)												
5	Buy Call, Sell Call, Sell Call, Buy Call												
6													
7													
8													
9													
10	Test	Four-Asset Strategies			Description (Trades Listed By Assets Having The Lowest To Highest Exercise Price)								Type
11	Yes	Buying a Butterfly Spread			"Buy Call, Sell Call, Sell Call, Buy Call" or "Buy Put, Sell Put, Sell Put, Buy Put"								Spread
12					with Assets 2 and 3 at the same exercise price								
13	No	Writing a Butterfly Spread			"Sell Call, Buy Call, Buy Call, Sell Call" or "Sell Put, Buy Put, Buy Put, Sell Put"								Spread
14					with Assets 2 and 3 at the same exercise price								
15	No	Other Strategies											

FIGURE 15.13 Buying a Butterfly Spread and Writing a Butterfly Spread.

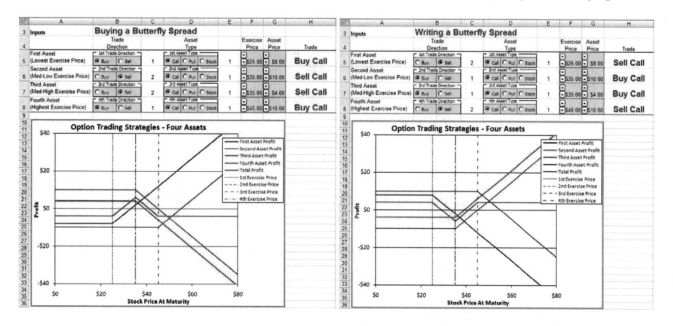

Buying a butterfly spread is betting that there will be less volatility than the rest of the market thinks. Writing a butterfly spread is the opposite.

Problems

1. There are three types of trading strategies involving options: (1) strategies involving a single option and a stock, (2) spreads involving options of one type (i.e., two or more calls or two or more puts), and (3) combinations involving both call(s) and put(s). Graph all of the trading strategies involving two assets. In particular, show the following strategies:

a. <u>First asset:</u>   Buy a call with an exercise price of $24.12 for a call price of $5.31 and
<u>Second asset:</u> Sell a call with an exercise price of $38.34 for a call price of $3.27 = Buying a bullish spread = Writing a bearish spread.

b. <u>First asset:</u>   Sell a call with an exercise price of $18.92 for a call price of $7.39 and
<u>Second asset:</u> Buy a call with an exercise price of $45.72 with a call price of $3.78 = Buying a bearish spread = Writing a bullish spread.

c. <u>First asset:</u>   Buy a call with an exercise price of $41.29 for a call price of $3.81 and
<u>Second asset:</u> Buy a put with an exercise price of $41.29 for a put price of $4.94 = Buying a straddle.

d. <u>First asset:</u>   Sell a call with an exercise price of $38.47 for a call price of $2.93 and
<u>Second asset:</u> Sell a put with an exercise price of $38.47 for a put price of $5.63 = Writing a straddle.

e. <u>First asset:</u>   Buy a call with an exercise price of $42.72 for a call price of $2.93 and
<u>Second asset:</u> Buy a put with an exercise price of $36.44 for a put price of $5.63 = Buying a strangle.

f. <u>First asset:</u>   Sell a call with an exercise price of $46.18 for a call price of $3.58 and
<u>Second asset:</u> Sell a put with an exercise price of $38.50 for a put price of $6.39 = Writing a strangle.

g. <u>First asset:</u>   Buy a stock for a stock price (asset price) of $41.25 and
<u>Second asset:</u> Sell a call with an exercise price of $47.39 for a call price of $5.83 = Buying a covered call.

h. <u>First asset:</u>   Sell a stock for a stock price (asset price) of $36.47 and
<u>Second asset:</u> Buy a call with an exercise price of $32.83 for a call price of $6.74 = Writing a covered call.

i. <u>First asset:</u>   Buy a stock for a stock price (asset price) of $43.72 and
<u>Second asset:</u> Buy a put with an exercise price of $47.87 for a put price of $7.31 = Buying a protective put.

j. <u>First asset:</u>   Sell a stock for a stock price (asset price) of $36.93 and
<u>Second asset:</u> Sell a put with an exercise price of $33.29 for a put price of $6.36 = Writing a protective put.

2. Graph all of the trading strategies involving four assets. In particular, show:

k. <u>First asset:</u>   Buy a call with an exercise price of $25.73 for a call price of $7.92 and
<u>Second asset:</u> Sell a call with an exercise price of $34.07 for a call price of

$10.15

Third asset: Sell a call with an exercise price of $34.07 for a call price of $3.96 and

Fourth asset: Buy a call with an exercise price of $41.83 for a call price of $9.23 = Buying a butterfly spread using calls.

l.   First asset: Sell a call with an exercise price of $23.84 for a call price of $5.39 and

Second asset: Buy a call with an exercise price of $36.19 for a call price of $6.98

Third asset: Buy a call with an exercise price of $36.19 for a call price of $3.36 and

Fourth asset: Sell a call with an exercise price of $47.28 for a call price of $8.34 = Writing a butterfly spread using calls.

m. First asset: Buy a put with an exercise price of $29.33 for a put price of $4.59 and

Second asset: Sell a put with an exercise price of $39.54 for a put price of $2.87

Third asset: Sell a put with an exercise price of $39.54 for a put price of $4.56 and

Fourth asset: Buy a put with an exercise price of $54.78 for a put price of $10.37 = Buying a butterfly spread using puts.

n.   First asset: Sell a put with an exercise price of $27.49 for a put price of $3.22 and

Second asset: Buy a put with an exercise price of $41.38 for a put price of $5.39

Third asset: Buy a put with an exercise price of $41.38 for a put price of $2.74 and

Fourth asset: Sell a put with an exercise price of $52.86 for a put price of $9.49 = Writing a butterfly spread using puts.

Chapter 16 Put-Call Parity

16.1 Basics

Problem. Consider a call option and put option on the same underlying stock with the same exercise price and time to maturity. The call price is $4.00, the underlying stock price is $43.00, the exercise price on both options is $40.00, the riskfree rate is 5.00%, the time to maturity on both options is 0.25 years, and the stock pays a $2.00 / share dividend in 0.10 years. What is the price of the put price now?

FIGURE 16.1 Excel Model of Put-Call Parity - Basics.

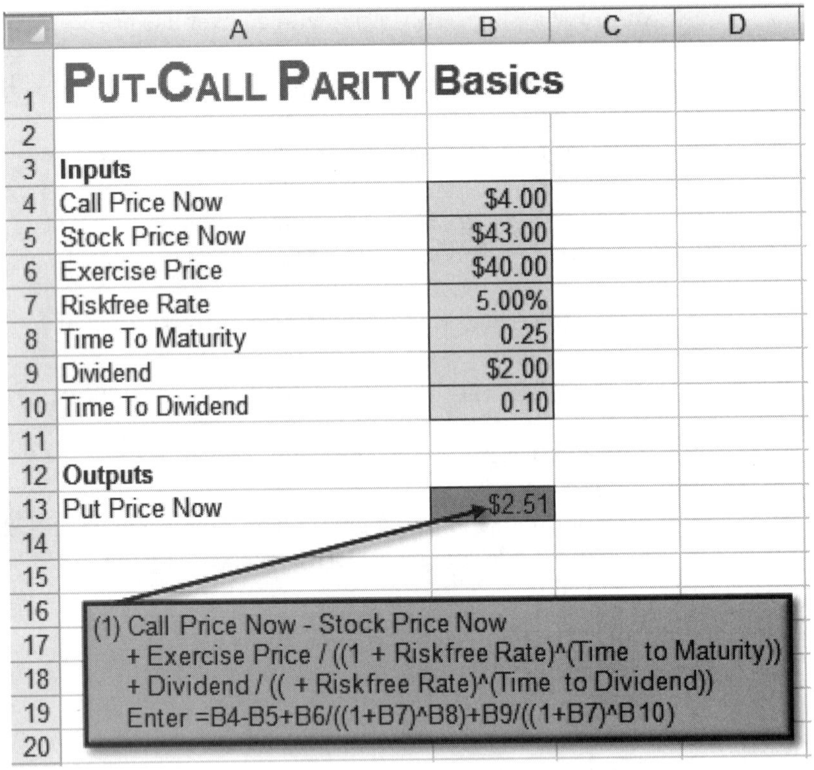

	A	B	C	D
1	**PUT-CALL PARITY Basics**			
2				
3	**Inputs**			
4	Call Price Now	$4.00		
5	Stock Price Now	$43.00		
6	Exercise Price	$40.00		
7	Riskfree Rate	5.00%		
8	Time To Maturity	0.25		
9	Dividend	$2.00		
10	Time To Dividend	0.10		
11				
12	**Outputs**			
13	Put Price Now	$2.51		
14				
15				
16	(1) Call Price Now - Stock Price Now			
17	+ Exercise Price / ((1 + Riskfree Rate)^(Time to Maturity))			
18	+ Dividend / ((+ Riskfree Rate)^(Time to Dividend))			
19	Enter =B4-B5+B6/((1+B7)^B8)+B9/((1+B7)^B10)			
20				

Put-Call Parity predicts the Put Price is $2.51.

16.2 Payoff Diagram

The Put-Call Parity equation claims that one Put Option is equivalent to a replicating portfolio consisting of one Call Option, short one Stock, and a Bond paying a face value equal to the exercise price of the put and call options. Construct a payoff diagram to determine if the payoff at maturity of the replicating portfolio is equivalent to the payoff at maturity of a put option.

FIGURE 16.2 Excel Model of Put-Call Parity - Payoff Diagram.

	A	B	C	D	E	F	G	H	I	J
1	**PUT-CALL PARITY** Payoff Diagram									
2										
3	**Inputs**									
4	Call Price Now	$4.00								
5	Stock Price Now	$43.00								
6	Exercise Price	$40.00								
7	Riskfree Rate	5.00%								
8	Time To Maturity	0.25								
9	Dividend	$2.00								
10	Time To Dividend	0.10								
11										
19	**Outputs**									
20	Stock Price at Maturity	$0.00	$8.00	$16.00	$24.00	$32.00	$40.00	$48.00	$56.00	$64.00
21										
22	Portfolio									
23	Call Payoff	$0.00	$0.00	$0.00	$0.00	$0.00	$0.00	$8.00	$16.00	$24.00
24	Short Stock Payoff	$0.00	-$8.00	-$16.00	-$24.00	-$32.00	-$40.00	-$48.00	-$56.00	-$64.00
25	Bond Payoff	$40.00	$40.00	$40.00	$40.00	$40.00	$40.00	$40.00	$40.00	$40.00
26	Total Portfolio Payoff	$40.00	$32.00	$24.00	$16.00	$8.00	$0.00	$0.00	$0.00	$0.00
27										
28	Put Payoff	$40.00	$32.00	$24.00	$16.00	$8.00	$0.00	$0.00	$0.00	$0.00

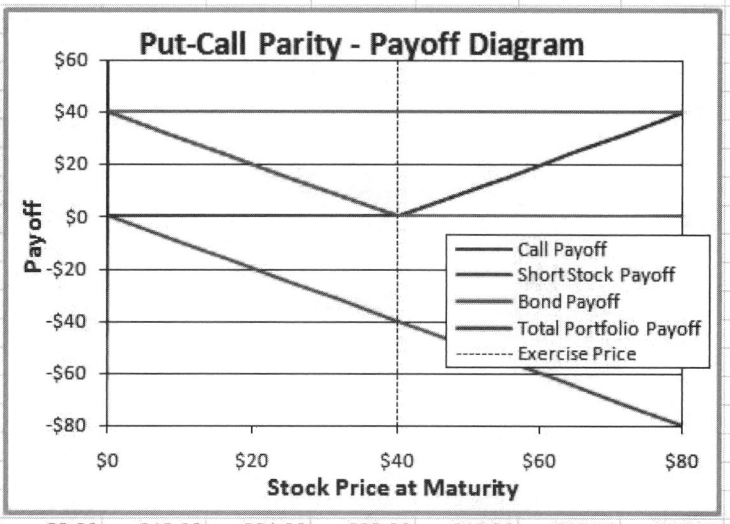

(1) Max(Stock Price at Maturity - Exercise Price, 0)
Enter =MAX(B20-$B$6,0) and copy across

(2) -(Stock Price at Maturity)
Enter =-B20 and copy across

(3) Exercise Price
Enter =$B$6 and copy across

(4) Sum of the portfolio assets
Enter =SUM(B23:B25) and copy across

(5) Max(Exercise Price - Stock Price at Maturity, 0)
Enter =MAX($B$6-B20,0) and copy across

FIGURE 16.3 Excel Model of Put-Call Parity - Payoff Diagram.

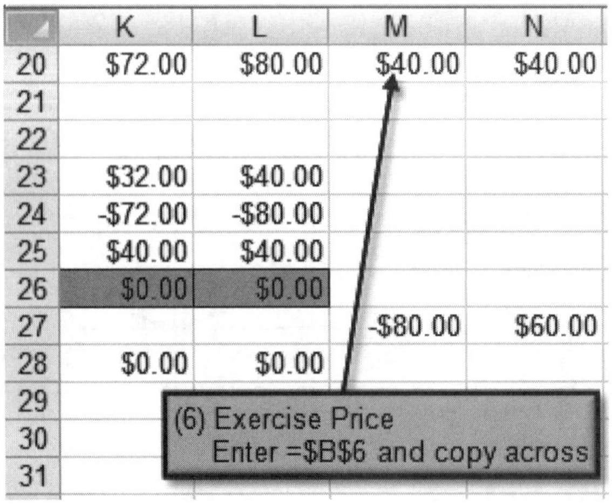

	K	L	M	N
20	$72.00	$80.00	$40.00	$40.00
21				
22				
23	$32.00	$40.00		
24	-$72.00	-$80.00		
25	$40.00	$40.00		
26	$0.00	$0.00		
27			-$80.00	$60.00
28	$0.00	$0.00		
29				
30				
31				

(6) Exercise Price
   Enter =$B$6 and copy across

Looking at the Total Portfolio Payoff (row **26**), we see that it matches the Put Payoff in row **28**. Looking at the Payoff Diagram we can see the payoff of each of the component of the replicating portfolio: (1) Call Payoff, (2) Short Stock Payoff, and (3) Bond Payoff. At each point on the X-axis, we vertically sum the three components to get the Total Payoff. The Payoff Diagram verifies that the Total Payoff has the same "hockey stick" payoff as a put option.

Problems

1. Consider a call option and put option on the same underlying stock with the same exercise price and time to maturity. The call price is $2.59, the underlying stock price is $28.63, the exercise price on both options is $26.18, the riskfree rate is 6.21%, the time to maturity on both options is 0.47 years, and the stock pays a $1.64 / share dividend in 0.28 years. Determine the price of the put price now.

2. The Put-Call Parity equation claims that one Put Option is equivalent to a replicating portfolio consisting of one Call Option, short one Stock, and a Bond paying a face value equal to the exercise price of the put and call options. Determine if the payoff at maturity of the replicating portfolio is equivalent to the payoff at maturity of a put option.

Chapter 17 Binomial Option Pricing

17.1 Estimating Volatility

The binomial option pricing model can certainly be used to price European calls and puts, but it can do much more. The Binomial Tree / Risk Neutral method can be extended to price *any* type of derivative security (European, American, etc.) on any underlying asset(s), with any underlying dividends or cash flows, with any derivative payoffs at maturity and/or payoffs before maturity. It is one of the most popular techniques on Wall Street for pricing and hedging derivatives.

Problem. What is the annual standard deviation of Amazon.com stock based on continuous returns?

Solution Strategy. Download three months of Amazon.com's daily stock price. Then calculate continuous returns. Finally, calculate the annual standard deviation of the continuous returns.

FIGURE 17.1 Binomial Option Pricing - Estimating Volatility.

	A	B	C	D	E	F	G	H
1	**BINOMIAL OPTION PRICING** Estimating Volatility							
2								
3			(1) Download three months of daily stock price data					
4								
5						(2) LN[(Price on date t) / (Price on date t-1)] Enter =LN(G11/G12) and copy down		
6	Stock:	Amazon						
7	Symbol:	AMZN						
8								
9								
10	Date	Open	High	Low	Close	Volume	Adjusted Close	Continuous Return
11	4/30/2010	$141.40	$141.40	$136.91	$137.10	6,102,200	$137.10	-3.32%
12	4/29/2010	$140.09	$142.45	$139.79	$141.73	6,314,200	$141.73	1.69%
13	4/28/2010	$142.59	$142.75	$138.69	$139.35	9,235,300	$139.35	-1.90%
14	4/27/2010	$145.55	$146.44	$141.11	$142.02	8,639,000	$142.02	-3.52%
71	2/3/2010	$117.12	$119.61	$116.56	$119.10	12,405,900	$119.10	0.83%
72	2/2/2010	$118.79	$118.98	$114.40	$118.12	23,079,700	$118.12	-0.63%
73	2/1/2010	$123.18	$124.86	$113.82	$118.87	37,774,400	$118.87	-5.36%
74	1/29/2010	$129.77	$131.85	$124.14	$125.41	29,471,300	$125.41	
75								
76						Standard Deviation (Daily)		2.02%
77						Standard Deviation (Annual)		38.67%
78								
79			(3) Standard Deviation of the Daily Return Series Enter =STDEV(H11:H73)					
80								
81								
82			(4) (Daily Standard Deviation) * (Square Root of Days in a Year) Enter =H76*SQRT(365)					
83								

We find that Amazon.com's annual standard deviation is 38.67%.

17.2 Single Period

Problem. At the close of trading on April 30, 2010, the stock price of Amazon.com was $137.10, the standard deviation of daily returns is 38.67%, the yield on a six-month U.S. Treasury Bill was 2.44%, the exercise price of an October 140 call on Amazon.com was $140.00, the exercise price of an October 140 put on Amazon.com was $140.00, and the time to maturity for both October 15, 2010 maturity options was 0.4583 years. The dividend yield is 1.00%. What is the price of an October 140 call and an October 140 put on Amazon.com?

FIGURE 17.2 Binomial Option Pricing - Single Period - Call Option.

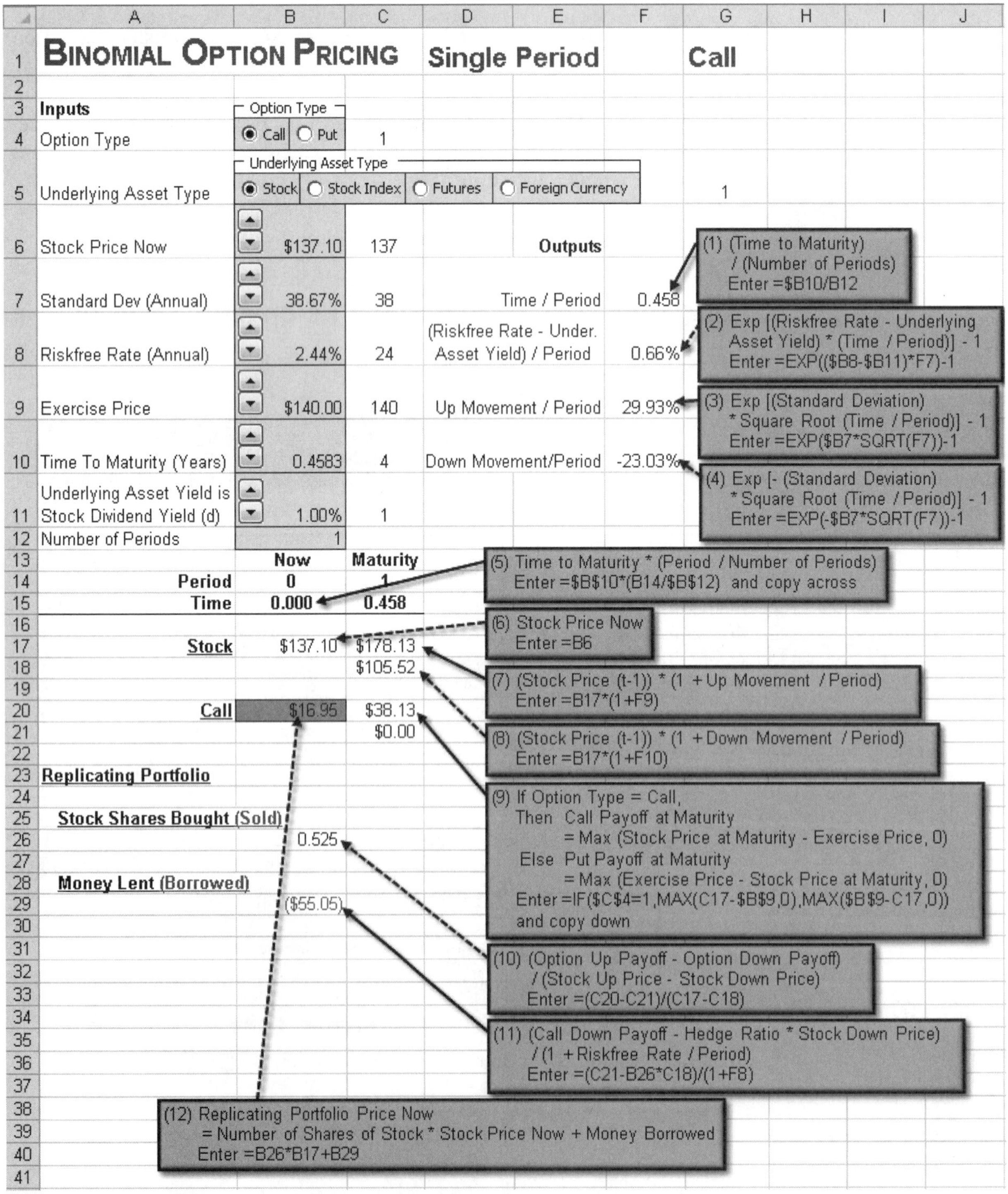

Solution Strategy. First, calculate the binomial tree parameters: time / period, riskfree rate / period, up movement / period, and down movement / period. Second, calculate the date 1, maturity date items: stock up price, stock down price, and the corresponding call and put payoffs. Third, calculate the shares of stock and money borrowed to create a replicating portfolio that replicates the option payoff at maturity. Finally, calculate the price now of the replicating portfolio and, in the absence of arbitrage, this will be the option price now.

Results. We see that the Binomial Option Pricing model predicts a one-period European call price of $16.95. The put price (below) is valued at $18.93.

FIGURE 17.3 Excel Model of Binomial Option Pricing - Single Period - Put

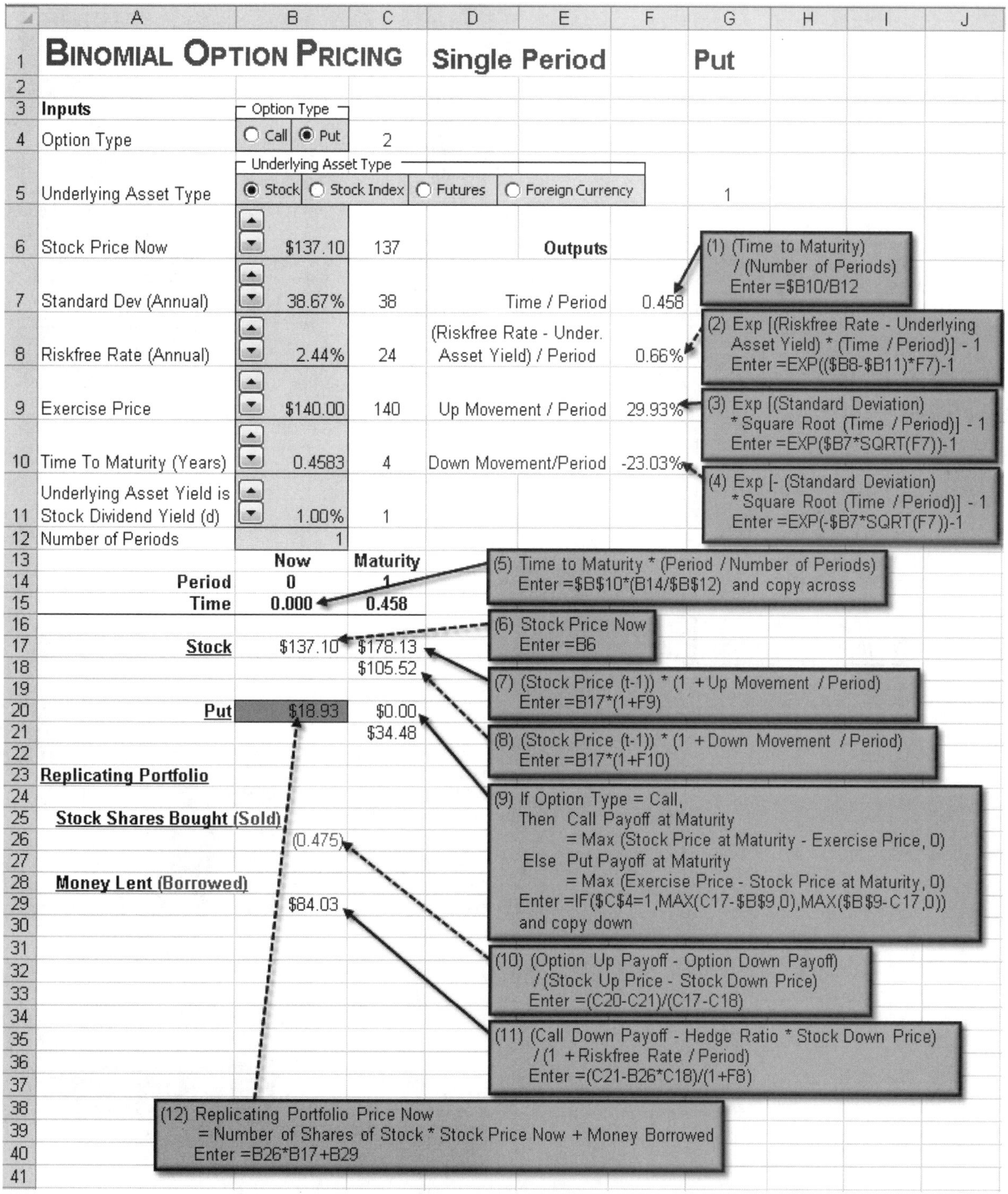

The model can handle three additional types of underlying asset (see **row 5**): (1) stock index, (2) futures, and (3) foreign currency. Then the underlying asset yield (see **row 11**) becomes: (1) the stock index dividend yield, (2) the riskfree rate, and (3) the foreign riskfree rate, respectively.

FIGURE 17.4 Binomial - Single Period – 3 Alternative Underlying Assets

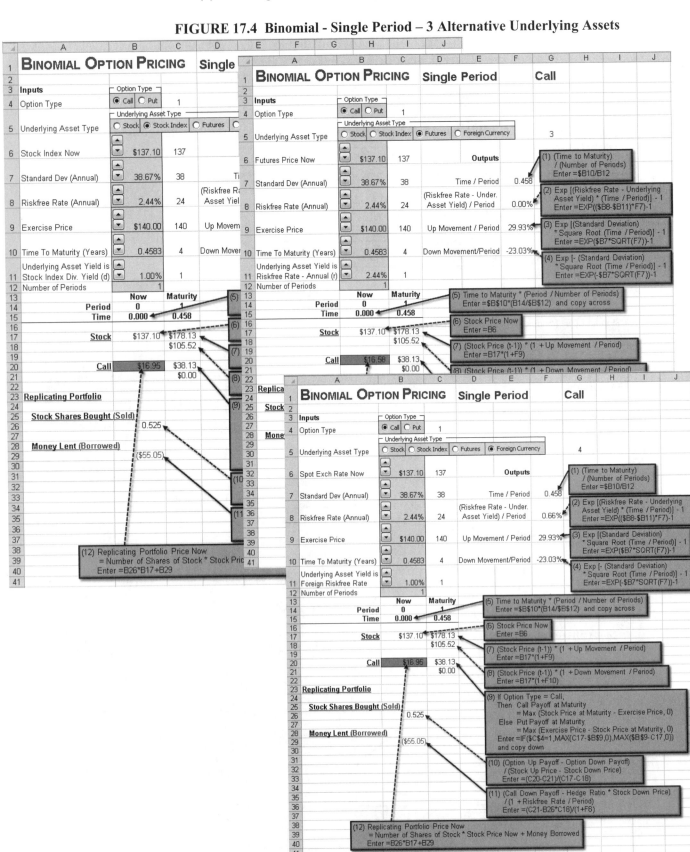

17.3 Multi-Period

Problem. Same as before, except we will use an eight-period model to evaluate it. At the close of trading on April 30, 2010, the stock price of Amazon.com was $137.10, the standard deviation of daily returns is 38.67%, the yield on a six-month U.S. Treasury Bill was 2.44%, the exercise price of an October 140 call on Amazon.com was $140.00, the exercise price of an October 140 put on Amazon.com was $140.00, and the time to maturity for both October 15, 2010 maturity options was 0.4583 years. The dividend yield is 1.00%. What is the price of an October 140 call and an October 140 put on Amazon.com?

FIGURE 17.5 Binomial Option Pricing - Multi-Period - Call.

	A	B	C	D	E	F	G	H	I	J
1	**BINOMIAL OPTION PRICING**			**Multi-Period**			**Call**			
2										
3	**Inputs**		— Option Type —							
4	Option Type	⦿ Call ○ Put	1							
5	Underlying Asset Type	⦿ Stock ○ Stock Index ○ Futures ○ Foreign Currency					1			
6	Stock Price Now	$137.10	137		**Outputs**					
7	Standard Dev (Annual)	38.67%	38	Time / Period		0.057				
8	Riskfree Rate (Annual)	2.44%	24	(Riskfree Rate - Under. Asset Yield) / Period		0.08%				
9	Exercise Price	$140.00	140	Up Movement / Period		9.70%				
10	Time To Maturity (Years)	0.4583	4	Down Movement/Period		-8.84%				
11	Underlying Asset Yield is Stock Dividend Yield (d)	1.00%	1							
12	Number of Periods	8								
13		**Now**								**Maturity**
14	**Period**	**0**	**1**	**2**	**3**	**4**	**5**	**6**	**7**	**8**
15	**Time**	**0.000**	**0.057**	**0.115**	**0.172**	**0.229**	**0.286**	**0.344**	**0.401**	**0.458**
16										
17	**Stock**	$137.10	$150.40	$164.98	$180.98	$198.53	$217.78	$238.90	$262.07	$287.48
18			$124.98	$137.10	$150.40	$164.98	$180.98	$198.53	$217.78	$238.90
19				$113.93	$124.98	$137.10	$150.40	$164.98	$180.98	$198.53
20					$103.86	$113.93	$124.98	$137.10	$150.40	$164.98
21						$94.68	$103.86	$113.93	$124.98	$137.10
22							$86.31	$94.68	$103.86	$113.93
23								$78.68	$86.31	$94.68
24									$71.72	$78.68
25										$65.38
36	**Call**	$13.32	$20.32	$30.09	$43.03	$59.20	$78.13	$99.13	$122.18	$147.48
37			$6.84	$11.29	$18.12	$28.10	$41.73	$58.76	$77.90	$98.90
38				$2.72	$4.97	$8.89	$15.49	$25.99	$41.09	$58.53
39					$0.64	$1.34	$2.78	$5.78	$12.01	$24.98
40						$0.00	$0.00	$0.00	$0.00	$0.00
41							$0.00	$0.00	$0.00	$0.00
42								$0.00	$0.00	$0.00
43									$0.00	$0.00
44										$0.00

(1) Copy the Outputs column from the previous sheet
Copy the range F7:F10 from the previous sheet to the range F7:F10 on this sheet

(2) Time to Maturity
* (Period / Number of Periods)
Enter =$B$10*(B14/$B$12)
and copy across

(3) Stock Price Now
Enter =B6

(4) If Cell to the Left = Blank,
  Then If Cell to the Left & Up One = Blank, Then Blank
    Else Down Price = (Stock Price to the Left & Up One) * (1+ Down Movement / Period)
  Else Up Price = (Stock Price to the Left) * (1 + Up Movement / Period)
Enter =IF(B17="",IF(B16="","",B16*(1+$F$10)),B17*(1+$F$9))
and copy to the range C17:J25

(5) If Option Type = Call,
  Then Call Payoff at Maturity = Max (Stock Price at Maturity - Exercise Price, 0)
  Else Put Payoff at Maturity = Max (Exercise Price - Stock Price at Maturity, 0)
Enter =IF($C$4=1,MAX(J17-$B$9,0),MAX($B$9-J17,0))
and copy to the range J37:J44

(8) If Cell to the Right & Down One = Blank, Then Blank
  Else Set Option Price = Price of the Corresponding Replicating Portfolio
  = Number of Shares of Stock * Stock Price + Money Borrowed
Enter =IF(C37="","",B52*B17+B63) and copy to the range B36:I43
Do NOT copy to column J, which contains the option payoffs at maturity

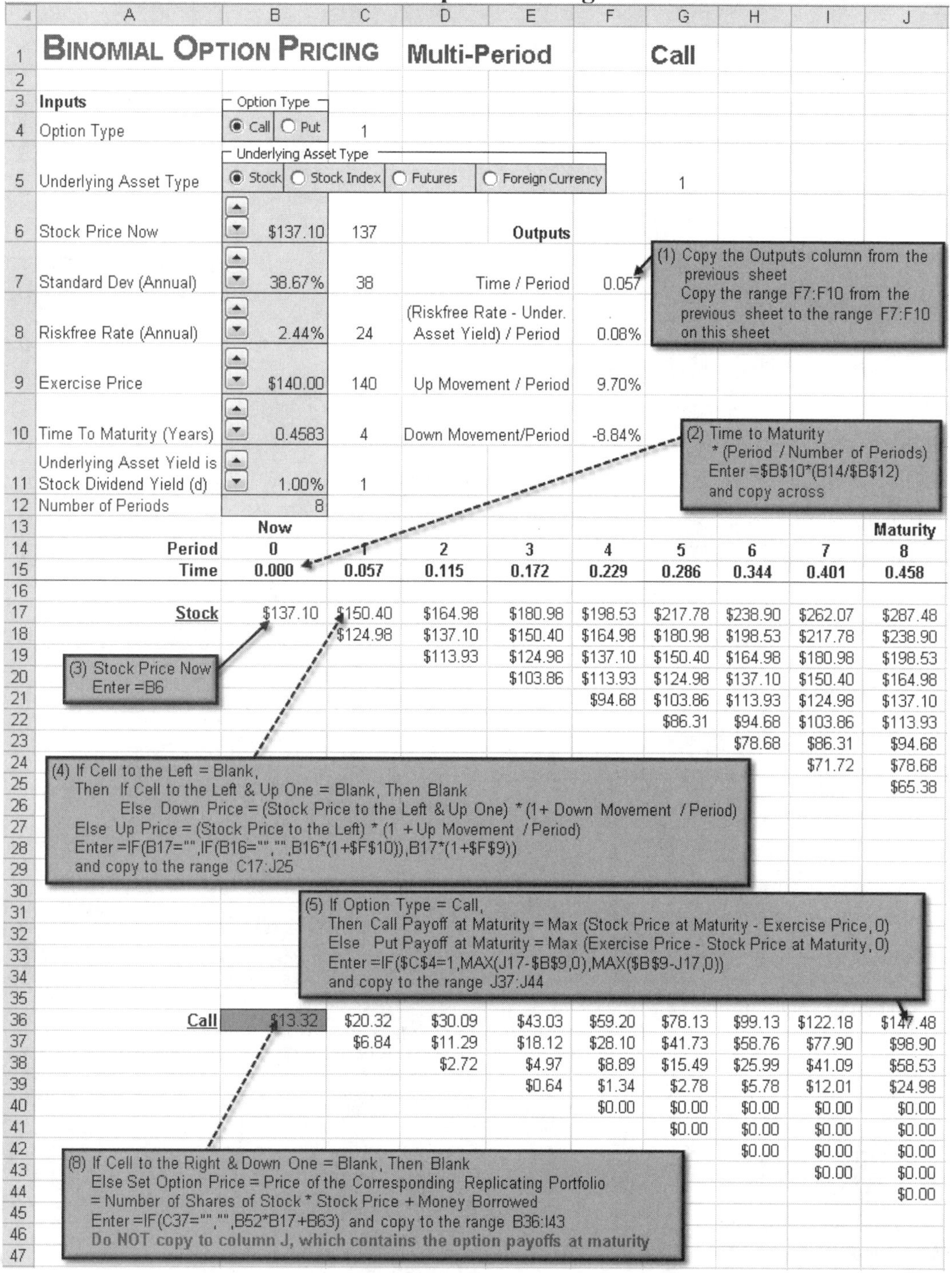

Solution Strategy. First, copy the binomial tree parameters from the single-period model. Second, build a multi-period tree of stock prices. Third, calculate call and put payoffs at maturity. Fourth, build the multi-period trees of the shares of stock and money borrowed to create a replicating portfolio that replicates the option period by period. Finally, build a multi-period tree of the value of the replicating portfolio and, in the absence of arbitrage, this will be the value of the option.

Results. We see that the Binomial Option Pricing model predicts an eight-period European call price of $13.32.

FIGURE 17.6 Binomial Option Pricing - Multi-Period - Call (Continued).

	A	B	C	D	E	F	G	H	I	J
1	**BINOMIAL OPTION PRICING**			**Multi-Period**			**Call**			
2										
3	**Inputs**		Option Type							
4	Option Type	● Call ○ Put	1							
5	Underlying Asset Type	Underlying Asset Type: ● Stock ○ Stock Index ○ Futures ○ Foreign Currency					1			
6	Stock Price Now	$137.10	137		**Outputs**					
7	Standard Dev (Annual)	38.67%	38		Time / Period	0.057				
8	Riskfree Rate (Annual)	2.44%	24	(Riskfree Rate - Under. Asset Yield) / Period		0.08%				
9	Exercise Price	$140.00	140	Up Movement / Period		9.70%				
10	Time To Maturity (Years)	0.4583	4	Down Movement/Period		-8.84%				
11	Underlying Asset Yield is Stock Dividend Yield (d)	1.00%	1							
12	Number of Periods		8							
13		**Now**								**Maturity**
14	**Period**	**0**	**1**	**2**	**3**	**4**	**5**	**6**	**7**	**8**
15	**Time**	**0.000**	**0.057**	**0.115**	**0.172**	**0.229**	**0.286**	**0.344**	**0.401**	**0.458**
48										
49	**Replicating Portfolio**									
50										
51	**Stock Shares Bought (Sold)**									
52		0.530	0.674	0.815	0.927	0.989	1.000	1.000	1.000	
53			0.370	0.518	0.689	0.858	0.977	1.000	1.000	
54				0.205	0.326	0.500	0.725	0.951	1.000	
55					0.069	0.132	0.249	0.473	0.896	
56						0.000	0.000	0.000	0.000	
57							0.000	0.000	0.000	
58								0.000	0.000	
59									0.000	
60										
61										
62	**Money Lent (Borrowed)**									
63		($59.40)	($81.08)	($104.30)	($124.74)	($137.15)	($139.65)	($139.77)	($139.88)	
64			($39.37)	($59.66)	($85.49)	($113.42)	($135.05)	($139.77)	($139.88)	
65				($20.61)	($35.79)	($59.70)	($93.54)	($130.88)	($139.88)	
66					($6.57)	($13.65)	($28.39)	($59.03)	($122.74)	
67						$0.00	$0.00	$0.00	$0.00	
68							$0.00	$0.00	$0.00	
69								$0.00	$0.00	
70									$0.00	
71										
72										

(1) Copy the Outputs column from the previous sheet
Copy the range F7:F10 from the previous sheet to the range F7:F10 on this sheet

(2) Time to Maturity
* (Period / Number of Periods)
Enter =$B$10*(B14/$B$12)
and copy across

(6) If Corresponding Option Down Price = Blank, Then Blank
Else Hedge Ratio = (Option Up Price - Option Down Price)
/ (Stock Up Price - Stock Down Price)
Enter =IF(C37="","",(C36-C37)/(C17-C18)) and copy to the range B52:I59

(7) If Corresponding Option Down Price = Blank, Then Blank
Else (Option Down Price - Hedge Ratio * Stock Down Price)
/ (1 + Riskfree Rate / Period)
Enter =IF(C37="","",(C37-B52*C18)/(1+$F$8)) and copy in range B63:I70

Now let's check the put.

FIGURE 17.7 Binomial Option Pricing - Multi-Period - Put.

	A	B	C	D	E	F	G	H	I	J
1	**BINOMIAL OPTION PRICING**			**Multi-Period**			**Put**			
2										
3	**Inputs**		Option Type							
4	Option Type	○ Call ● Put	2							
5	Underlying Asset Type	Underlying Asset Type ● Stock ○ Stock Index ○ Futures ○ Foreign Currency					1			
6	Stock Price Now	$137.10	137		**Outputs**					
7	Standard Dev (Annual)	38.67%	38		Time / Period	0.057				
8	Riskfree Rate (Annual)	2.44%	24	(Riskfree Rate - Under. Asset Yield) / Period		0.08%				
9	Exercise Price	$140.00	140	Up Movement / Period		9.70%				
10	Time To Maturity (Years)	0.4583	4	Down Movement/Period		-8.84%				
11	Underlying Asset Yield is Stock Dividend Yield (d)	1.00%	1							
12	Number of Periods	8								
13		**Now**								**Maturity**
14	**Period**	**0**	**1**	**2**	**3**	**4**	**5**	**6**	**7**	**8**
15	**Time**	**0.000**	**0.057**	**0.115**	**0.172**	**0.229**	**0.286**	**0.344**	**0.401**	**0.458**
16										
17	**Stock**	$137.10	$150.40	$164.98	$180.98	$198.53	$217.78	$238.90	$262.07	$287.48
18			$124.98	$137.10	$150.40	$164.98	$180.98	$198.53	$217.78	$238.90
19				$113.93	$124.98	$137.10	$150.40	$164.98	$180.98	$198.53
20					$103.86	$113.93	$124.98	$137.10	$150.40	$164.98
21						$94.68	$103.86	$113.93	$124.98	$137.10
22							$86.31	$94.68	$103.86	$113.93
23								$78.68	$86.31	$94.68
24									$71.72	$78.68
25										$65.38
36	**Put**	$15.30	$9.12	$4.42	$1.48	$0.21	$0.00	$0.00	$0.00	$0.00
37			$21.05	$13.50	$7.15	$2.66	$0.40	$0.00	$0.00	$0.00
38				$28.10	$19.41	$11.33	$4.75	$0.78	$0.00	$0.00
39					$36.21	$26.94	$17.45	$8.45	$1.50	$0.00
40						$44.86	$35.79	$25.84	$14.90	$2.90
41							$53.35	$45.09	$36.02	$26.07
42								$61.09	$53.58	$45.32
43									$68.16	$61.32
44										$74.62

Callout boxes:

(1) Copy the Outputs column from the previous sheet
Copy the range F7:F10 from the previous sheet to the range F7:F10 on this sheet

(2) Time to Maturity
* (Period / Number of Periods)
Enter =$B$10*(B14/$B$12)
and copy across

(3) Stock Price Now
Enter =B6

(4) If Cell to the Left = Blank,
Then If Cell to the Left & Up One = Blank, Then Blank
Else Down Price = (Stock Price to the Left & Up One) * (1+ Down Movement / Period)
Else Up Price = (Stock Price to the Left) * (1 + Up Movement / Period)
Enter =IF(B17="",IF(B16="","",B16*(1+$F$10)),B17*(1+$F$9))
and copy to the range C17:J25

(5) If Option Type = Call,
Then Call Payoff at Maturity = Max (Stock Price at Maturity - Exercise Price, 0)
Else Put Payoff at Maturity = Max (Exercise Price - Stock Price at Maturity, 0)
Enter =IF($C$4=1,MAX(J17-$B$9,0),MAX($B$9-J17,0))
and copy to the range J37:J44

(8) If Cell to the Right & Down One = Blank, Then Blank
Else Set Option Price = Price of the Corresponding Replicating Portfolio
= Number of Shares of Stock * Stock Price + Money Borrowed
Enter =IF(C37="","",B52*B17+B63) and copy to the range B36:I43
Do NOT copy to column J, which contains the option payoffs at maturity

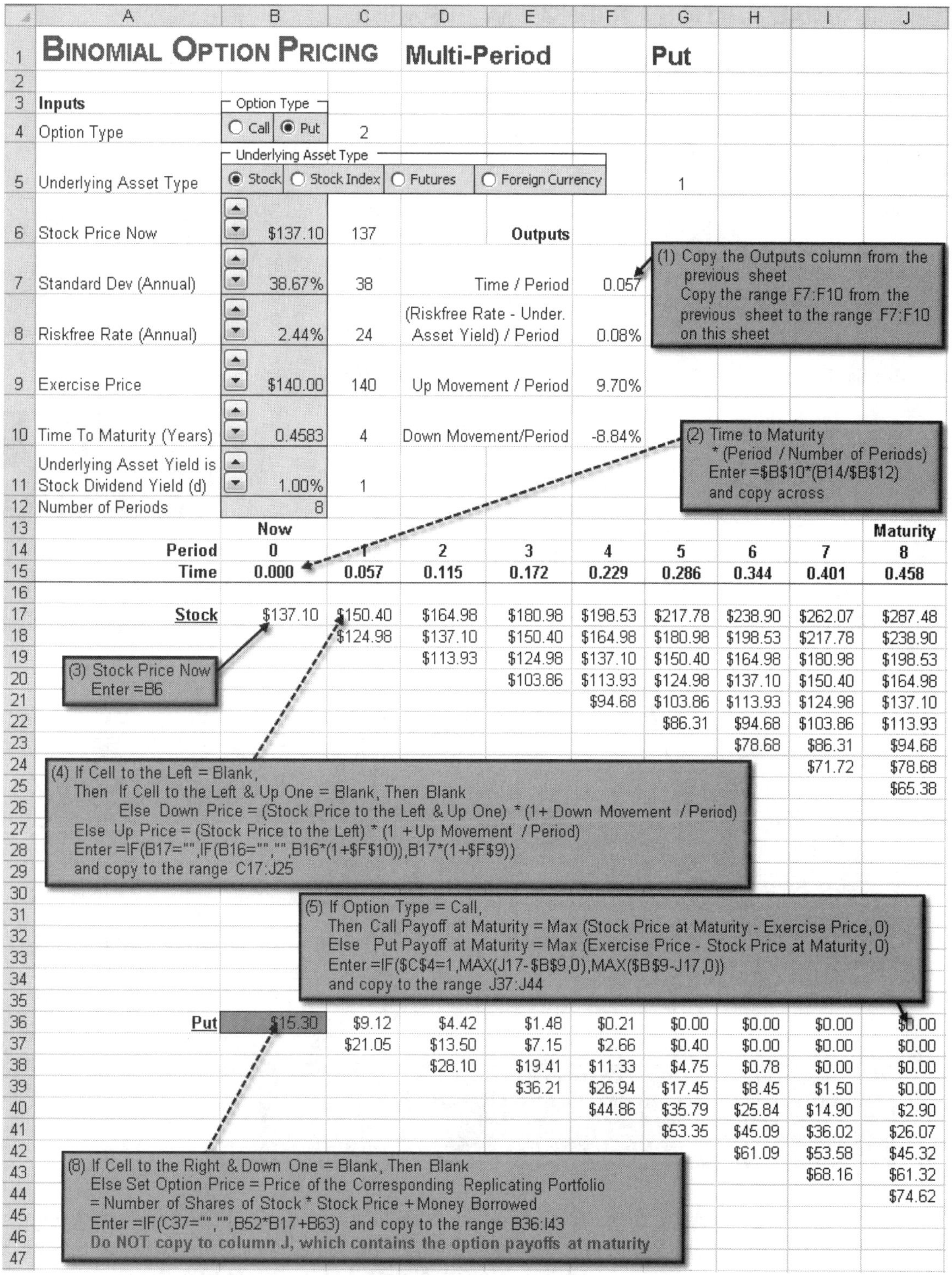

We see that the Binomial Option Pricing model predicts an eight-period European put price of $15.30.

FIGURE 17.8 Binomial Option Pricing - Multi-Period - Put (Continued).

	A	B	C	D	E	F	G	H	I	J
1	**BINOMIAL OPTION PRICING**			**Multi-Period**			**Put**			
2										
3	**Inputs**	⌐ Option Type ⌐								
4	Option Type	○ Call ● Put	2							
5	Underlying Asset Type	⌐ Underlying Asset Type ● Stock ○ Stock Index ○ Futures ○ Foreign Currency					1			
6	Stock Price Now	▲ ▼ $137.10	137		**Outputs**					
7	Standard Dev (Annual)	▲ ▼ 38.67%	38	Time / Period		0.057				
8	Riskfree Rate (Annual)	▲ ▼ 2.44%	24	(Riskfree Rate - Under. Asset Yield) / Period		0.08%				
9	Exercise Price	▲ ▼ $140.00	140	Up Movement / Period		9.70%				
10	Time To Maturity (Years)	▲ ▼ 0.4583	4	Down Movement/Period		-8.84%				
11	Underlying Asset Yield is Stock Dividend Yield (d)	▲ ▼ 1.00%	1							
12	Number of Periods	8								
13		**Now**								**Maturity**
14	**Period**	**0**	**1**	**2**	**3**	**4**	**5**	**6**	**7**	**8**
15	**Time**	**0.000**	**0.057**	**0.115**	**0.172**	**0.229**	**0.286**	**0.344**	**0.401**	**0.458**
48										
49	**Replicating Portfolio**									
50										
51	**Stock Shares Bought (Sold)**									
52		(0.470)	(0.326)	(0.185)	(0.073)	(0.011)	0.000	0.000	0.000	
53			(0.630)	(0.482)	(0.311)	(0.142)	(0.023)	0.000	0.000	
54				(0.795)	(0.674)	(0.500)	(0.275)	(0.049)	0.000	
55					(0.931)	(0.868)	(0.751)	(0.527)	(0.104)	
56						(1.000)	(1.000)	(1.000)	(1.000)	
57							(1.000)	(1.000)	(1.000)	
58								(1.000)	(1.000)	
59									(1.000)	
60										
61										
62	**Money Lent (Borrowed)**									
63		$79.68	$58.12	$35.01	$14.68	$2.39	$0.00	$0.00	$0.00	
64			$99.82	$79.65	$53.94	$26.11	$4.61	$0.00	$0.00	
65				$118.70	$103.64	$79.84	$46.12	$8.89	$0.00	
66					$132.86	$125.89	$111.27	$80.74	$17.15	
67						$139.54	$139.65	$139.77	$139.88	
68							$139.65	$139.77	$139.88	
69								$139.77	$139.88	
70									$139.88	
71										
72										

Callout notes in figure:

(1) Copy the Outputs column from the previous sheet
Copy the range F7:F10 from the previous sheet to the range F7:F10 on this sheet

(2) Time to Maturity
* (Period / Number of Periods)
Enter =$B$10*(B14/$B$12)
and copy across

(6) If Corresponding Option Down Price = Blank, Then Blank
Else Hedge Ratio = (Option Up Price - Option Down Price)
/ (Stock Up Price - Stock Down Price)
Enter =IF(C37="","",(C36-C37)/(C17-C18)) and copy to the range B52:I59

(7) If Corresponding Option Down Price = Blank, Then Blank
Else (Option Down Price - Hedge Ratio * Stock Down Price)
/ (1 + Riskfree Rate / Period)
Enter =IF(C37="","",(C37-B52*C18)/(1+$F$8)) and copy in range B63:I70

As in the single period case, replicating a Call option requires **Buying** Shares of Stock and **Borrowing** Money, whereas a Put option requires **Selling** Shares of Stock and **Lending** Money. Notice that the quantity of Money Borrowed or Lent and the quantity of Shares Bought or Sold changes over time and differs for up nodes vs. down nodes. This process of changing the replicating portfolio every period based on the realized up or down movement in the underlying stock price is called dynamic replication.

Price accuracy can be increased by subdividing the option's time to maturity into more periods (15, 30, etc.). Typically, from 50 to 100 periods are required in order to achieve price accuracy to the penny.

17.4 Risk Neutral

The previous Excel model, **Binomial Option Pricing Multi-Period**, determined the price of an option by constructing a replicating portfolio, which combines a stock and a bond to replicate the payoffs of the option. An alternative way to price an option is the Risk Neutral method. Both techniques give you the same answer. The main advantage of the Risk Neutral method is that it is faster and easier to implement. The Replicating Portfolio method required the construction of four trees (stock prices, shares of stock **bought (sold)**, money **lent (borrowed)**, and option prices). The Risk Neutral method will only require two trees (stock prices and option prices).

Problem. Same as before, except we will use the risk neutral method to evaluate it. At the close of trading on April 30, 2010, the stock price of Amazon.com was $137.10, the standard deviation of daily returns is 38.67%, the yield on a six-month U.S. Treasury Bill was 2.44%, the exercise price of an October 140 call on Amazon.com was $140.00, the exercise price of an October 140 put on Amazon.com was $140.00, and the time to maturity for both October 15, 2010 maturity options was 0.4583 years. The dividend yield is 1.00%. What is the price of an October 140 call and an October 140 put on Amazon.com?

Solution Strategy. First, copy the binomial tree parameters, stock price tree, and option payoffs at maturity from the multi-period model. Second, calculate the risk neutral probability. Finally, build a option value tree using the risk neutral probability.

Results. We see that the Risk Neutral method predicts an eight-period European call price of $13.32. This is identical to previous section's Replicating Portfolio Price. Next let's check the put.

FIGURE 17.9 Binomial Option Pricing – Risk Neutral - Call.

	A	B	C	D	E	F	G	H	I	J
1	**BINOMIAL OPTION PRICING**				Risk Neutral		Call			
2										
3	**Inputs**	Option Type								
4	Option Type	● Call ○ Put	1							
5	Underlying Asset Type	● Stock ○ Stock Index ○ Futures ○ Foreign Currency					1			
6	Stock Price Now	$137.10	137		**Outputs**					
7	Standard Dev (Annual)	38.67%	38		Time / Period	0.057				
8	Riskfree Rate (Annual)	2.44%	24	(Riskfree Rate - Under. Asset Yield) / Period		0.08%				
9	Exercise Price	$140.00	140	Up Movement / Period		9.70%				
10	Time To Maturity (Years)	0.4583	4	Down Movement/Period		-8.84%				
11	Underlying Asset Yield is Stock Dividend Yield (d)	1.00%	1	Risk Neutral Probability		48.13%				
12	Number of Periods	8								
13		**Now**								**Maturity**
14	**Period**	**0**	**1**	**2**	**3**	**4**	**5**	**6**	**7**	**8**
15	**Time**	**0.000**	**0.057**	**0.115**	**0.172**	**0.229**	**0.286**	**0.344**	**0.401**	**0.458**
16										
17	**Stock**	$137.10	$150.40	$164.98	$180.98	$198.53	$217.78	$238.90	$262.07	$287.48
18			$124.98	$137.10	$150.40	$164.98	$180.98	$198.53	$217.78	$238.90
19				$113.93	$124.98	$137.10	$150.40	$164.98	$180.98	$198.53
20					$103.86	$113.93	$124.98	$137.10	$150.40	$164.98
21						$94.68	$103.86	$113.93	$124.98	$137.10
22							$86.31	$94.68	$103.86	$113.93
23								$78.68	$86.31	$94.68
24									$71.72	$78.68
25										$65.38
26										
27										
28										
29										
30										
31										
32										
33										
34										
35										
36	**Call**	$13.32	$20.32	$30.09	$43.03	$59.20	$78.13	$99.13	$122.18	$147.48
37			$6.84	$11.29	$18.12	$28.10	$41.73	$58.76	$77.90	$98.90
38				$2.72	$4.97	$8.89	$15.49	$25.99	$41.09	$58.53
39					$0.64	$1.34	$2.78	$5.78	$12.01	$24.98
40						$0.00	$0.00	$0.00	$0.00	$0.00
41							$0.00	$0.00	$0.00	$0.00
42								$0.00	$0.00	$0.00
43									$0.00	$0.00
44										$0.00
45										
46										
47										
48										
49										
50										
51										

Annotations:

(1) Copy the Outputs column from the previous sheet
Copy the range F7:F10 from the previous sheet to the range F7:F10 on this sheet

(2) (Riskfree Rate / Period
 - Down Movement / Period)
/ (Up Movement / Period
 - Down Movement / Period)
Enter =(F8-F10)/(F9-F10)

(3) Copy the Stock Price Tree from the previous sheet
Copy the range B17:J25 from the previous sheet to the range B17:J25 on this sheet

(4) Copy the Payoffs at Maturity from the previous sheet
Copy the range J36:J44 from the previous sheet to the range J36:J44 on this sheet

(5) If Cell to the Right & Down One = Blank, Then Blank
 Else Expected Value of Option Price Next Period (using the Risk Neutral Probability)
 Discounted at the Riskfree Rate
 = [(Risk Neutral Probability) * (Stock Up Price) + (1 - Risk Neutral Probability) * (Stock Down Price)]
 / (1+ Riskfree Rate / Period)
 Enter =IF(C37="","",($F$11*C36+(1-$F$11)*C37)/(1+$F$8)) and copy to the range B36:I43
 Do NOT copy to column J, which contains the option payoffs at maturity

FIGURE 17.10 Binomial Option Pricing – Risk Neutral - Put.

	A	B	C	D	E	F	G	H	I	J
1	**BINOMIAL OPTION PRICING**			**Risk Neutral**			**Put**			
2										
3	**Inputs**	Option Type								
4	Option Type	○ Call ● Put	2							
5	Underlying Asset Type	● Stock ○ Stock Index ○ Futures ○ Foreign Currency					1			
6	Stock Price Now	$137.10	137		**Outputs**					
7	Standard Dev (Annual)	38.67%	38	Time / Period		0.057				
8	Riskfree Rate (Annual)	2.44%	24	(Riskfree Rate - Under. Asset Yield) / Period		0.08%				
9	Exercise Price	$140.00	140	Up Movement / Period		9.70%				
10	Time To Maturity (Years)	0.4583	4	Down Movement/Period		-8.84%				
11	Underlying Asset Yield is Stock Dividend Yield (d)	1.00%	1	Risk Neutral Probability		48.13%				
12	Number of Periods	8								
13		**Now**								**Maturity**
14	**Period**	**0**	**1**	**2**	**3**	**4**	**5**	**6**	**7**	**8**
15	**Time**	**0.000**	**0.057**	**0.115**	**0.172**	**0.229**	**0.286**	**0.344**	**0.401**	**0.458**
16										
17	**Stock**	$137.10	$150.40	$164.98	$180.98	$198.53	$217.78	$238.90	$262.07	$287.48
18			$124.98	$137.10	$150.40	$164.98	$180.98	$198.53	$217.78	$238.90
19				$113.93	$124.98	$137.10	$150.40	$164.98	$180.98	$198.53
20					$103.86	$113.93	$124.98	$137.10	$150.40	$164.98
21						$94.68	$103.86	$113.93	$124.98	$137.10
22							$86.31	$94.68	$103.86	$113.93
23								$78.68	$86.31	$94.68
24									$71.72	$78.68
25										$65.38
36	**Put**	$15.30	$9.12	$4.42	$1.48	$0.21	$0.00	$0.00	$0.00	$0.00
37			$21.05	$13.50	$7.15	$2.66	$0.40	$0.00	$0.00	$0.00
38				$28.10	$19.41	$11.33	$4.75	$0.78	$0.00	$0.00
39					$36.21	$26.94	$17.45	$8.45	$1.50	$0.00
40						$44.86	$35.79	$25.84	$14.90	$2.90
41							$53.35	$45.09	$36.02	$26.07
42								$61.09	$53.58	$45.32
43									$68.16	$61.32
44										$74.62

Callout notes:

(1) Copy the Outputs column from the previous sheet
Copy the range F7:F10 from the previous sheet to the range F7:F10 on this sheet

(2) (Riskfree Rate / Period - Down Movement / Period) / (Up Movement / Period - Down Movement / Period)
Enter =(F8-F10)/(F9-F10)

(3) Copy the Stock Price Tree from the previous sheet
Copy the range B17:J25 from the previous sheet to the range B17:J25 on this sheet

(4) Copy the Payoffs at Maturity from the previous sheet
Copy the range J36:J44 from the previous sheet to the range J36:J44 on this sheet

(5) If Cell to the Right & Down One = Blank, Then Blank
Else Expected Value of Option Price Next Period (using the Risk Neutral Probability)
Discounted at the Riskfree Rate
= [(Risk Neutral Probability) * (Stock Up Price) + (1 - Risk Neutral Probability) * (Stock Down Price)] / (1 + Riskfree Rate / Period)
Enter =IF(C37="","",($F$11*C36+(1-$F$11)*C37)/(1+$F$8)) and copy to the range B36:I43
Do NOT copy to column J, which contains the option payoffs at maturity

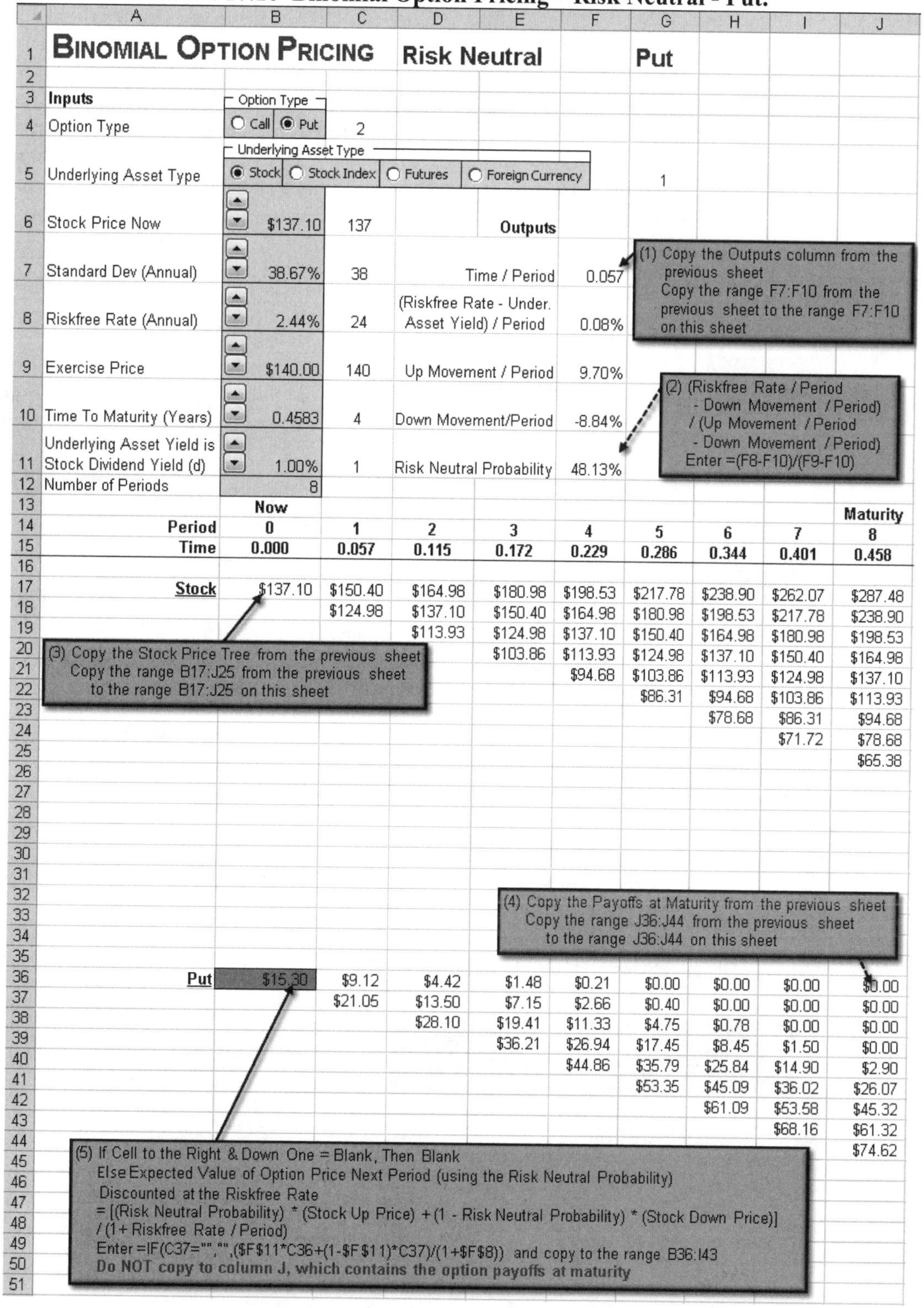

We see that the Risk Neutral method predicts an eight-period European put price of $13.49. This is identical to previous section's Replicating Portfolio Price. Again, we get the same answer either way. The advantage of the Risk Neutral method is that we only have to construct two trees, rather than four trees.

17.5 Average of N and N-1

Problem. Same as before, except we will use the average of N and N-1 method to evaluate it. At the close of trading on April 30, 2010, the stock price of Amazon.com was $137.10, the standard deviation of daily returns is 38.67%, the yield on a six-month U.S. Treasury Bill was 2.44%, the exercise price of an October 140 call on Amazon.com was $140.00, the exercise price of an October 140 put on Amazon.com was $140.00, and the time to maturity for both October 15, 2010 maturity options was 0.4583 years. The dividend yield is 1.00%. What is the price of an October 140 call and an October 140 put on Amazon.com?

FIGURE 17.11 Binomial Option Pricing – Ave of N and N-1 - Call.

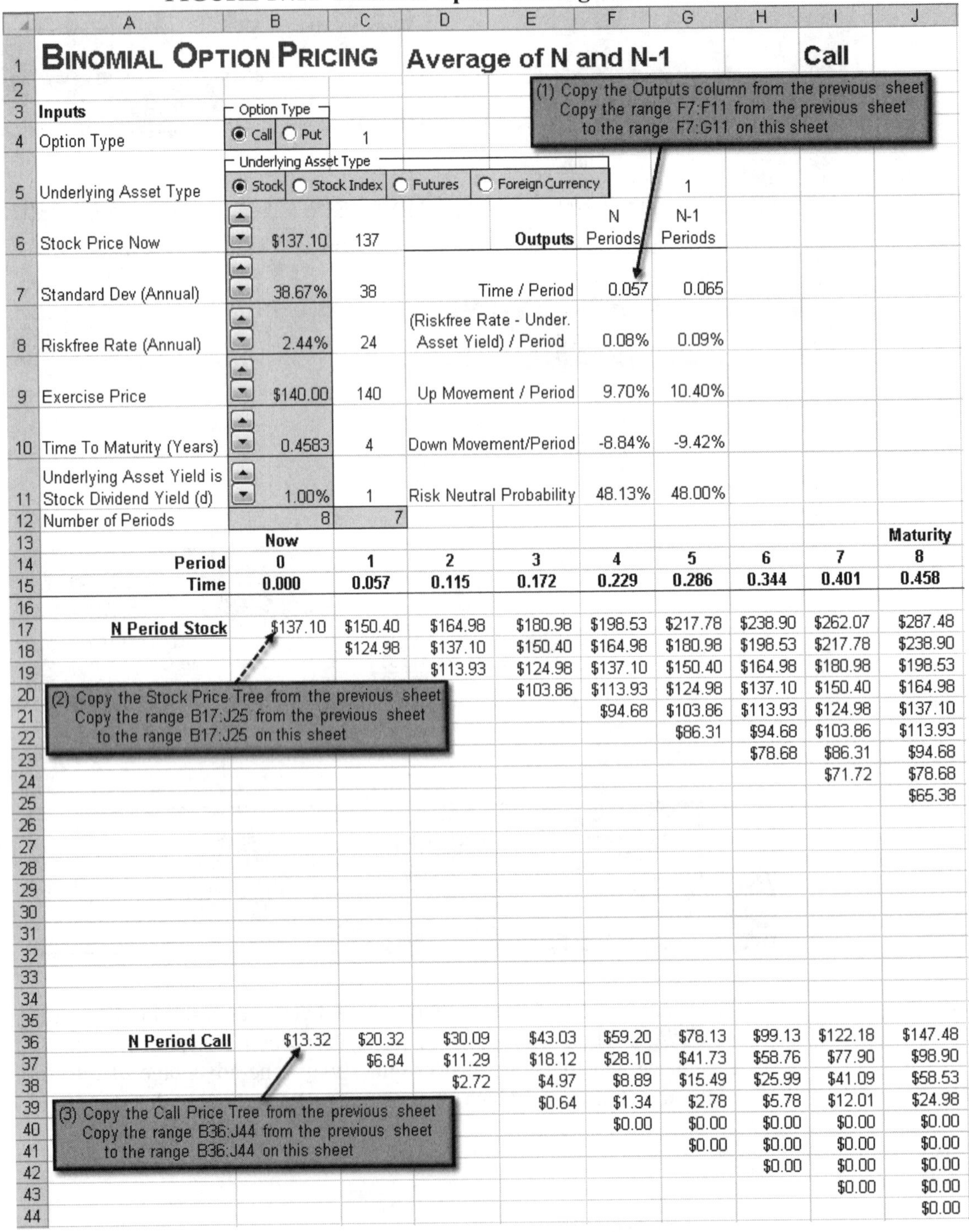

	A	B	C	D	E	F	G	H	I	J
1	**BINOMIAL OPTION PRICING**			**Average of N and N-1**					**Call**	
2										
3	**Inputs**	Option Type				(1) Copy the Outputs column from the previous sheet Copy the range F7:F11 from the previous sheet to the range F7:G11 on this sheet				
4	Option Type	⦿ Call ○ Put	1							
5	Underlying Asset Type	Underlying Asset Type ⦿ Stock ○ Stock Index ○ Futures ○ Foreign Currency				1				
6	Stock Price Now	$137.10	137		**Outputs**	N Periods	N-1 Periods			
7	Standard Dev (Annual)	38.67%	38	Time / Period		0.057	0.065			
8	Riskfree Rate (Annual)	2.44%	24	(Riskfree Rate - Under. Asset Yield) / Period		0.08%	0.09%			
9	Exercise Price	$140.00	140	Up Movement / Period		9.70%	10.40%			
10	Time To Maturity (Years)	0.4583	4	Down Movement/Period		-8.84%	-9.42%			
11	Underlying Asset Yield is Stock Dividend Yield (d)	1.00%	1	Risk Neutral Probability		48.13%	48.00%			
12	Number of Periods	8	7							
13		**Now**								**Maturity**
14	**Period**	**0**	**1**	**2**	**3**	**4**	**5**	**6**	**7**	**8**
15	**Time**	**0.000**	**0.057**	**0.115**	**0.172**	**0.229**	**0.286**	**0.344**	**0.401**	**0.458**
16										
17	**N Period Stock**	$137.10	$150.40	$164.98	$180.98	$198.53	$217.78	$238.90	$262.07	$287.48
18			$124.98	$137.10	$150.40	$164.98	$180.98	$198.53	$217.78	$238.90
19				$113.93	$124.98	$137.10	$150.40	$164.98	$180.98	$198.53
20	(2) Copy the Stock Price Tree from the previous sheet Copy the range B17:J25 from the previous sheet to the range B17:J25 on this sheet				$103.86	$113.93	$124.98	$137.10	$150.40	$164.98
21						$94.68	$103.86	$113.93	$124.98	$137.10
22							$86.31	$94.68	$103.86	$113.93
23								$78.68	$86.31	$94.68
24									$71.72	$78.68
25										$65.38
26										
27										
28										
29										
30										
31										
32										
33										
34										
35										
36	**N Period Call**	$13.32	$20.32	$30.09	$43.03	$59.20	$78.13	$99.13	$122.18	$147.48
37			$6.84	$11.29	$18.12	$28.10	$41.73	$58.76	$77.90	$98.90
38				$2.72	$4.97	$8.89	$15.49	$25.99	$41.09	$58.53
39	(3) Copy the Call Price Tree from the previous sheet Copy the range B36:J44 from the previous sheet to the range B36:J44 on this sheet				$0.64	$1.34	$2.78	$5.78	$12.01	$24.98
40						$0.00	$0.00	$0.00	$0.00	$0.00
41							$0.00	$0.00	$0.00	$0.00
42								$0.00	$0.00	$0.00
43									$0.00	$0.00
44										$0.00

Solution Strategy. First, copy the 8-period binomial model from the prior section. Second, create an analogous 7-period binominal model. Finally, compute the average derivate price from the 8-period price and 7-period price.

FIGURE 17.12 Binomial Option Pricing – Ave of N and N-1 - Call.

	A	B	C	D	E	F	G	H	I
		Now							**Maturity**
47									
48	Period	0	1	2	3	4	5	6	7
49	Time	0.000	0.065	0.131	0.196	0.262	0.327	0.393	0.458
50									
51	**N-1 Period Stock**	$137.10	$151.36	$167.10	$184.48	$203.67	$224.85	$248.24	$274.06
52			$124.18	$137.10	$151.36	$167.10	$184.48	$203.67	$224.85
53				$112.48	$124.18	$137.10	$151.36	$167.10	$184.48
54					$101.89	$112.48	$124.18	$137.10	$151.36
55						$92.29	$101.89	$112.48	$124.18
56							$83.59	$92.29	$101.89
57								$75.72	$83.59
58									$68.59

(4) Stock Price Now Enter =B6

(5) Copy the N Period Stock fromula from above, edit the formula, and copy to the full N-1 Period Stock tree
* Copy cell C17 to cell C51
* Edit the formula to substitute $G$10 for $F$10 and $G$9 for $F$9 to obtain:
=IF(B51="",IF(B50="","",B50*(1+$G$10)),B51*(1+$G$9))
* Copy the cell C49 to the range C51:I58

(6) Copy the Payoffs at Maturity from N Period Call tree
Copy the cell J36 to the range I70:I77

	A	B	C	D	E	F	G	H	I
70	**N-1 Period Call**	$13.88	$21.38	$31.96	$46.16	$64.06	$85.12	$108.37	$134.06
71			$6.98	$11.65	$18.91	$29.71	$44.75	$63.80	$84.85
72				$2.69	$4.96	$8.98	$15.89	$27.23	$44.48
73					$0.60	$1.25	$2.61	$5.45	$11.36
74						$0.00	$0.00	$0.00	$0.00
75							$0.00	$0.00	$0.00
76								$0.00	$0.00
77									$0.00

(7) Copy the N Period Call fromula from above, edit the formula, and copy to the full N-1 Period Call tree
* Copy cell B36 to cell B70
* Edit the formula to substitute $G$11 for $F$11 and $G$8 for $F$8 to obtain:
=IF(C71="","",($G$11*C70+(1-$G$11)*C71)/(1+$G$8))
* Copy the cell B70 to the range B70:H76

	A	B
86	**Average of N Period and N-1 Period Call**	$13.60

(8) (N Period Call +N-1 Period Call) /2
Enter =(B36+B70)/2

Results. The 8-period price is $13.32 and the 7-period price is $13.88. The average of these two prices is $13.60. This is a much more accurate estimate true option price, because the binomial model alternates between overshooting the true price and undershooting the true price as additional periods are added.

17.6 Convergence to Normal

Problem. At the close of trading on April 30, 2010, the stock price of Amazon.com was $137.10, the standard deviation of daily returns is 38.67%, and the option time to maturity was 0.4583 years. Show what happens to the stock price at maturity distribution of the binomial stock price tree as the number of periods increases. Show what happens to the continuous cumulative return distribution of the binomial stock price tree as the number of periods increases.

Solution Strategy. Given a number of periods, compute the stock price at maturity for each terminal node of the binomial tree. Given the stock price at maturity for each node, compute the corresponding continuous cumulative return and the probability of each terminal node. Then see what happens to the stock price at maturity graph and continuous cumulative return graph as the number of periods increases.

FIGURE 17.13 Binomial Option Pricing – Convergence To Normal.

	A	B	C	D	E	F	G	H	I	J	K	L	M
1	**BINOMIAL OPTION PRICING**			**Convergence to Normal**									
2				(2) If Node Number > Number of Periods, Then NA()									
3				Else (Stock Price Now) * (1 + Up Movement/Period)^(Node Number)									
4				* (1 + Down Movement/Period)^(Number of Periods - Node Number)									
5	Inputs			Enter =IF(B14>$B$12,NA(),$B$6*((1+$F$9)^B14)*((1+$F$10)^($B$12-B14)))									
				and copy across									
6	Stock Price Now	$137.10	137	**Outputs**			(1) Copy the Outputs column from the previous sheet						
7	Standard Dev (Annual)	38.67%	38	Time / Period		0.458	Copy the range F7:F10 from the previous sheet						
							to the range F7:F10 on this sheet						
8													
9				Up Movement / Period		29.93%							
10	Time To Maturity (Years)	0.4583	4	Down Movement/Period		-23.03%	(4) If Node Number > Number of Periods, Then NA()						
11							Else COBIN(Number of Periods, Node Number)*(0.5^Node Number)						
				(3) LN(Price(t) / Stock price now)			* (0.5^(Number of Periods - Node Number))						
12	Number of Periods	1		Enter =LN(B15/$B$6)			Enter =IF(B14>$B$12,NA(),COMBIN($B$12,B14)*(0.5^B14)						
				and copy across			*(0.5^($B$12-B14))) and copy across						
13													
14	Node Number	0	1	2	3	4	5	6	7	8	9	10	11
15	Price	$105.52	$178.13	#N/A	#N/A	#N/A	#N/A	#N/A	#N/A	#N/A	#N/A	#N/A	#N/A
16	Contin. Cumulative Return	-26.2%	26.2%	#N/A	#N/A	#N/A	#N/A	#N/A	#N/A	#N/A	#N/A	#N/A	#N/A
17	Probability	50.0%	50.0%	#N/A	#N/A	#N/A	#N/A	#N/A	#N/A	#N/A	#N/A	#N/A	#N/A

FIGURE 17.14 Number of periods = 1. Two nodes with a 50%-50% chance.

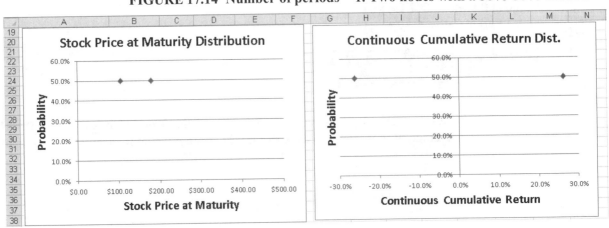

FIGURE 17.15 Number of periods = 4. Five nodes. 6.3%-25%-37.5%-%-25%-6.3% chance.

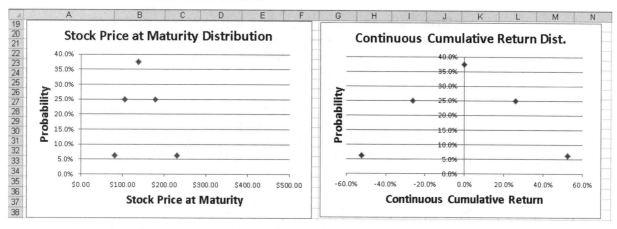

FIGURE 17.16 Number of periods = 13. Fourteen nodes.

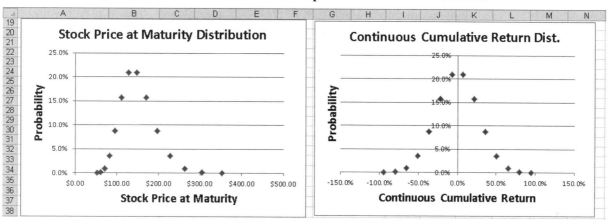

FIGURE 17.17 Number of periods = 33. Thirty-four nodes.

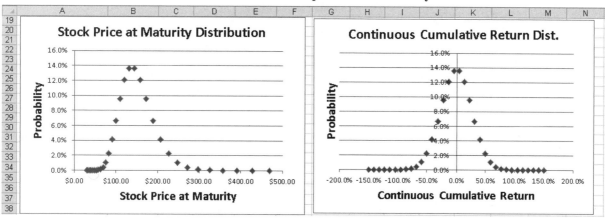

At the number of periods of the binomial model increases, the stock price at maturity converges to a left-skewed, lognormal distribution and the continuous cumulative return converges to the normal distribution.

17.7 American With Discrete Dividends

Problem. Same as before, except we will value American options where the underlying stock pays dividends. At the close of trading on April 30, 2010, the stock price of Amazon.com was $137.10, the standard deviation of daily returns is 38.67%, the yield on a six-month U.S. Treasury Bill was 2.44%, the exercise price of an October 140 call on Amazon.com was $140.00, the exercise price of an October 140 put on Amazon.com was $140.00, and the time to maturity for both October 15, 2010 maturity options was 0.4583 years. Assume that Amazon.com pays certain, riskfree $4.00 dividends on the periods show below. What is the price of an American October 140 call and an American October 140 put on Amazon.com?

Solution Strategy. First, copy the binomial tree parameters, the risk neutral probability, stock price tree, and option payoffs at maturity from the risk neutral model. Second, calculate the total stock price as the sum of the risky stock price plus the discounted value of future dividends. Finally, build a option value tree using the risk neutral probability and accounting for optimal early exercise.

FIGURE 17.18 Binomial – American With Discrete Dividends – Call.

	A	B	C	D	E	F	G	H	I	J
1	**BINOMIAL OPTION PRICING**			**American With Discrete Dividends**						**Call**
2										
3	**Inputs**	Option Type				Early Exercise				
4	Option Type	● Call ○ Put	1	Early Exercise		○ European ● American	2			
5	Underlying Asset Type	Underlying Asset Type ● Stock ○ Stock Index ○ Futures ○ Foreign Currency					1			
6	Stock Price Now	$137.10	137		**Outputs**					
7	Standard Dev (Annual)	38.67%	38	Time / Period		0.057				
8	Riskfree Rate (Annual)	2.44%	24	(Riskfree Rate - Under. Asset Yield) / Period		0.08%				
9	Exercise Price	$140.00	140	Up Movement / Period		9.70%				
10	Time To Maturity (Years)	0.4583	4	Down Movement/Period		-8.84%				
11	Underlying Asset Yield is Stock Dividend Yield (d)	1.00%	1	Risk Neutral Probability		48.13%				
12	Number of Periods	8								
13		**Now**								**Maturity**
14	**Period**	**0**	**1**	**2**	**3**	**4**	**5**	**6**	**7**	**8**
15	**Time**	**0.000**	**0.057**	**0.115**	**0.172**	**0.229**	**0.286**	**0.344**	**0.401**	**0.458**
16										
17	**Risky Part of the Stock**	$137.10	$150.40	$164.98	$180.98	$198.53	$217.78	$238.90	$262.07	$287.48
18			$124.98	$137.10	$150.40	$164.98	$180.98	$198.53	$217.78	$238.90
19				$113.93	$124.98	$137.10	$150.40	$164.98	$180.98	$198.53
20					$103.86	$113.93	$124.98	$137.10	$150.40	$164.98
21						$94.68	$103.86	$113.93	$124.98	$137.10
22							$86.31	$94.68	$103.86	$113.93
23								$78.68	$86.31	$94.68
24									$71.72	$78.68
25										$65.38
26										
27	**Riskfree Dividends**		$0.00	$0.00	$0.00	$4.00	$0.00	$0.00	$4.00	$0.00
28										
29	**Cum. Pres Value Factor**	100.00%	97.62%	95.29%	93.02%	90.81%	88.64%	86.53%	84.47%	82.46%
30										
31	**Total Stock Price**	$144.11	$157.58	$172.34	$188.52	$202.25	$221.59	$242.80	$262.07	$287.48
32			$132.16	$144.46	$157.93	$168.70	$184.79	$202.43	$217.78	$238.90
33				$121.29	$132.52	$140.82	$154.21	$168.88	$180.98	$198.53
34					$111.40	$117.65	$128.79	$141.00	$150.40	$164.98
35						$98.40	$107.67	$117.84	$124.98	$137.10
36							$90.12	$98.58	$103.86	$113.93
37								$82.58	$86.31	$94.68
38									$71.72	$78.68
39										$65.38

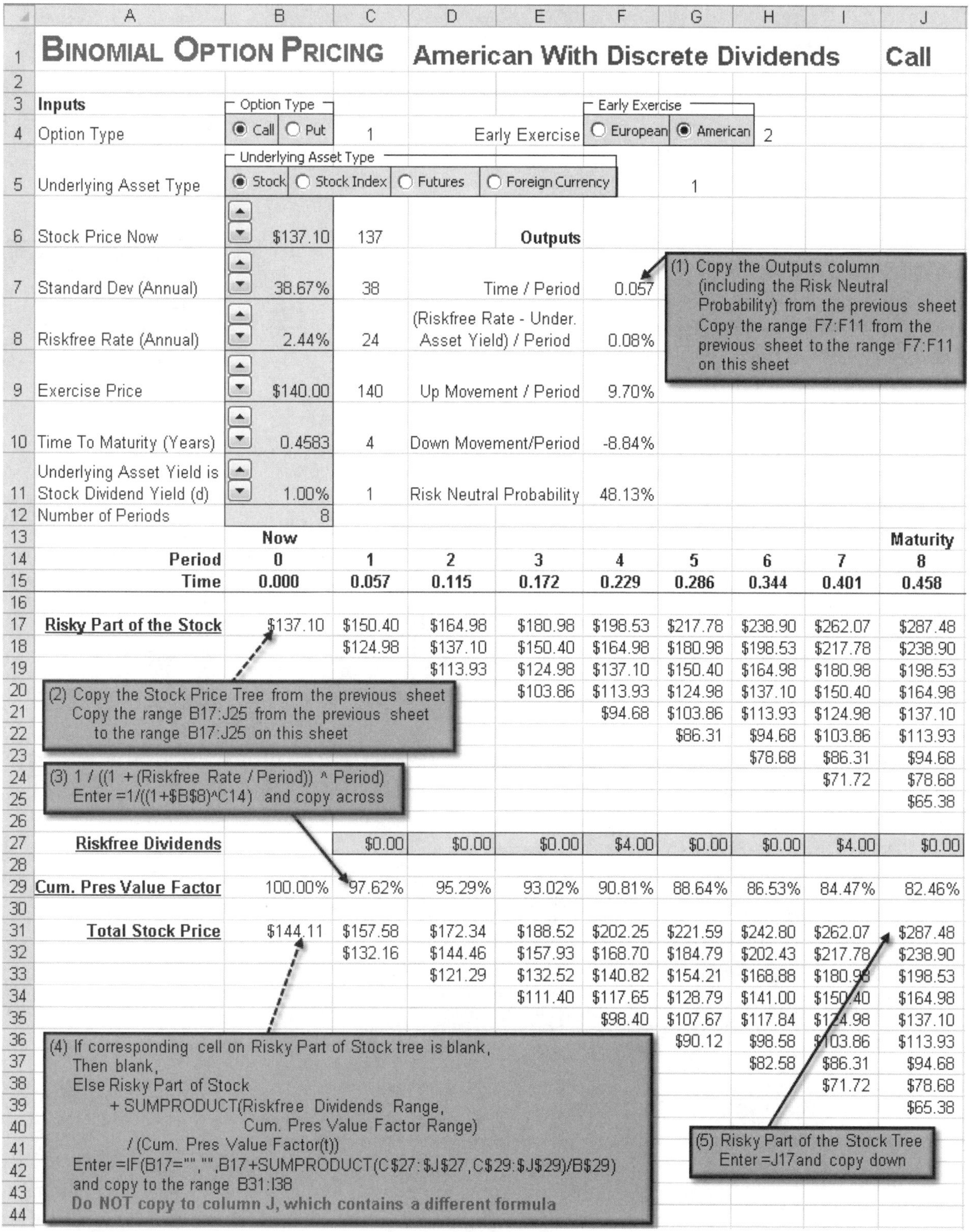

Annotations:

(1) Copy the Outputs column (including the Risk Neutral Probability) from the previous sheet Copy the range F7:F11 from the previous sheet to the range F7:F11 on this sheet

(2) Copy the Stock Price Tree from the previous sheet Copy the range B17:J25 from the previous sheet to the range B17:J25 on this sheet

(3) 1 / ((1 + (Riskfree Rate / Period)) ^ Period) Enter =1/((1+$B$8)^C14) and copy across

(4) If corresponding cell on Risky Part of Stock tree is blank,
Then blank,
Else Risky Part of Stock
     + SUMPRODUCT(Riskfree Dividends Range,
                        Cum. Pres Value Factor Range)
     / (Cum. Pres Value Factor(t))
Enter =IF(B17="","",B17+SUMPRODUCT(C$27:$J$27,C$29:$J$29)/B$29)
and copy to the range B31:I38
Do NOT copy to column J, which contains a different formula

(5) Risky Part of the Stock Tree Enter =J17 and copy down

FIGURE 17.19 Binomial – American With Discrete Dividends - Call.

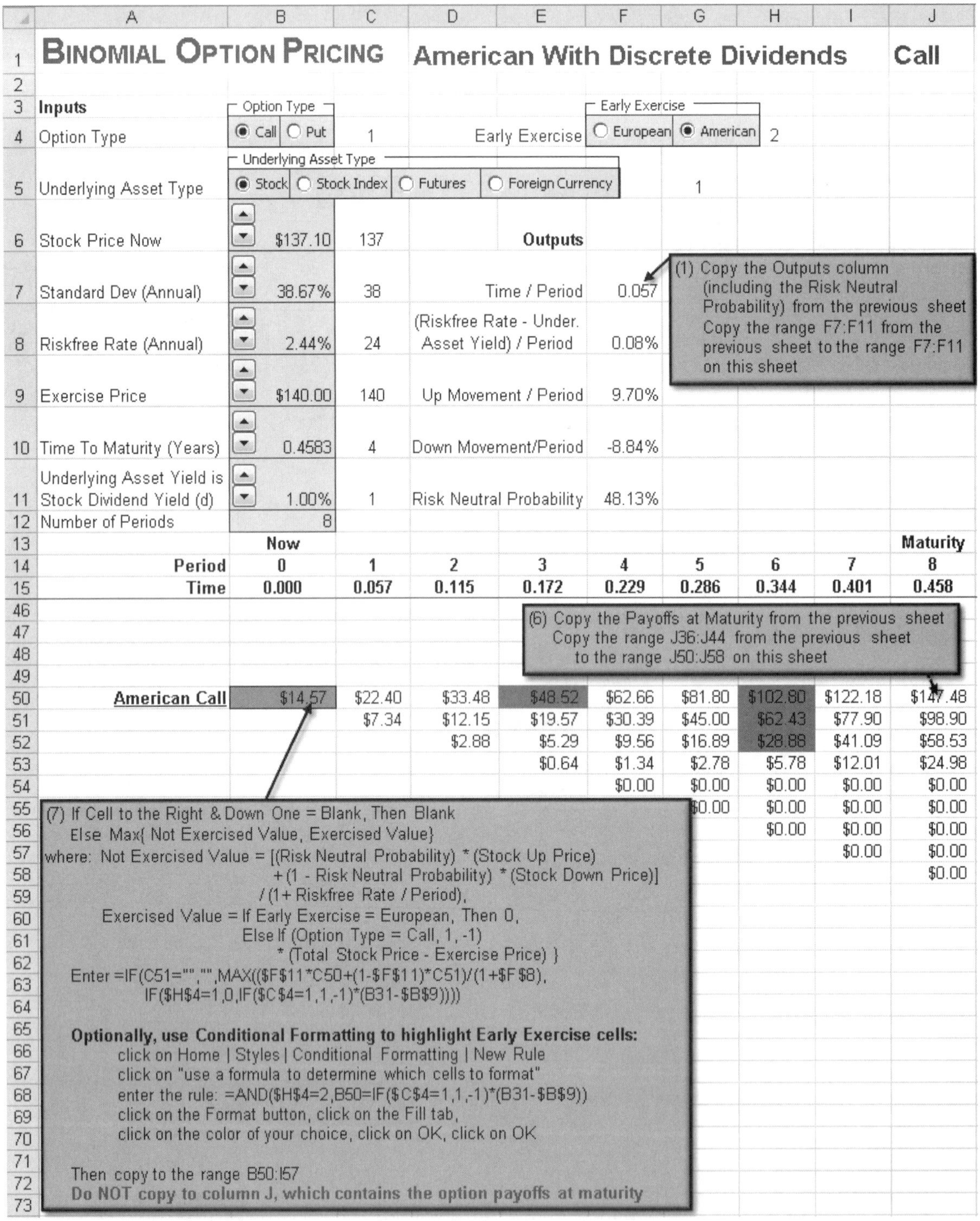

	A	B	C	D	E	F	G	H	I	J
1	**BINOMIAL OPTION PRICING**			American With Discrete Dividends						**Call**
2										
3	**Inputs**	Option Type				Early Exercise				
4	Option Type	◉ Call ○ Put	1		Early Exercise	○ European ◉ American		2		
5	Underlying Asset Type	Underlying Asset Type ◉ Stock ○ Stock Index ○ Futures ○ Foreign Currency					1			
6	Stock Price Now	$137.10	137		**Outputs**					
7	Standard Dev (Annual)	38.67%	38		Time / Period	0.057				
8	Riskfree Rate (Annual)	2.44%	24	(Riskfree Rate - Under. Asset Yield) / Period		0.08%				
9	Exercise Price	$140.00	140	Up Movement / Period		9.70%				
10	Time To Maturity (Years)	0.4583	4	Down Movement/Period		-8.84%				
11	Underlying Asset Yield is Stock Dividend Yield (d)	1.00%	1	Risk Neutral Probability		48.13%				
12	Number of Periods	8								
13		**Now**								**Maturity**
14	Period	0	1	2	3	4	5	6	7	8
15	Time	0.000	0.057	0.115	0.172	0.229	0.286	0.344	0.401	0.458
46										
47										
48										
49										
50	**American Call**	$14.57	$22.40	$33.48	$48.52	$62.66	$81.80	$102.80	$122.18	$147.48
51			$7.34	$12.15	$19.57	$30.39	$45.00	$62.43	$77.90	$98.90
52				$2.88	$5.29	$9.56	$16.89	$28.88	$41.09	$58.53
53					$0.64	$1.34	$2.78	$5.78	$12.01	$24.98
54						$0.00	$0.00	$0.00	$0.00	$0.00
55							$0.00	$0.00	$0.00	$0.00
56								$0.00	$0.00	$0.00
57									$0.00	$0.00
58										$0.00

(1) Copy the Outputs column (including the Risk Neutral Probability) from the previous sheet Copy the range F7:F11 from the previous sheet to the range F7:F11 on this sheet

(6) Copy the Payoffs at Maturity from the previous sheet Copy the range J36:J44 from the previous sheet to the range J50:J58 on this sheet

(7) If Cell to the Right & Down One = Blank, Then Blank
Else Max{ Not Exercised Value, Exercised Value}
where: Not Exercised Value = [(Risk Neutral Probability) * (Stock Up Price)
+ (1 - Risk Neutral Probability) * (Stock Down Price)]
/ (1+ Riskfree Rate / Period),
Exercised Value = If Early Exercise = European, Then 0,
Else If (Option Type = Call, 1, -1)
* (Total Stock Price - Exercise Price) }
Enter =IF(C51="","",MAX(($F$11*C50+(1-$F$11)*C51)/(1+$F$8),
IF($H$4=1,0,IF($C$4=1,1,-1)*(B31-$B$9))))

Optionally, use Conditional Formatting to highlight Early Exercise cells:
click on Home | Styles | Conditional Formatting | New Rule
click on "use a formula to determine which cells to format"
enter the rule: =AND($H$4=2,B50=IF($C$4=1,1,-1)*(B31-$B$9))
click on the Format button, click on the Fill tab,
click on the color of your choice, click on OK, click on OK

Then copy to the range B50:I57
Do NOT copy to column J, which contains the option payoffs at maturity

The purple-shading highlights the periods and call prices where it is optimal to exercise the American call early. Notice that it is optimal to exercise an American call early just before a dividend is paid, which will reduce the value of the underlying stock and thus reduce the value of an unexercised call option. We see that the model predicts an eight-period American call price of $14.57.

FIGURE 17.20 American With Discrete Dividends - Put.

▲	A	B	C	D	E	F	G	H	I	J
1	**BINOMIAL OPTION PRICING**			**American With Discrete Dividends**						**Put**
2										
3	**Inputs**	┌ Option Type ┐				┌ Early Exercise ┐				
4	Option Type	○ Call ● Put	2		Early Exercise	○ European ● American		2		
5	Underlying Asset Type	┌ Underlying Asset Type ┐ ● Stock ○ Stock Index ○ Futures ○ Foreign Currency					1			
6	Stock Price Now	$137.10	137		**Outputs**					
7	Standard Dev (Annual)	38.67%	38		Time / Period	0.057				
8	Riskfree Rate (Annual)	2.44%	24	(Riskfree Rate - Under. Asset Yield) / Period		0.08%				
9	Exercise Price	$140.00	140	Up Movement / Period		9.70%				
10	Time To Maturity (Years)	0.4583	4	Down Movement/Period		-8.84%				
11	Underlying Asset Yield is Stock Dividend Yield (d)	1.00%	1	Risk Neutral Probability		48.13%				
12	Number of Periods	8								
13		**Now**								**Maturity**
14	**Period**	**0**	**1**	**2**	**3**	**4**	**5**	**6**	**7**	**8**
15	**Time**	**0.000**	**0.057**	**0.115**	**0.172**	**0.229**	**0.286**	**0.344**	**0.401**	**0.458**

(1) Copy the Outputs column (including the Risk Neutral Probability) from the previous sheet Copy the range F7:F11 from the previous sheet to the range F7:F11 on this sheet

(6) Copy the Payoffs at Maturity from the previous sheet Copy the range J36:J44 from the previous sheet to the range J50:J58 on this sheet

▲	A	B	C	D	E	F	G	H	I	J
50	**American Put**	**$15.36**	$9.16	$4.44	$1.49	$0.21	$0.00	$0.00	$0.00	$0.00
51			$21.13	$13.56	$7.19	$2.67	$0.40	$0.00	$0.00	$0.00
52				$28.20	$19.49	$11.39	$4.78	$0.78	$0.00	$0.00
53					$36.32	$27.05	$17.54	$8.51	$1.50	$0.00
54						$44.98	$35.91	$25.95	$15.02	$2.90
55							$53.46	$45.21	$36.14	$26.07
56								$61.21	$53.69	$45.32
57									$68.28	$61.32
58										$74.62

(7) If Cell to the Right & Down One = Blank, Then Blank
Else Max{ Not Exercised Value, Exercised Value}
where: Not Exercised Value = [(Risk Neutral Probability) * (Stock Up Price)
+ (1 - Risk Neutral Probability) * (Stock Down Price)]
/ (1 + Riskfree Rate / Period),
Exercised Value = If Early Exercise = European, Then 0,
Else If (Option Type = Call, 1, -1)
* (Total Stock Price - Exercise Price) }
Enter =IF(C51="","",MAX(($F$11*C50+(1-$F$11)*C51)/(1+$F$8),
IF($H$4=1,0,IF($C$4=1,1,-1)*(B31-$B$9))))

Optionally, use Conditional Formatting to highlight Early Exercise cells:
click on Home | Styles | Conditional Formatting | New Rule
click on "use a formula to determine which cells to format"
enter the rule: =AND($H$4=2,B50=IF($C$4=1,1,-1)*(B31-$B$9))
click on the Format button, click on the Fill tab,
click on the color of your choice, click on OK, click on OK

Then copy to the range B50:I57
Do NOT copy to column J, which contains the option payoffs at maturity

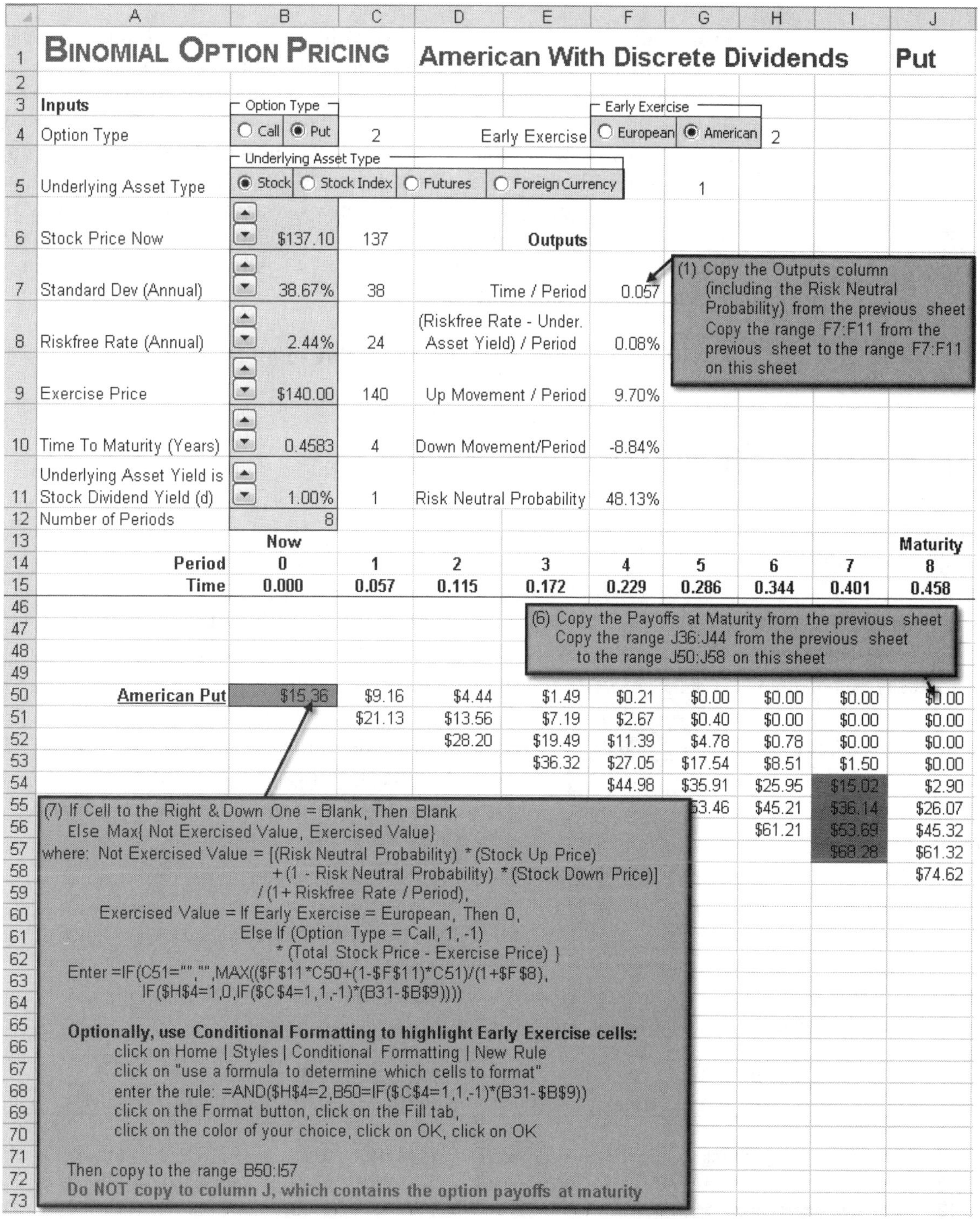

The purple-shading highlights the periods and call prices where it is optimal to exercise the American put early. Notice that it is optimal to exercise an American put early just when a dividend is paid, which will reduce the value of the underlying stock and thus increases the value of the put option. We see that the model predicts an eight-period American put price of $15.36.

17.8 Full-Scale

Problem. Same as before, except we will use a fifty-period model to evaluate it in order to increase accuracy. At the close of trading on April 30, 2010, the stock price of Amazon.com was $137.10, the standard deviation of daily returns is 38.67%, the yield on a six-month U.S. Treasury Bill was 2.44%, the exercise price of an October 140 call on Amazon.com was $140.00, the exercise price of an October 140 put on Amazon.com was $140.00, and the time to maturity for both October 15, 2010 maturity options was 0.4583 years. Assume that Amazon.com pays certain, riskfree $4.00 dividends on the periods show below. What is the price of an American October 140 call and an American October 140 put on Amazon.com?

FIGURE 17.21 Binomial Option Pricing - Full-Scale - Call.

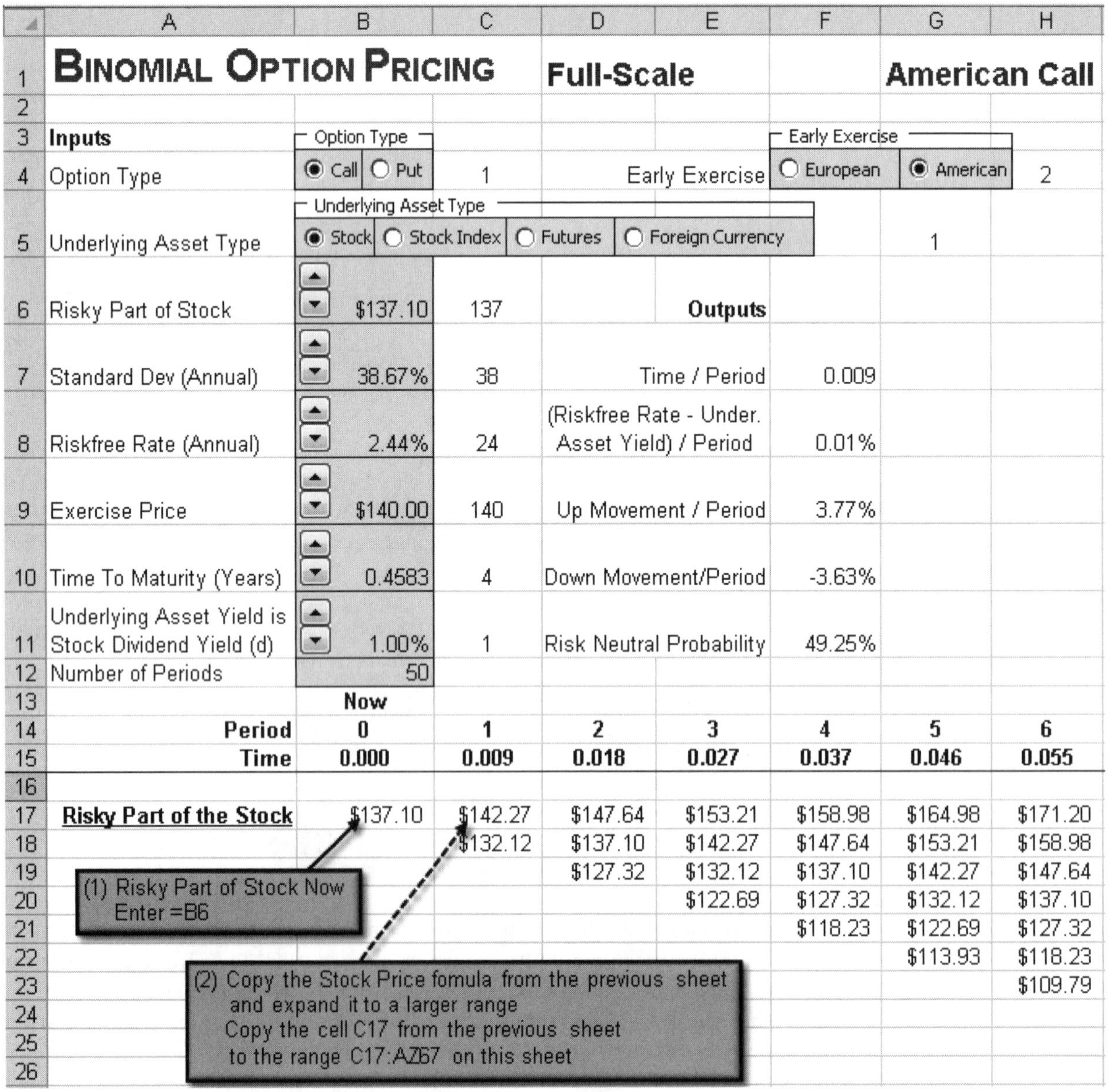

	A	B	C	D	E	F	G	H
1	**BINOMIAL OPTION PRICING**			**Full-Scale**			**American Call**	
2								
3	**Inputs**	Option Type				Early Exercise		
4	Option Type	◉ Call ○ Put	1	Early Exercise		○ European ◉ American	2	
5	Underlying Asset Type	Underlying Asset Type ◉ Stock ○ Stock Index ○ Futures ○ Foreign Currency					1	
6	Risky Part of Stock	$137.10	137		**Outputs**			
7	Standard Dev (Annual)	38.67%	38	Time / Period		0.009		
8	Riskfree Rate (Annual)	2.44%	24	(Riskfree Rate - Under. Asset Yield) / Period		0.01%		
9	Exercise Price	$140.00	140	Up Movement / Period		3.77%		
10	Time To Maturity (Years)	0.4583	4	Down Movement/Period		-3.63%		
11	Underlying Asset Yield is Stock Dividend Yield (d)	1.00%	1	Risk Neutral Probability		49.25%		
12	Number of Periods	50						
13		**Now**						
14	**Period**	**0**	**1**	**2**	**3**	**4**	**5**	**6**
15	**Time**	**0.000**	**0.009**	**0.018**	**0.027**	**0.037**	**0.046**	**0.055**
16								
17	**Risky Part of the Stock**	$137.10	$142.27	$147.64	$153.21	$158.98	$164.98	$171.20
18			$132.12	$137.10	$142.27	$147.64	$153.21	$158.98
19				$127.32	$132.12	$137.10	$142.27	$147.64
20					$122.69	$127.32	$132.12	$137.10
21						$118.23	$122.69	$127.32
22							$113.93	$118.23
23								$109.79
24								
25								
26								

(1) Risky Part of Stock Now Enter =B6

(2) Copy the Stock Price fomula from the previous sheet and expand it to a larger range
Copy the cell C17 from the previous sheet to the range C17:AZ67 on this sheet

Solution Strategy. First, copy the binomial tree parameters, the risk neutral probability, stock price tree, and option payoffs at maturity from the risk neutral model. Second, calculate the total stock price as the sum of the risky stock price plus the discounted value of future dividends. Finally, build a option value tree using the risk neutral probability and accounting for optimal early exercise.

FIGURE 17.22 Binomial Option Pricing - Full-Scale - Call (Continued).

	A	B	C	D	E	F	G	H
1	**BINOMIAL OPTION PRICING**			**Full-Scale**			**American Call**	
2								
3	**Inputs**	Option Type				Early Exercise		
4	Option Type	◉ Call ○ Put	1		Early Exercise	○ European	◉ American	2
5	Underlying Asset Type	Underlying Asset Type: ◉ Stock ○ Stock Index ○ Futures ○ Foreign Currency					1	
6	Risky Part of Stock	$137.10	137		**Outputs**			
7	Standard Dev (Annual)	38.67%	38		Time / Period	0.009		
8	Riskfree Rate (Annual)	2.44%	24	(Riskfree Rate - Under. Asset Yield) / Period		0.01%		
9	Exercise Price	$140.00	140	Up Movement / Period		3.77%		
10	Time To Maturity (Years)	0.4583	4	Down Movement/Period		-3.63%		
11	Underlying Asset Yield is Stock Dividend Yield (d)	1.00%	1	Risk Neutral Probability		49.25%		
12	Number of Periods	50						
13		**Now**						
14	**Period**	**0**	**1**	**2**	**3**	**4**	**5**	**6**
15	**Time**	**0.000**	**0.009**	**0.018**	**0.027**	**0.037**	**0.046**	**0.055**
64								
65	(3) (Cum. Pres Value Factor(t-1)) * EXP(- (Riskfree Rate / Period))							
66	Enter =B71*EXP(-$F$8) and copy across							
67								
68								
69	**Riskfree Dividends**		$0.00	$0.00	$0.00	$0.00	$5.00	$0.00
70								
71	**Cum. Pres Value Factor**	100.000%	99.987%	99.974%	99.960%	99.947%	99.934%	99.921%
72								
73	**Total Stock Price**	$152.06	$157.23	$162.60	$168.17	$173.95	$174.95	$181.17
74			$147.08	$152.06	$157.24	$162.61	$163.18	$168.96
75				$142.28	$147.08	$152.07	$152.24	$157.61
76					$137.65	$142.28	$142.09	$147.07
77						$133.20	$132.66	$137.29
78	(4) If corresponding cell on Risky Part of Stock tree is blank,						$123.90	$128.20
79	Then blank,							$119.76
80	Else Risky Part of Stock							
81	+ SUMPRODUCT(Riskfree Dividends Range,							
82	Cum. Pres Value Factor Range)							
83	/ (Cum. Pres Value Factor(t))							
84	Enter =IF(B17="","",B17+SUMPRODUCT(C$69:$AZ$69,C$71:$AZ$71)/B$71)							
85	and copy to the range B73:AY122							
86	Do NOT copy to column AZ, which contains a different formula							

The up movement / period and down movement / period are calibrated to correspond to the stock's annual standard deviation. It is not necessary to calibrate them to the stock's expected return.[6]

FIGURE 17.23 Binomial Option Pricing - Full-Scale - Call (Continued).

	AU	AV	AW	AX	AY	AZ
13						Maturity
14	45	46	47	48	49	50
15	0.412	0.422	0.431	0.440	0.449	0.458
64			$24.06	$24.97	$25.91	$26.89
65				$23.19	$24.06	$24.97
66			(5) Risky Part of the Stock Tree		$22.35	$23.19
67			Enter =AZ17 and copy down			$21.53
68						
69	$0.00	$0.00	$0.00	$0.00	$0.00	$0.00
70						
71	99.408%	99.395%	99.382%	99.368%	99.355%	99.342%
72						
73	$725.40	$752.75	$781.15	$810.61	$841.18	$872.91
74	$673.62	$699.03	$725.40	$752.75	$781.15	$810.61
75	$625.55	$649.14	$673.62	$699.03	$725.40	$752.75

FIGURE 17.24 Binomial Option Pricing - Full-Scale - Call (Continued).

	AR	AS	AT	AU	AV	AW	AX	AY	AZ
13									Maturity
14	42	43	44	45	46	47	48	49	50
15	0.385	0.394	0.403	0.412	0.422	0.431	0.440	0.449	0.458
120						$24.06	$24.97	$25.91	$26.89
121							$23.19	$24.06	$24.97
122		(6) If Option Type = Call,						$22.35	$23.19
123		Then Call Payoff at Maturity = Max (Stock Price at Maturity - Exercise Price, 0)							$21.53
124		Else Put Payoff at Maturity = Max (Exercise Price - Stock Price at Maturity, 0)							
125		Enter =IF($C$4=1,MAX(AZ73-$B$9,0),MAX($B$9-AZ73,0))							
126		and copy to the range AZ128:AZ177							
127	$509.29	$533.75	$559.14	$585.49	$612.83	$641.20	$670.64	$701.20	$732.91
128	$462.96	$485.68	$509.25	$533.72	$559.10	$585.45	$612.79	$641.16	$670.61
129	$419.94	$441.03	$462.92	$485.64	$509.21	$533.68	$559.07	$585.41	$612.75

[6] At full-scale (50 periods), the binomial option price is very insensitive to the expected return of the stock. For example, suppose that you calibrated this Amazon.com case to an annual expected return of 10%. Just add **.1*F7** to the formulas for the up and down movements / period. So the up movement / period in cell **F9** would become **=EXP(.1*F7+B7*SQRT(F7))-1** and the down movement / period in cell **F10** would become **=EXP(.1*F7-B7*SQRT(F7))-1**. This changes the option price by less than 1/100th of one penny! In the (Black-Scholes) limit as the number of (sub)periods goes to infinity, the option price becomes totally insensitive to the expected return of the stock. Because of this insensitivity, the conventions for calculating the up movement / period and down movement / period ignore the expected return of the stock.

FIGURE 17.25 Binomial Option Pricing - Full-Scale - Call (Continued).

	A	B	C	D	E	F	G	H
1	**BINOMIAL OPTION PRICING**			**Full-Scale**			**American Call**	
2								
3	**Inputs**	⌐ Option Type ⌐				⌐ Early Exercise		
4	Option Type	◉ Call ○ Put	1		Early Exercise	○ European	◉ American	2
5	Underlying Asset Type	⌐ Underlying Asset Type ◉ Stock ○ Stock Index ○ Futures ○ Foreign Currency					1	
6	Risky Part of Stock	▲▼ $137.10	137		**Outputs**			
7	Standard Dev (Annual)	▲▼ 38.67%	38		Time / Period	0.009		
8	Riskfree Rate (Annual)	▲▼ 2.44%	24	(Riskfree Rate - Under. Asset Yield) / Period		0.01%		
9	Exercise Price	▲▼ $140.00	140	Up Movement / Period		3.77%		
10	Time To Maturity (Years)	▲▼ 0.4583	4	Down Movement/Period		-3.63%		
11	Underlying Asset Yield is Stock Dividend Yield (d)	▲▼ 1.00%	1	Risk Neutral Probability		49.25%		
12	Number of Periods	50						
13		**Now**						
14	**Period**	**0**	**1**	**2**	**3**	**4**	**5**	**6**
15	**Time**	**0.000**	**0.009**	**0.018**	**0.027**	**0.037**	**0.046**	**0.055**
126								
127	**American Call**	$15.59	$19.09	$23.25	$28.19	$33.95	$36.29	$41.98
128			$12.20	$15.05	$18.47	$22.61	$26.01	$30.77
129				$9.44	$11.73	$14.46	$17.67	$21.40
130					$7.21	$9.08	$11.35	$14.06
131						$5.39	$6.89	$8.72
132							$3.95	$5.11
133								$2.82

(7) If Cell to the Right & Down One = Blank, Then Blank
Else Max{ Not Exercised Value, Exercised Value}
where: Not Exercised Value = [(Risk Neutral Probability) * (Stock Up Price)
+ (1 - Risk Neutral Probability) * (Stock Down Price)]
/ (1 + Riskfree Rate / Period),
Exercised Value = If Early Exercise = European, Then 0,
Else If (Option Type = Call, 1, -1)
* (Total Stock Price - Exercise Price) }
Enter =IF(C128="","",MAX(($F$11*C127+(1-$F$11)*C128)/(1+$F$8),
IF($H$4=1,0,IF($C$4=1,1,-1)*(B73-$B$9))))

Optionally, use Conditional Formatting to highlight Early Exercise cells:
click on Home | Styles | Conditional Formatting | New Rule
click on "use a formula to determine which cells to format"
enter the rule: =AND($H$4=2,B127=IF($C$4=1,1,-1)*(B73-$B$9))
click on the Format button, click on the Fill tab,
click on the color of your choice, click on OK, click on OK

Then copy to the range B127:AY176
Do NOT copy to column AZ, which contains the option payoffs at maturity

Again, optimal early exercise for an American call occurs just before a dividend is paid. We see that the Full-Scale model predicts an American call price of $15.59. Now let's check the put.

FIGURE 17.26 Binomial Option Pricing - Full-Scale - Put Option.

	AJ	AK	AL	AM	AN	AO	AP
14	34	35	36	37	38	39	40
15	0.312	0.321	0.330	0.339	0.348	0.357	0.367
68							
69	$0.00	$5.00	$0.00	$0.00	$0.00	$0.00	$0.00
70							
147	$30.44	$26.52	$22.58	$18.68	$14.88	$11.29	$8.03
148	$38.05	$34.25	$30.35	$26.38	$22.37	$18.36	$14.46
149	$45.30	$41.75	$38.04	$34.22	$30.28	$26.25	$22.16
150	$52.06	$48.76	$45.32	$41.75	$38.04	$34.20	$30.23
151	$58.34	$55.27	$52.08	$48.76	$45.32	$41.75	$38.04
152	$64.16	$61.32	$58.35	$55.27	$52.08	$48.76	$45.32
153	$69.57	$66.94	$64.16	$61.32	$58.35	$55.27	$52.08
154	$74.60	$72.15	$69.59	$66.94	$64.18	$61.32	$58.35
155	$79.26	$76.99	$74.62	$72.15	$69.59	$66.94	$64.18
156	$83.60	$81.49	$79.28	$76.99	$74.62	$72.15	$69.59
157	$87.62	$85.67	$83.62	$81.49	$79.28	$76.99	$74.62
158	$91.36	$89.54	$87.64	$85.67	$83.62	$81.49	$79.28
159	$94.83	$93.14	$91.38	$89.54	$87.64	$85.67	$83.62
160	$98.05	$96.49	$94.85	$93.14	$91.38	$89.54	$87.64
161	$101.04	$99.59	$98.07	$96.49	$94.85	$93.14	$91.38
162		$102.48	$101.06	$99.59	$98.07	$96.49	$94.85
163			$103.84	$102.48	$101.06	$99.59	$98.07
164			$105.16	$103.84	$102.48	$101.06
165				$106.42	$103.84	$105.16	$103.84
166					$107.64	$106.42
167							$108.82

Optimal early exercise for an American put often occurs on the date that the dividend is paid. More generally, it is optimal to exercise an American put option when the underlying stock price is very low for a given amount of time to maturity.

FIGURE 17.27 Binomial Option Pricing - Full-Scale - Put (Continued).

	A	B	C	D	E	F	G	H
1	**BINOMIAL OPTION PRICING**			**Full-Scale**			**American Put**	
2								
3	**Inputs**	Option Type				Early Exercise		
4	Option Type	○ Call ◉ Put	2		Early Exercise	○ European ◉ American		2
5	Underlying Asset Type	Underlying Asset Type ◉ Stock ○ Stock Index ○ Futures ○ Foreign Currency					1	
6	Risky Part of Stock	$137.10	137		**Outputs**			
7	Standard Dev (Annual)	38.67%	38	Time / Period	0.009			
8	Riskfree Rate (Annual)	2.44%	24	(Riskfree Rate - Under. Asset Yield) / Period	0.01%			
9	Exercise Price	$140.00	140	Up Movement / Period	3.77%			
10	Time To Maturity (Years)	0.4583	4	Down Movement/Period	-3.63%			
11	Underlying Asset Yield is Stock Dividend Yield (d)	1.00%	1	Risk Neutral Probability	49.25%			
12	Number of Periods	50						
13		**Now**						
14	Period	0	1	2	3	4	5	6
15	Time	0.000	0.009	0.018	0.027	0.037	0.046	0.055
126								
127	**American Put**	$15.50	$13.07	$10.85	$8.85	$7.08	$5.55	$4.25
128			$17.87	$15.24	$12.80	$10.57	$8.57	$6.81

We see that the Full-Scale model predicts an American put price of $15.5002.

Problems

1. Download three months of daily stock price for any stock that has listed options on it. What is the annual standard deviation of your stock based on continuous returns?

2. Lookup the current stock price of your stock, use the standard deviation of daily returns you computed, lookup the yield on a six-month U.S. Treasury Bill, lookup the exercise price of a call on your stock that matures in approximately six months, lookup the exercise price of a put on your stock that matures in approximately six months, and compute the time to maturity for both options in fractions of a year. For the call and put that you identified on your stock, determine the replicating portfolio and the price of the call and put using a single-period, replicating portfolio model.

3. For the same inputs as problem 2, determine the replicating portfolio and the price of the call and put using an eight-period, replicating portfolio model.

4. For the same inputs as problem 3, determine the price of the call and put using an eight-period, risk neutral model.

5. For the same inputs as problem 4 determine the price of the call and put using the average of N and N-1 method to evaluate them.

6. For the same inputs as problem 4, show what happens to the stock price at maturity distribution of the binomial stock price tree as the number of periods increases. Show what happens to the continuous cumulative return distribution of the binomial stock price tree as the number of periods increases.

7. Use the same inputs as problem 4. Further, forecast the dividends that you stock pays or make an assumption about the dividends that your stock pays. What is the price of an American call and an American put using an eight-period, risk neutral model of American options with discrete dividends?

8. For the same inputs as problem 7, determine the price of an American call and an American put using a fifty-period, risk neutral model of American options with discrete dividends?

9. Extend the Binomial Option Pricing model to analyze Digital Options. The only thing which needs to be changed is the option's payoff at maturity.
   (a.) For a Digital Call, the Payoff At Maturity

   $$= \$1.00 \text{ When Stock Price At Mat} > \text{Exercise Price}$$
   $$\text{Or } \$0.00 \text{ Otherwise.}$$

   (b.) For a Digital Put, the Payoff At Maturity

   $$= \$1.00 \text{ When Stock Price At Mat} < \text{Exercise Price}$$
   $$\text{Or } \$0.00 \text{ Otherwise.}$$

10. Extend the **Binomial Option Pricing – Full-Scale** model to determine how fast the binomial option price converges to the price in the **Black-Scholes**

Option Pricing – Basics model. Reduce the Full-Scale model to a 10 period model and to a 20 period model. Increase the 50 period model to a 100 period model. Then for the same inputs, compare call and put prices of the 10 period, 20 period, 50 period, 100 period, and Black-Scholes models.

11. Extend the **Binomial Option Pricing – Full-Scale** model to determine how fast the binomial option price with averaging of adjacent odd and even numbers of periods converges to the price in the **Black-Scholes Option Pricing – Basics** model. As you increase the number of periods in the binomial model, it oscillates between overshooting and undershooting the true price. A simple technique to increase price efficiency is to average adjacent odd and even numbers of periods. For example, average the 10 period call price and the 11 period call price. Reduce the Full-Scale model to a 10 period, 11 period, 20 period, and 21 period model. Increase the 50 period model to a 51 period, 100 period, and 101 period model. Then for the same inputs, compare call and put prices of the average of the 10 and 11 period models, 20 and 21 period models, 50 and 51 period models, 100 and 101 period models, and Black-Scholes model.

Chapter 18 Black-Scholes Option Pricing

18.1 Basics

Problem. At the close of trading on April 30, 2010, the stock price of Amazon.com was $137.10, the standard deviation of daily returns is 38.67%, the yield on a six-month U.S. Treasury Bill was 2.44%, the exercise price of an October 140 call on Amazon.com was $140.00, the exercise price of an October 140 put on Amazon.com was $140.00, and the time to maturity for both October 15, 2010 maturity options was 0.4583 years. What is the price of an October 140 call and an October 140 put on Amazon.com?

FIGURE 18.1 Excel Model for Black-Scholes Option Pricing - Basics.

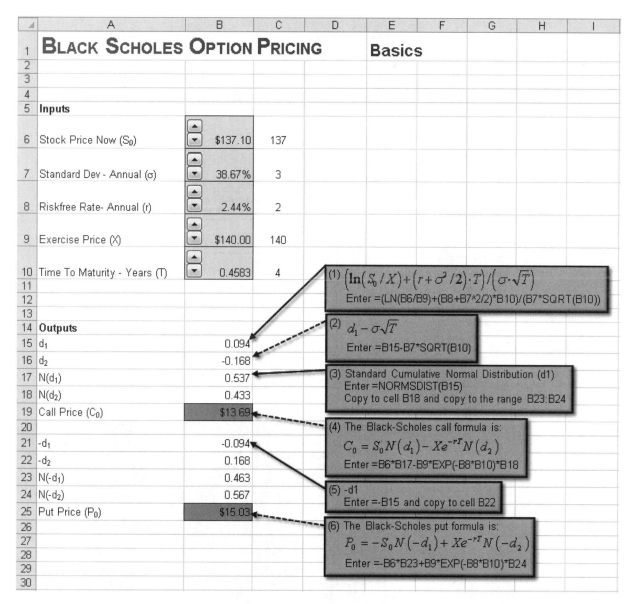

The Black-Scholes model predicts a call price of $13.69. This is four cents different than what the Binominal Option Pricing - Full-Scale Estimation model predicts for a *European* call with identical inputs (including no dividends). The Black-Scholes model predicts a put price of $15.03. This is four cents different than what the Binominal Option Pricing - Full-Scale Estimation model predicts for a *European* put with identical inputs (including no dividends).. The advantage of the Black-Scholes model and its natural analytic extensions is they are quick and easy to calculate. The disadvantage is that they are limited to a narrow range of derivatives (such as *European* options only, etc.).

18.2 Continuous Dividend

Problem. Suppose that Amazon.com paid dividends in tiny amounts on a continuous basis throughout the year at a 1.0% / year rate. What would be the new price of the call and put?

FIGURE 18.2 Black-Scholes – Cont Div Yield and Alt Under Assets – Call

	A	B	C	D	E	F	G	H	I	J
1	**BLACK SCHOLES OPTION PRICING**					**Continuous Dividend Yield and Alternative Underlying Assets**				
3	**Inputs**	Option Type								
4	Option Type	⊙ Call ○ Put	1							
5	Underlying Asset Type	Underlying Asset Type: ⊙ Stock ○ Stock Index ○ Futures ○ Foreign Currency				1				
6	Stock Price Now (S(0))	$137.10	137							
7	Standard Dev - Annual (σ)	38.67%	3							
8	Riskfree Rate- Annual (r)	2.44%	2							
9	Exercise Price (X)	$140.00	140							
10	Time To Maturity - Yrs (T)	0.4583	4							
11	Underlying Asset Yield is Stock Dividend Yield (d)	1.00%	1							
14	**Outputs**									
15	d_1	0.076								
16	d_2	-0.186								
17	$N(d_1)$	0.530								
18	$N(d_2)$	0.426								
19	Call Price (C_0)	$13.35								
21	$-d_1$	-0.076								
22	$-d_2$	0.186								
23	$N(-d_1)$	0.470								
24	$N(-d_2)$	0.574								
25	Put Price (P_0)	$15.32								

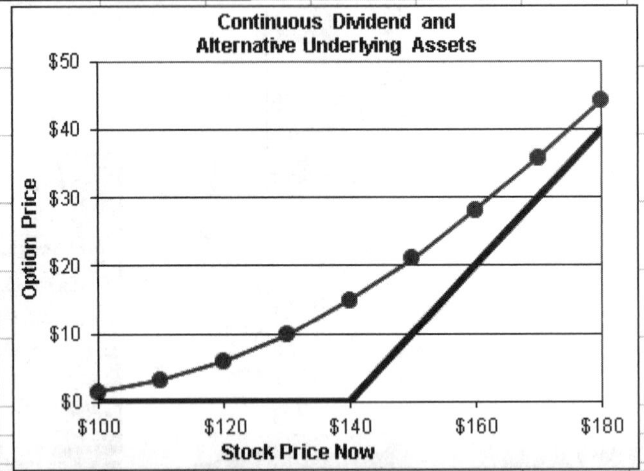

(1) Copy the basic Black-Scholes formulas from the previous sheet. Copy the range B15:B25 from the previous sheet to the range B15:B25

(2) Add dividend yield (*d*) to the d_1 formula:
$$\left(\ln(S_0/X) + \left(r - d + \sigma^2/2\right) \cdot T \right) / \left(\sigma \cdot \sqrt{T}\right)$$
Enter =(LN(B6/B9)+(B8-B11+B7^2/2)*B10)/(B7*SQRT(B10))

(3) Add dividend yield (*d*) to the call formula:
$$C_0 = S_0 e^{-dT} N(d_1) - Xe^{-rT} N(d_2)$$
Enter =B6*EXP(-B11*B10)*B17-B9*EXP(-B8*B10)*B18

(4) Add dividend yield (*d*) to the put formula:
$$P_0 = -S_0 e^{-dT} N(-d_1) + Xe^{-rT} N(-d_2)$$
Enter =-B6*EXP(-B11*B10)*B23+B9*EXP(-B8*B10)*B24

Solution Strategy. Modify the basic Black-Scholes formulas from the previous sheet to include the continuous dividend.

Results. We see that the continuous dividend model predicts a call price of $13.35. This is a drop of 34 cents from the no dividend version. The continuous dividend model predicts a put price of $15.32. This is a rise of 29 cents from the no dividend version. To create a dynamic chart, we have a few more steps.

FIGURE 18.3 Black-Scholes – Cont Div Yield and Alt Under Assets – Call

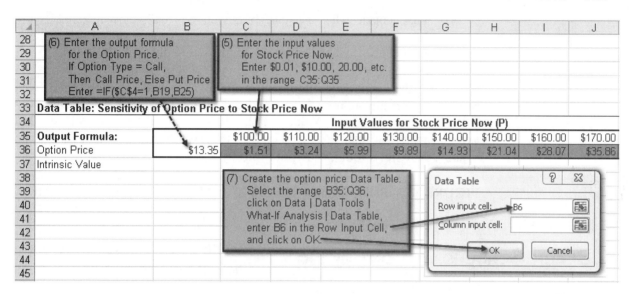

FIGURE 18.4 Black-Scholes – Cont Div Yield and Alt Under Assets – Call

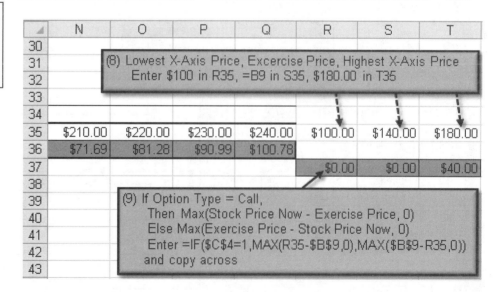

Excel 97-2003 Equivalent

To call up a Data Table in Excel 2003, click on **Data | Table**.

The spin buttons allows you to change Black-Scholes inputs and instantly see the impact on a graph of the option price and intrinsic value. This allows you to perform instant experiments on the Black-Scholes option pricing model. Here is a list of experiments that you might want to perform:

- What happens when the standard deviation is increased?

- What happens when the time to maturity is increased?

- What happens when the exercise price is increased?

- What happens when the riskfree rate is increased?

- What happens when the dividend yield is increased?

- What happens when the standard deviation is really close to zero?

- What happens when the time to maturity is really close to zero?

Notice that the Black-Scholes option price is usually greater than the payoff you would obtain if the option was maturing today (the "intrinsic value"). This extra value is called the "Time Value" of the option. Given your result in the last experiment above, can you explain *why* the extra value is called the "Time Value"? Now let's look at the put option.

FIGURE 18.5 Black-Scholes – Cont Div Yield and Alt Under Assets - Put

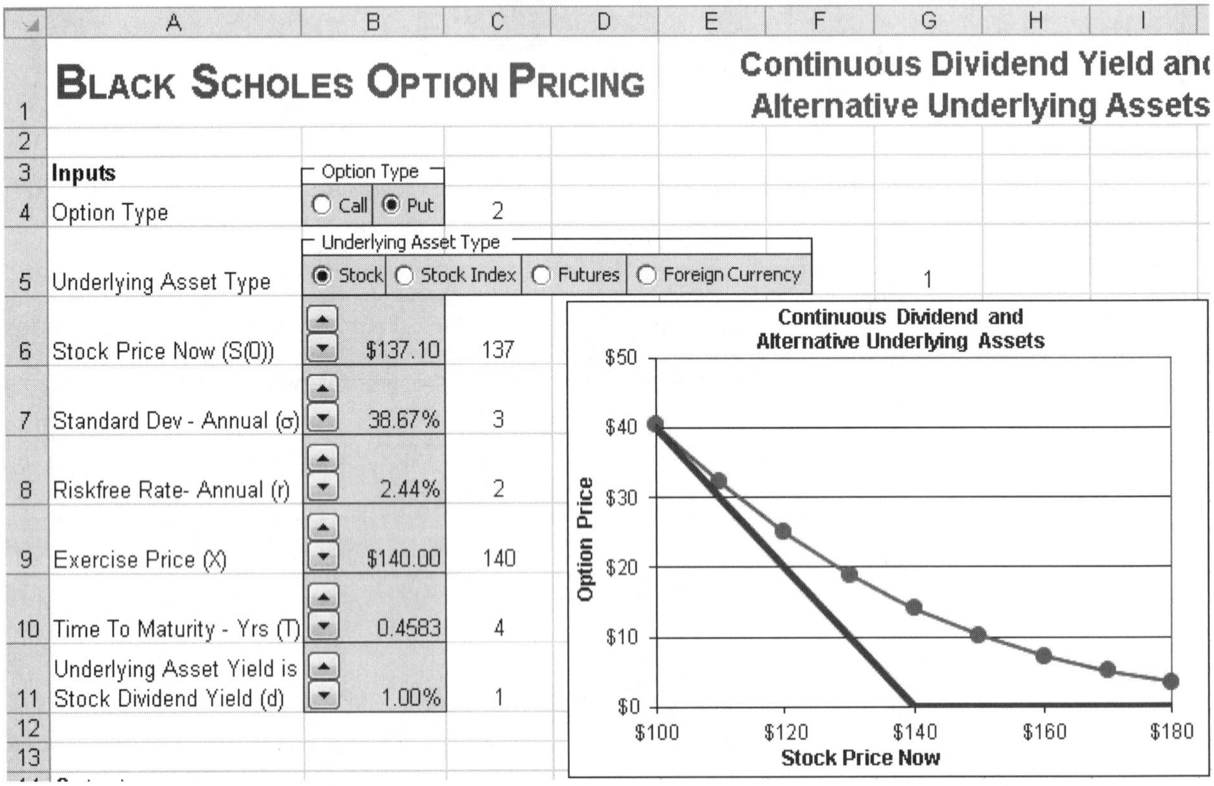

The put option value sometime drops below the intrinsic value. To understand why, try increasing the riskfree rate and see what happens. Then decrease the riskfree rate to zero and see what happens. You can perform many similar experiments on the put option.

The model can handle three additional types of underlying asset (see **row 5**): (1) stock index, (2) futures, and (3) foreign currency. Then the underlying asset yield (see **row 11**) becomes: (1) the stock index dividend yield, (2) the riskfree rate, and (3) the foreign riskfree rate, respectively.

FIGURE 18.6 Black-Scholes – Cont Div Yield and Alt Under Assets – Call

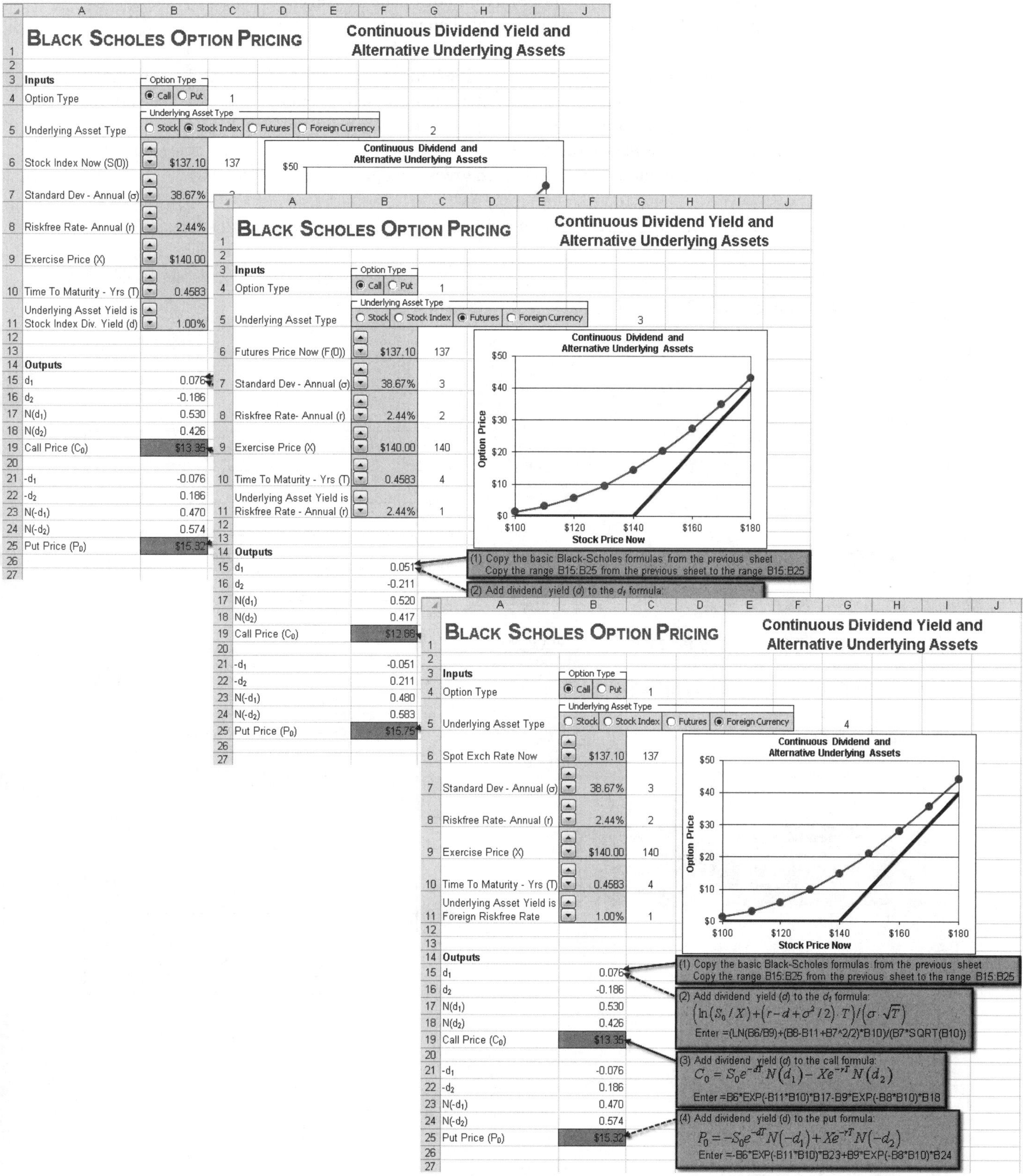

BLACK SCHOLES OPTION PRICING — Continuous Dividend Yield and Alternative Underlying Assets

Sheet 1 (Stock Index):

Row	A	B	C
3	Inputs	Option Type	1
4	Option Type	● Call ○ Put	
5	Underlying Asset Type	○ Stock ● Stock Index ○ Futures ○ Foreign Currency	2
6	Stock Index Now (S(0))	$137.10	137
7	Standard Dev - Annual (σ)	38.67%	
8	Riskfree Rate- Annual (r)	2.44%	
9	Exercise Price (X)	$140.00	
10	Time To Maturity - Yrs (T)	0.4583	
11	Underlying Asset Yield is Stock Index Div. Yield (d)	1.00%	
13	Outputs		
15	d_1	0.076	
16	d_2	-0.186	
17	$N(d_1)$	0.530	
18	$N(d_2)$	0.426	
19	Call Price (C_0)	$13.35	
21	$-d_1$	-0.076	
22	$-d_2$	0.186	
23	$N(-d_1)$	0.470	
24	$N(-d_2)$	0.574	
25	Put Price (P_0)	$15.32	

Sheet 2 (Futures):

Row	A	B	C
3	Inputs	Option Type	1
4	Option Type	● Call ○ Put	
5	Underlying Asset Type	○ Stock ○ Stock Index ● Futures ○ Foreign Currency	3
6	Futures Price Now (F(0))	$137.10	137
7	Standard Dev - Annual (σ)	38.67%	3
8	Riskfree Rate- Annual (r)	2.44%	2
9	Exercise Price (X)	$140.00	140
10	Time To Maturity - Yrs (T)	0.4583	4
11	Underlying Asset Yield is Riskfree Rate - Annual (r)	2.44%	1
14	Outputs		
15	d_1	0.051	
16	d_2	-0.211	
17	$N(d_1)$	0.520	
18	$N(d_2)$	0.417	
19	Call Price (C_0)	$12.88	
21	$-d_1$	-0.051	
22	$-d_2$	0.211	
23	$N(-d_1)$	0.480	
24	$N(-d_2)$	0.583	
25	Put Price (P_0)	$15.75	

(1) Copy the basic Black-Scholes formulas from the previous sheet. Copy the range B15:B25 from the previous sheet to the range B15:B25

(2) Add dividend yield (d) to the d_1 formula:

Sheet 3 (Foreign Currency):

Row	A	B	C
3	Inputs	Option Type	1
4	Option Type	● Call ○ Put	
5	Underlying Asset Type	○ Stock ○ Stock Index ○ Futures ● Foreign Currency	4
6	Spot Exch Rate Now	$137.10	137
7	Standard Dev - Annual (σ)	38.67%	3
8	Riskfree Rate- Annual (r)	2.44%	2
9	Exercise Price (X)	$140.00	140
10	Time To Maturity - Yrs (T)	0.4583	4
11	Underlying Asset Yield is Foreign Riskfree Rate	1.00%	1
14	Outputs		
15	d_1	0.076	
16	d_2	-0.186	
17	$N(d_1)$	0.530	
18	$N(d_2)$	0.426	
19	Call Price (C_0)	$13.35	
21	$-d_1$	-0.076	
22	$-d_2$	0.186	
23	$N(-d_1)$	0.470	
24	$N(-d_2)$	0.574	
25	Put Price (P_0)	$15.32	

(1) Copy the basic Black-Scholes formulas from the previous sheet. Copy the range B15:B25 from the previous sheet to the range B15:B25

(2) Add dividend yield (d) to the d_1 formula:

$$\left(\ln\left(S_0/X\right)+\left(r-d+\sigma^2/2\right)\cdot T\right)/\left(\sigma\cdot\sqrt{T}\right)$$

Enter =(LN(B6/B9)+(B8-B11+B7^2/2)*B10)/(B7*SQRT(B10))

(3) Add dividend yield (d) to the call formula:

$$C_0 = S_0 e^{-dT} N\left(d_1\right) - X e^{-rT} N\left(d_2\right)$$

Enter =B6*EXP(-B11*B10)*B17-B9*EXP(-B8*B10)*B18

(4) Add dividend yield (d) to the put formula:

$$P_0 = -S_0 e^{-dT} N\left(-d_1\right) + X e^{-rT} N\left(-d_2\right)$$

Enter =-B6*EXP(-B11*B10)*B23+B9*EXP(-B8*B10)*B24

Charts (all three sheets): *Continuous Dividend and Alternative Underlying Assets* — Option Price ($0–$50) vs Stock Price Now ($100–$180).

18.3 Greeks

Problem. What is the sensitivity of the call price to changes in the stock price, time, standard deviation, and the riskfree rate? What is the sensitivity of the sensitivity of the call price to changes in the stock price? And same questions with respect to the put price? How does each sensitivity change by stock price now and how does each sensitivity change by time to maturity?

Solution Strategy. These sensitivities are the so-called "Greeks," because each sensitivity is called by a greek letter, such as Delta, Gamma, etc. Each sensitivity has a specific formula and it is just a matter of entering each formula in turn. Then create a data table to see how each greek changes by stock price now and another data table to see how each greek changes by time to maturity.

FIGURE 18.7 Excel Model for Black-Scholes Option Pricing - Greeks.

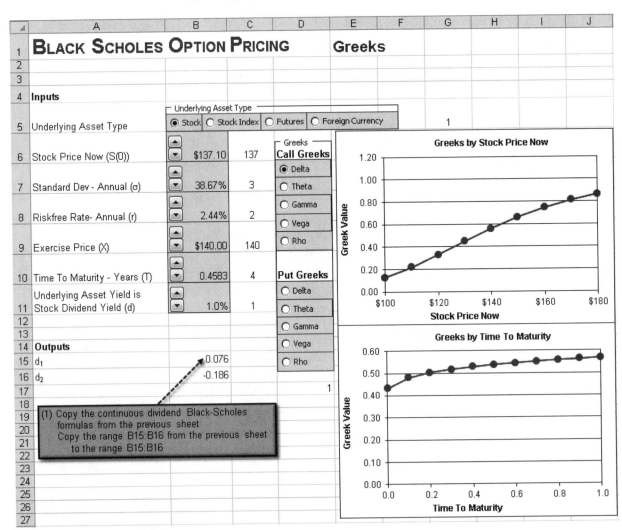

FIGURE 18.7 Excel Model for Black-Scholes Option Pricing - Greeks.

(2) $Delta = e^{-dT} N(d_1)$
Enter =EXP(-B11*B10)*NORMSDIST(B15)

(3) $Theta = -\dfrac{S_0 N'(d_1)\sigma e^{-dT}}{2\sqrt{T}} + dS_0 N(d_1)e^{-dT} - rXe^{-rT}N(d_2)$

where $N'(d_1)$ = normal *density* evaluated at d_1
Enter =-(B6*NORMDIST(B15,0,1,FALSE)*B7*EXP(-B11*B10))/(2*SQRT(B10))
+B11*B6*NORMDIST(B15)*EXP(-B11*B10)
-B8*B9*EXP(-B8*B10)*NORMSDIST(B16)

Call Greeks

Delta (∂Call / ∂Stock Price)	0.528
Theta (-∂Call / ∂Time To Mat)	-16.221
Gamma (∂²Call / ∂Stock Price²	0.011
Vega (∂Call / ∂Std Dev)	36.751
Rho (∂Call / ∂Riskfree Rate)	27.052

(4) $Gamma = \dfrac{N'(d_1)e^{-dT}}{S_0 \sigma \sqrt{T}}$

where $N'(d_1)$ = normal *density* evaluated at d_1
Enter =(NORMDIST(B15,0,1,FALSE)*EXP(-B11*B10))/(B6*B7*SQRT(B10))

Put Greeks

Delta (∂Put / ∂Stock Price)	-0.468
Theta (-∂Put / ∂Time To Mat)	-14.208
Gamma (∂²Put / ∂Stock Price²	0.011
Vega (∂Put / ∂Std Dev)	36.751
Rho (∂Put / ∂Riskfree Rate)	-36.396

(5) $Vega = S_0 \sqrt{T} N'(d_1)e^{-dT}$

where $N'(d_1)$ = normal *density* evaluated at d_1
Enter =B6*SQRT(B10)*NORMDIST(B15,0,1,FALSE)*EXP(-B11*B10)

(6) $Rho = XTe^{-rT}N(d_2)$
Enter =B9*B10*EXP(-B8*B10)*NORMSDIST(B16)

(9) *Call Gamma*
Enter =B38

(10) *Call Vega*
Enter =B39

(7) $Delta = -e^{-dT}N(-d_1)$
Enter =-EXP(-B11*B10)*NORMSDIST(-B15)

(8) $Theta = -\dfrac{S_0 N'(d_1)\sigma e^{-dT}}{2\sqrt{T}} - dS_0 N(d_1)e^{-dT} + rXe^{-rT}N(d_2)$

where $N'(d_1)$ = normal *density* evaluated at d_1
Enter =-(B6*NORMDIST(B15,0,1,FALSE)*B7*EXP(-B11*B10))/(2*SQRT(B10))
-B11*B6*NORMDIST(-B15)*EXP(-B11*B10)
+B8*B9*EXP(-B8*B10)*NORMSDIST(-B16)

(11) $Rho = -XTe^{-rT}N(-d_2)$
Enter =-B9*B10*EXP(-B8*B10)*NORMSDIST(-B16)

(13) Enter the output formula for the Selected Greek.
CHOOSE(Greek Index, Call Delta, Call Theta, ..., Put Rho)
Enter =CHOOSE($D$17,B$36,B$37,B$38,B$39,B$40,
B$43,B$44,B$45,B$46,B$47)
and copy to cell B87

(12) Enter the input values for Stock Price Now.
Enter $100, $110, 120, etc. in the range C67:Q67

Data Table: Sensitivity of the Selected Greek to Stock Price Now

		Input Values for Stock Price Now							
Output Formula:		$100.00	$110.00	$120.00	$130.00	$140.00	$150.00	$160.00	$170.00
Selected Greek	0.528	0.129	0.221	0.331	0.447	0.559	0.660	0.744	0.812

(14) Create the option price Data Table.
Select the range B67:Q68,
click on Data | Data Tools |
What-If Analysis | Data Table,
enter B6 in the Row Input Cell,
and click on OK.

Data Table — Row input cell: B6 — Column input cell: — OK — Cancel

Excel 97-2003 Equivalent

To call up a Data Table in Excel 97-2003, click on **Data | Table**

(15) Time To Maturity Index / 10
Enter =C86/10 and copy across

(16) Enter the input values for Time To Maturity Index.
Enter 0.01, 1.00, 2.00, etc. in the range C86:M86

Time To Maturity		0.001	0.1	0.2	0.3	0.4	0.5	0.6	0.7

Data Table: Sensitivity of the Selected Greek to Time To Maturity Index

		Input Values for Time To Maturity Index							
Output Formula:		0.01	1.00	2.00	3.00	4.00	5.00	6.00	7.00
Selected Greek	0.528	0.434	0.482	0.503	0.517	0.528	0.537	0.544	0.551

(17) Create the option price Data Table.
Select the range B86:M87,
click on Data | Data Tools |
What-If Analysis | Data Table,
enter C10 in the Row Input Cell,
and click on OK.

Data Table — Row input cell: C10 — Column input cell: — OK — Cancel

It is interesting to see how each greek changes by stock price now and by time to maturity (see the graphs below).

FIGURE 18.9 Black-Scholes – Greeks – Call Delta and Theta.

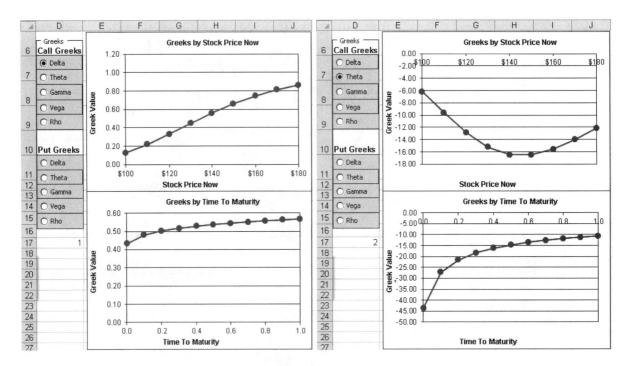

FIGURE 18.10 Black-Scholes – Greeks – Call Gamma and Vega.

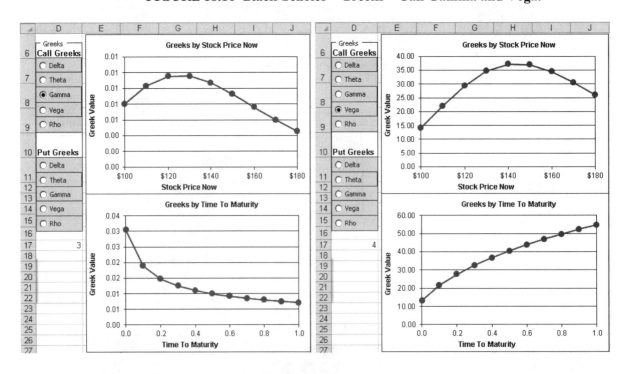

FIGURE 18.11 Black-Scholes – Greeks – Call Rho and Put Delta.

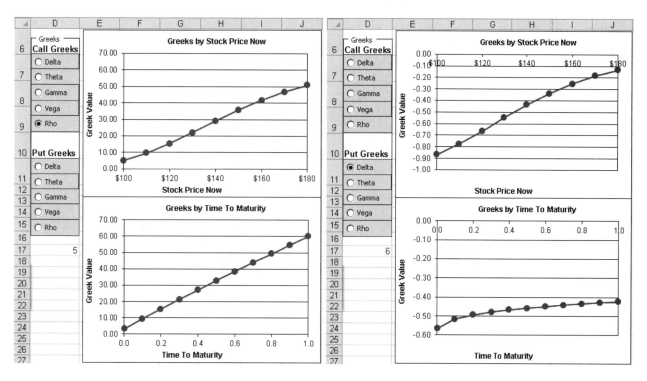

FIGURE 18.12 Black-Scholes – Greeks – Put Theta and Gamma.

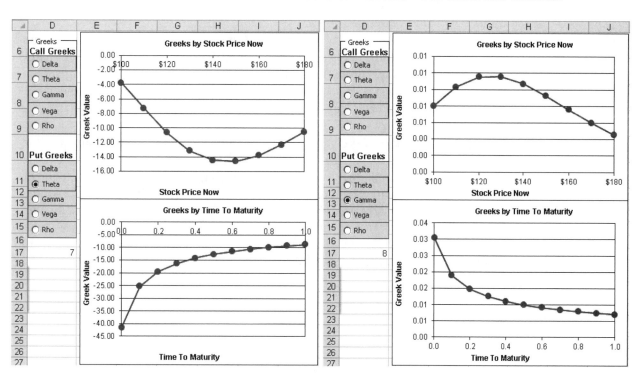

FIGURE 18.13 Black-Scholes – Greeks – Put Vega and Rho.

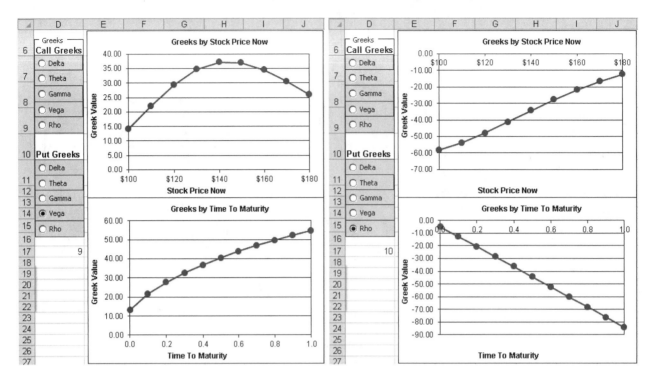

18.4 Daily Delta Hedging

Problem. Suppose that you want to buy 500 October 140 Amazon.com calls on day 0, hold them for 30 days, and then sell all 500 on day 30. How many shares do you need to buy (or sell) each day in order to create a portfolio that is delta neutral and how many dollars would the resulting portfolio be over (or under) the perfect-hedged value on day 30?

Solution. Use normally-distributed random numbers to track the evolution of the stock price day-by-day. Use the Black-Scholes formula to value the call option. Determine the number of shares that must be bought or sold to adjust the delta of the portfolio to zero each day. The bond category is where you keep track of the net cost of each daily portfolio adjustment. Value the actual portfolio and value the hypothetical perfect-hedged portfolio to determine the amount over or under the target value. Press **F9** to recalculate the spreadsheet and see how the day 30 over or under amount changes with different stock realizations.

FIGURE 18.14 Black-Scholes Option Pricing – Daily Delta Hedging.

	A	B	C	D	E	F	G	H	I
1	**BLACK SCHOLES OPTION PRICING**				**Daily Delta Hedging**				
2									
3	Inputs							Outputs	
4	Stock Price Now (S$_0$)	$137.10	137					Time / Period	0.015
5	Standard Dev - Annual (σ)	38.67%	3						
6	Riskfree Rate- Annual (r)	2.44%	2						
7	Exercise Price (X)	$140.00	140						
8	Time To Maturity - Years (T)	0.4583	4						
9	Dividend Yield (d)	1.0%	1						
10	Number of Periods	30							
11									
12	Day	0	1	2	3	4	5	6	7
13	Time to Maturity	0.4583	0.4556	0.4528	0.4501	0.4473	0.4446	0.4419	0.4391
14	Stock Price	$137.10	$137.72	$140.96	$139.92	$138.93	$138.63	$136.78	$143.22
15									
16	d$_1$	0.078	0.0928	0.181	0.153	0.125	0.115	0.063	0.241
17	d$_2$	-0.186	-0.168	-0.079	-0.107	-0.134	-0.142	-0.194	-0.015
18	N(d$_1$)	0.530	0.5370	0.572	0.561	0.550	0.546	0.525	0.595
19	N(d$_2$)	0.426	0.433	0.469	0.457	0.447	0.443	0.423	0.494
20	Call Price (C$_0$)	$13.35	$13.64	$15.38	$14.75	$14.16	$13.94	$12.91	$16.46
21	Call Delta	0.528	0.535	0.569	0.558	0.547	0.544	0.523	0.593
22									

(1) Initial Time To Maturity - # of Days /365
Enter =$B$8-B$12/365 and copy across

(2) Stock Price Now
Enter =$B$4 and copy across

(3) $S_0 Exp\left[(r-d-\sigma^2/2)\Delta t + \sigma\sqrt{\Delta t}\,\varepsilon\right]$
Enter =B14*EXP(($B$6-$B$9-($B$5^2)/2)*$I$4
+$B$5*SQRT($I$4)*NORMSINV(RAND())) and copy across

(4) $\left(\ln(S_0/X) + (r-d+\sigma^2/2)\cdot T\right)/(\sigma\cdot\sqrt{T})$
Enter =(LN(B14/$B$7)+($B$6-$B$9+$B$5^2/2)*B13)
/($B$5*SQRT(B13) and copy across

(5) $d_1 - \sigma\sqrt{T}$
Enter =B16-$B$5*SQRT(B13)

(6) Standard Cumulative Normal Distribution (d1)
Enter =NORMSDIST(B16) and copy to the range B18:AF19

(7) The continuous dividend Black-Scholes call formula is:
$$C_0 = S_0 e^{-dT} N(d_1) - Xe^{-rT} N(d_2)$$
Enter =B14*EXP(-$B$9*B13)*B18-$B$7*EXP(-$B$6*B13)*B19
and copy across

(8) $Delta = e^{-dT} N(d_1)$
Enter =EXP(-$B$9*B13)*NORMSDIST(B16) and copy across

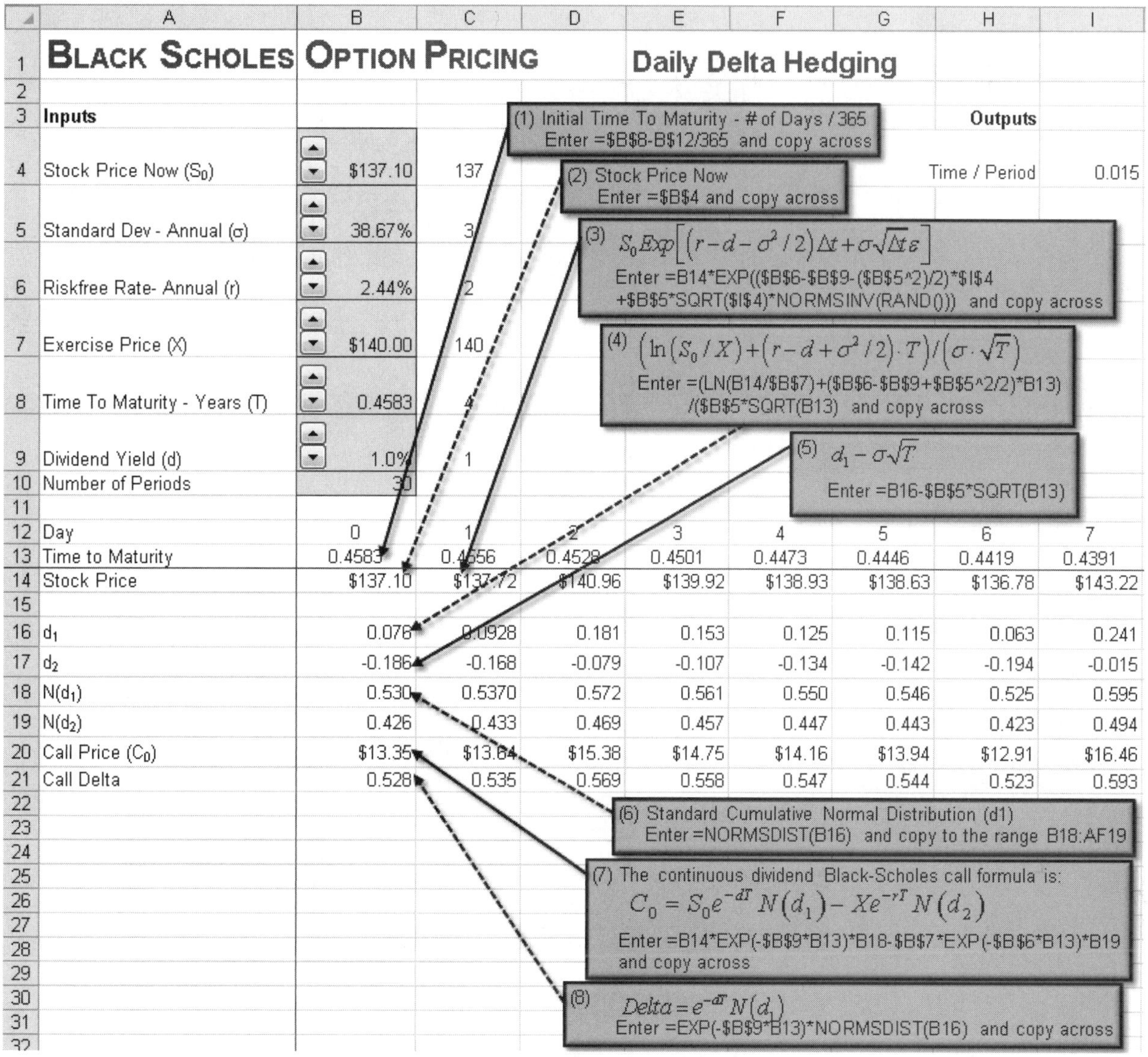

Results. Given this particular stock price realization, the day 30 portfolio over or under amount is $2,525. Press **F9** to recalculate the spreadsheet and see how this amount changes with different stock realizations. The variability of the over or under amount indicates how imperfect the hedge it.

FIGURE 18.15 Black-Scholes Option Pricing – Daily Delta Hedging.

	A	B	C	D	E	F	G	H	I
33	(9) Calls Before Trade + Calls Bought								
34	Enter =B43+B44, copy to B53, and copy both across								
35									
36	(10) Calls After Trade								
37	Enter =B45, copy to C47, and copy both across								
38	(11) Shares Delta-Hedged Target - Shares Before Trade								
39	Enter =B49-B47 and copy across								
40									
41	(12) -Calls After Trade * Call Delta								
42	Enter =-B45*B21 and copy across								
43	Calls: Before Trade	0	500	500	500	500	500	500	500
44	Calls: Bought (Sold)	500	0	0	0	0	0	0	0
45	Calls: After Trade	500	500	500	500	500	500	500	500
46									
47	Shares: Before Trade	0	-264	-267	-285	-279	-274	-272	-261
48	Shares: Bought (Sold)	-264	-3	-17	6	5	2	10	-35
49	Shares: Delta-Hedged Target	-264	-267	-285	-279	-274	-272	-261	-296
50									
51	Bonds: Before Trade	-$29,514	$0	$456	$2,913	$2,122	$1,362	$1,112	-$313
52	Bonds: Bought (Sold)	$29,514	$455	$2,457	-$791	-$760	-$250	-$1,425	$5,018
53	Bonds: After Trade	$0	$455	$2,913	$2,122	$1,362	$1,112	-$313	$4,705
54									
55	Portfolio: Actual Value	-$29,514	-$29,535	-$29,529	-$29,549	-$29,568	-$29,591	-$29,604	-$29,513
56	Portfolio: Perfect-Hedged Value	-$29,514	$29,515	-$29,517	-$29,519	-$29,521	-$29,523	-$29,525	-$29,527
57	Portfolio: Over (Under) Target	$0	-$19	-$12	-$29	-$47	-$67	-$79	$15
58									
59	Portfolio Delta	0.0000	0.0000	0.0000	0.0000	0.0000	0.0000	0.0000	0.0000
60									
61	(17) Portfolio Actual Value		(13) -Bonds Bought						
62	- Portfolio Perfect-Hedged Value		Enter =-$B$52 and copy to B56						
63	Enter =B55-B56 and copy across		(14) Bonds Befor Trade(t-1) * EXP(Riskfree Rate * (1/365))						
64	(18) Shares Delta-Hedged Target * 1		Enter =B53*EXP($B$6*(1/365)), copy to C56, and copy both across						
65	+ Calls After Trade * Call Delta		(15) -Calls Bought * Call Price - Shares Bought * Share Price						
66	Enter =B49*1+B45*B21 and copy across		Enter =-B44*B20-B48*B14 and copy across						
67									
68			(16) Calls Before Trade * Call Price						
69			+ Shares Before Trade * Share Price + Bonds Before Trade						
70			Enter =B43*B20+B47*B14+B51 and copy across						

FIGURE 18.16 Black-Scholes Option Pricing – Daily Delta Hedging.

	A	AA	AB	AC	AD	AE	AF
12	Day	25	26	27	28	29	30
13	Time to Maturity	0.3898	0.3871	0.3843	0.3816	0.3788	0.3761
43	Calls: Before Trade	500	500	500	500	500	500
44	Calls: Bought (Sold)	0	0	0	0	0	-500
45	Calls: After Trade	500	500	500	500	500	0
46							
47	Shares: Before Trade	-120	-97	-111	-130	-158	-130
48	Shares: Bought (Sold)	22	-14	-19	-28	29	130
49	Shares: Delta-Hedged Target	-97	-111	-130	-158	-130	0
50							
51	Bonds: Before Trade	-$15,422	-$17,878	-$16,316	-$14,103	-$10,695	-$14,039
52	Bonds: Bought (Sold)	-$2,455	$1,563	$2,214	$3,409	-$3,343	-$13,019
53	Bonds: After Trade	-$17,877	-$16,315	-$14,102	-$10,694	-$14,038	-$27,057
54							
55	Portfolio: Actual Value	-$27,289	-$27,286	-$27,270	-$27,222	-$27,172	-$27,057
56	Portfolio: Perfect-Hedged Value	-$29,563	-$29,565	-$29,567	-$29,569	-$29,571	-$29,573
57	Portfolio: Over (Under) Target	$2,273	$2,279	$2,297	$2,347	$2,399	$2,515
58							
59	Portfolio Delta	0.0000	0.0000	0.0000	0.0000	0.0000	

18.5 Trading Strategies Over Any Horizon

Problem. What is the profit on trading strategies that combine multiple options, stocks, bonds, and futures? Consider trading strategies with as many as eight assets that are either held to maturity or held to any other date.

FIGURE 18.17 Black-Scholes – Trading Strategies Over Any Horizon.

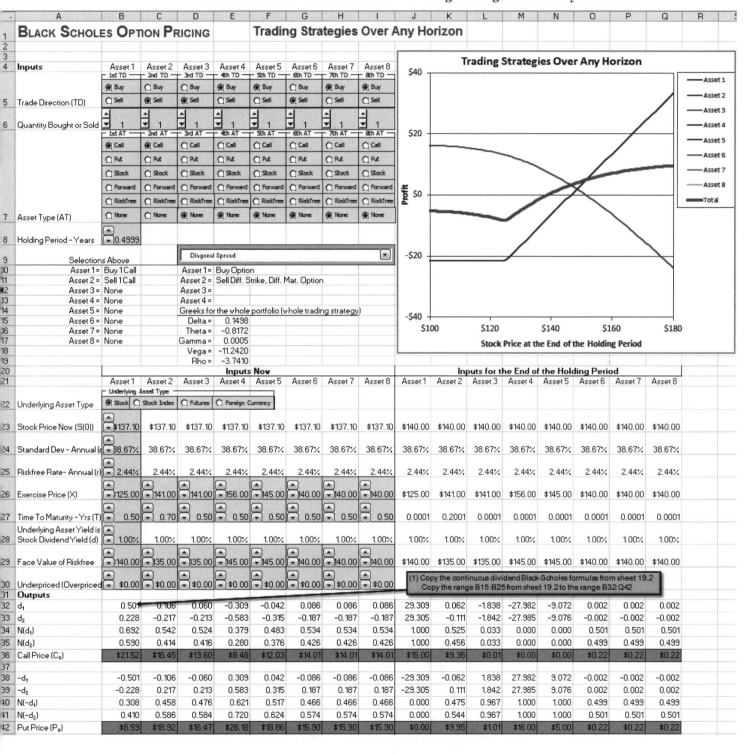

Solution Strategy. For as many as eight asset, value the assets today and value the assets at the end of a holding period (which may or may not be the maturity date) as a function of the stock price at the end of the holding period. Graph the profit on each asset and of the portfolio by the stock price at the end of the holding period. A database of 50 trading strategies is provided. It includes bullish strategies, bearish strategies, high volatility strategies, low volatility strategies, combined directional and volatility strategies, and arbitrage strategies.

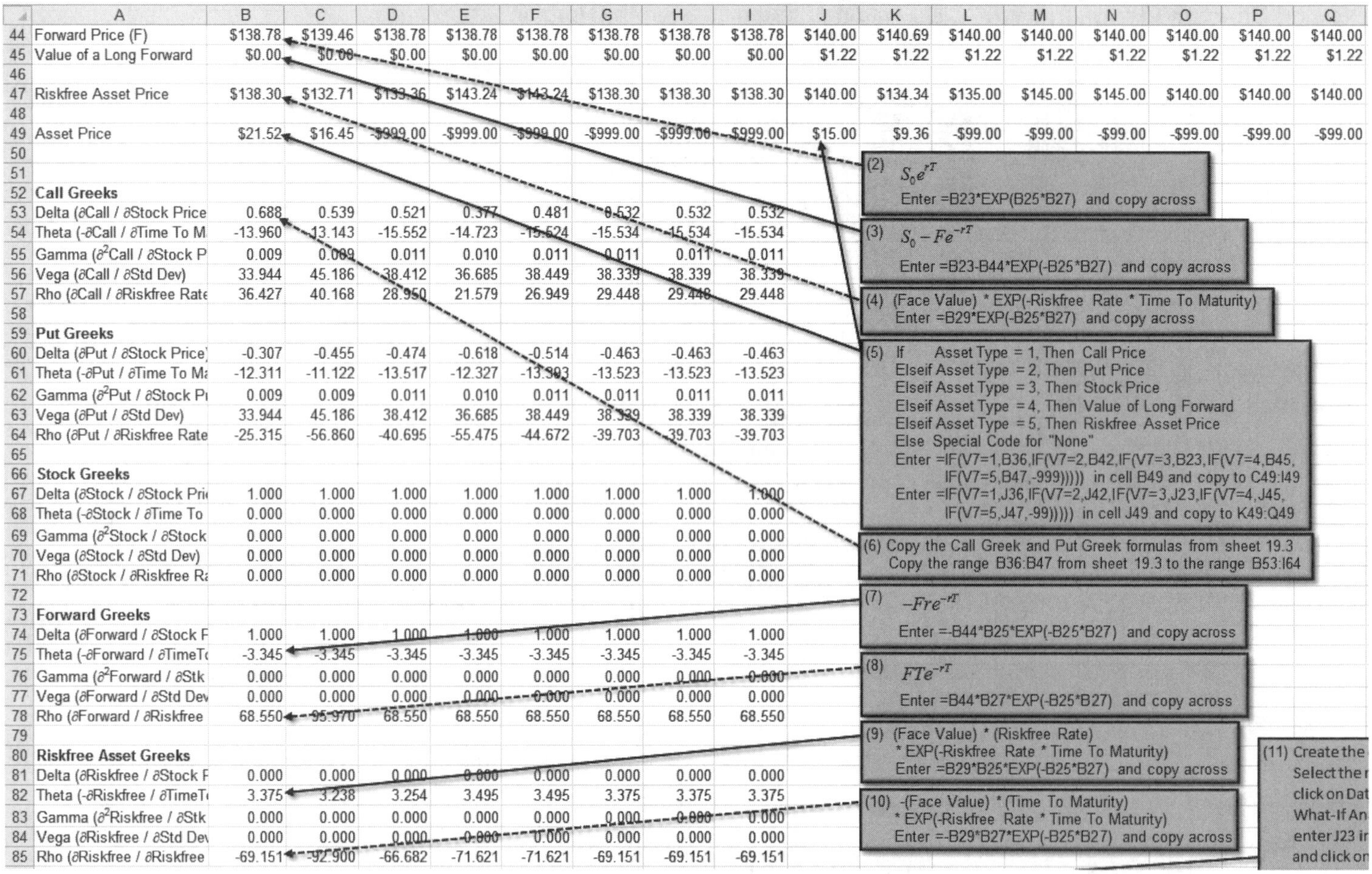

FIGURE 18.18 Black-Scholes – Trading Strategies Over Any Horizon.

	A	B	C	D	E	F	G	H	I
44	Forward Price (F)	$138.78	$139.46	$138.78	$138.78	$138.78	$138.78	$138.78	$138.78
45	Value of a Long Forward	$0.00	$0.00	$0.00	$0.00	$0.00	$0.00	$0.00	$0.00
46									
47	Riskfree Asset Price	$138.30	$132.71	$133.36	$143.24	$143.24	$138.30	$138.30	$138.30
48									
49	Asset Price	$21.52	$16.45	-$999.00	-$999.00	-$999.00	-$999.00	-$999.00	-$999.00
50									
51									
52	**Call Greeks**								
53	Delta (∂Call / ∂Stock Price	0.688	0.539	0.521	0.377	0.481	0.532	0.532	0.532
54	Theta (-∂Call / ∂Time To M	-13.960	-13.143	-15.552	-14.723	-15.624	-15.534	-15.534	-15.534
55	Gamma (∂²Call / ∂Stock P	0.009	0.009	0.011	0.010	0.011	0.011	0.011	0.011
56	Vega (∂Call / ∂Std Dev)	33.944	45.186	38.412	36.685	38.449	38.339	38.339	38.339
57	Rho (∂Call / ∂Riskfree Rate	36.427	40.168	28.950	21.579	26.949	29.448	29.448	29.448
58									
59	**Put Greeks**								
60	Delta (∂Put / ∂Stock Price)	-0.307	-0.455	-0.474	-0.618	-0.514	-0.463	-0.463	-0.463
61	Theta (-∂Put / ∂Time To Ma	-12.311	-11.122	-13.517	-12.327	-13.393	-13.523	-13.523	-13.523
62	Gamma (∂²Put / ∂Stock Pr	0.009	0.009	0.011	0.010	0.011	0.011	0.011	0.011
63	Vega (∂Put / ∂Std Dev)	33.944	45.186	38.412	36.685	38.449	38.339	38.339	38.339
64	Rho (∂Put / ∂Riskfree Rate	-25.315	-56.860	-40.695	-55.475	-44.672	-39.703	-39.703	-39.703
65									
66	**Stock Greeks**								
67	Delta (∂Stock / ∂Stock Pri	1.000	1.000	1.000	1.000	1.000	1.000	1.000	1.000
68	Theta (-∂Stock / ∂Time To	0.000	0.000	0.000	0.000	0.000	0.000	0.000	0.000
69	Gamma (∂²Stock / ∂Stock	0.000	0.000	0.000	0.000	0.000	0.000	0.000	0.000
70	Vega (∂Stock / ∂Std Dev)	0.000	0.000	0.000	0.000	0.000	0.000	0.000	0.000
71	Rho (∂Stock / ∂Riskfree Ra	0.000	0.000	0.000	0.000	0.000	0.000	0.000	0.000
72									
73	**Forward Greeks**								
74	Delta (∂Forward / ∂Stock F	1.000	1.000	1.000	1.000	1.000	1.000	1.000	1.000
75	Theta (-∂Forward / ∂TimeTo	-3.345	-3.345	-3.345	-3.345	-3.345	-3.345	-3.345	-3.345
76	Gamma (∂²Forward / ∂Stk	0.000	0.000	0.000	0.000	0.000	0.000	0.000	0.000
77	Vega (∂Forward / ∂Std Dev	0.000	0.000	0.000	0.000	0.000	0.000	0.000	0.000
78	Rho (∂Forward / ∂Riskfree	68.550	95.970	68.550	68.550	68.550	68.550	68.550	68.550
79									
80	**Riskfree Asset Greeks**								
81	Delta (∂Riskfree / ∂Stock F	0.000	0.000	0.000	0.000	0.000	0.000	0.000	0.000
82	Theta (-∂Riskfree / ∂TimeTo	3.375	3.238	3.254	3.495	3.495	3.375	3.375	3.375
83	Gamma (∂²Riskfree / ∂Stk	0.000	0.000	0.000	0.000	0.000	0.000	0.000	0.000
84	Vega (∂Riskfree / ∂Std Dev	0.000	0.000	0.000	0.000	0.000	0.000	0.000	0.000
85	Rho (∂Riskfree / ∂Riskfree	-69.151	-92.900	-66.682	-71.621	-71.621	-69.151	-69.151	-69.151

	A	J	K	L	M	N	O	P	Q
44	Forward Price (F)	$140.00	$140.69	$140.00	$140.00	$140.00	$140.00	$140.00	$140.00
45	Value of a Long Forward	$1.22	$1.22	$1.22	$1.22	$1.22	$1.22	$1.22	$1.22
47	Riskfree Asset Price	$140.00	$134.34	$135.00	$145.00	$145.00	$140.00	$140.00	$140.00
49	Asset Price	$15.00	$9.36	-$99.00	-$99.00	-$99.00	-$99.00	-$99.00	-$99.00

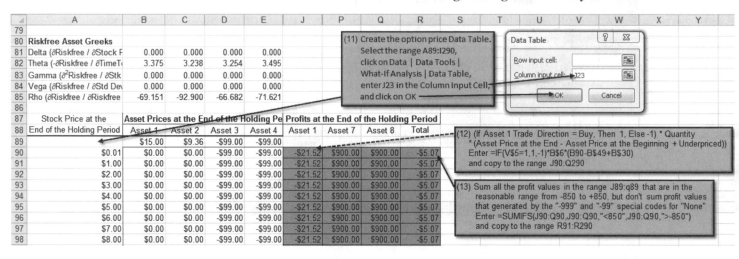

FIGURE 18.19 Black-Scholes – Trading Strategies Over Any Horizon.

	A	B	C	D	E	J	P	Q	R
79									
80	**Riskfree Asset Greeks**								
81	Delta (∂Riskfree / ∂Stock F	0.000	0.000	0.000	0.000				
82	Theta (-∂Riskfree / ∂TimeTo	3.375	3.238	3.254	3.495				
83	Gamma (∂²Riskfree / ∂Stk	0.000	0.000	0.000	0.000				
84	Vega (∂Riskfree / ∂Std Dev	0.000	0.000	0.000	0.000				
85	Rho (∂Riskfree / ∂Riskfree	-69.151	-92.900	-66.682	-71.621				
86									
87	Stock Price at the	**Asset Prices at the End of the Holding Pe**				**Profits at the End of the Holding Period**			
88	End of the Holding Period	Asset 1	Asset 2	Asset 3	Asset 4	Asset 1	Asset 7	Asset 8	Total
89		$15.00	$9.36	-$99.00	-$99.00				
90	$0.01	$0.00	$0.00	-$99.00	-$99.00	-$21.52	$900.00	$900.00	-$5.07
91	$1.00	$0.00	$0.00	-$99.00	-$99.00	-$21.52	$900.00	$900.00	-$5.07
92	$2.00	$0.00	$0.00	-$99.00	-$99.00	-$21.52	$900.00	$900.00	-$5.07
93	$3.00	$0.00	$0.00	-$99.00	-$99.00	-$21.52	$900.00	$900.00	-$5.07
94	$4.00	$0.00	$0.00	-$99.00	-$99.00	-$21.52	$900.00	$900.00	-$5.07
95	$5.00	$0.00	$0.00	-$99.00	-$99.00	-$21.52	$900.00	$900.00	-$5.07
96	$6.00	$0.00	$0.00	-$99.00	-$99.00	-$21.52	$900.00	$900.00	-$5.07
97	$7.00	$0.00	$0.00	-$99.00	-$99.00	-$21.52	$900.00	$900.00	-$5.07
98	$8.00	$0.00	$0.00	-$99.00	-$99.00	-$21.52	$900.00	$900.00	-$5.07

The drop down box in the range D9:I9 provides a list of 50 trading strategies in six broad categories: bullish strategies, bearish strategies, high volatility strategies, low volatility strategies, combined directional and volatility strategies, and arbitrage strategies.

FIGURE 18.20 Black-Scholes – Trading Strategies Over Any Horizon.

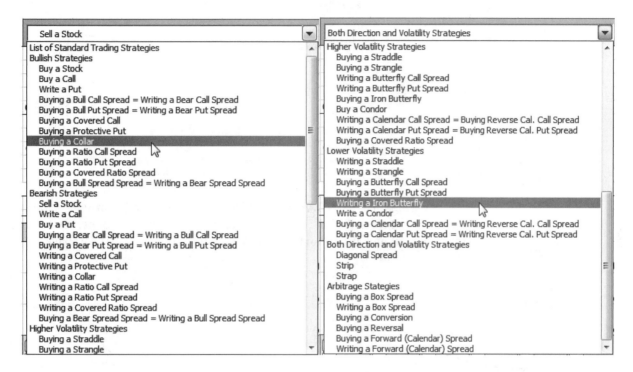

Select any trading strategy from the database and it tells you what that strategy means. For example, if you select "Writing a Butterfly Call Spread," then the range D10:I13 displays that this means sell a low strike call, buy a medium strike call, buy the same medium strike call, and sell a high strike call.

FIGURE 18.21 Black-Scholes – Trading Strategies Over Any Horizon.

	D	E	F	G	H	I
9	Writing a Butterfly Call Spread					
10	Asset 1 = Sell Low Strike Call					
11	Asset 2 = Buy Medium Strike Call					
12	Asset 3 = Buy Same Medium Strike Call					
13	Asset 4 = Sell High Strike Call					

Below are some interesting trading strategies that take full advantage of the ability to trade many assets in any quantity and analyze positions before their maturity dates.

FIGURE 18.22 DIAGONAL SPREAD – Left: Buy Long Maturity, Low Strike Call and Sell Short Maturity High Strike Call; Right: Buy Short Maturity, Low Strike Call and Sell Long Maturity, High Strike Call.

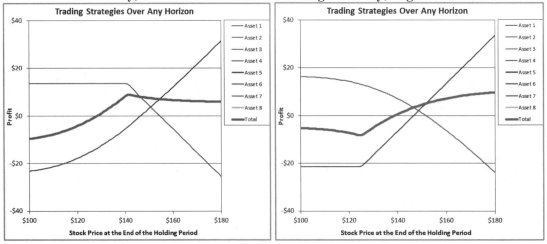

FIGURE 18.23 CALENDAR SPREAD – Left: Buy Long Maturity Call and Sell Short Maturity Call with the Same Strike Price; Right: Sell Long Maturity Call and Buy Short Maturity Call with the Same Strike Price.

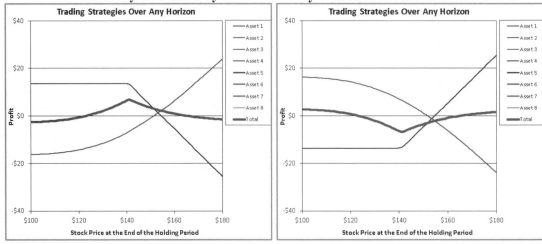

FIGURE 18.24 BULL SPREAD BEFORE MATURITY – Left: Buy Low Strike Call and Sell High Strike Call One Month Before Maturity; Right: Same Position Four Months Before Maturity.

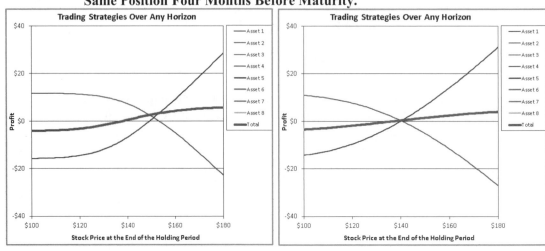

FIGURE 18.25 STRIP AND STRAP – Left: STRIP = Buy One Call and Sell Two Same Strike, Same Maturity Puts; Right: STRAP = Buy Two Calls and Sell One Same Strike, Same Maturity Put.

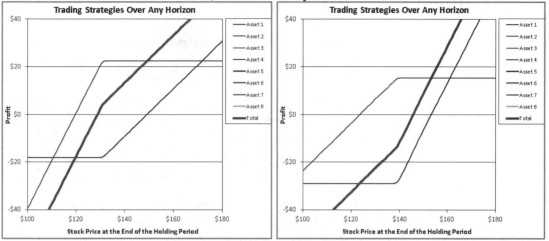

FIGURE 18.26 ARBITRAGE BOX SPREAD – Left: Buy Low Strike Call, Sell High Strike Call, Sell Same Low Strike Put, Buy Same High Strike Put Makes No Profit When All Assets Are Correctly Priced; Right: Same Position Makes a Riskfree Arbitrage Profit When One Asset is Mispriced.

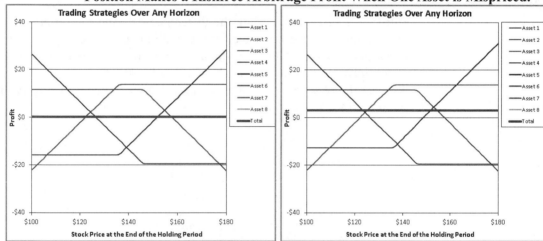

FIGURE 18.27 ARBITRAGE CONVERSION – Left: Buy Stock With Div Yield = 0, Sell Call, Buy Same Strike and Maturity Put, Sell Riskfree With Face Value = Same Strike and Same Maturity Makes No Profit When All Assets Are Correctly Priced; Right: Same Position Makes a Riskfree Arbitrage Profit When One Asset is Mispriced.

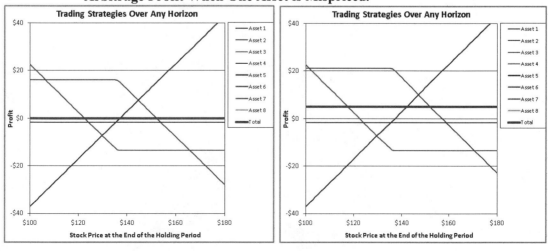

18.6 Implied Volatility

Problem. At the close of trading on April 30, 2010, SPX, a security based on the S&P 500 index, traded at 1,186.69. European call and put options on SPX with the exercise prices shown below traded for the following prices:

Exercise price	1,175	1,195	1,200	1,225	1,250
Call price	$58.50	$47.16	$44.30	$32.41	$22.30
Exercise price	1,100	1,125	1,150	1,195	1,200
Put price	$27.50	$34.10	$38.00	$54.60	$59.10

These call options mature on August 20, 2010, which is in 0.3056 years. The S&P 500 portfolio pays a continuous dividend yield of 1.89% per year and the annual yield on a Treasury Bill which matures on August 15th is 0.16% per year. What is the implied volatility of each of these calls and puts? What pattern do these implied volatilities follow across exercise prices and between calls vs. puts?

Solution Strategy. Calculate the difference between the observed option price and the option price predicted by the continuous dividend yield version of the Black-Scholes model using a dummy value for the stock volatility. Have the Excel Solver tool adjust the stock volatility by trial and error until the difference between the observed price and the model price is equal to zero (within a very small error tolerance).

FIGURE 18.28 Excel Model of Black-Scholes - Implied Volatility.

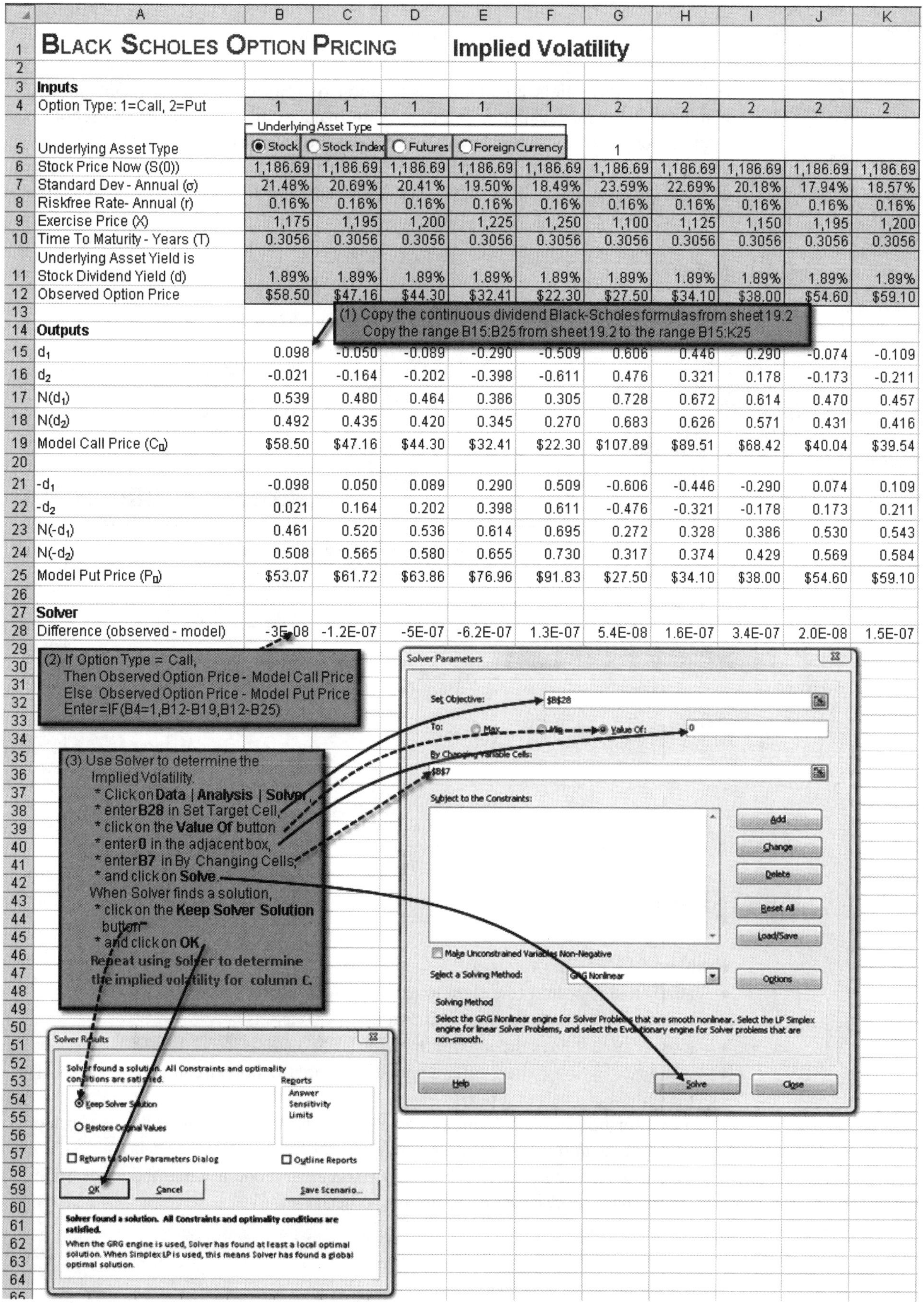

	A	B	C	D	E	F	G	H	I	J	K
1	**BLACK SCHOLES OPTION PRICING**				**Implied Volatility**						
2											
3	**Inputs**										
4	Option Type: 1=Call, 2=Put	1	1	1	1	1	2	2	2	2	2
5	Underlying Asset Type	⊙Stock ○Stock Index ○Futures ○Foreign Currency					1				
6	Stock Price Now (S(0))	1,186.69	1,186.69	1,186.69	1,186.69	1,186.69	1,186.69	1,186.69	1,186.69	1,186.69	1,186.69
7	Standard Dev - Annual (σ)	21.48%	20.69%	20.41%	19.50%	18.49%	23.59%	22.69%	20.18%	17.94%	18.57%
8	Riskfree Rate- Annual (r)	0.16%	0.16%	0.16%	0.16%	0.16%	0.16%	0.16%	0.16%	0.16%	0.16%
9	Exercise Price (X)	1,175	1,195	1,200	1,225	1,250	1,100	1,125	1,150	1,195	1,200
10	Time To Maturity - Years (T)	0.3056	0.3056	0.3056	0.3056	0.3056	0.3056	0.3056	0.3056	0.3056	0.3056
11	Underlying Asset Yield is Stock Dividend Yield (d)	1.89%	1.89%	1.89%	1.89%	1.89%	1.89%	1.89%	1.89%	1.89%	1.89%
12	Observed Option Price	$58.50	$47.16	$44.30	$32.41	$22.30	$27.50	$34.10	$38.00	$54.60	$59.10
13											
14	**Outputs**										
15	d_1	0.098	-0.050	-0.089	-0.290	-0.509	0.606	0.446	0.290	-0.074	-0.109
16	d_2	-0.021	-0.164	-0.202	-0.398	-0.611	0.476	0.321	0.178	-0.173	-0.211
17	$N(d_1)$	0.539	0.480	0.464	0.386	0.305	0.728	0.672	0.614	0.470	0.457
18	$N(d_2)$	0.492	0.435	0.420	0.345	0.270	0.683	0.626	0.571	0.431	0.416
19	Model Call Price (C_0)	$58.50	$47.16	$44.30	$32.41	$22.30	$107.89	$89.51	$68.42	$40.04	$39.54
20											
21	$-d_1$	-0.098	0.050	0.089	0.290	0.509	-0.606	-0.446	-0.290	0.074	0.109
22	$-d_2$	0.021	0.164	0.202	0.398	0.611	-0.476	-0.321	-0.178	0.173	0.211
23	$N(-d_1)$	0.461	0.520	0.536	0.614	0.695	0.272	0.328	0.386	0.530	0.543
24	$N(-d_2)$	0.508	0.565	0.580	0.655	0.730	0.317	0.374	0.429	0.569	0.584
25	Model Put Price (P_0)	$53.07	$61.72	$63.86	$76.96	$91.83	$27.50	$34.10	$38.00	$54.60	$59.10
26											
27	**Solver**										
28	Difference (observed - model)	-3E-08	-1.2E-07	-5E-07	-6.2E-07	1.3E-07	5.4E-08	1.6E-07	3.4E-07	2.0E-08	1.5E-07

(1) Copy the continuous dividend Black-Scholes formulas from sheet 19.2
Copy the range B15:B25 from sheet 19.2 to the range B15:K25

(2) If Option Type = Call,
Then Observed Option Price - Model Call Price
Else Observed Option Price - Model Put Price
Enter =IF(B4=1,B12-B19,B12-B25)

(3) Use Solver to determine the
Implied Volatility.
  * Click on **Data | Analysis | Solver**
  * enter **B28** in Set Target Cell,
  * click on the **Value Of** button
  * enter **0** in the adjacent box,
  * enter **B7** in By Changing Cells,
  * and click on **Solve**.
When Solver finds a solution,
  * click on the **Keep Solver Solution** button
  * and click on **OK**.
Repeat using Solver to determine
the implied volatility for column C.

Solver Parameters

Set Objective: $B$28

To: ○ Max ○ Min ⊙ Value Of: 0

By Changing Variable Cells: $B$7

Subject to the Constraints:
[Add] [Change] [Delete] [Reset All] [Load/Save]

☐ Make Unconstrained Variables Non-Negative

Select a Solving Method: GRG Nonlinear [Options]

Solving Method
Select the GRG Nonlinear engine for Solver Problems that are smooth nonlinear. Select the LP Simplex engine for linear Solver Problems, and select the Evolutionary engine for Solver problems that are non-smooth.

[Help] [Solve] [Close]

Solver Results

Solver found a solution. All Constraints and optimality conditions are satisfied.

Reports
Answer
Sensitivity
Limits

⊙ Keep Solver Solution
○ Restore Original Values

☐ Return to Solver Parameters Dialog
☐ Outline Reports

[OK] [Cancel] [Save Scenario...]

Solver found a solution. All Constraints and optimality conditions are satisfied.

When the GRG engine is used, Solver has found at least a local optimal solution. When Simplex LP is used, this means Solver has found a global optimal solution.

To install the Analysis ToolPak, click on File , click on Options , click on **Add-Ins**, highlight the **Solver** in the list of Inactive Applications, click on **Go**, check the **Solver**, and click on **OK**.

If the market's beliefs about the distribution of returns of the S&P 500 Index matched the theoretical distribution of returns assumed by the Black-Scholes model, then all of the implied volatilities would be the same. From the graph we see this is not the case. The implied volatility pattern declines sharply with the exercise price and puts have lower implied volatilities than calls. In the '70s and '80s, the typical implied volatility pattern was a U-shaped, "Smile" pattern. In the '90s and 2000s, it is more typical to see a downward-sloping, "Scowl" pattern.

FIGURE 18.29 Graph of the "Scowl" Pattern of Implied Volatilities.

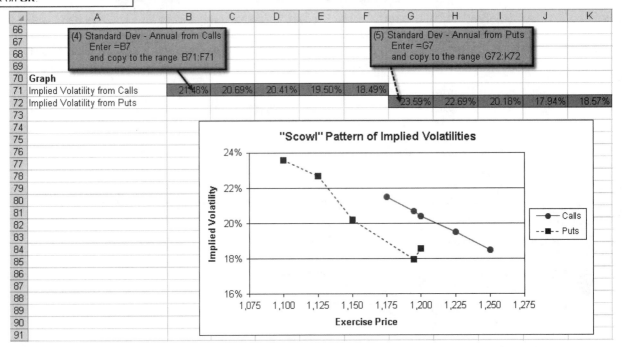

18.7 Exotic Options

Problem. What is the value of:
- an exchange option (the right to exchange one asset for another asset)?
- a security that pays the minimum value of two assets?
- a security that pays the maximum value of two assets?
- a chooser option (where after a specified time, the holder can choose whether the option is a call or a put)?
- a cash-or-nothing call (which pays a fixed cash amount when the asset price is greater than the strike price or nothing otherwise)?
- a cash-or-nothing put (which pays a fixed cash amount when the asset price is less than the strike price or nothing otherwise)?

- an asset-or-nothing call (which pays the asset price when the asset price is greater than the strike price or nothing otherwise)?
- an asset-or-nothing put (which pays the asset price when the asset price is less than the strike price or nothing otherwise)?
- a gap call (which pays the asset price minus the strike price when the asset price is greater than a trigger price and nothing otherwise)?
- a gap put (which pays the strike price minus the asset price when the asset price is less than the trigger price and nothing otherwise)?
- a supershare (which pays the asset price when the asset price is between an upper and lower bound and nothing otherwise)?

FIGURE 18.30 Excel Model of Black-Scholes – Exotic Options.

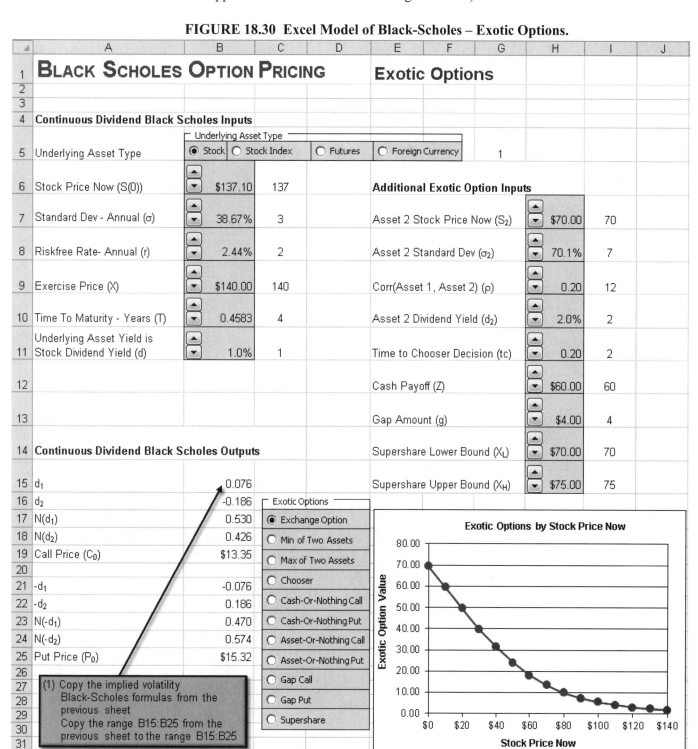

FIGURE 18.31 Excel Model of Black-Scholes – Exotic Options.

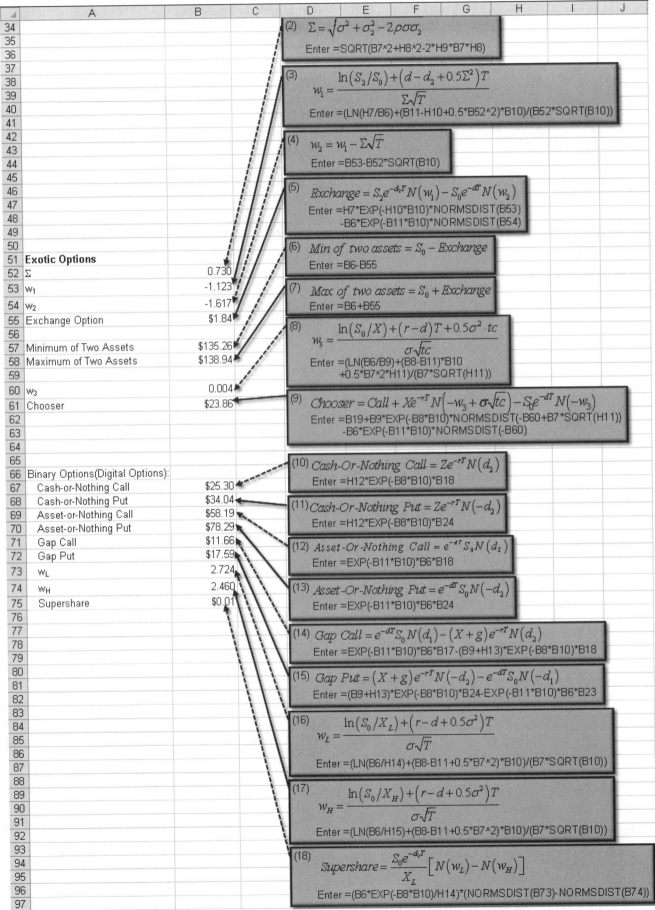

Solution Strategy. Each exotic option has a specific formula and it just a matter of entering each formula in turn. Then create a data table to see how each exotic option changes by the stock price now.

FIGURE 18.32 Excel Model of Black-Scholes – Exotic Options.

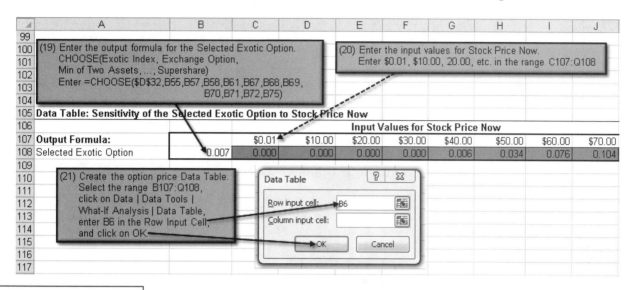

Data Table: Sensitivity of the Selected Exotic Option to Stock Price Now

		Input Values for Stock Price Now							
Output Formula:		$0.01	$10.00	$20.00	$30.00	$40.00	$50.00	$60.00	$70.00
Selected Exotic Option	0.007	0.000	0.000	0.000	0.000	0.006	0.034	0.076	0.104

It is interesting to see how each exotic option changes by the stock price now. The graphs below show each exotic option by stock price now.

FIGURE 18.33 Exotic Options – Exchange Option and Min of Two Assets.

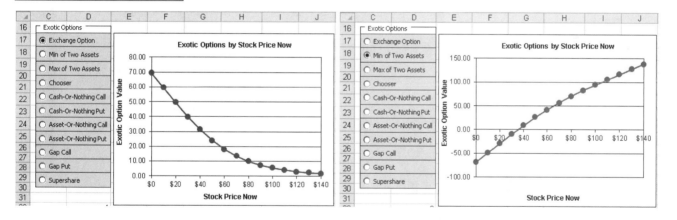

FIGURE 18.34 Exotic Options –Max of Two Assets and Chooser.

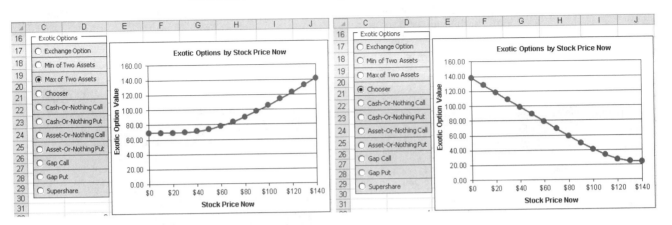

FIGURE 18.35 Exotic Options –Cash-Or-Nothing Call and Put.

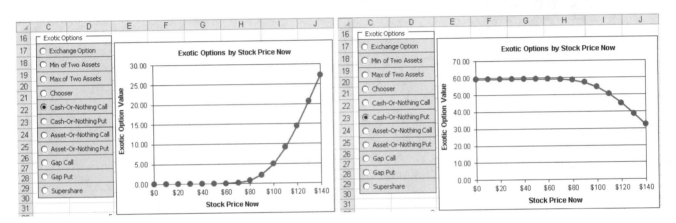

FIGURE 18.36 Exotic Options –Asset-Or-Nothing Call and Put.

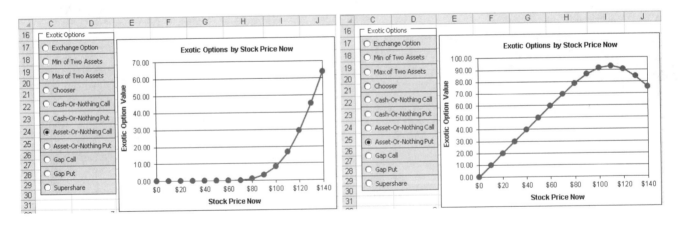

FIGURE 18.37 Exotic Options –Gap Call and Put.

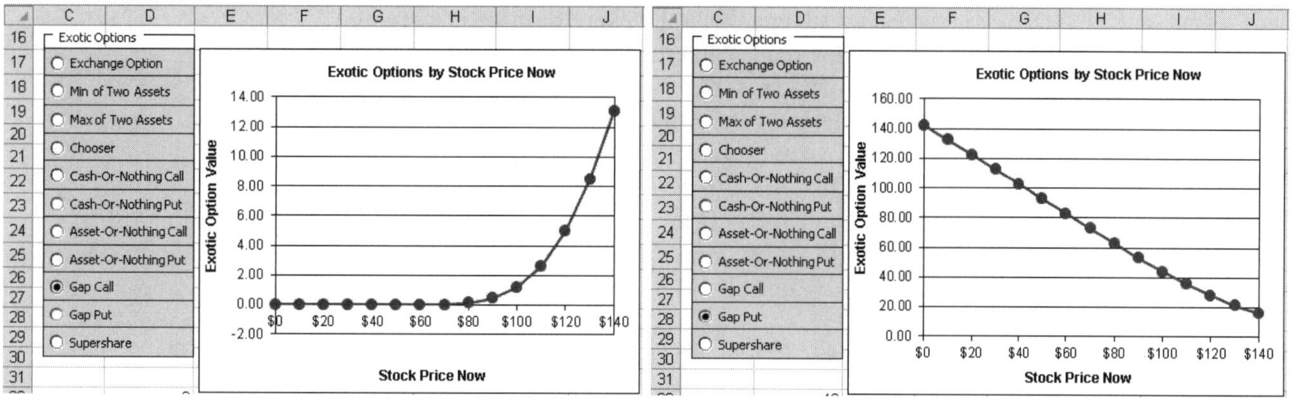

FIGURE 18.38 Exotic Options –Supershare.

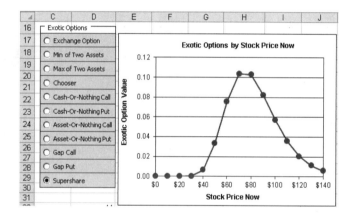

Problems

1. Download three months of daily stock price for any stock that has listed options on it and compute the standard deviation of daily returns. Lookup the current stock price of your stock, use the standard deviation of daily returns you just computed, lookup the yield on a six-month U.S. Treasury Bill, lookup the exercise price of a call on your stock that matures in approximately six months, lookup the exercise price of a put on your stock that matures in approximately six months, and compute the time to maturity for both options in fractions of a year. For the call and put that you identified on your stock, determine the price of the call and put using the Black-Scholes basics model.

2. Use the same inputs as problem 1. Forecast the continuous dividend that your stock pays or make an assumption about the continuous dividend that your stock pays. Determine the price of the call and put using the Black-Scholes continuous dividend model.

3. Perform instant experiments on whether changing various inputs causes an increase or decrease in the Call Price and in the Put Price and by how much.

(a.) What happens when the standard deviation is increased?
(b.) What happens when the time to maturity is increased?
(c.) What happens when the exercise price is increased?
(d.) What happens when the riskfree rate is increased?
(e.) What happens when the dividend yield is increased?
(f.) What happens when the standard deviation is really close to zero?
(g.) What happens when the time to maturity is really close to zero?

4. What is the sensitivity of the call price to changes in the stock price, time, standard deviation, and the riskfree rate? What is the sensitivity of the sensitivity of the call price to changes in the stock price? And same questions with respect to the put price? How does each sensitivity change by stock price now and how does each sensitivity change by time to maturity?

5. The S&P 500 index closes at 2000. European call and put options on the S&P 500 index with the exercise prices shown below trade for the following prices:

Exercise price	1,950	1,975	2,000	2,025	2,050
Call price	$88	$66	$47	$33	$21
Put price	$25	$26	$32	$44	$58

All options mature in 88 days. The S&P 500 portfolio pays a continuous dividend yield of 1.56% per year and the annual yield on a Treasury Bill which matures on the same day as the options is 4.63% per year. Determine what is the implied volatility of each of these calls and puts. What pattern do these implied volatilities follow across exercise prices and between calls vs. puts?

6. What is the value of:
   - an exchange option (the right to exchange one asset for another asset)?
   - a security that pays the minimum value of two assets?
   - a security that pays the maximum value of two assets?
   - a chooser option (where after a specified time, the holder can choose whether the option is a call or a put)?
   - a cash-or-nothing call (which pays a fixed cash amount when the asset price is greater than the strike price or nothing otherwise)?
   - a cash-or-nothing put (which pays a fixed cash amount when the asset price is less than the strike price or nothing otherwise)?
   - an asset-or-nothing call (which pays the asset price when the asset price is greater than the strike price or nothing otherwise)?
   - an asset-or-nothing put (which pays the asset price when the asset price is less than the strike price or nothing otherwise)?
   - a gap call (which pays the asset price minus the strike price when the asset price is greater than a trigger price and nothing otherwise)?
   - a gap put (which pays the strike price minus the asset price when the asset price is less than the trigger price and nothing otherwise)?
   - a supershare (which pays the asset price when the asset price is between an upper and lower bound and nothing otherwise)?

Chapter 19 Futures

19.1 Spot-Futures Parity (Cost of Carry)

Problem. Suppose we recorded the monthly spot price of the S&P 500 index and corresponding futures price over a seven month period for a stock index futures contract maturing in month 7. Here are the prices in index points:

Month	1	2	3	4	5	6	7
Spot price	1,417.8	1,436.3	1,426.6	1,456.8	1,455.5	1,460.2	1,476.6
Futures price	1,452.7	1,467.9	1,451.4	1,472.8	1,466.7	1,467.1	1,476.6

Suppose that the riskfree rate is 0.42% per month. Suppose that the round trip transaction cost for doing an index arbitrage trade is 1.60 index points. Compute the basis, to the price difference (the futures price implied by Spot-Futures Parity minus the observed futures price), and the arbitrage profit net of transaction costs.

Solution Strategy. First calculate the basis. Then substitute the spot price into the Spot-Futures Parity to determine the model futures price. Then calculate the price difference between the model futures price and the actual futures price. Finally, the arbitrage profit net of transactions costs is the amount (if any) by which the absolute value of the price difference exceeds transaction costs.

Results. Notice that the basis is a substantial positive value and steadily declines over time before finally reaching zero when the futures contract matures, which is called "price convergence." By contrast, the price difference is very small value and fluctuates between positive and negative values before going to zero when the futures contract matures. Most of the time the price difference was inside the transaction cost boundaries, so there wasn't an arbitrage opportunity. However in month 4, the price difference went outside the boundaries by rising above the upper bound. Thus, an arbitrage profit could made in month 4 by selling in the stock index portfolio in the spot market, using the proceeds to invest at the riskfree rate, and taking a long position in stock index futures.

FIGURE 19.1 Futures – Spot-Futures Parity (Cost of Carry).

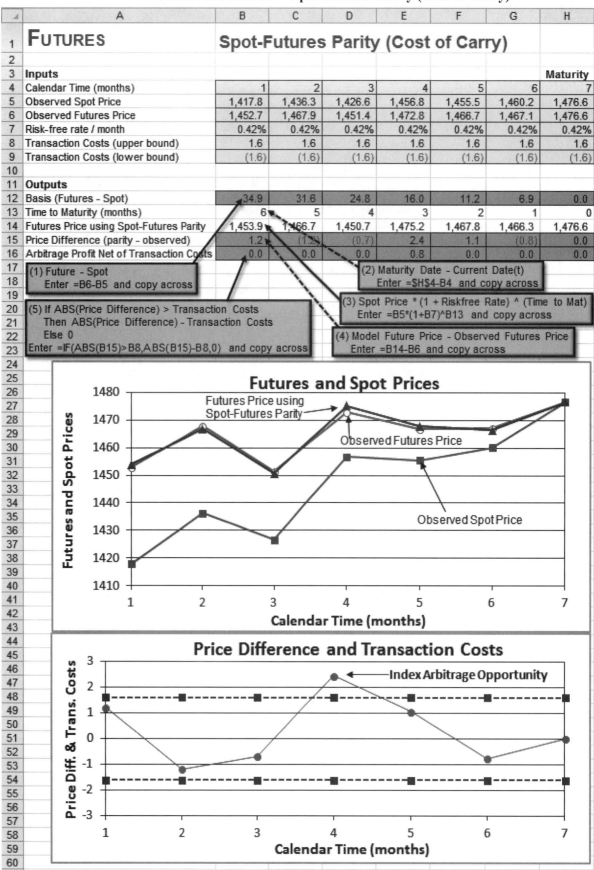

19.2 Margin

Problem. Suppose that you buy 50 futures contracts, where each contract is on 1,000 units of the underlying asset. The initial margin is $5,000 and the maintenance margin is $3,000. The riskfree rate is 4.31%. The standard deviation of the futures price is 63.00%. Each day is 1/365 = 0.0027 of a year. The future price on day 0 is $42.93. Develop a model of margin calls and excess margin.

Solution Strategy. First model the random changes in the futures price. Then determine the daily gain (or loss) on your futures position that is added to (or subtracted from) your margin account at the end of the day. Finally, determine if you margin account balance has fallen below the maintenance level generating a margin call to add more money or risen above the initial level providing excess margin that can be withdrawn.

FIGURE 19.2 Futures – Margin.

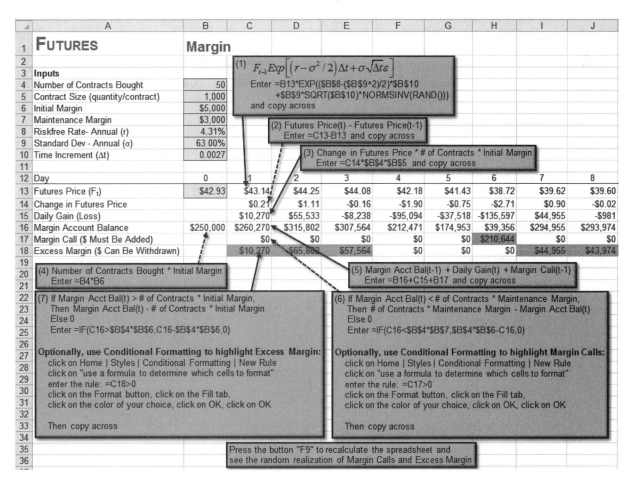

Problems

1. Suppose we recorded the monthly spot price of the S&P 500 index and corresponding futures price over a seven month period for a stock index futures contract maturing in month 7. Here are the prices in index points:

Month	1	2	3	4	5	6	7
Spot price	1539.21	1552.95	1587.44	1603.48	1659.12	1653.47	1693.59
Futures price	1590.33	1593.68	1619.93	1630.37	1679.38	1661.81	1693.59

Suppose that the riskfree rate is 0.63% per month. Suppose that the round trip transaction cost for doing an index arbitrage trade is 1.30 index points. Compute the basis, to the price difference (the futures price implied by Spot-Futures Parity minus the observed futures price), and the arbitrage profit net of transaction costs.

2. Suppose that you buy 84 futures contracts, where each contract is on 800 units of the underlying asset. The initial margin is $9,500 and the maintenance margin is $6,700. The riskfree rate is 3.84%. The standard deviation of the futures price is 47.00%. Each day is 1/365 = 0.0027 of a year. The future price on day 0 is $42.93. Develop a model of margin calls and excess margin.

Chapter 20 Pricing By Simulation

20.1 Path-Independent Derivatives

Problem. At the close of trading on April 30, 2010, the stock price of Amazon.com was $137.10, the standard deviation of daily returns is 38.67%, the yield on a six-month U.S. Treasury Bill was 2.44%, the exercise price of an October 140 call on Amazon.com was $140.00, the exercise price of an October 140 put on Amazon.com was $140.00, and the time to maturity for both October 15, 2010 maturity options was 0.4583 years. The cash payoff for cash-or-nothing options is $15.00. Using the simulation method, what is the price of the following path-independent derivatives: (1) European Call, (2) European Put, (3) Cash-or-Nothing Call, (4) Cash-or-Nothing Put, (5) Asset-or-Nothing Call, and (6) Asset-or-Nothing Put?

Solution Strategy. Make 1,000 draws of the stock price at maturity under the risk neutral process using Excel's random number function. Then compute the payoff of the six path-independent derivatives for all 1,000 draws. Then discount all 1,000 payoffs back to the present at the riskfree rate under risk neutral valuation method. Finally, take the average of all 1,000 discounted values to value the six path-independent derivatives.

Results. In the screen shot below, a European Call is valued at $13.67. If you push the F9 button to recalculate the spreadsheet, you will get a new set of 1,000 draws and thus a new derivative value. Upon recalculating, the next five valuations I obtained were: $13.86, $13.66, $13.42, $14.13, and $12.70. As you can see, there is considerable variation in these valuations. You can improve the accuracy of your estimate by dramatically increasing the number of draws to, say, 10,000 draws or even 100,000 draws. This is easy to accomplish by simply copying the formulas in columns **B**, **C**, **F**, and **G** further down the spreadsheet and updating the formula in cell **K5** to average over all of the values in column **F**.

FIGURE 20.1 Pricing By Simulation – Path-Independent Derivatives.

PRICING BY SIMULATION   Path-Independent Derivatives   European Call

Inputs

Input	Value	
Stock Price Now (S_0)	$137.10	137
Standard Dev - Annual (σ)	38.67%	3
Riskfree Rate- Annual (r)	2.44%	2
Exercise Price (X)	$140.00	140
Time To Maturity - Yrs (T)	0.4583	4
Number of Periods	1	

Derivative

- ● European Call
- ○ European Put
- ○ Cash-or-Nothing Call
- ○ Cash-or-Nothing Put
- ○ Asset-or-Nothing Call
- ○ Asset-or-Nothing Put

1

Outputs

Time / Period (Δt)   0.458

European Call Price $13.67

(5) Average of Derivative Price Now
Enter =AVERAGE(F14:F1013)

More Inputs: Cash Payoff (Z) $15.00

	Now	Maturity		Now	Maturity
Period	0	1	Period	0	1
Time	0.000	0.458	Time	0.000	0.458

	Stock		European Call		
Stock	$137.10	$188.18	**European Call**	$47.65	$48.18
	$137.10	$154.06		$13.90	$14.06
	$137.10	$85.16		$0.00	$0.00
	$137.10	$177.14		$36.73	$37.14
	$137.10	$90.17		$0.00	$0.00
	$137.10	$197.87		$57.23	$57.87
	$137.10	$149.30			

(1) Stock Price Now
Enter =$B$4 and copy
to the range B15:B1013

(4) Derivative Price at Maturity
* Exp(-r * T)
Enter =G14*EXP(-$B$6*$B$8)
and copy to the range F15:F1013

(2) $$S_0 Exp\left[\left(r-\sigma^2/2\right)\Delta t+\sigma\sqrt{\Delta t}\,\varepsilon\right]$$

Enter =B14*EXP(($B$6-($B$5^2)/2)*$K$4
+$B$5*SQRT($K$4)*NORMSINV(RAND()))
and copy to the range C15:C1013

(3) If   Derivative = European Call,   Then Max(S(T) - X, 0)
Elseif Derivative = European Put,   Then Max(X - S(T), 0)
Elseif Derivative = Cash-or-Nothing Call, Then If S(T) > X, Then Z, Else 0
Elseif Derivative = Cash-or-Nothing Put, Then If S(T) < X, Then Z, Else 0
Elseif Derivative = Asset-or-Nothing Call, Then If S(T) > X, Then S(T), Else 0
Else   If S(T) < X, Then S(T), Else 0

Enter =IF($G$4=1,MAX(C14-$B$7,0),
    IF($G$4=2,MAX($B$7-C14,0),
    IF($G$4=3,IF(C14>$B$7,$K$7,0),
    IF($G$4=4,IF(C14<$B$7,$K$7,0),
    IF($G$4=5,IF(C14>$B$7,C14,0),
        IF(C14<$B$7,C14,0))))))
and copy to the range G15:G1013

	$137.10	$150.25	
	$137.10	$148.06	
	$137.10	$238.24	
	$137.10	$184.99	
	$137.10	$190.77	
	$137.10	$123.76	
	$137.10	$152.81	
	$137.10	$140.54	

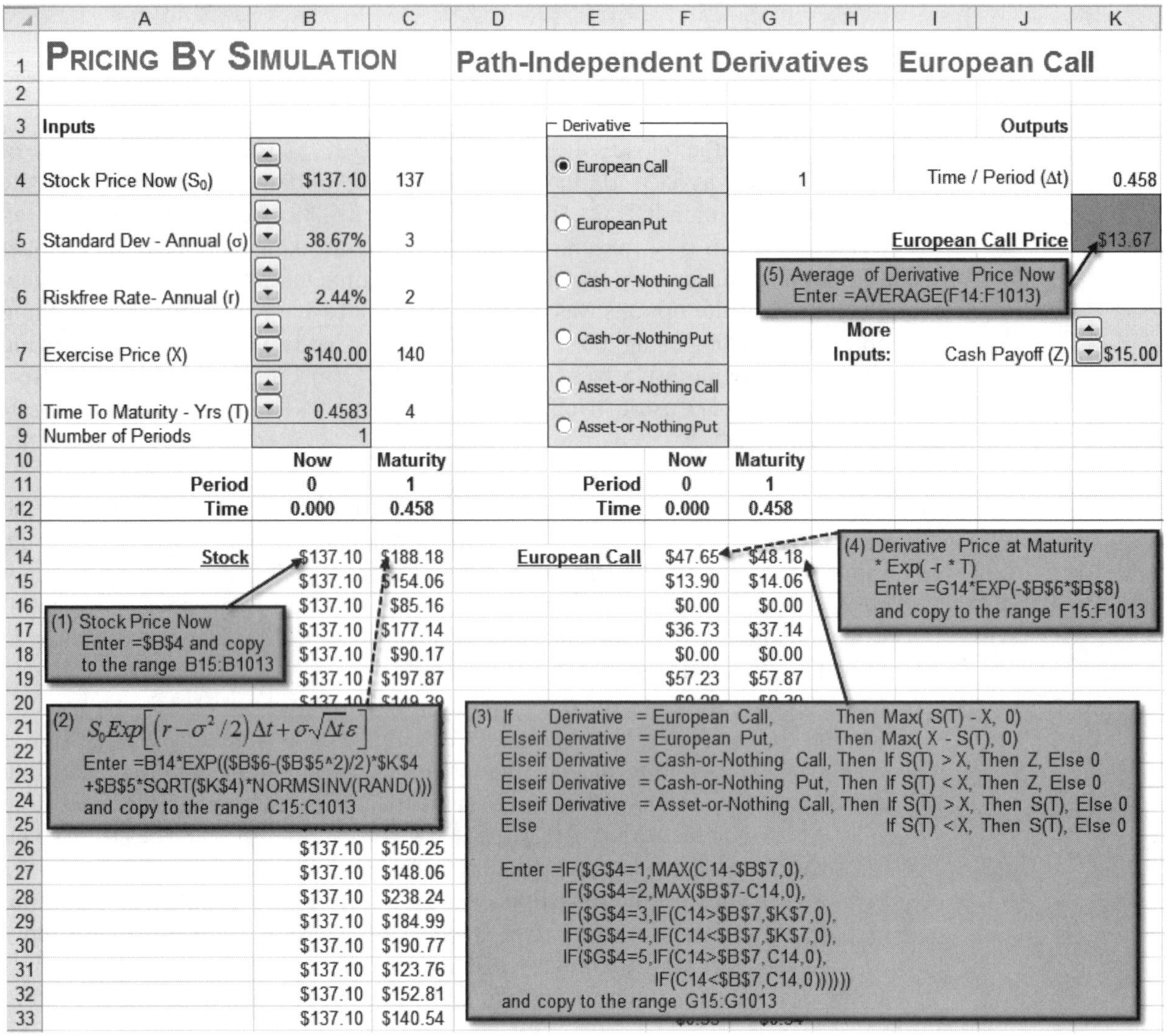

20.2 Path-Independent Derivatives With Jumps

Problem. At the close of trading on April 30, 2010, the stock price of Amazon.com was $137.10, the standard deviation of daily returns is 38.67%, the yield on a six-month U.S. Treasury Bill was 2.44%, the exercise price of an October 140 call on Amazon.com was $140.00, the exercise price of an October 140 put on Amazon.com was $140.00, and the time to maturity for both October 15, 2010 maturity options was 0.4583 years. The cash payoff for cash-or-nothing options is $15.00. The annual jump rate is 1.3840, the jump mean is 7.0%, and the jump standard deviation is 30.0%. Using a jump-diffusion process evaluated by simulation, what is the price of the following path-independent derivatives: (1) European Call, (2) European Put, (3) Cash-or-Nothing Call, (4) Cash-or-Nothing Put, (5) Asset-or-Nothing Call, and (6) Asset-or-Nothing Put?

FIGURE 20.2 Pricing By Simulation – Path-Indep Derivatives With Jumps.

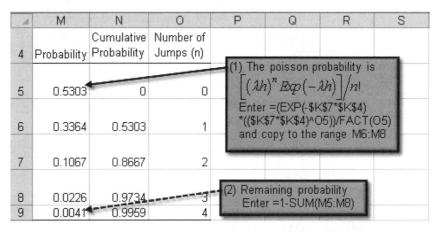

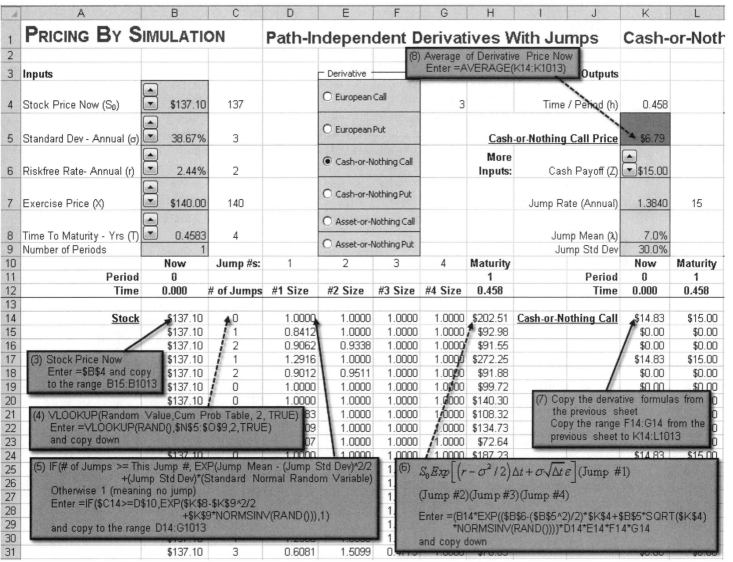

Solution Strategy. In 1,000 cases, determine the stock price at maturity under the risk neutral process by: (1) determining the number of jumps by taking a draw from a Poisson distribution, (2) determining the size of each jump to as many as four jumps, and (3) combining the jumps with the non-jump diffusion process. Then compute the payoff of the six path-independent derivatives for all 1,000 cases. Then discount all 1,000 payoffs back to the present at the riskfree rate under risk neutral valuation method. Finally, take the average of all 1,000 discounted values to value the six path-independent derivatives.

Results. A Cash-or-Nothing Call is valued at $6.79. Again, there is considerable variation in the valuation if you press F9 to recalculate the spreadsheet. Increased accuracy can be obtained by dramatically increasing the number of draws of all of the random variables (# of jumps, jump #1, etc.).

20.3 Path-Independent Derivatives With Stratified Sampling

Problem. At the close of trading on April 30, 2010, the stock price of Amazon.com was $137.10, the standard deviation of daily returns is 38.67%, the yield on a six-month U.S. Treasury Bill was 2.44%, the exercise price of an October 140 call on Amazon.com was $140.00, the exercise price of an October 140 put on Amazon.com was $140.00, and the time to maturity for both October 15, 2010 maturity options was 0.4583 years. The cash payoff for cash-or-nothing options is $15.00. Using the simulation method with stratified sampling to improve accuracy, what is the price of the following path-independent derivatives: (1) European Call, (2) European Put, (3) Cash-or-Nothing Call, (4) Cash-or-Nothing Put, (5) Asset-or-Nothing Call, and (6) Asset-or-Nothing Put?

Solution Strategy. Determine 1,000 "representative" values of the standard normal distribution that are each one-tenth of a percentile. Use these values to determine 1,000 cases of the stock price at maturity under the risk neutral process. Then compute the payoff of the six path-independent derivatives for all 1,000 cases. Then discount all 1,000 payoffs back to the present at the riskfree rate under risk neutral valuation method. Finally, take the average of all 1,000 discounted values to value the six path-independent derivatives.

Results. A European call option is valued at $13.68. This compares to a Black-Scholes price of $13.69 for the same inputs. Clearly there is an enormous gain in accuracy by using stratified sampling. Accuracy can be increased further, by increasing the number of "representative" values up to 10,000 or even 100,000. This is easy to accomplish by simply copying the formulas in columns **B**, **C**, **D**, **E**, **H**, and **I** further down the spreadsheet, updating the number of draws in cell **K8** and updating the formula in cell **K5** to average over all of the values in column **H**.

FIGURE 20.3 Pricing By Sim – Path-Indep Deriv With Stratified Sampling.

	A	B	C	D	E	F	G	H	I	J	K	L	M
1	**PRICING BY SIMULATION**				**Path-Independent Derivatives European Call**								
2					**With Stratified Sampling**								
3	Inputs				┌ Derivative ─					Outputs			
4	Stock Price Now (S₀)	$137.10	137		◉ European Call		1			Time / Period	0.458		
5	Standard Dev - Annual (σ)	38.67%	3		○ European Put					**European Call Price**	$13.68		
6	Riskfree Rate- Annual (r)	2.44%	2		○ Cash-or-Nothing Call								
7	Exercise Price (X)	$140.00	140		○ Cash-or-Nothing Put			**More Inputs:**		Cash Payoff (Z)	$15.00	15	
8	Time To Maturity - Yrs (T)	0.4583	4		○ Asset-or-Nothing Call					Number of Draws	1,000		
9	Number of Periods	1			○ Asset-or-Nothing Put								
10		**Now**			**Maturity**			**Now**	**Maturity**	(5) Average of Derivative Price Now			
11	**Period**	0	Draw	Draw	1		**Period**	0	1	Enter =AVERAGE(H14:H1013)			
12	**Time**	0.000	**Number**	**Value**	0.458		**Time**	0.000	0.458				
13													
14	**Stock**	$137.10	1	-3.2905	$56.61	**European Call**		$0.00	$0.00				
15		$137.10	2	-2.9677	$61.60			$0.00	$0.00				
16	(1) Stock Price Now	$137.10	3	-2.8070	$64.25			$0.00	$0.00				
17	Enter =$B$4 and copy to the range B15:B1013	$137.10	4	-2.6968	$66.13			$0.00	$0.00				
18		$137.10	5	-2.6121	$67.61			$0.00	$0.00	(4) Copy the derivative formulas from			
19		$137.10	6	-2.5427	$68.85			$0.00	$0.00	the previous sheet			
20	(2) NORMSINV((Draw Number - 0.5)							$0.00	$0.00	Copy the range K14:L14 from the previous sheet to H14:I1013			
21	/ (Number of Draws))			$S_0 Exp\left[(r-\sigma^2/2)\Delta t + \sigma\sqrt{\Delta t}\,\varepsilon\right]$				$0.00	$0.00				
22	Enter =NORMSINV((C14-0.5)/$K$8)			Enter =B14*EXP(($B$6-($B$5^2)/2)*$K$4				$0.00	$0.00				
23	and copy to the range B15:B1013			+$B$5*SQRT($K$4)*D14)				$0.00	$0.00				
24		$137.10		and copy to the range E15:E1013				$0.00	$0.00				
25		$137.10						$0.00	$0.00				

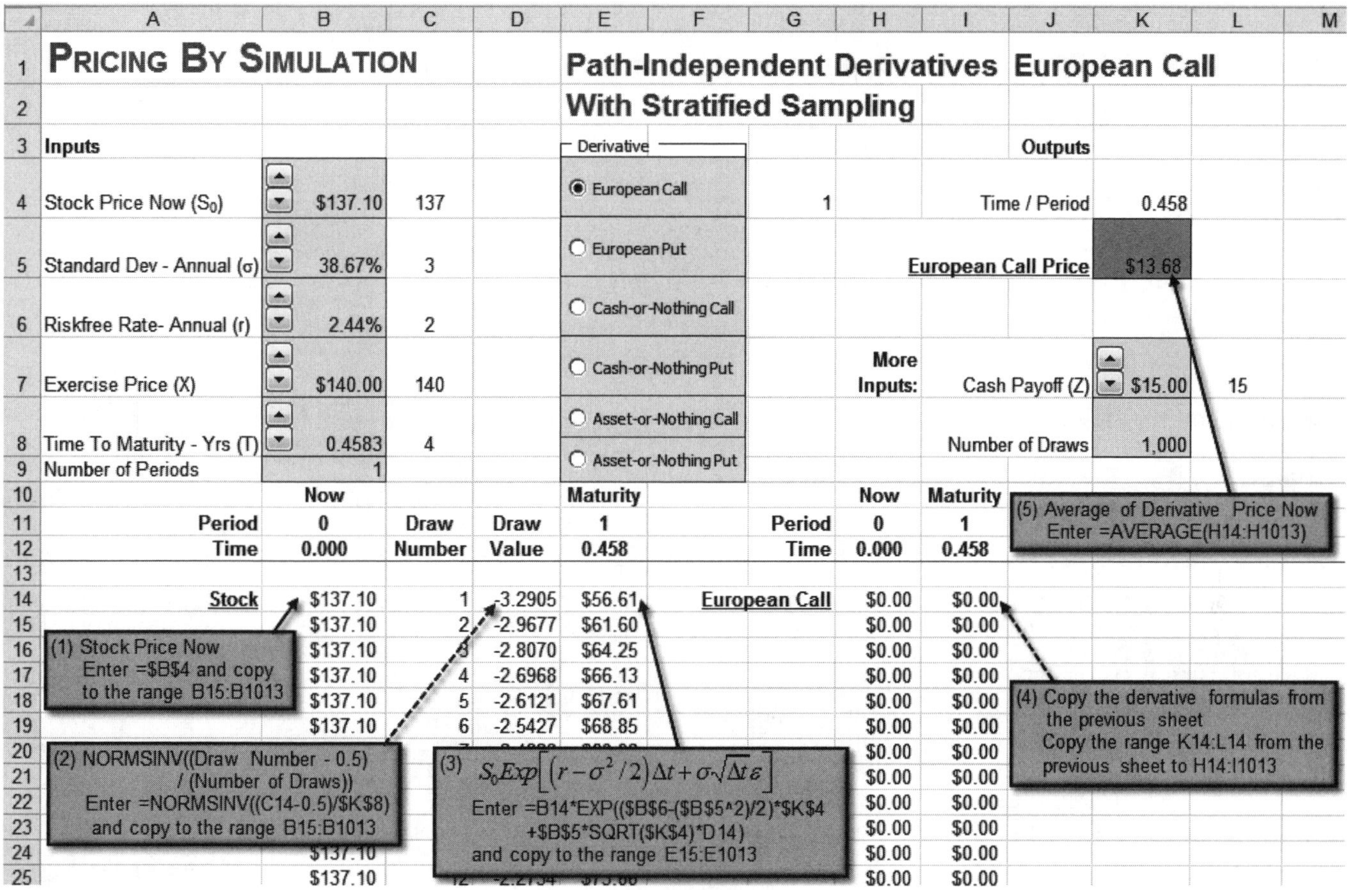

20.4 Path-Dependent Derivatives

Problem. At the close of trading on April 30, 2010, the stock price of Amazon.com was $137.10, the standard deviation of daily returns is 38.67%, the yield on a six-month U.S. Treasury Bill was 2.44%, the exercise price of an October 140 call on Amazon.com was $140.00, the exercise price of an October 140 put on Amazon.com was $140.00, and the time to maturity for both October 15, 2010 maturity options was 0.4583 years. For barrier options, the barrier is $125.00. Using the simulation method, what is the price of the following path-dependent derivatives: (1) Asian Call, (2) Asian Put, (3) Lookback Call, (4) Lookback Put, (5) Down-And-Out Call, and (6) Down-And-In Put?

Solution Strategy. Make 1,000 draws of the period 1 shock to compute the period 1 price under the risk neutral process using Excel's random number function. Do the same for periods 2 through 8. Then compute the payoff of the six path-dependent derivatives for all 1,000 period 8 prices. Then discount all 1,000 payoffs back to the present at the riskfree rate under risk neutral valuation method. Finally, take the average of all 1,000 discounted values to value the six path-dependent derivatives.

FIGURE 20.4 Pricing By Simulation – Path-Dependent Derivatives.

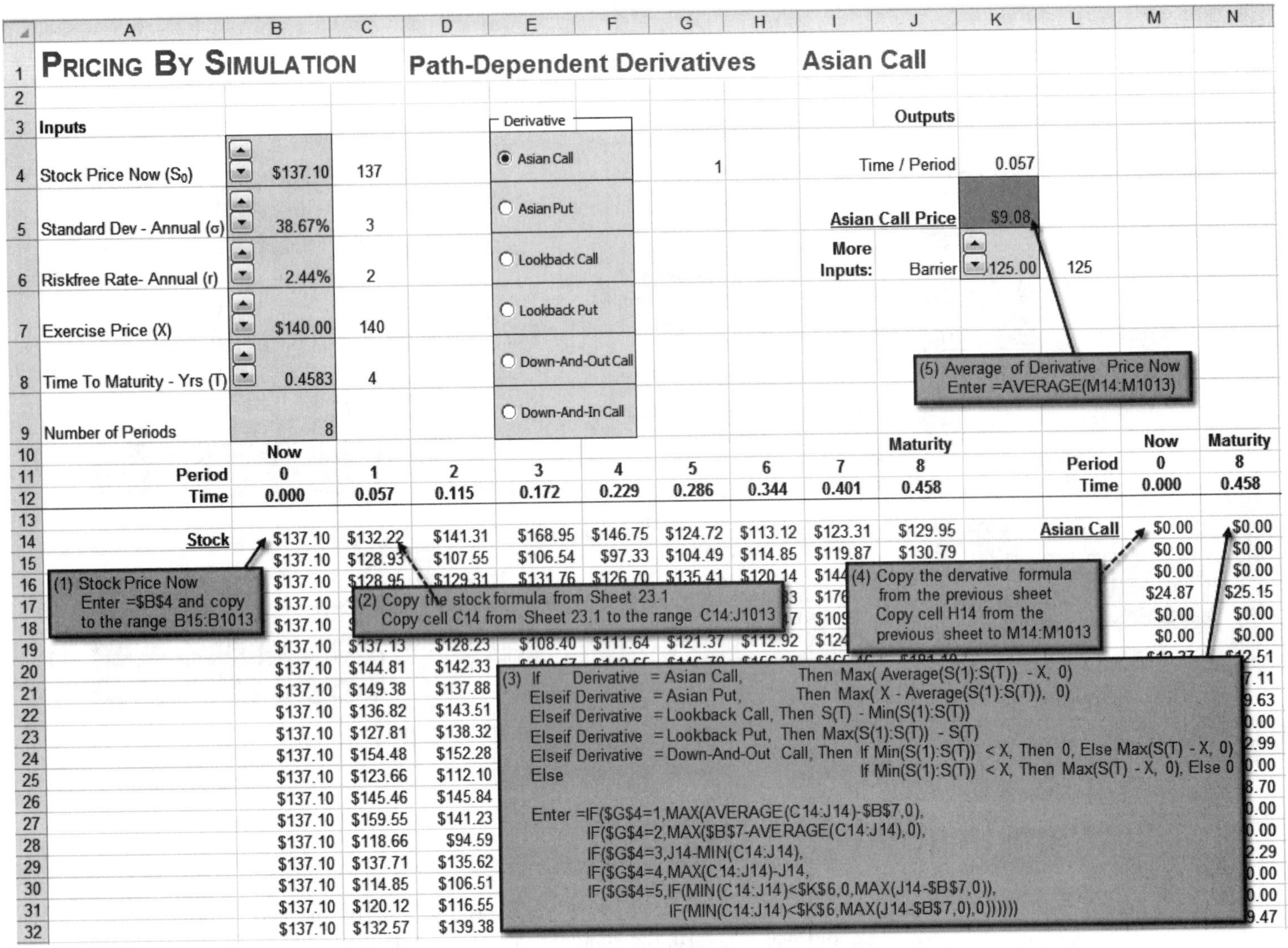

An Asian Call is valued at $9.08. Again, there is considerable variation in the valuation if you press F9 to recalculate the spreadsheet. Increased accuracy can be obtained by dramatically increasing the number of draws of all of the random variables (period 1 shock, period 2 shock, etc.).

20.5 Path-Dependent Derivatives With Jumps

Problem. At the close of trading on April 30, 2010, the stock price of Amazon.com was $137.10, the standard deviation of daily returns is 38.67%, the yield on a six-month U.S. Treasury Bill was 2.44%, the exercise price of an October 140 call on Amazon.com was $140.00, the exercise price of an October 140 put on Amazon.com was $140.00, and the time to maturity for both October 15, 2010 maturity options was 0.4583 years. For barrier options, the barrier is $125.00. The annual jump rate is 1.3840 and the jump size is 5.00%. Using a jump-diffusion process evaluated by simulation, what is the price of the following path-dependent derivatives: (1) Asian Call, (2) Asian Put, (3) Lookback Call, (4) Lookback Put, (5) Down-And-Out Call, and (6) Down-And-In Put?

Solution Strategy. Make 1,000 draws of the period 1 shock to compute the period 1 price under the risk neutral process using Excel's random number function. Do the same for periods 2 through 8. Then compute the payoff of the six path-dependent derivatives for all 1,000 period 8 prices. Then discount all 1,000 payoffs back to the present at the riskfree rate under risk neutral valuation method. Finally, take the average of all 1,000 discounted values to value the six path-dependent derivatives.

FIGURE 20.5 Pricing By Simulation – Path-Dep Derivatives With Jumps.

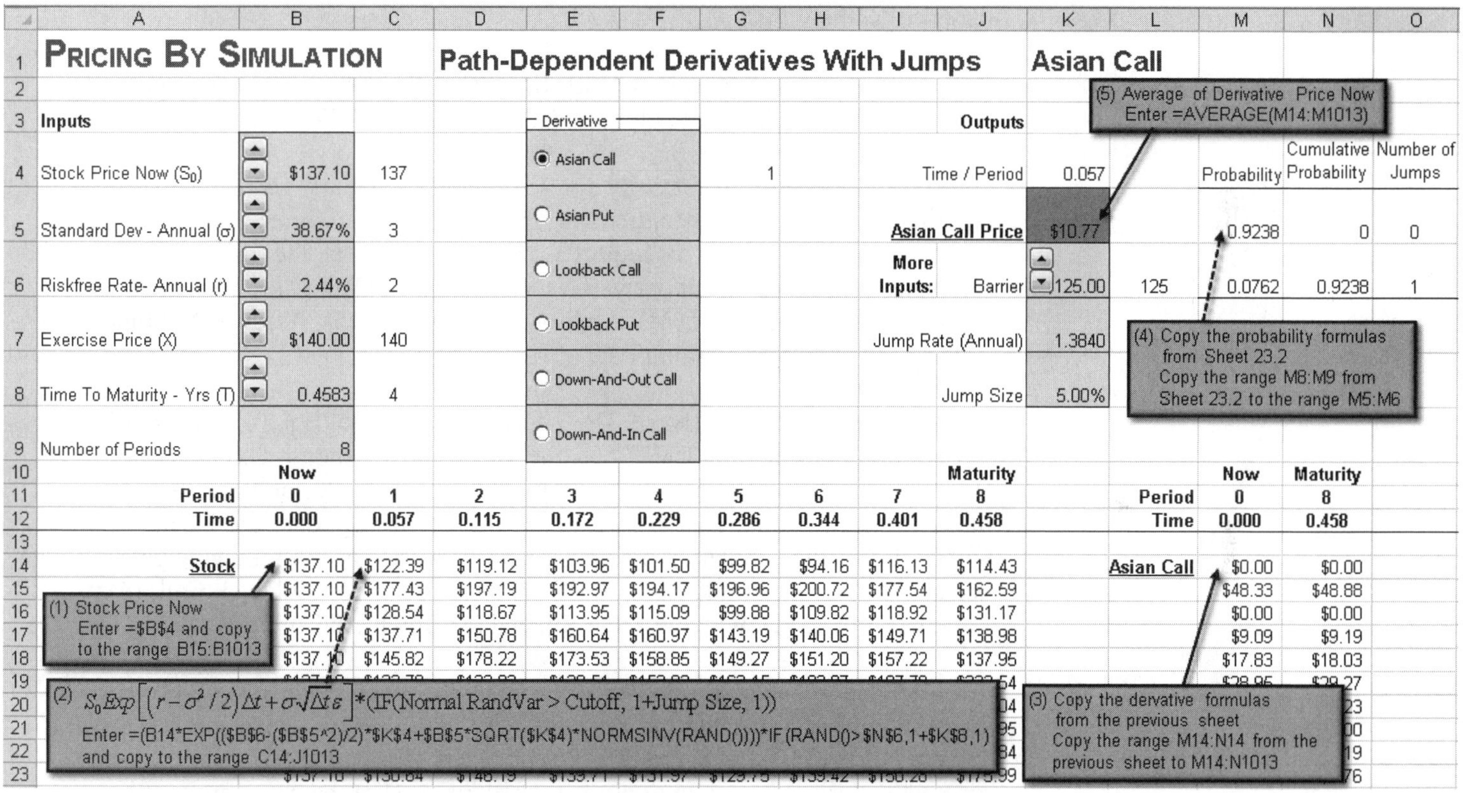

An Asian Call on a multi-period jump-diffusion process is valued at $10.77. Again, there is considerable variation in the valuation if you press F9 to recalculate the spreadsheet. Increased accuracy can be obtained by dramatically increasing the number of draws of all of the random variables (period 1 shock, period 1 jump draw, period 2 shock, period 2 jump draw, etc.).

Problems

1. **Path-independent Derivatives.** The stock price is $45.83, the standard deviation of daily returns is 52.70%, the yield on a six-month U.S. Treasury Bill was 3.91%, the exercise price for all options $40.00, and the time to maturity for all options is 0.8247 years. The cash payoff for cash-or-nothing

options is $34.00. Using the simulation method, what is the price of the following path-independent derivatives: (1) European Call, (2) European Put, (3) Cash-or-Nothing Call, (4) Cash-or-Nothing Put, (5) Asset-or-Nothing Call, and (6) Asset-or-Nothing Put?

2. **Path-independent Derivatives With Jumps.** The stock price is $32.15, the standard deviation of daily returns is 31.36%, the yield on a six-month U.S. Treasury Bill was 1.75%, the exercise price for all options $35.00, and the time to maturity for all options is 0.6429 years. The cash payoff for cash-or-nothing options is $42.00. The annual jump rate is 1.7391, the jump mean is 6.3%, and the jump standard deviation is 46.0%. Using a jump-diffusion process evaluated by simulation, what is the price of the following path-independent derivatives: (1) European Call, (2) European Put, (3) Cash-or-Nothing Call, (4) Cash-or-Nothing Put, (5) Asset-or-Nothing Call, and (6) Asset-or-Nothing Put?

3. **Path-independent Derivatives With Stratified Sampling.** The stock price is $63.84, the standard deviation of daily returns is 28.73%, the yield on a six-month U.S. Treasury Bill was 3.41, the exercise price for all options $60.00, and the time to maturity for all options is 0.4384 years. The cash payoff for cash-or-nothing options is $18.00. Using the simulation method with stratified sampling to improve accuracy, what is the price of the following path-independent derivatives: (1) European Call, (2) European Put, (3) Cash-or-Nothing Call, (4) Cash-or-Nothing Put, (5) Asset-or-Nothing Call, and (6) Asset-or-Nothing Put?

4. **Path-dependent Derivatives.** The stock price is $57.91, the standard deviation of daily returns is 72.35%, the yield on a six-month U.S. Treasury Bill was 2.63%, the exercise price for all options $60.00, and the time to maturity for all options is 0.6481 years. For barrier options, the barrier is $50.00. Using the simulation method, what is the price of the following path-dependent derivatives: (1) Asian Call, (2) Asian Put, (3) Lookback Call, (4) Lookback Put, (5) Down-And-Out Call, and (6) Down-And-In Put?

5. **Path-dependent Derivatives With Jumps.** The stock price is $53.82, the standard deviation of daily returns is 46.62%, the yield on a six-month U.S. Treasury Bill was 4.27%, the exercise price for all options $55.00, and the time to maturity for all options is 0.6419 years. For barrier options, the barrier is $45.00. The annual jump rate is 1.7392 and the jump size is 9.00%. Using a jump-diffusion process evaluated by simulation, what is the price of the following path-dependent derivatives: (1) Asian Call, (2) Asian Put, (3) Lookback Call, (4) Lookback Put, (5) Down-And-Out Call, and (6) Down-And-In Put?

Chapter 21 Corporate Bonds

21.1 Two Methods

Problem. The Value of the Firm (V) is $340 million, the Face Value of the Debt (B) is $160 million, the time to maturity of the debt (t) is 2.00 years, the riskfree rate (k_{RF}) is 5.0%, and the standard deviation of the return on the firm's assets (σ) is 50.0%. There are two different methods for valuing the firm's equity and risky debt based in an option pricing framework. Using both methods, what is the firm's Equity Value (E) and Risky Debt Value (D)? Do both methods produce the same result?

Solution Strategy. In the first method, equity is considered to be a call option. Thus, E = Call Price. For this call option, the underlying asset is the Value of the Firm (V) and the exercise price is the face value of the debt (B). Hence, the call price is calculated from the Black-Scholes call formula by substituting V for P and B for X. The rationale is that if V > B, then the equityholders gain the net profit V-B. However, if V < B, then the equityholders avoid the loss by declaring bankruptcy, turning V over to the debtholders, and walking away with zero rather than owing money. Thus, the payoff to equityholders is Max (V - B, 0), which has the same payoff form as a call option. Further, we can use the fact that Debt plus Equity equals Total Value of Firm (D + E = V) and obtain the value of debt D = V - E = V - Call.

In the second method, Risky Debt is considered to be Riskfree Debt minus a Put option. Thus, D = Riskfree Debt - Put. For this put option, the underlying asset is also the Value of the Firm (V) and the exercise price is also the face value of the debt (B). Hence, the put price is calculated from the Black-Scholes put formula by substituting V for P and B for X. The rationale is that the put option is a *Guarantee* against default in repaying the face value of the debt (B). Specifically, if V > B, then the equityholders repay the face value B in full and the value of the guarantee is zero. However, if V < B, then the equityholders only pay V and default on the rest, so the guarantee must pay the balance B - V. Thus, the payoff on the guarantee is Max (B - V, 0), which has the same payoff form as a put option. Further, we can use the fact that Debt plus Equity equals Total Value of Firm (D + E = V) and obtain E = V - Risky Debt = V - (Riskfree Debt - Put).

FIGURE 20.1 Excel Model for Stocks and Risky Bonds.

	A	B	C	D	E	F	G	H	I	J
1	**CORPORATE BONDS**			**Two Methods**						
2										
3	**Inputs**			**Analogous Inputs for a Black-Scholes Call Option on a Stock**						
4	Value of Firm (V)	$340.00	Stock Price							
5	Firm Asset Std Dev (σ)	50.0%	Stock Std Dev							
6	Risk-free Rate (k$_{RF}$)	5.0%	Risk-free Rate							
7	Face Value of Debt (B)	$160.00	Exercise Price							
8	Time to Maturity (t)	2.00	Time to Maturity							
9										
10	**Outputs**									
11	**Black-Scholes Option Pricing**									
12	d1	1.561								
13	d2	0.854								
14	N(d1)	0.941								
15	N(d2)	0.803								
16	Call Price	$203.54			(1) (Face Value of Debt) * Exp[- (Risk-free Rate) * (Time to Maturity)]					
17					Enter =B7*EXP(-B6*B8)					
18	-d1	-1.561								
19	-d2	-0.854		(2) Call Price						
20	N(-d1)	0.059		Enter =B16						
21	N(-d2)	0.197								
22	Put Price	$8.31		(3) V - Call Price						
23				Enter =B4-B16						
24	**Merton Model**									
25	Riskfree Debt Value	$144.77		(4) Equity + Risky Debt						
26				Enter =C30+C32						
27			**Method One:**		**Method Two (equivalent by Put-Call Parity):**					
28			**Equity is a Call**		**Risky Debt is Riskfree Debt minus Put**					
29										
30	Equity Value (E)	= Call	$203.54		= V - Riskfree Debt + Put	$203.54	(5) V - Riskfree Debt Value + Put Price			
31							Enter =B4-B25+B22			
32	Risky Debt Value (D)	= V - Call	$136.46		= Riskfree Debt - Put	$136.46				
33							(6) Riskfree Debt Value - Put Price			
34	Total Value of Firm (V)	= V	$340.00		= V	$340.00	Enter =B25-B22			
35										
36							(7) Equity + Risky Debt			
37							Enter =F30+F32			

Both methods of doing the calculation find that the Equity Value (E) = $203.54 and the Risky Debt Value (D) = $136.46. We can verify that both methods should always generate the same results. Consider what we get if we equate the Method One and Method Two expressions for the Equity Value (E): **Call Price = V – Riskfree Bond Value + Put Price**. You may recognize this as an alternative version of Put-Call Parity. The standard version of Put-Call Parity is: **Call Price = Stock Price - Bond Price + Put Price**. To get the alternative version, just substitute V for the Stock Price and substitute the Riskfree Bond Value for the Bond Price. Consider what we get if we equate the Method One and Method Two expressions for the Risky Debt Value (D): **V - Call Price = Riskfree Bond - Put Price**. This is simply a rearrangement of the alternative version of Put-Call Parity. Since Put-Call Parity is always true, then both methods of valuing debt and equity will always yield the same result!

20.2 Impact of Risk

Problem. What impact does the firm's risk have upon the firm's Debt and Equity valuation? Specifically, if you increased Firm Asset Standard Deviation, then what would happen to the firm's Equity Value and Risky Debt Value?

Solution Strategy. Create a **Data Table** of Equity Value and Risky Debt Value for different input values for the Firm's Asset Standard Deviation. Then graph the results and interpret it.

FIGURE 20.2 Excel Model of the Sensitivity of Equity Value and Risky Debt Value.

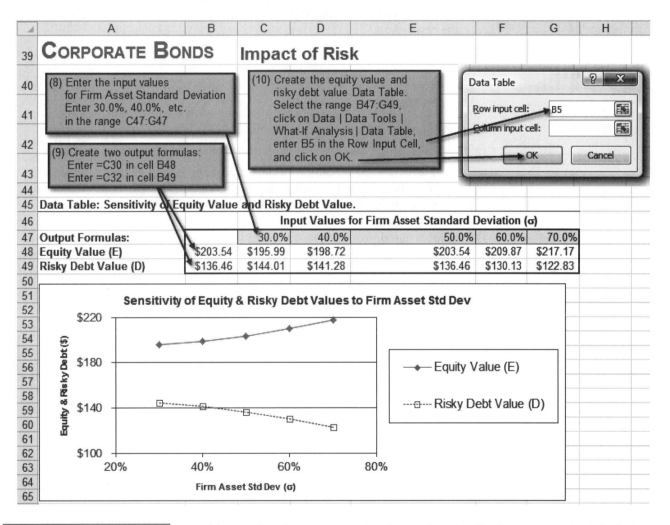

Excel 97-2003
Equivalent

To call up a Data Table in Excel
97-2003, click on **Data | Table**

Looking at the chart, we see that increasing the firm's asset standard deviation causes a wealth transfer from debtholders to equityholders. This may seem surprising, but this is a direct consequence of equity being a call option and debt being V *minus* a call option. We know that increasing the standard deviation makes a call more valuable, so equivalently increasing the firm's asset standard deviation makes the firm's Equity Value more valuable and reduces the Risky Debt Value by the same amount.

The intuitive rationale for this is that an increase in standard deviation allows equityholders to benefit from more frequent and bigger increases in V, while not being hurt by more frequent and bigger decreases in V. In the later case, the equityholders are going to declare bankruptcy anyway so they don't care how much V drops. Debtholders are the mirror image. They do *not* benefit from more frequent and bigger increases in V since repayment is capped at B, but they are *hurt* by more frequent and bigger decreases in V. In the latter case, the size of the repayment default (B – V) increases as V drops more.

The possibility of transferring wealth from debtholders to equityholders (or visa versa) illustrates the potential for conflict between equityholders and debtholders. Equityholders would like the firm to take on riskier projects, but debtholders would like the firm to focus on safer projects. Whether the firm ultimately decides to take on risky or safe projects will determine how wealth is divided between the two groups.

Problems

1. The Value of the Firm (V) is $780 million, the Face Value of the Debt (B) is $410 million, the time to maturity of the debt (t) is 1.37 years, the riskfree rate (k_{RF}) is 3.2%, and the standard deviation of the return on the firm's assets (σ) is 43.0%. Using both methods of debt and equity valuation, what is the firm's Equity Value (E) and Risky Debt Value (D)? Do both methods produce the same result?

2. Determine what impact an increase in the Firm Asset Standard Deviation has on the firm's Equity Value and Risky Debt Value.

PART 7 EXCEL SKILLS

Chapter 22 Useful Excel Tricks

22.1 Quickly Delete The Instruction Boxes and Arrows

Task. Quickly get rid of all of the instruction boxes and arrows after you are done building the Excel model.

How To. All of the instruction boxes and arrows are *objects* and there is an easy way to select all of them at once. Click on **Home | Editing | Find & Select**

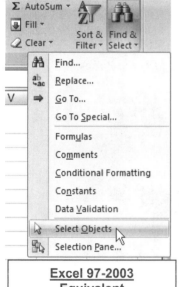

down-arrow | Select Objects. This causes the cursor to become a pointer   .
Then point to a **location above and to the left** of the instruction boxes and arrows, continue to hold down the left mouse button while you drag the pointer to a **location below and to the right** of the instruction boxes and arrows, and then let go of the left mouse button. This selects *all* of the instruction boxes and arrows (see example below). Then just press the **Delete** key and they are all gone!

**Excel 97-2003
Equivalent**

To get the Select Objects cursor in Excel 97-2003, click on the **Drawing** icon on the Standard toolbar and then click on the **Select Objects** icon (which looks like pointer) on the Drawing toolbar in the lower-left corner of the screen.

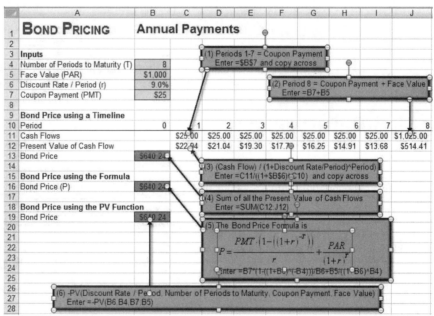

22.2 Freeze Panes

Task. Freeze column titles at the top of the columns and/or freeze row titles on the left side of the rows. This is especially useful for large spreadsheets.

How To. In the example below, suppose you want to freeze the column titles from row 8 and above (freezing Barrick over column B, Hanson over column C, etc.) and you want to freeze the row titles in column A. Select cell **B9** (as shown), because cell **B9** is just below row 8 that you want to freeze and just to the right of column A that you want to freeze.

	A	B	C	D	E	F	G	H
1	ASSET PRICING		Static CAPM Using Fama-MacBeth Method					
2								
3	Inputs							
4	Market Portfolio Benchmark	Market Portfolio Benchmark: ○ SPDR ETF ◉ CRSP VWMR ○ DJ World Stock			2			
5	Asset Type	Asset Type: ○ Stock ◉ US Port ○ Country Port			2			
6								
7		Stock	Stock	Stock	Stock	Stock	Stock	US Portfolio
8		Barrick	Hanson	IBM	Nokia	Telefonos	YPF	Small-Growth
9	Monthly Returns							
10	Dec 2006	-3.50%	-0.24%	2.06%	8.76%	8.63%	0.50%	-0.59%
11	Nov 2006	-2.37%	4.88%	5.69%	0.51%	9.01%	-0.95%	2.58%
12	Oct 2006	1.79%	3.78%	-0.12%	1.70%	-1.08%	3.49%	5.87%
13	Sep 2006	0.92%	-3.49%	12.69%	0.93%	3.14%	7.02%	1.09%
14	Aug 2006	-8.23%	14.36%	1.20%	-5.68%	6.76%	-3.83%	3.22%

Then click on **View | Window | Freeze Panes down-arrow | Freeze Panes**.

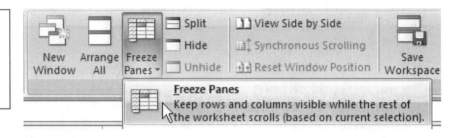

Excel 97-2003 Equivalent

To Freeze Paines in Excel 97-2003, click on **Window | Freeze Panes**.

22.3 Spin Buttons and the Developer Tab

Excel 2007 Equivalent

To view the macro in Excel 2007, click on the **Office** button, click on the **Excel Options** button, check the **Show Developer tab in the Ribbon** checkbox, and click **OK**.

Task. Add a spin button to make an input interactive.

How To. Spin buttons and other so-called "form controls" are located on the Developer tab Developer. If the Developer tab is not visible, you can display it by clicking on File, click on Options, click on **Customize Ribbon**, check the **Developer** checkbox, and click **OK**.

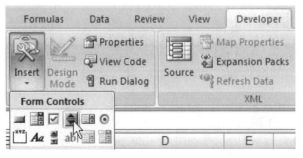

Then click on **Developer | Controls | Insert down-arrow | Form Controls | Spin Button**.

Excel 97-2003 Equivalent

To insert a Spin Button in Excel 97-2003, click on **View | Toolbars | Forms**. Then click on the **Spinner** icon on the Forms Toolbar.

Then point the cursor crosshairs to the upper-left corner of where you want the spin button to be, click and drag to the lower-right corner, and release. You get a

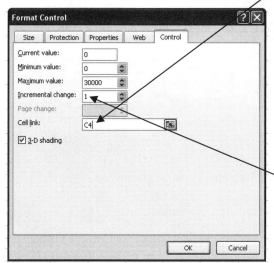

spin button 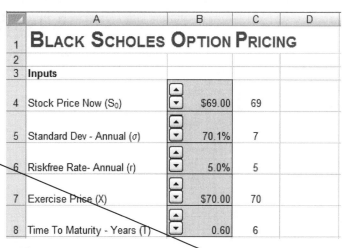. Now place the cursor over the top of the spin button, right-click, and select **Format Control** from the pop-up menu. On the **Control** tab of the **Format Control** dialog box, enter **C4** in the **Cell Link** entry box, and click **OK**.

Now when you click on the spin button, the value in cell **C4** will increase or decrease by 1. For convenience, I scale the spin button output to the appropriate scale of the input. For example, in the spreadsheet below the spin button in cell **B6** is linked to the cell **C6** and creates the integer value **5**. The formula in cell B6 is =**C6/100** and this create the value **5.0%** for the riskfree rate.

	A	B	C	D
1	**BLACK SCHOLES OPTION PRICING**			
2				
3	**Inputs**			
4	Stock Price Now (S$_0$)	$69.00	69	
5	Standard Dev - Annual (σ)	70.1%	7	
6	Riskfree Rate- Annual (r)	5.0%	5	
7	Exercise Price (X)	$70.00	70	
8	Time To Maturity - Years (T)	0.60	6	

Unfortunately, Spin Buttons are only allowed to have **Incremental Changes** that are integers (1, 2, 3, etc.). It would be convenient if they could have **Incremental Changes** of any value, such as .01 or -.0043.

22.4 Option Buttons and Group Boxes

Task. Add option buttons to allow input choices.

Excel 97-2003 Equivalent

To insert a Option Button in Excel 97-2003, click on **View | Toolbars | Forms**. Then click on the **Option Button** icon on the Forms Toolbar.

How To. Option buttons and other so-called "form controls" are located on the Developer tab. If you don't see a Developer tab, then you need to take a simple step to make it visible (see the section above).

Then click on **Developer | Controls | Insert down-arrow | Form Controls | Option Button**.

Then point the cursor crosshairs to the upper-left corner of where you want the option button to be, click and drag to the lower-right corner, and release. You get a option button 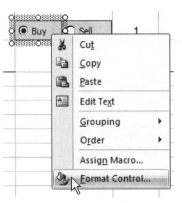. Repeat this process to get more option buttons.

Now place the cursor over the top of the first option button, right-click, then click over the blank text area, click a second time over the blank text area, delete any unwanted text (e.g., "Option Button1"), enter a text description of the choice (e.g., "Buy"), and then click outside the option button to finish. Repeat this process for the other option buttons (e.g., "Sell").

Now place the cursor over the top of the first option button, right-click, and select **Format Control** from the pop-up menu. On the **Control** tab of the **Format Control** dialog box, enter **C5** in the **Cell Link** entry box, and click **OK**.

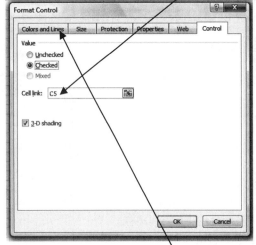

Now when the first option button is clicked, then the cell **C5** will show a **1**, and when the second option button is clicked, then the cell **C5** will show a **2**. Optionally, you click on the **Colors and Lines** tab of **Format Control** dialog box and specify the option button's fill color, line color, etc.

If you just want to have *one set* of option buttons on a spreadsheet, then you are done. However, if you want to have two or more sets of option buttons (the example below has four sets of option buttons), then you need to use **Group Boxes** to indicate which option buttons belong to which set.

	A	B	C	D	E
1	Oᴘᴛɪᴏɴ Tʀᴀᴅɪɴɢ Sᴛʀᴀᴛᴇɢɪᴇs Two Assets				
2					
3	Inputs	Buying a Bullish Spread			
4		Trade Direction		Asset Type	
5	First Asset (Lowest Exercise Price)	1st Trade Direction ◉ Buy ○ Sell	1	1st Asset Type ◉ Call ○ Put ○ Stock	1
6	Second Asset (Highest Exercise Price)	2nd Trade Direction ○ Buy ◉ Sell	2	2nd Asset Type ◉ Call ○ Put ○ Stock	1

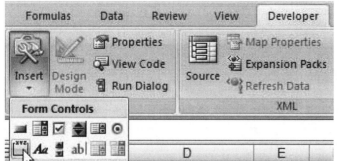

Click on **Developer | Controls | Insert down-arrow | Form Controls | Group Box**.

Then point the cursor crosshairs above and left of the first option button, click and drag to below and right of the second option button (or last option button in the set), and release. A Group Box is created which surrounds the option buttons. Click on the title of the Group Box, delete any unwanted text (e.g., "Group Box 1"), enter a text description (e.g., "1st Trade Direction"). Now when you click on the Buy or Sell option button in cell **B5** of the example above, then the linked cell **C5** changes to 1 or 2. Repeat the process of creating option buttons and surrounding them by group boxes to create all of the sets of option buttons that you want.

Excel 97-2003 Equivalent

To insert a Group Box in Excel 97-2003, click on **View | Toolbars | Forms**. Then click on the **Group Box** icon on the Forms Toolbar.

22.5 Scroll Bar

Excel 97-2003 Equivalent

To insert a Scroll Bar in Excel 97-2003, click on **View | Toolbars | Forms**. Then click on the **Scroll Bar** icon on the Forms Toolbar.

Task. Add a scroll bar call option to make big or small changes to an input.

How To. Option buttons and other so-called "form controls" are located on the Developer tab. If you don't see a Developer tab, then you need to take a simple step to make it visible (see two sections above).

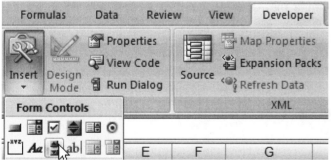

Then click on **Developer | Controls | Insert down-arrow | Form Controls | Scroll Bar**.

Then point the cursor crosshairs to the upper-left corner of where you want the option button to be, click and drag to the lower-right corner, and release. You get a scroll bar.

Now place the cursor over the top of the scroll bar, right-click, and select **Format Control** from the pop-up menu. On the **Control** tab of the **Format Control** dialog box, enter **I7** in the **Cell Link** entry box, and click **OK**. Optionally, you can specify the **Page Change** amount, which is the change in the cell link when you click on the white space of the scroll bar. In this example, a ~~Page Change of~~ 12 months jumps a year ahead.

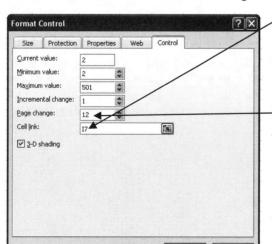

The advantage of a scroll bar is that you can make big or small changes (see example below). Clicking on the left or right arrow lowers or raises the value in cell **I7** by 1. Clicking on the white space of the scroll bar, lowers or raises the value in cell **I7** by 12 (the Page Change). Sliding the position bar allows you to rapidly scroll through the entire range of values.

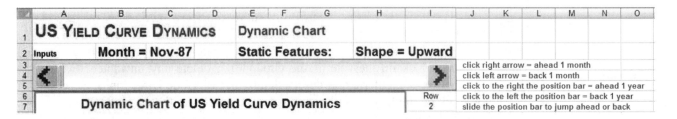

22.6 Install Solver or the Analysis ToolPak

Task. Install Solver or the Analysis ToolPak.

How To. Excel provides several special tools, such as Solver and the Analysis ToolPak, which need to be separately installed. Solver is a sophisticated, yet easy to use optimizer. The Analysis ToolPak contains advanced statistical programs and advanced functions.

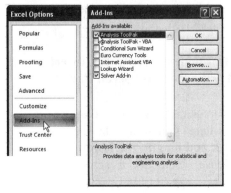

To install the Analysis ToolPak, click on the **Office** button , click on the $\boxed{\text{Excel Options}}$ button at the bottom of the drop-down window, click on **Add-Ins**, highlight the **Analysis ToolPak** $\boxed{\text{Analysis ToolPak}}$ in the list of Inactive Applications, click on **Go** $\boxed{\underline{Go...}}$ near the bottom of the dialog box, check the **Analysis ToolPak**, and click on **OK**.

To install Solver, do the same steps except substitute **Solver** in place of **Analysis ToolPak** along the way.

22.7 Format Painter

Task. Apply formatting from one cell to other cells.

How To. Select the cell(s) whose format you want to copy (e.g., select **D5:E5** in the example below). Then click on **Home | Clipboard | Format Painter** $\checkmark$ **Format Painter**. The cursor now includes a paint brush. Then select the range that you want to apply the formatting to (e.g., range **D6:E17** in the example below). Notice that Format Painter copies all of the formatting, including number type (percentage), number of decimals, background color, and border color.

Before

	A	B	C	D	E
1	THE YIELD CURVE	Obtaining and Using It			
2		Maturity	Time To	Yield To	Forward
3	Yield Curve Inputs	Date	Maturity	Maturity	Rates
4	Today's Date	5/22/2007			
5	One Month Treasury Bill	6/22/2007	0.08	4.90%	4.90%
6	Three Month Treasury Bill	8/22/2007	0.25	0.0477	0.0471
7	Six Month Treasury Bill	11/22/2007	0.50	0.0481	0.0485
8	One Year Treasury Strip	5/15/2008	0.98	0.0489	0.0497
9	Two Year Treasury Strip	8/15/2009	2.23	0.0482	0.0477
10	Three Year Treasury Strip	8/15/2010	3.23	0.0474	0.0456
11	Four Year Treasury Strip	8/15/2011	4.23	0.0472	0.0466
12	Five Year Treasury Strip	8/15/2012	5.23	0.0471	0.0467
13	Ten Year Treasury Strip	8/15/2017	10.23	0.0493	0.0516
14	Fifteen Year Treasury Bond	8/15/2022	15.23	0.0514	0.0557
15	Twenty Year Treasury Bond	8/15/2027	20.23	0.0511	0.0502
16	Twenty Five Year Treasury Bond	8/15/2032	25.23	0.0497	0.0441
17	Thirty Year Treasury Bond	2/15/2037	29.73	0.0495	0.0484

After

	A	B	C	D	E
1	THE YIELD CURVE	Obtaining and Using It			
2		Maturity	Time To	Yield To	Forward
3	Yield Curve Inputs	Date	Maturity	Maturity	Rates
4	Today's Date	5/22/2007			
5	One Month Treasury Bill	6/22/2007	0.08	4.90%	4.90%
6	Three Month Treasury Bill	8/22/2007	0.25	4.77%	4.71%
7	Six Month Treasury Bill	11/22/2007	0.50	4.81%	4.85%
8	One Year Treasury Strip	5/15/2008	0.98	4.89%	4.97%
9	Two Year Treasury Strip	8/15/2009	2.23	4.82%	4.77%
10	Three Year Treasury Strip	8/15/2010	3.23	4.74%	4.56%
11	Four Year Treasury Strip	8/15/2011	4.23	4.72%	4.66%
12	Five Year Treasury Strip	8/15/2012	5.23	4.71%	4.67%
13	Ten Year Treasury Strip	8/15/2017	10.23	4.93%	5.16%
14	Fifteen Year Treasury Bond	8/15/2022	15.23	5.14%	5.57%
15	Twenty Year Treasury Bond	8/15/2027	20.23	5.11%	5.02%
16	Twenty Five Year Treasury Bond	8/15/2032	25.23	4.97%	4.41%
17	Thirty Year Treasury Bond	2/15/2037	29.73	4.95%	4.84%

22.8 Conditional Formatting

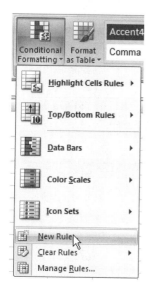

Task. Conditionally format a cell. This allows the displayed format to change based upon the results of a formula calculation.

How To. Suppose you want to use special formatting to highlight the best portfolio in constrained portfolio optimization (see example below). Select cell M166. Click on **Home | Styles | Conditional Formatting down-arrow | New Rule**. Then click on Use a formula to determine which cells to format

▶ Use a formula to determine which cells to format . In the text entry box, enter **=M166=1**. This checks whether the value of cell M166 is equal to one. Formulas for conditional fomatting must begin with an equal sign, so oddly you end up with two equal signs in the formula. Then click on the **Format** button. In the **Format Cells** dialog box, click on the **Fill** tab, select the **color** you like, click **OK**, and then click **OK** again. Finally, copy this new conditional format down the column using Format Painter. Click on **Home | Clipboard | Format Painter**

✔ Format Painter . The cursor now includes a paint brush. Then select the range **M167:M181**. In this example, the cell **M173** turns orange because it is the highest ranking (#1) portfolio. If you changed one of the problem inputs, then a different portfolio might be ranked #1 and the cell corresponding to the new #1 would be highlighted in orange.

Edit the Rule Description:

Format values where this formula is true:

=M166=1

Edit the Rule Description:

Format values where this formula is true:

=M166=1

Preview: No Format Set Format...

Excel 97-2003 Equivalent

To invoke Conditional Formatting in Excel 97-2003, click on the **Format | Conditional Formatting**.

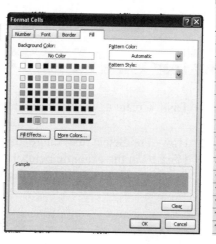

	L	M
54	Investor Utility	Portfolio Ranking
166	0.555%	15
167	0.568%	13
168	0.578%	11
169	0.587%	9
170	0.594%	7
171	0.599%	5
172	0.603%	3
173	0.604%	1
174	0.604%	2
175	0.602%	4
176	0.598%	6
177	0.593%	8
178	0.585%	10
179	0.576%	12
180	0.565%	14
181	0.552%	16

22.9 Fill Handle

Task. Fill in row 10 with integers from 0 to 8 to create the timeline (see example below). This fill technique works for wide range of patterns.

How To. Enter **0** in cell **B10** and **1** in cell **C10**. Select the range **B10:C10**, then hover the cursor over the fill handle ▬▪ (the square in the lower-right corner) of cell **C10** and the cursor turns to a plus symbol ╬. Click, drag the plus symbol to cell **J10**, and release. The range fills up with the rest the pattern from 2 to 8.

Before

	A	B	C	D	E	F	G	H	I	J
1	BOND PRICING	Annual Payments								
2										
3	Inputs									
4	Number of Periods to Maturity (T)	8								
5	Face Value (PAR)	$1,000								
6	Discount Rate / Period (r)	9.0%								
7	Coupon Payment (PMT)	$25								
8										
9	Bond Price using a Timeline									
10	Period	0	1							
11	Cash Flows		$25.00	$25.00	$25.00	$25.00	$25.00	$25.00	$25.00	$1,025.00
12	Present Value of Cash Flow		$22.94	$25.00	$25.00	$25.00	$25.00	$25.00	$25.00	$1,025.00
13	Bond Price	########								

After

	A	B	C	D	E	F	G	H	I	J
1	BOND PRICING	Annual Payments								
2										
3	Inputs									
4	Number of Periods to Maturity (T)	8								
5	Face Value (PAR)	$1,000								
6	Discount Rate / Period (r)	9.0%								
7	Coupon Payment (PMT)	$25								
8										
9	Bond Price using a Timeline									
10	Period	0	1	2	3	4	5	6	7	8
11	Cash Flows		$25.00	$25.00	$25.00	$25.00	$25.00	$25.00	$25.00	$1,025.00
12	Present Value of Cash Flow		$22.94	$21.04	$19.30	$17.71	$16.25	$14.91	$13.68	$514.41
13	Bond Price	$640.24								

22.10 2-D Scatter Chart

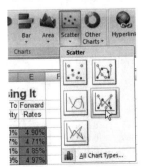

Task. Create a two-dimensional Scatter Chart.

How To. Select the range that has the data you wish to graph (e.g., select **C5:E17** in the example below). Click on **Insert | Charts | Scatter down-arrow | Scatter with Straight Lines and Markers**.

	A	B	C	D	E
1	THE YIELD CURVE	Obtaining and Using It			
2		Maturity	Time To	Yield To	Forward
3	**Yield Curve Inputs**	Date	Maturity	Maturity	Rates
4	Today's Date	5/22/2007			
5	One Month Treasury Bill	6/22/2007	0.08	4.90%	4.90%
6	Three Month Treasury Bill	8/22/2007	0.25	4.77%	4.71%
7	Six Month Treasury Bill	11/22/2007	0.50	4.81%	4.85%
8	One Year Treasury Strip	5/15/2008	0.98	4.89%	4.97%
9	Two Year Treasury Strip	8/15/2009	2.23	4.82%	4.77%
10	Three Year Treasury Strip	8/15/2010	3.23	4.74%	4.56%
11	Four Year Treasury Strip	8/15/2011	4.23	4.72%	4.66%
12	Five Year Treasury Strip	8/15/2012	5.23	4.71%	4.67%
13	Ten Year Treasury Strip	8/15/2017	10.23	4.93%	5.16%
14	Fifteen Year Treasury Bond	8/15/2022	15.23	5.14%	5.57%
15	Twenty Year Treasury Bond	8/15/2027	20.23	5.11%	5.02%
16	Twenty Five Year Treasury Bond	8/15/2032	25.23	4.97%	4.41%
17	Thirty Year Treasury Bond	2/15/2037	29.73	4.95%	4.84%

A rough version of the 2-D Scatter Chart appears.

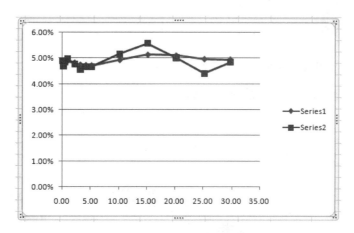

As long as the Chart is selected, three new tabs appear that provide lots of chart options for Design, Layout, and Formatting.

Chart Tools

Design   Layout   Format

Alternatively, you can right-click on parts of the chart to get pop-up menus with formatting choices. Here is what a fully-formatted 2-D Scatter Chart looks like.

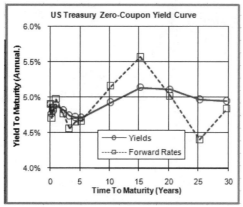

22.11 3-D Surface Chart

Task. Create a three-dimensional Surface Chart.

How To. Select the range that has the data you wish to graph (e.g., select C94:G98 in the example below). Click on **Insert | Charts | Other Charts down-arrow | Surface | 3-D Surface**.

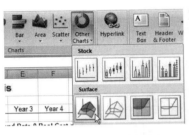

Excel 97-2003 Equivalent

To insert a 3-D Surface Chart in Excel 97-2003, click on the **Insert | Chart | Surface | 3-D Surface**.

	A	B	C	D	E	F	G
1	PROJECT NPV	Sensitivity Analysis					
2	(in thousands of $)						
3		Year 0	Year 1	Year 2	Year 3	Year 4	Year 5
90							
91	Data Table: Sensitivity of the Net Present Value to Unit Sales and Date 0 Real Cost of Capital						
92			Input Values for Unit Sales Scale Factor				
93	Out Formula: Net Present Value	$3,180	80%	90%	100%	110%	120%
94		9.0%	($1,324)	$1,667	$4,658	$7,649	$10,640
95	Input Values for	11.0%	($2,336)	$422	$3,180	$5,938	$8,696
96	Date 0 Real Cost of Capital	13.0%	($3,246)	($698)	$1,851	$4,399	$6,947
97		15.0%	($4,065)	($1,706)	$652	$3,010	$5,369
98		17.0%	($4,804)	($2,617)	($431)	$1,755	$3,941

A rough version of the 3-D Surface Chart appears.

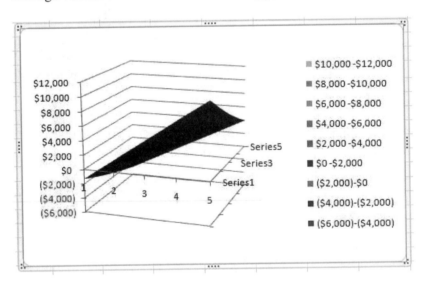

As long as the Chart is selected, three new tabs appear that provide lots of chart options for Design, Layout, and Formatting.

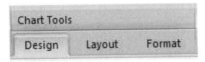

Alternatively, you can right-click on parts of the chart to get pop-up menus with formatting choices.

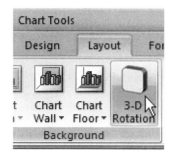

It is often useful to rotate a 3-D chart. To do this, click on **Layout | Background | 3-D Rotation**. 3-D Rotation provides the ability to rotate the surface in the X-axis direction, Y-axis direction, or Z-axis direction.

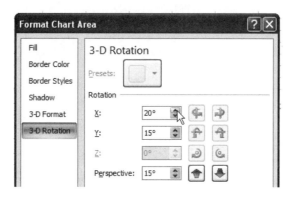

Here is what a fully-formatted 3-D Surface Chart looks like.

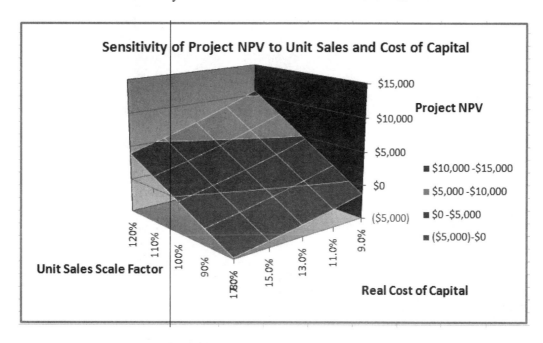